Culture, Philanthropy and the Poor in Late-Victorian London

The Late-Victorian cultural mission to London's slums was a peculiar effort towards social reform that today is largely forgotten or misunderstood. The philanthropy of middle- and upper-class social workers saw hundreds of art exhibitions, concerts of fine music, evening lectures, clubs and socials, debates and excursions mounted for the benefit of impoverished and working-class Londoners. Ginn's vivid and provocative book captures many of these in detail for the first time.

In refreshing our understanding of this obscure but eloquent activism, Ginn approaches cultural philanthropy not simply as a project of class self-interest, nor as fanciful 'missionary aestheticism'. Rather, he shows how liberal aspirations towards adult education and civic community can be traced in a number of centres of moralising voluntary effort. Concentrating on Toynbee Hall in Whitechapel, the People's Palace in Mile End, Red Cross Hall in Southwark and the Bermondsey Settlement, the discussion identifies the common impulses animating practical reformers across these settings.

Drawing on new primary research to clarify reformers' underlying intentions and strategies, Ginn shows how these were shaped by a distinctive diagnosis of urban deprivation and anomie. In rebutting the common view that cultural philanthropy was a crudely paternalistic attempt to impose 'rational recreation' on the poor, this volume explores its sources in a liberal-minded social idealism common to both religious and secular conceptions of social welfare in this period. *Culture, Philanthropy and the Poor in Late-Victorian London* appeals to students and researchers of Victorian culture, moral reform, urbanism, adult education and philanthropy, who will be fascinated by this underrated but lively aspect of the period's social activism.

Geoffrey A. C. Ginn teaches modern British history and heritage studies at the School of Historical and Philosophical Inquiry, University of Queensland, Australia. His research focuses on urban history, historical museology and public history, with particular interests in the Victorians, colonial cities, the history of religion, and public culture.

Perspectives in Economic and Social History

Series Editors: Andrew August and Jari Eloranta

Culture, Philanthropy and the Poor in Late-Victorian London

Geoffrey A. C. Ginn

Routledge
Taylor & Francis Group

LONDON AND NEW YORK

First published 2017 by Routledge

2 Park Square, Milton Park, Abingdon, Oxfordshire OX14 4RN
52 Vanderbilt Avenue, New York, NY 10017

Routledge is an imprint of the Taylor & Francis Group, an informa business

First issued in paperback 2019

British Library Cataloguing in Publication Data
A catalogue record for this book is available from the British Library

Library of Congress Cataloging in Publication Data
Names: Ginn, Geoffrey A. C., author.
Title: Culture, philanthropy and the poor in late-Victorian London /
Geoffrey A.C. Ginn.
Description: Abingdon, Oxon ; New York, NY : Routledge, 2017. | Includes
bibliographical references and index.
Identifiers: LCCN 2016052835 | ISBN 9781848936089 (hardback) |
ISBN 9781315184999 (ebook)
Subjects: LCSH: Social service--Great Britain--History--19th century. |
Poor--Services for–Great Britain--History–19th century. | Arts--Great
Britain--History–19th century. | Great Britain--Cultural policy--History--
19th century. | Great Britain--Civilization--19th century.
Classification: LCC HV245 .G467 2017 | DDC 362.5/5709421--dc23
LC record available at https://lccn.loc.gov/2016052835

ISBN: 978-1-8489-3608-9 (hbk)
ISBN: 978-0-367-35676-7 (pbk)

Typeset in Times New Roman
by Taylor & Francis Books

To Anna,
and the memory of our first conversation

For 'respectables' to settle in such slums,
    Where toil hums,
And to dwell amidst much dirt, and noise, and vice,
    Is not 'nice'...
But here Culture, in the spirit of true neighbour,
    Lives with Labour;
And with wisdom, love, and unsectarian piety,
    Lends variety
To that gloom which for poor workers and their wives,
    Spoils their lives.
There are lectures, classes, clubs, 'larks' not a few,
    Outings too!
In- and out-door recreation they all share,
    For their care
Is to 'chum in' with poor folk in grief *or* joy, –
    Girl and boy!

Punch, 21 December 1895, p. 298.

Contents

Figures

Acknowledgments

My first thanks go to three advisors and mentors over the years of work on this book: Emeritus Professor Paul Crook, Professor Daniel Pick, and Emeritus Professor Peter Spearritt for their guidance and commentary throughout the research, writing and revision.

Many others have helped shape this work one way or another, and in particular I thank Seth Koven, Malcolm Thomis, Simon Devereaux, Gareth Stedman Jones, Andrea McKenzie, Sean Brady, Lucinda Matthews-Jones, Margaret Higgs, Adam Bowles, Andrew Bonnell, Dolly MacKinnon, Patrick Jory, Martin Crotty, Lisa Featherstone, Ian Hesketh, Tom Aechtner, Leigh Penman, Malcolm Catchpole, Michael Westaway, George Megalogenis, Richard Gray, John McGuire, Fiona Sinclair, Ron McKenzie, my stepfather Matt and my father Geoff. At London House a very special group of friends helped make the initial research such a pleasure: Victor Tschudi, Annastacia Palaszczuk, Les Joynes, Simone Murray, Kimberley Amman, Jason Wong and Theo Hong. Andrew August, Janka Romero, Emily Kindleysides, Laura Johnson, Alaina Christensen and Kris Wischenkamper all provided wonderful advice and professionalism during the publishing process.

The breadth of research undertaken would not have been possible without funding from a number of sources. An Australian Postgraduate Research Award sustained my initial doctoral work in Australia, further supported by a Chevening Scholarship awarded by the Foreign and Commonwealth Office for research in London. Later research occurred through study leave from the University of Queensland and as a Visiting Fellow at the Institute of Historical Research, University of London.

My sincere thanks also go to many librarians and archivists. In particular, Anselm Nye, Lorraine Screene, and Nicola Wood of the Queen Mary University of London Library; Harriet Jones at the London Metropolitan Archives; Chris Lloyd at the Tower Hamlets Local History Library; Penny Fussell at the Drapers' Company Archives, Drapers' Hall; and Patricia Dark and Stephen Potter at the Southwark Local History Library. I am also grateful to the editors of *The London Journal* for permission to use material previously published in that journal in Chapters 4, and 5, to Queen Mary, University of London, for permission to reproduce images of the People's Palace, Museums Sheffield and the Collection of the Guild of St George for the portrait of Octavia Hill, the National Portrait Gallery, London for the portrait of Walter Besant, to the Hampstead Garden Suburb Trust for the portrait of Samuel and Henrietta Barnett, and to the Southwark Local History Library for assistance with reproducing materials in their collection.

Abbreviations

Bod. L	Bodleian Library
BL	British Library
BLPES	British Library of Political and Economic Science
COS	Charity Organisation Society
CRU	Church Reform Union
DRO	Derbyshire Record Office
DCA	Drapers' Company Archives, Drapers' Hall
ELA	*East London Advertiser*
ELO	*East London Observer*
KCAC	King's College (Cambridge) Archives Centre
LCC	London County Council
LMA	London Metropolitan Archives
LPL	Lambeth Palace Library
LSEUT	London Society for the Extension of University Teaching
Parlt. P.	Parliamentary Papers
PMG	*Pall Mall Gazette*
PES	People's Entertainment Society
PP	People's Palace
QMUL	Queen Mary, University of London Library
SPCK	Society for Promoting Christian Knowledge
SLHL	Southwark Local History Library
THLHL	Tower Hamlets Local History Library
TNA	The National Archives, Kew
TTC	Toynbee Travellers' Club
UEJ	*University Extension Journal*
ULL	University of London Library
VAM	Victoria and Albert Museum
WAC	Westminster Archives Centre
WEA	Workers' Educational Association

1   A good young man in a shiny top hat

In mid-February 1893, at the tail end of a London winter, the aspiring writer Henry Nevinson visited a new London County Council (LCC) lodging-house near Camden Town for Charles Booth's poverty survey. His guide, evidently a supervisor there and unimpressed by the expensive electric lights and thermal heating, 'thought the place was much too good, and complained very much that it was impossible to get the men up in the morning'. Nevinson was intrigued to see that the new doss-house catered to metaphysical needs, too. Its sitting room had a fresco above the fireplace in the style of Walter Crane, 'smiths and carpenters and ploughmen ideally dressed and employed', evoking truth, beauty, moral dignity and social well-being. But as he wrote in his diary that night,

> it would have been impossible to find a subject of which the occupants who crowded round the fire knew less. Seedy, demi-semi respectable cadgers and literary hacks with relics of top hats they looked. On a platform at one end stood a good new piano, [a] gift of Earl Compton, on which a good young man in a very shiny top hat, perhaps Compton himself, was playing tiny bits from Beethoven and Chopin to the indifferent dossers.[1]

We might agree with Nevinson that the scene, and by extension the reforming aspirations it embodied, is little short of bizarre. Yet the recital was not an unusual event at the artistic doss-house; at least thirty-five musical concerts and recitals were given there between 1893 and 1895.[2] Most were delivered by volunteers, but the relevant LCC sub-committee received a letter in January 1895 from a Mr J. A. Wieppart requesting payment 'for playing the piano and accompanying singers at the lodging-house'. Around this time the committee decided to purchase three oil lamps to illuminate the fresco Nevinson had found so strangely misplaced.

This book explains the strand of late-Victorian social work embodied by the doss-house fresco, by Lord Compton's piano, and by the good young man in the shiny top hat playing fragments from Beethoven and Chopin to homeless men. We might see little evidence of it now, but at the end of Queen Victoria's reign, in the restless, troubled twilight of the nineteenth century, hundreds of social workers devoted countless hours and enormous energy to supply cultural opportunities and experiences to Britain's urban poor. This activism was especially pronounced in London, and resulted in symbolically-charged settings such as the frescoed sitting room at Parker Street and contrived events such as the good young man's piano recital. It prompted educated, affluent men and women to mount classical music concerts in impoverished neighbourhoods, and to show and explain fine art through philanthropic loan exhibitions. Their efforts were much more widespread and sustained than we might think, embedded in local voluntary action and historically obscure as a consequence. Their cultural philanthropy encompassed art exhibitions, musical concerts, reading groups in poetry and drama, evening lectures, debating clubs and subscriber libraries, social occasions like dinner dances, *conversaziones* and *soirées*, excursions and educational day trips, social interactions and opportunities intended to refine and improve.[3]

Considered in isolation as 'missionary aestheticism' this mode of reforming activism is easily misunderstood or caricatured.[4] We find it easy to marvel at the apparent naivety of these social workers and their quixotic mission. But a clearer sense of late-Victorian cultural philanthropy emerges if we appreciate its extent, its sources and context. To that end, this book introduces this work of cultural provision broadly, but then concentrates on several centres of philanthropic social work in late-nineteenth century London. North of the Thames, in the East End, we consider the Anglican parish of St Jude's, Whitechapel and its pioneering university settlement Toynbee Hall established in 1884, comparing it to the Beaumont Trust's flamboyant scheme to build a People's Palace three years later further out on Mile End Road. Across the river in South London, we examine the Bermondsey Settlement established by Methodist interests in 1891 and Octavia Hill's Red Cross Hall in Southwark.

Taking a broad purview, but with a closer look at these telling examples, we explore the ideas, strategies and outlook of the men and women who laboured in these vineyards as we consider the motives that inspired them, the schemes they implemented, the activities they hosted. Rather than treating individual enterprises in isolation, and rather than highlighting their cosmetic differences, we explore underlying patterns of late-Victorian improving moralism, grounded in an urban imaginary of social crisis, that help us to grasp cultural philanthropy as a distinct mode of late-Victorian urban reform and social work. No matter how delusional, elitist or self-serving they might appear at first glance, this book contends that the late-century philanthropic efforts to educate the urban poor through cultural opportunity demand closer attention. To contemporaries they were not necessarily far-fetched or marginal, and many found their schemes entirely worthy and practical. The cultural philanthropists were easily mocked by critics, then and now, but they also called out great numbers of energetic, capable, intelligent men and women who willingly put their shoulders to the wheel. This book aims to re-capture and re-comprehend that practical effort, in order to draw out its underlying coherence and develop a better appreciation of its circumstances and logic.

* * *

We begin with the bland but necessary observation that cultural philanthropy was part of the broad 'moralising mission' directed at the urban poor by social workers and active reformers, male and female, from largely middle-class backgrounds. Charity work and voluntary philanthropy were every-where in nineteenth-century Britain, most of it undertaken by the 'respectable' and well-to-do in partnership with churches, reform societies, charities and benevolent agencies of all kinds. 'For every public gesture', James Walvin writes, 'there were thousands of hours of modest but practical work, as Vic-torians sought to put right the wrongs of the world around them'.

> Not all their efforts were directed at obvious physical human needs. They helped animal welfare (think of the surviving drinking fountains for horses), they built libraries, large numbers of which still stand, they staffed the thousands of classes in local Sunday and ragged schools. There were few aspects of contemporary social life which failed to lure Victorians to their charitable stations.[5]

The fault-lines of social class were particularly evident as Britain's labouring poor 'were subjected to a package deal from those above them; inspired principally by members of middle class minority groups, with occasional noble or gentry parti-cipation'.[6] By the mid-1870s this activity was reaching a crescendo in the gen-eration which asked, as Anthony Wohl puts it, 'not what is to be done, but what can *I* do' about widespread, visible and troubling urban poverty.[7]

  The first historians to assess nineteenth-century social work were preoccupied by the gradual evolution of state-sponsored welfare and a shift from individualist to collective solutions to poverty and its circumstances.[8] But clearly, as Frank Prochaska observes, 'the tendency to see [modern British philanthropy] as a stage in the development of the statutory social services has not been helpful to our appreciation of its persistence and variety. The provision of welfare is central to philanthropy, but it is far from being its sole concern.'[9] The flawed teleology of the old approach has spurred an academic rediscovery of a 'mixed economy of welfare' (in both contemporary and historical terms) with renewed attention to the voluntary sector in Britain and its history.[10] The older scholarship also failed to supply a sense of how philanthropic impulses and relationships suffused Victorian life and society, a theme that has now been treated abundantly.[11] The resulting picture is rich and complex. 'Humanitarian impulses were certainly a character-istic of charitable activists', Prochaska writes, 'but in a culture so profoundly voluntarist, philanthropy was an essential sphere of politics and social relations, an expression of local democracy and civic pride, of individual hope and aspira-tion'.[12] Landmark studies highlight key women as primary agents of charity work in the late-Victorian and Edwardian periods, and clarify important points of intersection with organised religion.[13] Scholars have demonstrated the extent to which philanthropic duties were central to middle class identity, particularly in provincial centres,[14] while urban historians have measured philanthropy's impact on the evolution of public space and amenity.[15] Problems of urban representation and the languages of social description favoured by social workers have also drawn attention.[16] These themes – gender, religion, civic identity, public space and urban consciousness – recur as focal points in the following chapters.

As might be expected, scholars have been particularly concerned with class, and with philanthropy as an element 'in the ongoing dialectic between the English middle class and its urban poor'.[17] The possessive note sounded here is deliberate: a perpetual theme in studies of nineteenth-century charity and social work has been the intrusion by middle-class reformers into the homes, lives and habits of the 'lower orders'. The early historians tended to argue, in Bernard Harris' summary, 'that the very nature of Victorian philanthropy was rooted in the characteristics of a deeply unequal society, and that it was designed primarily to salve the consciences of the rich and reinforce their control over the poor'.[18] Attempts to encourage associations among working men and women through the Club and Institute Union, for example, have been dismissed as patronising efforts at social control, despite the very real advantages and benefits they fostered.[19] This book seeks a better, more nuanced understanding of the active business of reform undertaken by social workers than is supplied by such a reductive approach. We take a fresh look at the perceptions, attitudes and actions of members of the educated professional sector of the middle class, those men and women 'responsible for the dominant discourse on charity and social policy in the period'.[20] Exploring the scope, character and purposes of middle-class social activism through the pregnant statements and actions of cultural philanthropists themselves, we continue the recent scholarly interest in 'the moral imperatives which lay behind Victorian philanthropy'.[21] As with the third part of Gareth Stedman Jones' magisterial *Outcast London*, then, the focus here is often on matters not as they *actually* existed, but as the reform-minded and socially active element of the middle and upper classes *conceived* them to exist.[22]

This is not to assume that charity was entirely the work of middle-class social workers and agencies. Prochaska urges attention to working-class benevolence, in part to complicate the standard picture of the poor as victims and passive recipients, and suggests that neighbourly giving was a major factor for social stability.[23] Perceptive observers of urban life were acutely aware of the informal benevolence that kept despair at bay and dignity intact. Samuel Barnett, for instance, noted 'a kind of communism' amid scenes of metropolitan poverty: 'They easily borrow and easily lend', he wrote of East Londoners. 'The women spend much time in gossiping, know intimately one another's affairs, and in times of trouble help willingly.'[24] Educational provision, too, was something that could be supplied in an autonomous and independent spirit by working people themselves.[25] Social historians have pursued the individual subjective experience of nineteenth-century poverty by real men, women and children in concrete historical circumstances, through the charity they received, the places they occupied and even the clothes they wore.[26] They are also keen to emphasise that charitable provision and its moral strictures were often resisted or defied.[27] After all, 'the poor were not statistics devoid of form and feeling. They were people, and they need to be seen from within their own communities as much as from without.'[28]

But the sources are frustratingly silent when we try to access plebeian experiences on the particular occasions discussed in this book. We have no accounts originating directly from working men and women that might illuminate the response of a dock labourer to the opening of the People's Palace, for example, a seamstress' experiences at a Toynbee Hall *conversazione*, or an evening Shakespeare class at the Bermondsey Settlement attended (or shunned) by the local unemployed. Despite the many thousands of visits made by ordinary working-class Londoners to libraries, art shows, evening classes and music concerts supplied by the cultural reformers, few accounts of these occasions give us any direct access to their responses. Those accounts that do exist, as we discuss below, emanate almost without exception from the self-improving, self-consciously educated stratum of skilled workers and the respectable working poor, and so tend to endorse the cultural and educational opportunities on offer.

Accordingly, this study does not follow recent scholarly attempts to re-construct the history of late-Victorian philanthropy as it was experienced 'from below'. But it is worth noting how brilliantly Jonathan Rose's *The Intellectual Life of the British Working Classes* recaptures the world of the nineteenth-century autodidact, demonstrating conclusively how adult education, cultural literacy, familiarity with literary classics, poetry, drama and fine music were all features of working-class life in the towns and cities of Victorian Britain. Rose concludes that knowledge, education and self-culture were highly prized by large numbers of the 'self-improving' working class, both male and female, especially in the golden age of the autodidact in the last decades of the nineteenth century. In part, this study develops Rose's insight that '[S]trictly speaking, settlement houses were not mutual improvement societies, they were university-sponsored institutions staffed by educated men and women. But the literary, musical and dramatic groups they hosted offered the same kind of collaborative working-class education.'[29] These opportunities in higher education and cultural literacy were genuinely valued by many in working class communities, and were not necessarily regarded as an alien culture of the governing elite imposed for largely self-interested reasons.

* * *

Added to the mix in the chapters below is a keen appreciation of the urban consciousness that is often overlooked in historical assessments of active social reform efforts. We examine the relationships between practical social work and late-Victorian civic ethics, the links between liberal culture and urban leisure that Meller and Beaven have explored in regional cities like Bristol and Coventry.[30] Here our attention returns to the metropolis to examine practical social activism in the notorious slum districts of late-Victorian London (see Figure 1.1).

A glittering imperial capital, a sprawling, congested metropolis; a source of pride, anxiety, fear and wonder all intermixed: London was the great laboratory of late-Victorian charitable activism. Its example dominated every debate that swirled around problems of poverty and its amelioration. In our period the 'social question' was 'peculiarly a London debate, using London organs of publicity, carried on by an intelligentsia of London professional men and provoked by the symptoms of a crisis specific to the London economy'.[31] It was textured by the experiences of London's social workers and given urgency and direction by their sense of the urban crisis gripping the metropolis. Charles Booth's monumental survey of London poverty, painstakingly accumulated street by street from 1886 and published in sequential volumes, captures this metropolitan primacy neatly for us, and although he used the term 'Darkest England', William Booth of the Salvation Army likewise generally confined his attention to London. A commentator like the novelist Walter Besant could admit to being familiar only with London (and in particular, East London) conditions, and yet still be considered an authority on urban poverty in general.[32]

By the 1880s London had experienced decades of convulsive physical growth, massive inflows of population and investment in its infrastructure accompanied by the physical deterioration of its inner residential neighbourhoods. The rapid development of a ring of middle-class suburbs, imagined as 'a great continent of petty villadom', had drained more affluent inhabitants out of the old central districts.[33] In notorious neighbourhoods like Marylebone, Camden Town, Whitechapel and the East End, Bermondsey, Southwark and Lambeth, the older housing stock, tumbledown courts and low-rise tenements had been sub-divided in ever smaller and denser tenancies.[34] Trade and industry in the capital experienced a severe cyclical downturn between 1884 and 1887, inducing acute unemployment amid a 'string of highly publicised events and scandals, between 1883 and 1888, [that] sustained the problem of poverty as a subject of concern for the educated reading public'.[35] Contemporary anxieties about 'Outcast London', the moral and social condition of the slum-dwelling poor and its implications, animated a sequence of interlocking debates over housing, sanitation, the sweat-shops, the evils of indiscriminate charity, unemployment and the insecurity of casual labour, and the prevalence of crime and vice.

Following Stedman Jones and others who have explored discursive representations of late-Victorian urban poverty, we can recognise 'Outcast London' itself as the great imaginative construct of this debate. As an imagined and mythologised landscape, it infused both the metropolitan poverty debate and the practical social work that quickened through this period. But where was it to be found, topographically speaking? What were its boundaries and main contours? It was often conflated with the 'East End', but many commentators were keen to point out that the same conditions and problems were just as evident south of the river.[36] Its boundaries might be vague, but the Thames was not one of them. And even when discussion concentrated on one district, the potential for confusion was high. Charles Booth wrestled with the problem directly as he sought to condense the colossal data sets of his survey into concise, accurate and empirically defensible statements about the character of poverty in each London neighbourhood. When he arrived at Bermondsey for his religious influences survey, for instance, observable fact and perception were hopelessly entangled. 'What is said...and what may be true of a part of the [South London] district', he wrote, 'is often assumed, either recklessly by the assertor or carelessly by the opponent, to be equally applicable to other parts or even to the whole district. The boundaries implied are very vague. Who can say what exactly may be meant by South London, or Southwark, or even Walworth or Bermondsey?'[37]

Stedman Jones primarily associated 'Outcast London' with concentrations of casual labour, especially in the dockside neighbourhoods either side of the river downstream of London Bridge. The labourers, carters, stevedores, warehousemen – the volatile casual labourers of the East London docks – leapt to attention during the period of aggravated unemployment and the Trafalgar Square demonstrations and riots in 1886 and 1887. But the industrial conditions of East London's sweated seamstresses and tailors were also sources of disquiet, as were the restless, intractable 'factory girls' of neighbourhoods like Bermondsey in South London favoured by food and jam manufacturers, the tannery labourers and basket makers that dominated local trades, and the boisterous street hawkers and carters of the market areas of nearby Southwark. The *Pall Mall Gazette* felt the urgent problem was 'the excessive overcrowding of enormous multitudes of the very poor in pestilential rookeries where it is a matter of physical impossibility to live a human life',[38] and following the graphic descriptions of celebrated slum correspondents like Andrew Mearns and George Sims attention focused on 'outcast' neighbourhoods where the housing was decrepit and the population crammed in like livestock. As Stedman Jones put it, 'lurid and sensational impressions of London slum life proliferated in the ensuing barrage of pamphlet literature, Parliamentary investigation, and press reportage'.[39] The repulsive exposés of child prostitution canvassed during W. T. Stead's 'Maiden Tribute' scandal of 1885 drew attention to the brothels, pimps and madams active in these notorious slums, where labyrinthine streets and narrow courts made official scrutiny difficult. Perhaps most conclusively, the gruesome Whitechapel murders of autumn 1888 seemed to confirm respectable London's worst fears of the vice, depravity and violence that festered in the capital's sensational, squalid neighbourhoods of crime and misery.

But, as we see in the following chapters, an alternative vein of urban description was sustained by the accounts of London poverty promulgated

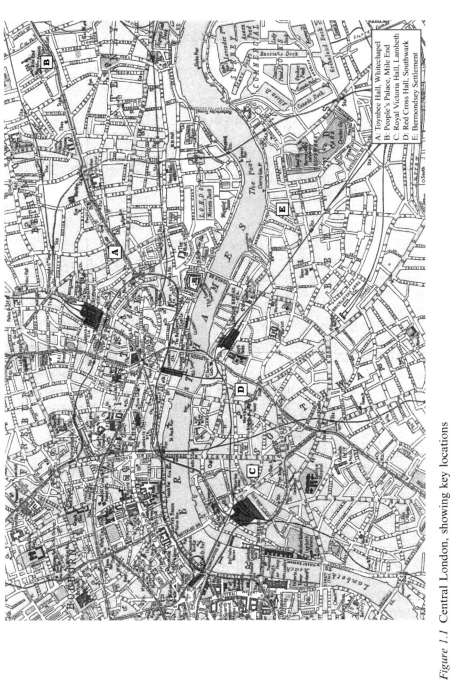

A: Toynbee Hall, Whitechapel
B: People's Palace, Mile End
C: Royal Victoria Hall, Lambeth
D: Red Cross Hall, Southwark
E: Bermondsey Settlement

Figure 1.1 Central London, showing key locations

directly by active social workers. Less prone to sensational hyperbole, these voluntary activists used their reports and speeches, sermons and pamphlets to depict London's impoverished neighbourhoods in very different terms. They described scenes that were less exaggerated, less highly coloured, but no less intended to demonstrate that these neighbourhoods demanded urgent action. But their remedies were directed not against sensational squalor and misery but rather an unremitting tedium of life-sapping urban monotony, against the alienation and isolation they feared was taking hold in modern cities. On this basis, they provided the kind of cultural experiences they felt would draw people together in mutual and life-affirming relationships as a liberal-minded mode of urban reform that was both practical and (to many contemporaries) entirely plausible.

In this way we see in the chapters that follow how beliefs about London's social character and condition directly shaped the practical work involved in the cultural mission to the metropolitan slums. Our discussion unpacks the relationship between, on the one hand, London as a material setting – as an urban context with a particular topographical form, with distinctive functions and relationships that we might describe as its social geography – and (on the other) the interpretations of that material setting and its social character that were so fundamentally a component of reformist schemes and interventions. Urban visions of various kinds did not simply accompany or promote reformist strategies of social intervention; in a sense they actually constituted them, and did so decisively. Values and assumptions about urban life did not simply give rise to actions, but rather the two were inter-related in complex but empirically recoverable ways. As urban historians have insisted, physical context, urban relationships, and ideas about cities are tripartite elements of a single whole; in Kevin Lynch's classic formulation, '[C]ity forms, their actual function, and the ideas and values that people attach to them make up a single phenomenon.'[40]

In this spirit our discussion explores the inter-connections involved when a host of middle-class late-Victorian men and women, each of them advocates of a cultural mission to London's impoverished neighbourhoods, embarked on their projects of practical activism. They brought frameworks of thinking to bear, a 'moral imagination' that when mobilised was indelibly marked by their diagnostic convictions about London as a site of urban crisis. As we will see, they set out to engineer certain types of material settings to conduct that work, and to orchestrate certain kinds of social relationships. Cultural philanthropy as a reformist project, this is all to say, was profoundly configured by the urban context in which it was conceptualised and enacted. The chapters below revisit that process of imaginative and practical configuration.

Following this introduction, Chapter Two complicates our picture of the sources of cultural philanthropy, establishing a broader scope for the discussion than scholars have typically favoured. Chapter Three sets out the London reformist *milieu*, excavating and highlighting the manifold schemes of cultural provision, large and small, that punctuated charitable effort between 1875 and the turn of the century. The three chapters that follow explore our three major case studies: in the East End, we look at Toynbee Hall and the People's Palace in detail through consecutive chapters, while in Chapter Six we turn south of the river to consider comparable efforts in Bermondsey, Southwark and Lambeth. Chapter Seven considers the material fabric of these philanthropic centres – and accounts of the audiences that attended their cultural events. The last two chapters highlight aspects of cultural philanthropy in action to emphasise its close relationship to classes, lectures, readings groups, clubs and recreation, and conclude with an encapsulation of this moralising effort as an expression of the period's social idealism.

* * *

Very few studies in the crowded literature of late-Victorian urban reform have grappled with late-Victorian cultural philanthropy as a mode of practical social work in a broad sense. Scholars tend rather to examine isolated instances of 'missionary aestheticism' (as Ian Fletcher called it) and cultural uplift without attempting a larger synthesis. The work of Manchester's art philanthropist T. C. Horsfall has garnered attention, for example, as have provincial art museums, the Home Arts and Industries Association founded in 1884, and Emma Cons' and Lucy Cavendish's work in recreation and adult education through the Royal Victoria Hall.[41] With their moralising delivery of art and aesthetics into impoverished homes and communities, these schemes arguably exemplified a fundamentally elitist determination that 'culture was to be deployed as a means of social engineering and control'.[42] But the considerable social distance between Miss Cons and Lady Cavendish (as we see below) should give us pause for thought. These reformist strategies, moreover, overlapped with those of militant social progressives, as demonstrated in Chris Waters' fine study of popular culture and late-Victorian and Edwardian socialism that explores socialist responses to cultural philanthropy.[43] Emphasising the commonalities between reformers like Beatrice Webb and Samuel Barnett, for example, Waters notes that many middle-class philanthropists shared with socialists a commitment to cultural provision for working-class communities, both as an antidote to the crass commercialism of popular leisure and as a means to renovate moral character. 'Even when critics remained sceptical of philanthropists who claimed that their "concerts for the people" or their country outings served to elevate the working class', he notes, 'they often praised the work of the Barnetts'.[44]

Other key studies have illuminated aspects of the cultural mission, but again without developing a full and rounded picture.[45] Seth Koven's compelling *Slumming: Sexual and Social Politics in Victorian London* concentrates on the homosocial gendering of settlement work and the opportunities such work presented reformers for the fashioning of selfhood and sexual identity through cross-class encounters. Standish Meacham's older *Toynbee Hall and Social Reform, 1880–1914*, a sharp analysis of the lineage and character of Barnett's Whitechapel settlement, privileges the contribution made to its work by the social ethics of T. H. Green and the men of Balliol College. In down-playing the contribution of Samuel and Henrietta Barnett's parochial activism in Whitechapel to Toynbee Hall's creed and ambitions, however, Meacham largely overlooks a pattern of work that was arguably more fundamental to the settlement than Oxford social theory. Among recent biographies, Alison Creedon's work on Henrietta Barnett, and Alan Turberfield's wide-ranging study of John Scott Lidgett's career draw together the many threads of busy lives in social work and activism; their provision of culture and higher edu-cation for the poor is only considered in passing. Regarding the settlement movement more broadly, Ruth Gilchrist explains how the arts, creative and applied, have featured in settlement work since Toynbee Hall's inception in 1884 to build community participation, overcome social isolation, encourage creativity and complement narrow school-teaching and skills training. These aspirations, she suggests, remain highly relevant to community-based social work today, and so urges a re-evaluation of the late-nineteenth century set-tlement model for present-day circumstances.[46] Others have treated Samuel Barnett sympathetically as an unjustly neglected figure in the history of ideas about urban renewal and citizenship. 'Rich and poor were to meet together', Helen Meller observes perceptively of Barnett's municipal idealism, 'under the auspices of cultural institutions and, in the pursuit of Liberal Culture in this arena, rich and poor were equal. Barnett hoped that he had found the means of restoring a sense of unity to modern British society which he felt large scale urbanization had done so much to destroy.'[47] His example crystallises the larger themes addressed in Brad Beaven's perceptive study of the politics of masculine leisure and social citizenship. '[F]or those in society keen to create a bond between individual and nation during this mass democratic age', Beaven observes, 'the diffusion of appropriate leisure activities became a means to achieve a more incorporated and civic-minded population'.[48]

But very few studies directly consider the work of the cultural philan-thropists in detail across a range of settings and institutions. Lucinda Mat-thews-Jones broadens the conventional focus by examining the construction of intimacy through domestic space at East End settlement houses; her recent comparison of the Barnetts' work at Toynbee Hall with parallel attempts to 'spiritualise' the East End at Oxford House in nearby Bethnal Green demon-strates the value of cross-institutional comparison.[49] By contrast Nigel Scot-land's *Squires in the Slums* provides a set of institutional histories of the major late-Victorian settlements and missions and evaluates their achievements, but does little to unlock and analyse the inner life that inspired their work of cultural provision.[50] Accounts of the origins of Toynbee Hall typically relate it to earlier, pioneering 'social mission' work in the 1860s, but the settlement's relationship to contemporary endeavours, and especially those beyond 'Oxford Idealism', has been less thoroughly considered. Koven's superb doc-toral thesis explored the conjuncture between reformist cultural theory and the everyday realities of slum life as a theme in the settlement house move-ment, but disregarded other reforming efforts such as the popular music societies and free libraries, polytechnics and recreational institutes, and brash charitable experiments like the People's Palace.[51] Historical treatments of this grandiose but now largely forgotten philanthropic folly, which along with Baroness Burdett-Coutts' vast and ill-fated Columbia Market of 1869 was perhaps the most elaborate and well-publicised charity scheme of the period, do not relate its purposes to wider patterns of reformist activism.[52]

This book challenges several conclusions of earlier scholars as it develops a more nuanced and contextualised view of the cultural mission to the slums. Frances Borzello's bracing survey of British notions of art as a social good provocatively (but quite implausibly) links the Whitechapel Fine Art Exhibitions – to date the emblematic activity of late-Victorian cultural philanthropy – to the enduring elitism of the Arts Council in the twentieth century.[53] Her sense that cultural provision for social amelioration remained irredeemably elitist as it crept from the philanthropic to the public sphere, an anti-democratic 'misuse of art', is challenged here. Similarly, the architectural readings developed by Deborah Weiner suggest that the settlement houses and early polytechnics were fundamentally mis-conceived and anachronistic, fantasies of pre-industrial hierarchy in an urban and democratic age that (in the case of the People's Palace) struggled to present a credible architectural face.[54] A rebuttal of Weiner's sweeping simplification of these schemes and their purposes appears in Chapter Six. Most recently, several scholars account for the late-Victorian cultural philanthropy as a 'missionary aestheticism' evident in a generation of 'disciples' who (in Maltz's verdict) un-problematically followed Ruskin's precepts as they 'descended into London's East End believing that gifts of beauty and culture would civilize and spiritually elevate the poor'. Following the art historians Ian Fletcher and Mark Girouard, Maltz argues that late-Victorian reformers 'institutionalized aestheticism as a species of philanthropy, employing both the rhetoric of aestheticism and actual manifestations of aesthetic style as remedies for urban degradation'.[55] Woodson-Bolton speaks in similar terms of a 'short-lived but deeply influential aesthetic ideology' deriving principally from Ruskin, 'that understood painting as able to communicate ideas directly to all audiences (even the uneducated)'.[56]

But given Stefan Collini's significant re-thinking of how intellectual formulations become influential in Victorian public life this approach seems inadequate: 'influential' ideas are properly understood as parasitic upon deeply ingrained habits of evaluation and response, as Collini put it.[57] We are also struck by several relevant facts: much of the improving social work of the active reformers discussed in this book did not relate to painting or aesthetics at all, and most cannot be described in any meaningful sense as Ruskinian 'aesthetes'. We need to dig more carefully for the animating motives and purposes they brought to their social work. Accordingly, the values and ideas we find embedded in everyday outlooks and mental habits – what we might describe, following Himmelfarb, as a 'moral imagination' infused with the endemic social idealism of the period rather than a set of ideas neatly labelled 'aestheticism', for example, codified in the work of Ruskin, or the cultural theory of Arnold, or the social ethics of T. H. Green – are invoked here to explain this remark-able late-century flowering of cultural reformism in the London slums.

* * *

Finally, what can be said of the historical approach adopted here? This book develops a contextually grounded treatment of the language used to promote and enact these schemes of cultural improvement. In considering the diagnostic interpretations that gave these interventions their direction and purpose, we concentrate on the way social workers described their own efforts, and their sense of the consequences that followed. We are interested in their mental landscape, as evoked in their own words.

A useful initial example of this approach might be the way Beatrice Potter (later Webb), the most celebrated social worker turned socialist reformer of the period, described the families of the unemployed she encountered as a voluntary housing supervisor in Whitechapel. In the February 1886 letter to the *Pall Mall Gazette* that launched her public career, she argued that rela-tively few of these families were foreign immigrants or remnants of the old artisanal population of the district, as many assumed. Rather, 'the great majority of the "unemployed" are those who have been pressed out of the working ranks in provincial towns and country neighbourhoods and who have thoughtlessly drifted to the great centre of odd jobs and indiscriminate charity'. This was Potter's diagnosis; her view in formulating a response at this time was that indiscriminate charity and work-for-dole schemes would only aggravate the problems stemming from unemployment, which was essen-tially structural (the decline of riverside occupations, the removal of the dock industries further downstream, and the inflow of job-seekers from provincial towns and rural districts) even if its individual manifestations had much to do with personal moral character. In her Fabian career she later disowned this mor-alist perspective, but the 1886 letter is nevertheless sharp-witted, observant and filled with all the assumptions and emphases of like-minded social reformers of the day. 'For the individual who is disabled either through lack of inclination, or from want of power for persistent and worthful work, for the ne'er do weel, the discontented and the genuinely unfortunate, London seems to offer the best chance of gaining a bare subsistence with comparatively little exertion', she wrote.

> Indefinite opportunities for picking up a livelihood (the expression may be understood literally and metaphorically), employment for wives and children, cheap living except for house room, and cheap pleasure. And in this wilderness of unconnected lives and severed classes those who have known a better state need feel no shame in a rapid decline to the low social and moral state surrounding them.[58]

Samuel and Henrietta Barnett, who worked with Potter's sister Kate at this time, applauded the diagnosis, writing to Beatrice that they thought she had 'said exactly the right thing and in a tone both judicial and considerate – Do it again.'[59]

This fragment captures how social workers like Potter and the Barnetts worked with a social geography in mind, a sense of social relationships in a larger urban context. As they went about their day-to-day round of charity work, practical reformers conceived the sprawling, formless morass of this 'great hungry sea', in Arthur Sherwell's imagery of 1901, in highly diagnostic terms that are historically very revealing. This London of the reformist imagination – an observed and interpreted topography of wealth, poverty, glittering achievement and miserable squalor, of individuals connected and alone, social groups cohering or antagonistic – comes alive for us in these sources. As they confronted the miserable, daunting neighbourhoods of 'Outcast London', reformers used and re-used a stock of tropes and interpretive elements as a language that helped make sense of the urban setting on their terms. Their work was sustained by this language, and essential elements of their activism can be recaptured through it. They had an urban imagination, we might say, articulated in a diagnostic language of social description that offered a justification of their work, and that became tangible through their practical interventions into the lives and circumstances of the poor.

Accordingly, in the chapters that follow, we pay close attention to the ideas, values and responses of historical individuals, to the extent that these are discernible in memoirs, letters, speeches and sermons. Rather than assuming the direct influence of thinkers such as Ruskin, Arnold or Green on active reformers, we excavate traces of a more elusive outlook. In taking up Collini's 'embedded' approach to the ideas and values of practical reformers, this study draws on contextualised approaches to the history of ideas that resist simplistic notions of influence and artificially sharp intellectual positions. 'The more their extensive writings on social issues are probed', wrote the historian of a similarly diffused and disjointed movement, Christian Socialism, through the Victorian period, 'the more it becomes clear that the social and political ideas of the Christian Socialists were derived from reformist currents of opinion within the educated classes rather than from their own theological learning'.[60] This book sets out to explain the diffuse, disjointed late-century effort to ameliorate urban poverty through cultural philanthropy in similar terms: as a pattern of activity grounded in a 'moral imagination' broadly shared between liberal-minded social reformers, that was given scope and direction by a coherent language of urban diagnosis.

A pattern of activity emerges as we absorb the evidence of charitable appeals, settlement reports, the philanthropic proposals and debates that peppered the periodicals and newspapers of the late Victorian period. A recognition grows that cultural philanthropy was a less aberrant, less marginal and less 'aesthetic' undertaking than it might seem at first sight.

Notes

1 Bod. L: Nevinson Papers, MSS Eng. Misc. e 610/1, [journal, 1893] ff. 24–5. Nevinson concluded that the facility was 'something between a prison and a palace', f. 25.

2 LMA: LCC/MIN/7784, ff. 80, 153.

3 The term 'cultural philanthropy' was likely coined by F. Borzello, *Civilising Caliban: The Misuse of Art 1875–1980* (London: Faber and Faber, 2014 [1987]), chapter 5 'The Theory of Cultural Philanthropy', pp. 32–9, and A. Anderson and E. Darling, 'The Hill Sisters: Cultural Philanthropy and the Embellishment of Lives in late-Nineteenth Century England' in E. Darley and L. Whitworth (eds), *Women and the Making of Built Space in England, 1870–1950* (Aldershot: Ashgate, 2007), pp. 51–68.

4 For 'missionary aestheticism' see I. Fletcher, 'Some Aspects of Aestheticism' in O. M. Brack (ed.), *Twilight of the Dawn: Studies in English Literature in Transition* (Tuscon: University of Arizona Press, 1987), pp. 1–33, and D. Maltz, *British Aestheticism and the Urban Working Classes, 1870–1900: Beauty for the People* (Basingstoke: Palgrave Macmillan, 2006).

5 J. Walvin, *Victorian Values* (London: Penguin, 1988), p. 96.

6 U. Henriques, *Before the Welfare State: Social Administration in Early Industrial Britain* (London: Longman, 1979), pp. 266–7. The terminologies of social class used in this book generally follow historical convention, although the complexities and ambiguities noted by leading scholars (see J. Harris, *Private Lives, Public Spirit: A Social History of Britain, 1870–1914* (Oxford: Oxford University Press, 1993), pp. 6–11 for example) are not ignored. As we are primarily concerned with the actions of middle class social workers, the terms of social description used often follow their practice.

7 A. S. Wohl, 'Octavia Hill and the Homes of the London Poor', *Journal of British Studies* 10:2 (1971), p. 131, f. n. 109.

8 D. Fraser, *The Evolution of the British Welfare State* (London: Macmillan, 1973), pp.115–34; see also D. Roberts, *Victorian Origins of the British Welfare State* (New Haven: Yale University Press, 1960); M. Bruce, *The Coming of the Welfare State* (London: Batsford, 1961).

9 F. Prochaska, *The Voluntary Impulse: Philanthropy in Modern Britain* (London: Faber and Faber, 1988), xiii. See also his 'Philanthropy' in F. M. L. Thompson (ed.), *The Cambridge Social History of Britain, 1750–1950* (vol. 3) (Cambridge: Cambridge University Press, 1990), pp. 357–93, and *Christianity and Social Service in Modern Britain: The Disinherited Spirit* (Oxford: Oxford University Press, 2006).

10 A. Kidd, 'Civil Society or the State? Recent Approaches to the History of Voluntary Welfare' *Journal of Historical Sociology* 15:3 (2002), pp. 328–42 and his *State, Society and the Poor in Nineteenth-Century England* (Basingstoke: Macmillan, 1999), chapter 1.

11 First encouraged by B. Harrison, 'Philanthropy and the Victorians' *Victorian Studies* 9 (1966), pp. 353–74.

12 F. Prochaska, *Royal Bounty: The Making of a Welfare Monarchy* (New Haven: Yale University Press, 1995), p. 67.

13 See especially F. Prochaska, *Women and Philanthropy in Nineteenth Century England* (Oxford: Clarendon Press, 1980); J. Lewis, *Women and Social Action in Victorian and Edwardian England* (Stanford: Stanford University Press, 1991); and E. Ross, *Love and Toil: Motherhood in Outcast London 1870–1918* (Oxford: Oxford University Press, 1993). On the religious dimension, an important early study was K. Inglis, 'English Nonconformity and Social Reform, 1880–1900' *Past and Present* 13 (April 1958), pp. 73–88; and see for example H. M. Wach, 'Unitarian Philanthropy and Cultural Hegemony in Comparative Perspective: Manchester and Boston, 1827–1848' *Journal of Social History* 26 (1993), pp. 539–57.

14 M. E. Rose, 'Culture, Philanthropy and the Manchester Middle Classes' in A. J. Kidd and K. W. Roberts (eds), *City, Class and Culture: Studies of Social Policy and Cultural Production in Victorian Manchester* (Manchester: Manchester

University Press, 1985), pp. 103–17; S. Gunn, 'The Ministry, the Middle Class and the "Civilizing Mission" in Manchester, 1850–80' *Social History* 21 (1996), pp. 22–36.

15 H. Malchow, 'Public Gardens and Social Action in Late Victorian London' *Victorian Studies* 29 (1985), pp. 97–124.

16 R. Livesey, 'Reading for Character: Women Social Reformers and Narratives of the Urban Poor in Late Victorian and Edwardian London' *Journal of Victorian Culture* 9:1 (2004), pp. 43–67; G. Ginn, 'Answering the "Bitter Cry": Urban Description and Social Reform in the Late-Victorian East End' *London Journal* 31:2 (2006), pp. 179–200.

17 R. Henkle, '*East End 1888*' (review essay) *Victorian Studies* 33:2 (1990), p. 365.

18 B. Harris, *The Origins of the British Welfare State: Society, State and Social Welfare in England and Wales, 1800–1945* (Basingstoke: Palgrave, 2004), p. 75. Key texts in this vein include P. Bailey, *Leisure and Class in Victorian England: Rational Recreation and the Contest for Control 1830–1885* (London: Routledge and Kegan Paul, 1978); and P. McCann, *Popular Education and Socialization in the Nineteenth Century* (London: Methuen, 1977). A. Chapman, 'The People's Palace for East London' (M.Phil. thesis, University of Hull, 1978) follows this line in presenting the People's Palace as an expression of the drive for 'rational recreation'.

19 See R. Price, 'The Working Men's Club Movement and Victorian Social Reform Ideology' *Victorian Studies* 15 (1971), pp. 117–47.

20 G. Stedman Jones, 'Preface to the 1984 Edition', *Outcast London: A Study in the Relationship between Classes in Victorian Society* (London: Penguin, 1992 [1971]), p. xv.

21 Harris, *The Origins of the British Welfare State*, p. 75.

22 Stedman Jones, *Outcast London*, p. 240.

23 Prochaska, *The Voluntary Impulse*, pp. 27–31.

24 S. Barnett, 'Distress in East London' *Nineteenth Century* 20 (November 1886), p. 682. Tebbutt explores the structured context of female oral culture in the formation of 'knowable communities' in *Women's Talk? A Social History of 'Gossip' in Working-class Neighbourhoods, 1880–1960* (Aldershot: Scolar Press, 1995).

25 For the provision of cultural amenities within the auspices of the Co-operative movement, see for example S. Drodge, 'Co-operative Society Libraries and Education in the Nineteenth Century: A Preliminary Assessment' *Studies in the Education of Adults* 20:1 (April 1988), pp. 49–59.

26 See essays in the collection *The Uses of Charity: The Poor on Relief in the Nineteenth-Century Metropolis* (Philadelphia: University of Pennsylvania Press, 1990) that explore how the uses of charity by recipients could be different to the purposes of donors; A. Davin, *Growing Up Poor: Home, School and Street in London 1870–1914* (London: Rivers Oram Press, 1996); V. Richmond, *Clothing the Poor in Nineteenth-Century England* (Cambridge: Cambridge University Press, 2013).

27 A. August, 'A culture of Consolation? Rethinking Politics in Working-class London, 1870–1914' *Historical Research* 74: 183 (2001), esp. pp. 202–5.

28 C. Chinn, *Poverty amid Prosperity: The Urban Poor in England, 1834–1914* (Manchester: Manchester University Press, 1995), p. 6.

29 J. Rose, *The Intellectual Life of the British Working Classes* (New Haven: Yale University Press, 2001), p. 80.

30 H. Meller, *Leisure and the Changing City, 1870–1914* (London: Routledge and Kegan Paul, 1976), esp. pp. 56–71; B. Beaven, *Leisure, Citizenship and Working-class Men in Britain, 1850–1945* (Manchester: Manchester University Press, 2005), esp. pp. 16–43.

31 E. P. Hennock, 'The Measurement of Urban Poverty: From the Metropolis to the Nation, 1880–1920' *Economic History Review* 2nd ser. 40:2 (1987), p. 212.

32 P. J. Keating, 'Fact and Fiction in the East End' in H. J. Dyos and M. Wolff (eds), *The Victorian City: Images and Realities* (vol. 2) (London: Routledge and Kegan Paul, 1973), p. 585.

33 H. J. Dyos and D. A. Reeder, 'Slums and Suburbs', in Dyos and Wolff, *The Victorian City* (vol. 1), p. 362.

34 For 'slum' terminology and the problem of representation, see A. Mayne, *The Imagined Slum: Newspaper Representation in Three Cities, 1870–1914* (Leicester: Leicester University Press, 1993) and the debate that followed in *Social History* during 1995.

35 Stedman Jones, *Outcast London*, pp. 281–2; J. Walkowitz, *City of Dreadful Delight: Narratives of Sexual Danger in Late-Victorian London* (Chicago: University of Chicago Press, 1992), p. 26.

36 Although the term 'East End' dated from mid-century it entered wider currency around 1880; see W. J. Fishman, *East End 1888: A Year in a London Borough among the Labouring Poor* (London: Duckworth, 1988), p. 1. Nick Draper explains how South London's character and identity were represented from mid-century in '"Across the Bridges": Representations of Victorian South London' *London Journal* 29:1 (2004), pp. 25–43.

37 C. Booth, *Life and Labour of the People in London: Third Series: Religious Influences* (vol. 4: Inner South London) (London: Macmillan and Co., 1902), p. 97.

38 'Is It Not Time?' *PMG* 16 October 1883, p. 1.

39 Stedman Jones, *Outcast London*, pp. 222–3.

40 K. Lynch, *Good City Form* (Cambridge, MA: MIT Press, 1984), p. 36.

41 M. Harrison, 'Art and Philanthropy: T. C. Horsfall and the Manchester Art Museum' in Kidd and Roberts (eds), *City, Class and Culture*, pp.120–47; A. Woodson-Boulton, '"Industry without Art is Brutality": Aesthetic Ideology and Social Practice in Victorian Art Museums' *Journal of British Studies* 46:1 (2007) pp. 47–71 and her *Transformative Beauty: Art Museums in Industrial Britain* (Stanford: Stanford University Press, 2012); A. Anderson, 'Victorian High Society and Social Duty: The Promotion of "Recreative Learning and Voluntary Teaching"' *History of Education* 31:4 (2002), pp. 311–34; A. Geddes Poole, *Philanthropy and the Construction of Victorian Women's Citizenship: Lady Frederick Cavendish and Miss Emma Cons* (Toronto: Toronto University Press, 2014), esp. chapters 4 and 5.

42 Anderson, 'Victorian High Society and Social Duty', p. 313.

43 C. Waters, *British Socialists and the Politics of Popular Culture, 1884–1914* (Stanford: Stanford University Press, 1990), chapter 3, 'Philanthropy and the Social Utility of Free Time', pp. 65–96.

44 Waters, *British Socialists and the Politics of Popular Culture*, p. 68.

45 S. Koven, *Slumming: Sexual and Social Politics in Victorian London* (New Haven: Yale University Press, 2004), esp. chapter 5; S. Meacham, *Toynbee Hall and Social Reform, 1880–1914: The Search for Community* (New Haven: Yale University Press, 1987); A. Creedon, *Only a Woman: Henrietta Barnett, Social Reformer and Founder of Hampstead Garden Suburb* (Chichester: Phillimore, 2006); A. Turberfield, *John Scott Lidgett: Archbishop of British Methodism?* (London: Epworth Press, 2003).

46 R. Gilchrist, 'Settlements and the Arts' in R. Gilchrist and T. Jeffs (eds), *Settlements, Social Change and Community Action: Good Neighbours* (London: Jessica Kingsley, 2001), pp. 173–93.

47 H. Meller, 'Urban Renewal and Citizenship: The Quality of Life in British Cities, 1890–1990' *Urban History* 22 (1995), p. 69.

48 Beaven, *Leisure, Citizenship and Working-class Men*, p. 1. 'The historian R. H. Tawney and social reformers like Samuel Barnett saw "social" citizenship as an activity that obliged the individual to engage in "public spiritedness" and carry out wider social and civic duties' (p. 8).

49 Matthews-Jones' 2009 University of Manchester thesis is now (2016) being pre-
    pared for publication under the title *Settling: Class and Urban Philanthropy in the
    British University Settlement Movement*.
50 N. Scotland, *Squires in the Slums: Settlements and Missions in Late-Victorian
    London* (London: I. B. Tauris, 2007).
51 S. Koven, 'Culture and Poverty: the London Settlement House Movement 1870 to
    1914' (Ph.D. thesis, Harvard University, 1987).
52 See G. P. Moss and M. V. Saville, *From Palace to College: An Illustrated History of
    Queen Mary College* (London: Queen Mary College, 1985); S. Joyce, 'Castles in
    the Air: the People's Palace, Cultural Reformism and the East End Working Class'
    Victorian Studies 39:4 (1996), pp. 513–38, and Chapman, 'The People's Palace for
    East London'.
53 Borzello, *Civilising Caliban*, especially chapter 16, 'The Legacy', pp. 130–9.
54 D. Weiner, *Architecture and Social Reform in Late-Victorian London* (Manchester:
    Manchester University Press, 1994).
55 Maltz, *British Aestheticism and the Urban Working Classes*, p. 2. See also S.
    Eagles, *After Ruskin: The Social and Political Legacies of a Victorian Prophet,
    1870–1920* (Oxford: Oxford University Press, 2010), chapter 3, and M. Girouard,
    Sweetness and Light: the 'Queen Anne' Movement 1860–1900 (Oxford: Clarendon
    Press, 1977), pp. 4–9.
56 Woodson-Boulton, 'Industry Without Art is Brutality', p. 50.
57 S. Collini, *Public Moralists: Political Thought and Intellectual Life in Britain*
    (Oxford: Clarendon Press, 1991), pp. 4–5.
58 B. Potter, 'A Lady's View of the Unemployed at the East', *PMG* 18 February 1886, p. 11.
59 BLPES: Passfield Papers, 2/1/2/8, f. 558, letter from S. A. Barnett, 26 February 1886.
60 E. Norman, *The Victorian Christian Socialists* (Cambridge: Cambridge University
    Press, 1987), p. 5.

2   Sources and explanations

So far we have outlined this book's intentions, indicated how it relates to the relevant scholarship, and explained our focus on London and the basic tenor of our approach. In this chapter we go on to clarify and frame key aspects of the central argument, starting with the fundamental sources of this apparently quixotic cultural activism in the slums. In a basic sense a deep and almost instinctive Romanticism would seem its ultimate origin. Clearly, this is not the place for a sustained account of this rich and complex tendency and its lingering afterlife through our period, but we do need to capture its presence in some elemental sense.[1] By the 1870s, late Romanticism was simultaneously an academic style in the visual arts, a consumer taste in homewares and furnishings, a poetic preoccupation with individual subjectivity, and a radical call for democratic arts and crafts among other things. Two particular aspects call for our attention as we consider how it might have infused so unlikely a quarter of public life as social work.

The first is the religious dimension, as the world-renouncing dogmatic piety of evangelicalism gave way to notions of spiritual immanence in the visible world that owed much to Romantic impulses. A pithy illustration of this appears in the 1888 bestseller *Robert Elsmere*, where the novelist Mary Ward – herself a sturdy and pragmatic liberal reformer – dramatised the religious and social dilemmas of contemporary clergy in her eponymous hero. Robert's first encounter with the trenchant evangelicalism of his future wife comes early on as Catherine frets over her sister's love of the violin. How could any Christian, she asks her suitor, 'spend the few short years of the earthly combat in any pursuit, however novel and exquisite, which merely aimed at the gratification of the senses, and implied in the pursuer the emphasising rather than the surrender of self?' Here Ward was looking to personify a larger dilemma: how was the evangelical to respond to the presence of beauty in the world? Robert responds, she explained to her readers,

> very much as Kingsley would have argued it...dwelling on the function of pure beauty in life, and on the influence of beauty on character, pointing out the value to the race of all individual development, and pressing home on her the natural religious question: How are the artistic aptitudes

to be explained unless the Great Designer meant them to have a use and function in His world?

The clincher comes as Elsmere rhapsodises about the practical work being undertaken on these lines in the London slums:

> Then he told her much that he knew about the humanising effect of music on the poor. He described to her the efforts of a London society, of which he was a subscribing member, to popularise the best music among the lowest class; he dwelt almost with passion on the difference between the joys to be got out of such things and the common brutalising joys of the workman….he was only talking the commonplaces of his day. But to her they were not commonplaces at all. She looked at him from time to time, her great eyes lightening and deepening as it seemed with every fresh thrust of his. 'I am grateful to you', she said at last with an involuntary outburst, 'I am *very* grateful to you!'[2]

This emphasis in religious life on humanity's intrinsically social being and the plethora of improving influences that might assist moral emancipation is one measure of Romanticism's contribution to social thought and activism in our period. Another is the explicit moral status given to nature and the natural world by educated opinion in this period, the 'naturalistic fallacy' of late Romanticism that sustained the provision of moralising beauty to the urban poor in a fundamental way. In 1890 a perceptive young American graduate, Robert Woods, encountered the cultural mission at its peak as he spent six months investigating the range and scope of British social work amid urban poverty. 'It is often thought that the ministry of beauty to the poor is a merely sentimental thing', Woods later declared in a lecture about his London experiences. 'No mistake could be greater.' His logic is worth recounting, capturing as it does the ethical convictions about nature's 'refining influence' that made this kind of social work possible.

> The reason for the mistake is that people who are not poor breathe in this refining influence as plentifully as they breathe the atmosphere, without thinking how necessary it is for the renewing of the better nature. Suppose you had never run in a green field, or walked down a shady lane. Suppose you had never looked over a broad landscape, had never seen the open sky – never really seen a sunset – never heard the distant murmur of the wind among the trees. No flowers, no brooks, no birds; save the mere change of temperature, no springtime. Suppose music and pictures were gone; or rather had never come – for we are supposing all these things banished not only from the present experience, but out of all your memory and out of all the subconscious influences of your life. Such an awful gloom is the common inheritance of the poor in great cities. If one

could imagine the moral element being developed under such circumstances, how could it be sustained, how could it find expression?[3]

A late-century persistence of Romantic thought and feeling was clearly important, then, but this insight does not take us very far in explaining the origins of the period's 'ministry of beauty' to urban neighbourhoods and the poor. Can we account for these more substantively, and with some degree of historical precision?

* * *

Part of the problem is that although 'culture' was a vehicle for moralising social reform in this period, social workers and practical reformers rarely set out systematically to define what they meant by it. Instead they relied on conventional contemporary meanings that were implicit and left unstated. For Raymond Williams, the founder of modern cultural studies, nineteenth-century usage posited culture as 'a state or process of human perfection, in terms of certain absolute or universal values'.[4] It subsisted in a range of moral and intellectual activities that, in Williams' phrase, were 'cultured' in the sense that they were '[separated] from the driven impetus of a new kind of society'. Accordingly, culture was closely aligned to nineteenth-century moral absolutes, serving as 'a court of human appeal, to be set over the processes of practical social judgement and yet to offer itself as a mitigating and rallying alternative'.[5] It supplied a plane of reference against which given human behaviour, endeavours and social arrangements could be measured for their intrinsic value.

Understood in this way as a reified set of values, the term 'culture' invoked conceptions of truth, beauty and goodness that were universal and timeless. They were truths, moreover, that for the Victorians had profound personal and social utility: making or re-making the individual, and through personal reform enacting a transformation of society through its human relations. In this way 'culture' was also understood as intrinsically active and progressive, as a process of self-cultivation with large social implications. For the *Quarterly Review* in 1874, grasping 'to extract from the new Culture, of which we hear so much, a precise account of its meaning', the answer lay in an active principle of self-cultivation found in German Idealism, modelled on the example of Goethe and popularised in Britain by Teutophiles like Thomas Carlyle.[6] It was in this sense that Edward Adolf Sonnenschein, a Latin scholar and newly installed Professor of Classics at Mason College, Birmingham, encapsulated the term 'culture' as 'the complete spiritual development of the individual' for a prize night audience in October 1885, for example.[7] But it is of course Matthew Arnold, the poet, critic and educationalist, who 'has exercised an immense, perhaps decisive, influence over our whole way of thinking about 'culture' and its role as a possible antidote or corrective to the cramping hold of the narrowly practical and mundane'.[8] Culture in Arnold's sense was a moral undertaking that he defined simply as 'a study of perfection. It moves by the force, not merely or primarily of the scientific passion for pure knowledge, but also of the moral and social passion for doing good.'[9] For this first great exponent of high culture in an increasingly democratic age, culture had a vast remit, 'lead[ing] us to conceive of true perfection, developing all sides of our humanity, and, as a general perfection, developing all parts of our society'.[10] Dismayed by ignorance, prejudice, class interest and narrow sectarianism, Arnold famously insisted upon culture's perfecting mission to society at large. Seeing it as a solvent to partiality and prejudice, he became perhaps the leading Victorian exponent of the social value of culture. 'Plenty of people', he wrote in another canonical passage,

> will try to indoctrinate the masses with the set of ideas and judgements constituting the creed of their own profession or party…but culture works differently. It does not try to teach down to the level of inferior classes; it does not try to win them for this or that sect of its own, with ready-made judgements and watchwords. It seeks to do away with classes; to make the best that has been thought and known in the world current everywhere; to make all men live in an atmosphere of sweetness and light, where they may use ideas, as it uses them itself, freely, – nourished and not bound by them.[11]

We think of these views as 'Arnoldian', and indeed they are poetically expressed, but they were far from idiosyncratic or unique. Rather, his pronouncements represent, as Turner observes, 'a set of more or less traditional English humanist values long employed to oppose commercialism, excessive religious zeal, dissent from Anglicanism, philosophical mechanism, political radicalism, subjective morality, and social individualism'.[12] Arnold's formulation became the most famous statement of these values, but he had no part in their coining. José Harris suggests the poet's 'championship of humanistic "Hellenism" at the expense of Nonconformist "Hebraism"' was symptomatic of the steadily declining credibility of strict evangelical, Puritan virtues among educated men and women since the advent of social and political reform in the 1820s. As Harris notes, by the close of the century Hellenistic ideals had been 'widely invoked to legitimise and dignify a vast range of social activities and institutions of the period, including boarding-schools, civic architecture, homosexual relationships, organized charity, mystical religion, and women's rights'.[13] This 'Hellenistic', 'Arnoldian' reification of truth and beauty embodied in fine art and in the force of intellect, the universal currency of 'the best that has been thought and known', was available, ready-at-hand, for philanthropic late-Victorians busy with their own 'moral and social passion for doing good' in their dealings with the poor.

When understood in terms of the development of the individual and their capacities, then, 'self-culture' supplied an active principle of self-improvement, an engine of ethical, scientific and social progress in human history and the rock on which the nineteenth-century's great expansion of educational provision rested. Taken in an immediate sense, as something that occupied an individual's time in a process of moral self-improvement, 'self-culture' came into general currency through the catchier term 're-creation', which always meant far more than simple leisure or entertainment. It implied a moral process of renewal and refreshment drawing on older associations with consolation and spiritual comfort. One of the key figures in this study, the Wesleyan social reformer John Scott Lidgett, captures the connection for us:

> What do we want for re-creation? We need to be taken out of our wonted surroundings; to have new interests awakened by which unused faculties may be called forth; to be brought into contact with things great and beautiful in the realms of Nature, Art, and Character, in presence of which we can forget ourselves, not only our frets and troubles, but our ambitions, and this in the company of kindred minds with whom we can share these interests and the joy and hilarity which they create....When we get out of ourselves, and after the weary pilgrimage of daily life plunge ourselves into the pure flood of truth and beauty and goodness round us, then we are refreshed.[14]

Social reformers among the late-Victorian generation imbued these ideals and attitudes as easily as they inhaled the air, so that we find versions of them widely shared and exchanged. In 1876, asking rhetorically what the future 'democratisation' of England would hold, one advocate of Sunday recreation responded to his own question in entirely conventional terms that '*the issue will mainly depend on the mental and moral culture of the custodians of political power*'.[15] And at the end of our period, trying to capture the passivity and alienation of London's urban masses, suffocated in their unvarying daily routine between city and suburb, the New Liberal social critic and South Londoner Charles Masterman flattered himself that he could explain 'our silence'. It was an apathetic silence and disaffection that turned its back on self-culture and moral re-creation:

> Kindly and enthusiastic millionaires build for us art galleries, collections of paintings and statuary, museums filled with stuffed beasts and the products of foreign lands. We gaze on their imposing façades as we hurry to work in the morning, or hurry at even to rest. Amiable young men elevate us by frequent lectures on the ethics of Dante, the poetry of the Renaissance, and similar pleasing topics....Lectures, sermons, the charms of oratory, impassioned debate, the *obiter dicta* of great and suave politicians preachers and philanthropists, art, science, foreign diplomacy, the ways and manners of men and nations, the vastness and variety of the universe – all these to us who work and devour and rest, and rest and devour and work, pass by us and over us and beyond us, the mere shadow of a dream.[16]

The spiritualising and moralising influences captured in the term 'culture' offered to ameliorate the grim daily realities of urban poverty in a host of ways. A vehicle for the moral and social improvement of individuals beset by poverty and its manifold curses, culture was seen as a powerful moralising antidote to pauperism, intemperance, brutishness and passive apathy. It had an environmental dimension, in that a cultured appreciation of art and beauty might mitigate the dreary settings and everyday routine of city life and repetitive labour, and perhaps inculcate an urge to renounce them. In leisure, moralising recreation promised to reduce patronage of the sordid pleasures of the public house, countering the siren vulgarities of music hall and the cheap street press and 'penny dreadfuls'. As a mode of education, self-culture sat alongside the enduring Victorian ethos of self-help through intellectual effort and improvement. An appreciation of the 'higher things' of human civilisation and achievement would develop personal character, engender self-discipline, and overcome prejudices and self-interest through an inculcated respect for moral order. It would establish a basis for civic identity, and membership in a collective life of the mind beyond narrow partisan interests.

These precepts – none of them, we immediately recognise, entirely free of what we might call middle-class assumptions, and all stamped with the characteristic moralising liberalism of their day – were key articles of faith for the cultural philanthropists we discuss in the following chapters. Although their work self-consciously aimed to intervene, moralise and thereby re-make plebeian identities and outlooks, their efforts were not entirely driven by the class self-interest that an earlier generation of historians regarded as intrinsic to Victorian 'rational recreation'.[17] Goldman demonstrates how the university-trained intellectuals of this period, for example, shared (rather than imposed) an anti-materialistic, idealist social outlook with working-class students in the labour movement and extension classes. We find similar parallels in the examples discussed here, and a similar emphasis, despite their unwavering moralism, 'on collective goals and social rather than individual enhancement'.[18] Although easily lost in their earnest statements of moralising intervention, the late-Victorian cultural reformers addressed genuine challenges of urban amenity and social equity by attempting to build affective communities of interest, something that today we might call 'social capital'.

* * *

Who were these cultural reformers? Many are today lost from view, obscure in their historical anonymity, and so the chapters that follow examine only the most prominent working in three iconic neighbourhoods of 'Outcast London' in the last quarter of the century. In the Whitechapel, Mile End and inner South London of the 1880s and 1890s clustered groups of reformers: men and women, clergymen, parish workers, earnest young spinsters and bachelor graduates, writers and utopians, dreamers and activists of all sorts. The most articulate and prolific of these rather dominate our discussion: key figures like clergyman Samuel Barnett and his wife Henrietta, the energetic Wesleyan John Scott Lidgett, the novelist Walter Besant, the businessman Sir Edmund Hay Currie and the housing reformer Octavia Hill. Attention to some of their lesser-known colleagues rounds out the work of active reformers in general, rather than these major figures alone.

How have historians tended to explain the methods and motives of these men and women? As a broad observation, they typically condense the complexity of motive and purpose involved. The main ideas of key Victorian thinkers such as Arnold, Ruskin, Carlyle, Charles Kingsley or William Morris (or, in the case of Toynbee Hall, T. H. Green and the Oxford Idealists) are briefly paraphrased as an 'influence' or an 'intellectual context' to explain the practical efforts of others.[19] The seductive accessibility of the ideas of the great thinkers has resulted in over-stated claims about their 'influence' on social activism. If a charity worker upheld the social utility of liberal culture, for example, historians routinely assume that he or she was implicitly Matthew Arnold's disciple, sharing his views or heavily in his debt. If they advocated fine art for general social wellbeing, by association they seem evidence of 'Ruskinian' thinking put to practical effect. Judith Walkowitz talks of Samuel Barnett and 'his new squirearchy of East London' who were 'imbued with Arnoldian conceptions of culture', for instance, but the precise terms of the relationship is not scrutinised.[20] Broad parallels in thinking are configured as a vague intellectual influence that is rarely traced in detail. According to Meacham, in another example, Barnett 'believed with Matthew Arnold in a hierarchy of cultural values and in the necessity for a disinterested elite to instil that hierarchy into the minds of working-class men and women by instilling it into their habits'.[21] Emily Abel maintains that Barnett 'followed Matthew Arnold in his criticism of the way of life of the upper classes, in his disdain for practical politics and above all in his determination to spread the best culture through all levels of society'.[22] But then Gavin Budge speaks casually of Ruskin, not Arnold, as the Barnetts' 'mentor in matters aesthetic', a line of argument pursued by Eagles, Maltz and Matthews-Jones.[23] The 'Arnoldian' tag has also been invoked to explain other cultural philanthropists such as Walter Besant. A literary scholar, having cited Besant's view that 'those who master any one of the Arts...have left once and for ever the ranks of disorder', comments that 'a practical and optimistic Matthew Arnold seems to be addressing us here'.[24]

But it is clear that far more diffuse conceptions than this shaped Toynbee Hall and kindred efforts at cultural provision. 'The underlying philosophy of the settlement was derived from various sources', José Harris observes insightfully, 'from Octavia Hill's desire to "elevate" the lives of the poor, from Matthew Arnold's belief in the civilizing power of "culture", from T. H. Green's doctrine of "personal service" and from the Christian socialist emphasis on "social reconciliation"'.[25] Similarly, Seth Koven suggests that '[s]ettlers drank deeply the teachings of Thomas Carlyle, F. D. Maurice, John Ruskin, Matthew Arnold and T. H. Green'.[26] In the case of Lidgett, one historian writes of the influence that reading the biographies of Charles Kingsley and F. D. Maurice had in turning Lidgett's theological training in a social direction.[27]

But name-dropping like this only takes us so far. It fails to explain how the formal pronouncements of leading intellectuals might later be manifested in the concrete social work undertaken by others. Undeniably, the great Victorian 'sages' were influential in quickening the moral sense of receptive readers and directing them towards practical endeavours. Octavia Hill's work in the Kyrle Society seems self-evidently derived from her artistic tutelage by Ruskin, and Sydney Cockerell's effervescent diary entries of the late 1880s, during his initial fixation with Ruskinian ideas, confirm their powerful inspirational force.[28] But 'influence' cannot be assumed unilaterally: individual commitment was always initiated in a range of ways, from a myriad of intertwined sources. The practical shape of that commitment was individually fixed by a personal mixture of beliefs, assumptions, values and motives. When Cockerell first met Octavia Hill in December 1886, for example, he was advised by her that Ruskin 'was to be taken rather as an inspiration than as a practical guide',[29] despite acknowledging her own enormous debt to him and his ideas. One suspects that most practical reformers regarded the influence of the great social commentators in similar terms. Walter Besant recalled being inspired by Carlyle as a young man, but it was an abstract and impractical influence:

> his readers were lifted by certain of his chapters or pages into regions of thought which were to them purely imaginary – the lovely creation of a mere dreamer; they wandered in those regions with the help and guidance of their prophet, but they never conceived the possibility of the dream being realised.[30]

Similarly, as a young curate Samuel Barnett was described as 'more inclined to sociology than theology and…a devoted disciple of Carlyle'[31] but his contemporaries agreed that his mature social thought was unfocused and unsystematic, owing as much to feeling and a genius for organising others as to intellectual conviction. The key here is that we need to be cautious in ascribing unilateral influence when presented with apparent affinities in outlook and expression.

The memoirs of many social workers also suggest less rarefied origins for their personal activism. Many were drawn into social work by encountering poverty and social conditions at first hand. The private exploration of urban slum districts (the practice easily mocked as 'slumming') was a common experience of this generation, as with Francis Fletcher Vane, an unusual Toynbee Hall resident in that he was a military man, a commissioned officer in the Scots Guards. 'It was my custom', he remembered, 'when there was little doing in the matter of parades and guards, sometimes accompanied by a brother officer, to seek adventures by fixing upon some district to explore.

Naturally this led me to explore the East End. At any rate this method...was more instructive than always loafing in well-known clubs.'[32] Stimulation also came from writers like George Sims, Andrew Mearns and the 'social problem' novelists. In Vane's case, he felt drawn to social activism by 'a general sympathy for suffering' and 'much reading of books respecting the poor, including Charles Booth's and the novels of Besant'.[33] Such prosaic accounts of social workers' first steps into practical activism are by no means rare. Yet historians are loath to seek the sources of personal activism in such commonplace experiences, and prefer to explain the beliefs of active social workers by reference to formal social theory. Helen Meller, for instance, acknowledges that reformers such as Samuel Barnett pursued 'immediately practical objectives', but invokes the views of the commentator James Bryce, the Oxford philosopher T. H. Green and the sociologist Patrick Geddes to amplify Barnett's views on urban problems.[34] Such treatment may help frame an intellectual context, but it can only ever be shorthand for the cast of mind and manners that we might call a 'moral imagination', treated here as an underlying and widely shared framework of evaluation and response that shaped the everyday activism of practical reformers.[35]

In this book, therefore, we proceed on the premise that ascribing the direct motivation of active Victorian social workers to the 'influence' of celebrated thinkers and social critics denies the historical situation its complexity. At best it only approximates, and at worst it distorts, our understanding of historical actions and their sources. Stefan Collini offers a better approach in his account of Victorian political attitudes. Against the conventional explanation that these 'should be seen as evidence of the "influence" of the most prominent theories of the period, such as Utilitarianism, or Social Darwinism or philosophical Idealism', Collini sets his sights upon a more diffuse object. 'My initial assumption has been, rather, that those theories acquired their prominence partly because they gave a coherent form and foundation to attitudes already widely, if unselfconsciously, entertained', he writes.

> In other words, political arguments, and their attempted systematisation as bodies of theory, must, if they are to have any persuasiveness, deploy, re-work, or otherwise make use of the shared evaluative language of those to whom they are addressed, and hence must appeal to the ideals and aspirations which that language represents. In this sense, political theories are parasitic upon the less explicit habits of response and evaluation that are deeply embedded in the culture.[36]

Lawrence Goldman poses a similar rejoinder to assumptions about the widespread influence of T. H. Green and his 'Oxford Idealism' in inspiring reform movements such as university extension and the settlements. 'Above all', he writes, 'in considering Green's influence and the influence of his ideas it needs to be remembered that, in many circumstances, it was not idealism that made a certain type of outlook and personality: it was a certain type of personality that was attracted to idealism'.[37] In a similar way this book considers the

relationship between the moral foundations of practical activism and the concrete schemes prosecuted by late-Victorian social reformers. Tracing the active
presence of a consistent framework of values constituting this 'moral imagination' reveals how practical social workers used (in Collini's terms) a 'shared
evaluative language' to sustain their 'habits of response and evaluation'.

* * *

Alternatively, a more limited explanation of the cultural mission to the slums
might simply acknowledge its resemblance to the 'social Christianity' associated with the Immanence theology of F. D. Maurice, and let the matter rest.
Recognising that Samuel Barnett's efforts in Whitechapel were distinctive but
not unique, we might be content to see it as an off-shoot of Broad Church
Anglican concepts of parochial welfare, inspired by Maurice's theology of
social redemption and pioneered in experimental parishes like St Mary's,
Bryanston Square, in the late 1860s.[38] Certainly the late-Victorian period saw
a rich crop of improving endeavours in city neighbourhoods sponsored by
local clergy, their volunteers and supporters: evening classes, reading groups,
social clubs, music recitals, youth groups and so on, all part of a 'diffusive
Christianity' optimistically sown across urban parishes and neighbourhoods
by church and chapel interests. This term was coined in 1903 by Edward
Talbot, Bishop of Rochester, to denote a social faith shorn of dogmatic
theology, visible in the penumbra of local social agencies radiating from the
parish offices of Anglicanism. Perhaps the new 'gospel of culture' was simply
a dimension of this effort?[39] But as we see below, just as cultural philanthropy's range extended well beyond the settlements and was undertaken by
men and women with little or no exposure to formal social theory, so too did
it flourish independently of local churches and chapels in what we might
describe as an entirely secular manner. Thus we cannot hold that it was
identical to these parish endeavours, or rose directly from their animating ideas
and purposes. Any explanation that rests as heavily on the social ethics of
Maurice can only be as partial and inadequate as those that lean on Ruskinian
aesthetics, or Green and the 'Balliol mode'.

Such explanations are just as reductive as the old accounts that emphasise
'rational recreation' as simply a matter of paternalistic class self-interest, as
when Chapman bluntly characterises the work of the People's Palace as
'designed to present acceptable standards of recreational behaviour into a
working-class area and to thereby act as a means of social control'.[40] Cultural
philanthropy was not a misuse of art, a fanciful mis-application of aesthetic
theory to social circumstances, or an expression of Ruskinian 'missionary
aestheticism' to the slums.[41] Nor was it a sentimental neo-Toryism simplistically understood as the neo-chivalric social crusade of 'squires in the slums'.[42]
It was more than just 'Oxford Idealism' put into action, or a simple 'secular-
ising' transference by Anglican clergy of their energies from the redeeming
power of doctrinal religion to a new 'gospel of culture'.

These are only partial explanations. This book argues more fully that cultural philanthropy was in fact a liberal-minded response to a long, slow crisis of nineteenth-century urbanism, rather than the urgent and short-term crisis of extreme poverty that dominates many historical treatments of social affairs in the 1880s in particular. As a mode of moralising intervention into the largely self-contained world of urban poverty, it responded to the deprivation, creeping materialism and social dislocation perceived in urban modernity with a humanistic evocation of what its advocates took to be enduring, eternal values of spiritual and social well-being. The central argument is that cultural philanthropy sprang from an underlying and essentially consistent outlook, one that we can identify as a moralising, liberal social idealism that had its 'Anglican' and 'Nonconformist' varieties, as well as its 'Oxford' and 'literary' expressions and many other shades besides.

We are not surprised by the moralising element, as nineteenth-century Britain had a vibrant tradition of moral reform for social improvement.[43] But this impulse ran deeper still. 'The social imagination of the late Victorians', as Gertrude Himmelfarb writes, 'the ideas and sentiments they brought to bear upon social affairs, was an eminently moral imagination'.[44] She shows how compassion was an essentially moral instinct, with its logic and rigour as well as its more familiar sentimental qualities.[45] Witness how the meaning of 'condescension' had evolved, as Daniel Siegel has recently demonstrated, so that the older idea of a generosity of spirit transcending the line between nobility and commoner had become a pejorative term for the false renunciation of such differences in order to subtly reinforce them. As older forms of social paternalism were increasingly challenged by the liberal ethos of self-determination, Siegel observes, 'condescension' became 'a sign of an outmoded ideology; it represented the grasping determination of a ruling elite to maintain status distinctions and stifle reform'.[46] Social workers had to be well-attuned to the dangers of assuming superiority in their personal relations with the urban poor; 'condescension' and all its associations were thus to be expunged from the modern practices of charitable relief and social work. This helps explain why active reformers valued sincerity so highly in their dealings with the poor, were acutely self-aware of their intrusion into the daily life of impoverished neighbourhoods, and idealised 'a genuine, reciprocal connection between rich and poor, one in which members of both classes would learn to recognize each other as fellow beings with a practical stake in one another's welfare'.[47]

Thus despite the much-trumpeted shift to abstracted principles of 'scientific' charity relief over old-fashioned, sentimental and unsystematic alms-giving, a commitment to personal activism and moral influence continued to be vital to late-Victorian social work. It inspired among many other things the Charity Organisation Society's (COS) insistence on casework and personal cross-class relations through welfare services.[48] Practical benevolence was only effective if it was carefully directed and manifestly personal, a conviction that inspired social workers to insist on the need for mutuality between rich and poor. This was nowhere more vital, it was asserted, than in the social regeneration of

'Outcast London', the dense neighbourhoods north and south of the river with their teeming, impenetrable populations of labouring men and women and their families. Samuel Barnett, for example, maintained early in his career the Society's emphasis on casework had opened new relationships between classes. The greatest gain in COS work, he maintained in an Oxford sermon on 'The New Charity' in 1877, 'is that the thought evoked in consultation, the interest awakened by visits, the love strengthened by action, links together the rich and poor as they were linked by no old system'.[49] Personal intervention was the key, and only the personal and moralising influence of 'life upon life' could achieve genuine social amelioration.

A sense of social relationships and active citizenship were other essential ingredients. As José Harris explains, an underlying social idealism, with a flavour of moral liberalism, decisively shaped social thought and activism in the decades around the turn of the century. 'It was for a time as popular and pervasive among the socially active middle classes as evangelism or utilitarianism had been in the [earlier] nineteenth century', she observes of this idealist outlook that 'subordinat[ed] the analysis of specific social problems to a vision of reconstructing the whole of British society, together with reform of the rational understanding and moral character of individual British citizens'.[50] Importantly, these precepts were not discrete; they were not confined to individual thinkers, and their 'influence' did not flow from their example alone. Frank Turner sees a 'vast idealist presence' that was deeper still, a set of values and critical responses at work behind social criticism, political theory and theology in the late nineteenth century. This presence crystallised in the work of major social commentators and was popularised and recycled by poets and writers, but it was perhaps most tangibly vented in the practical work of active social reformers. Its ultimate source is obscure, but perhaps can be traced *inter alia*, Harris suggests, to the ongoing currency of classical Platonism, the reaction against positivist modes of thought exemplified by the mechanistic theories of the 1834 New Poor Law, 'and by the search for a "modernist" reformulation (or an ethical substitute for) traditional Christianity'.[51] Whatever its sources, by the end of the century, Turner writes,

> idealism represented an outlook that emphasized metaphysical questions in philosophy, historicist analysis of the past, the spiritual character of the world, the active powers of the human mind, intuitionism, subjective religiosity, the responsibility of individuals for undertaking moral choice and action, the relative or even absolute importance of communities and communal institutions over individual action or rights, and the shallowness of any mode of reductionist thought.[52]

This outlook galvanised the work of popular education gathering momentum through this period, and in concentrating here on the cultural mission to the slums we trace the ripples and eddies as this undercurrent manifested in schemes of practical social work. We follow Harris in seeing social idealism's essence as 'an emphasis on corporate identity, individual altruism, ethical imperatives and active citizen-participation'.[53] When it shaded into politics and social life, as Goodlad explains, this outlook was part of a liberal tradition that was 'more demanding in its conception of citizenship and, at the same time, more likely to view the state as a potential aid to individual and social welfare'. Amid the manifold tensions and paradoxes of Victorian liberalism Goodlad sees a

> remarkably durable liberal mythology – the ideals, vocabulary, and assumptions – to which contemporaries consciously and unconsciously subscribed. Although many Victorians did not regard themselves as political liberals, most were responsive to the overall projects of liberating individuals from illegitimate authority while simultaneously ensuring their moral and spiritual growth.[54]

The formal social theory that bolstered 'New Liberalism', ideas taking shape in the 1870s and 1880s through Green's 'lay sermons' and the political economists Arnold Toynbee and Alfred Marshall, absorbed these diffuse themes and forged them into a concrete intellectual position. These thinkers took the circumstances and condition of the labouring poor as an essential social problem needing redress. They were social optimists, believing themselves surrounded by ample evidence of a moral and material improvement in the character and circumstances of the working class and labouring poor.[55] In this sense they were the intellectual wing of the reform movement, sharing its pre-occupation with the 'social question' of poverty amidst plenty. But as Himmelfarb notes, 'it was the poor, rather than the very poor, who were the beneficiaries of most of the reforms of the late-Victorian and Edwardian periods'. She reminds us that it was the social condition of the labourers and semi-skilled, rather than the urban underclass, that attracted most attention:

> Instead of yet another revision of the Poor Law dealing with paupers, Parliament enacted laws for the benefit of the labouring poor: housing, workmen's compensation, extended schooling, school meals, old age pensions, cheap trains, labor exchanges, unemployment and health insurance. And instead of new and improved workhouses for paupers, philanthropists concentrated on new and improved houses for workers: 'model dwellings' and renovated flats and houses, supervised by rent collectors who doubled as social workers.[56]

It is a salutary reminder. Historians tend to jump at lurid apparitions, in this case the underclass of demoralised casual labourers, vagrants, the destitute and inevitably often criminal *lumpenproletariat* that periodically stoked the anxiety of respectable late-Victorians. As Stedman Jones famously demonstrated, much energy was spent seeking to isolate and eradicate this threatening 'residuum', often in ways that were frightfully illiberal such as labour colonies, housing segregation and forced emigration. This emphasis dominated his *Outcast London*, but it had a corollary in his comparatively truncated attention to the attempts by social theorists and charity activists to win over aspirational working people to a broadly New Liberal social programme. Stedman Jones emphasised a desire for working-class participation in poor relief through service as guardians, as well as schemes such as non-contributory pensions and subsidised housing for the 'deserving poor'.[57]

In a similar way liberal-minded philanthropic work in the 1880s and 1890s also involved positive efforts to build relationships across the boundaries of social class, between middle-class reformers and respectable men and women of the labouring poor (but also, as we will see, within these groups) by the moralising and redeeming potential of culture. The latter belonged to Classes C and D in Charles Booth's survey, 'whose lives and aspirations', Stedman Jones writes, 'have more or less escaped the attention of historians'. They were rarely secure in their work, rarely joining trade unions and vulnerable to unemployment if trade declined or relations with their employers went sour. 'But they were not for that beyond the sphere of associational life', he goes on.

> These were the members of the humbler friendly societies, of the militias, and of the clubs operating under the aegis of the churches, the missions, and the university or public-school settlements. Unlike the skilled and the better paid, they could not afford the luxury of rejecting the patronage of those above them and probably did not see the point of doing so.[58]

They rarely featured in sensational depictions of 'Outcast London'; on the contrary, as one settlement worker acknowledged to the Booth inquiry, they 'were leading quite quiet respectable lives before Oxford House came [to be established]'.[59] But nevertheless they were crucial to the New Liberal reformist project. When Beatrice Potter wanted to assess a Whitechapel relief scheme that paid unemployed men two shillings a day to sweep the streets, for example, she took the issue up with this 'better class' of East Ender. At this time a conventional moralist in social policy, Potter was inclined to regard the limited enrolments in the scheme as evidence of pervasive demoralisation. 'But in discussing the matter quietly with the men attending the reading-room of Katherine Buildings', she explained in a letter to Joseph Chamberlain,

> we found that there was a strong feeling among the better class that unless they were prepared to sink permanently into the ranks of unskilled labour, acceptance of this work would injure their chance (some said irretrievably) of gaining employment in their own trade. I confess, I do not attach much importance to this objection: still it was urged by men who were themselves in work.[60]

Such men were avid self-improvers, alert to the benefits of education and ready to seize opportunities to develop their cultural literacy. The East End bookbinder and autodidact Frederick Rogers, whose *Labour, Life and Literature* presents a classic account of late-Victorian working-class self-improvement, is perhaps archetypical. Ordinary working people of his ilk, in regular employment as artisans, tradesmen and factory hands were a receptive constituency for adult education and cultural philanthropy alike. Remembering the dim evenings of Whitechapel's University Extension classes on English history, for example, Rogers recalled the scholarly figure of S. R. Gardiner, professor of modern history at King's College, London, and the moment when 'standing quietly before his audience, without note or gesture, he began to talk to them about the nation of which they were a part'. 'I had dreamed of what scholarship might be', Rogers wrote with feeling, 'and perhaps I had fancied myself a scholar; but now I was face to face with true scholarship, and I sat silent and with bowed head'.[61]

Perhaps this response embodies social control in action, as the working-class autodidact bows his head reverently to the cultural authority of his social betters. But there is also a rich complexity of interaction and response that is overlooked by such reductionist readings of the historical situation. Even in the 1970s, in moderating the claims of the 'social control' school then in vogue, enthusiasts for the concept accepted that identifying social control processes in middle-class charity work 'is not to assert that the control element within each is necessarily its main characteristic, still less its only meaning'.[62] Social workers' commitment to personal 'influence' and moralising improvement across the social divide was in a basic sense a paternalistic intrusion into the everyday lives and habits of working men and women. But the picture is a little more complicated than that, with a complexity that cannot be encapsulated so baldly. As F. M. L. Thompson neatly observed during that earlier debate, 'many improvers and reformers were socializers rather than controllers, peddling recipes for better survival in a changing environment rather than weaving webs of subordination'.[63] There are many ingredients to be considered in the mix if we are to better understand their recipes for moralising improvement through cultural philanthropy.

* * *

To summarise the argument, then: this book contends that the cultural mission to the London poor was not the 'expression' of a discrete idea put into action, whether that be Arnoldian 'culture', or Ruskinian 'art for the people', or the social metaphysics of Green implanted at Balliol College, to take the three usual suspects. Nor in its essence was it simply an aspect of the 'social gospel' descended from Maurice and the Christian Socialists, a substitution of culture for doctrine and liturgy to 'spiritualise' the poor. Rather it was a practical embodiment of the broader, underlying social idealism and moral liberalism that flavoured so much of the social criticism of this period. Importantly, this set of values rested at the intersection of secular and religious modes of social intervention, and consequently the cultural mission exemplifies for us 'the mesh of subtle interconnections between social and religious thought through much of the nineteenth century'.[64] Proceeding from a 'secular' perspective, we might privilege the importance of civic idealism, citizenship, popular education and municipal reform as the cultural mission's defining *milieu*. Or alternatively, proceeding from a 'religious' point of view, we might just as easily focus on immanence theology, on the influence of Maurice and 'Social Christianity', the liberal 'Forward Movement' in Nonconformity or 'Broad Church' social inclusion in Anglicanism.

Either way, when seen properly at this intersection, cultural philanthropy resolves for us as part of two distinct but overlapping systems of values and practice that were themselves in a state of flux in this period. Between 1875 and the turn of the century, the social welfare of organised religion on the one hand, and the modern 'secular' provision of adult education and public culture on the other were both rapidly evolving to face new circumstances, pressures and expectations. Seen in the moment, synchronically, the cultural mission seems an expression of a 'diffusionist' social Christianity, but one that overlapped with conceptions of municipal provision for education and social reform that were part of what historians tend to think of as the New Liberalism. Seen dia-chronically in hindsight, it re-appears as part of the creeping secularisation of modern British life, obscure in its details but undeniable in its broad con-sequences, as responsibility for the 'civilising mission' slowly passed from chur-ches and the voluntarist charities influenced by their ideologies to the state, either in national public-funded bodies or in local municipal institutions.

Seen in this way, as an expression of the overlap between 'diffusionist religion' and an emerging pattern of adult education, cultural philanthropy as a mode of voluntarist social work could only be sustained relatively briefly. It was only pos-sible *after* the stern individualist moralism of the earlier Victorians and the 'Age of Atonement' had softened, and *before* conceptions of the modern state had evolved sufficiently to broaden out its functions to include cultural enrichment through public agencies. That window, it seems, opened and quietly closed again in the quarter century between 1875 and 1900. As part of the threshold to the modern framework of adult education and public cultural policy, the cultural mission shared the liberal idealism that is highly visible in university extension just as it shared the quasi-religious, moralising impulses of voluntary philanthropy. Cer-tainly it was decisively shaped by the moralising assumptions of its day: as we will see, for example, class assumptions were never far away and in practice the gift of culture was carefully policed to discriminate between 'deserving' and 'undeserving' recipients. But its full historical complexity eludes us if only viewed through the lens of class interest as a narrow project of 'social control', or as the social expres-sion of the ideas of Arnold, Ruskin or Green. The philanthropic provision of cul-ture to the late-Victorian urban poor was not entirely self-interested, patronising or misguided, and nor was it narrowly conceived: in fact it resulted in solutions that were both substantial in their time and pregnant with long-term implications.

Notes

1 The classic older text is G. Hough, *The Last Romantics* (London: Methuen, 1961 [1947]), but see also S. Mencher, 'The Influence of Romanticism on Nineteenth-Century British Social Work' *Social Service Review* 38:2 (1964), pp. 174–90.

2 M. Ward, *Robert Elsmere* (Oxford: Oxford University Press, 1987 [1888]), pp. 85–6.
3 R. A. Woods, *English Social Movements* (London: Swan Sonnenschein and Co., 1892), pp. 204–5.
4 R. Williams, *The Long Revolution* (London: Chatto and Windus, 1961), p. 41.
5 R. Williams, *Culture and Society 1780–1950* (Harmondsworth: Penguin Books, 1961), p. 17.
6 'Modern Culture' *Quarterly Review* 137 (October 1874), p. 391.
7 E. A. Sonnenschein, 'Culture and Science' *Macmillan's Magazine* 53 (November 1885), p. 5.
8 S. Collini, *Arnold* (Oxford: Oxford University Press, 1988), p. 3. See J. Carroll, *The Cultural Theory of Matthew Arnold* (Berkeley: University of California Press, 1982).
9 M. Arnold, 'Culture and Its Enemies' *Cornhill Magazine* 16:91 (July 1867), p. 38.
10 As cited in 'Modern Culture' *Quarterly Review* 137 (October 1874), p. 394.
11 M. Arnold, *Culture and Anarchy* (J. Dover Wilson ed.) (Cambridge: Cambridge University Press, 1960), p. 70.
12 F. Turner, *The Greek Heritage in Victorian Britain* (New Haven: Yale University Press, 1981), p. 21.
13 J. Harris, *Private Lives, Public Spirit: A Social History of Britain 1870–1914* (Oxford: Oxford University Press, 1993), p. 247.
14 J. S. Lidgett, 'Ideals of the Settlement, and How to Realise Them: III – Recreation', *Monthly Record* 2:1 (January 1896), p. 2.
15 F. W. Dyer, 'The Claims of Culture' *The Sunday Review* 1 (October 1876), p. 48 (emphasis in original).
16 C. F. G. Masterman, *From the Abyss: Of Its Inhabitants by One of Them* (London: R. B. Johnson, 1902), pp. 22–3.
17 See P. Bailey, *Leisure and Class in Victorian England: Rational Recreation and the Contest for Control, 1830–1885* (London: Routledge and Kegan Paul, 1978).
18 L. Goldman, 'Intellectuals and the English Working Class 1870–1945: The Case of Adult Education' *History of Education* 29:4 (2000), p. 296.
19 See S. Koven, 'Culture and Poverty: the London Settlement House Movement 1870 to 1914' (Ph.D. thesis, Harvard University, 1987), pp. 1–27.
20 J. Walkowitz, *City of Dreadful Delight: Narratives of Sexual Danger in Late-Victorian London* (Chicago: University of Chicago Press, 1992), p. 59.
21 S. Meacham, *Toynbee Hall and Social Reform, 1880–1914: The Search for Community* (New Haven: Yale University Press, 1987), p. 39.
22 E. Abel, 'Canon Barnett and the First Thirty Years of Toynbee Hall' (Ph.D. thesis, University of London, 1969), p. 91.
23 G. Budge, 'Poverty and the Picture Gallery: The Whitechapel Exhibitions and the Social Project of Ruskinian Aesthetics' *Visual Culture in Britain* 1:2 (2000), p. 43; Eagles, *After Ruskin*, pp. 114–33; D. Maltz, *British Aestheticism and the Urban Working Classes, 1870–1900: Beauty for the People* (Basingstoke: Palgrave Macmillan, 2006), pp. 67–97; L. Matthews-Jones, 'Lessons in Seeing: Art, Religion and Class in the East End of London, 1881–1898', *Journal of Victorian Culture* 16:3 (2011), pp. 385–403.
24 W. Neetens, 'Problems of a "Democratic Text": Walter Besant's Impossible Story' *Novel* 23 (1990), p. 247.
25 J. Harris, *William Beveridge: A Biography* (Oxford: Clarendon Press, 1977), p. 44.
26 Koven, 'Culture and Poverty', p. iv. Koven's first chapter (pp. 1–41) captures the formal intellectual context that nurtured the late-Victorian settlement impulse.
27 B. Frost, 'God Cares Also for Minds: John Scott Lidgett, the Bermondsey Settlement and Methodist Educationalists' in his *Pioneers of Social Passion: London's Cosmopolitan Methodism* (Peterborough: Epworth Press, 2006), p. 46.
28 BL: Cockerell Papers, Add. Mss. 52621–2.

36 *Sources and explanations*

29 BL: Cockerell Papers, Add. Mss. 52623 (Diary, 1886) f. 70; entry of Thursday 16 December.
30 W. Besant, 'On University Settlements' in W. Reason (ed.), *University and Social Settlements* (London: Methuen, 1898), p. 5.
31 Meacham, *Toynbee Hall and Social Reform*, p. 27.
32 F. Fletcher Vane, *Agin the Governments: Memories and Adventures* (London: Sampson, Low, Marston and Co., 1929), p. 57.
33 Vane, *Agin the Governments*, p. 55.
34 H. Meller, *Leisure and the Changing City, 1870–1914* (London: Routledge and Kegan Paul, 1976), pp. 9–11.
35 G. Himmelfarb, *Poverty and Compassion: The Moral Imagination of the Late Victorians* (New York: Alfred A. Knopf, 1991).
36 S. Collini, *Public Moralists: Political Thought and Intellectual Life in Britain* (Oxford: Clarendon Press, 1991), pp. 4–5.
37 L. Goldman, *Dons and Workers: Oxford and Adult Education since 1850* (Oxford: Clarendon Press, 1995), p. 55.
38 See L. E. Nettleship, 'William Fremantle, Samuel Barnett and the Broad Church Origins of Toynbee Hall' *Journal of Ecclesiastical History* 33 (1982), pp. 564–79.
39 See J. Cox, *The English Churches in a Secular Society: Lambeth, 1870–1930* (New York: Oxford University Press, 1982), esp. chapter 4; and H. Schlossberg, *Conflict and Crisis in the Religious Life of Late Victorian England* (New Brunswick: Transaction Publishers, 2009), chapter 6.
40 A. Chapman, 'The People's Palace for East London: A Study of Victorian Philanthropy' (M.Phil. thesis, University of Hull, 1978), p. 73.
41 As argued in Borzello, *Civilising Caliban*, and Maltz, *British Aestheticism and the Urban Working Classes*.
42 N. Scotland, *Squires in the Slums: Settlements and Missions in Late-Victorian London* (London: I. B. Tauris, 2007).
43 See M. Roberts, *Making English Morals: Voluntary Associations and Moral Reform in England, 1787–1886* (Cambridge: Cambridge University Press, 2004).
44 Himmelfarb, *Poverty and Compassion*, p. 7.
45 Himmelfarb, *Poverty and Compassion*, esp. introduction: 'Compassion "Properly Understood"', pp. 3–18.
46 D. Siegel, *Charity and Condescension: Victorian Literature and the Dilemmas of Philanthropy* (Athens: Ohio University Press, 2012), p. 4.
47 Siegel, *Charity and Condescension*, p. 106.
48 See *Outcast London*, pp. 256–7, and J. Fido, 'The Charity Organisation Society and Social Casework in London 1869–1900' in A.P. Donajgrodzki (ed.), *Social Control in Nineteenth Century Britain* (London: Croom Helm, 1977), pp. 207–30.
49 LMA: Barnett Papers, F/BAR/498, f. 147.
50 J. Harris, 'Political Thought and the Welfare State 1870–1940: An Intellectual Framework for British Social Policy' *Past and Present* 135 (1992), pp. 138, 126.
51 Harris, 'Political Thought and the Welfare State', p. 124.
52 F. Turner, 'The Triumph of Idealism in Victorian Classical Studies' in his *Contesting Cultural Authority: Essays in Victorian Intellectual Life* (Cambridge: Cambridge University Press, 1993), p. 322.
53 Harris, 'Political Thought and the Welfare State', p. 137.
54 L. Goodlad, *Victorian Literature and the Victorian State: Character and Governance in a Liberal Society* (Baltimore: Johns Hopkins University Press, 2003), p. viii.
55 See M. Freeden, *The New Liberalism: An Ideology of Social Reform* (Oxford: Clarendon Press, 1978), P. Weiler, *The New Liberalism: Liberal Social Theory in Great Britain 1889–1914* (New York: Garland Publishing, 1982) and J. Offer, *An*

Intellectual History of British Social Policy: Idealism versus non-Idealism (Bristol: Policy Press, 2006).

56 Himmelfarb, *Poverty and Compassion*, p. 12.
57 Stedman Jones, *Outcast London*, pp. 302–3.
58 G. Stedman Jones, 'The "Cockney" and the Nation, 1780–1988', in D. Feldman and G. Stedman Jones (eds), *Metropolis London: Histories and Representations since 1800* (London: Routledge, 1989), p. 309.
59 BLPES: Booth Collection, B/225, fol.139, information of A. W. Bailward.
60 N. MacKenzie (ed.), *The Letters of Sidney and Beatrice Webb: Volume 1: Apprenticeships 1873–1892* (Cambridge: Cambridge University Press, 1978), p. 53, letter of early March 1886.
61 F. Rogers, *Labour, Life and Literature: Some Memories of Sixty Years* (London: Smith, Elder and Co., 1913), p. 81.
62 A. P. Donajgrodzki, 'Introduction' in A. P. Donajgrodzki (ed.), *Social Control in Nineteenth Century Britain* (London: Croom Helm, 1977), p. 15.
63 F. M. L. Thompson, 'Social Control in Victorian Britain' *Economic History Review* 34:2 (1981), p. 207. See also G. Stedman Jones, 'Class Expression versus Social Control? A Critique of Recent Trends in the Social History of Leisure' in his *Languages of Class: Studies in English Working Class History, 1832–1982* (Cambridge: Cambridge University Press, 1983), pp. 76–89.
64 P. T. Phillips, *A Kingdom on Earth: Anglo-American Social Christianity, 1880–1940* (University Park: Pennsylvania State University Press, 1996), p. xxv.

3   Social work, sweetness and light

'Outcast London' was the setting for voluntary philanthropy on a truly vast scale in the last decades of the nineteenth century. 'This age may have its faults, but it is not a lazy age', observed one lady activist in 1884,[1] as a host of social workers committed themselves to an array of charities and relief schemes large and small, sporadic or sustained, that aimed to assist the London poor. By the end of that decade, Simon Joyce comments, such was the level of middle-class interest and activism that 'sections of the city (and especially Whitechapel) must have seemed positively overrun by the bourgeoisie, in their various guises as rent collectors, clergymen and Salvation Army evangelicals, housing and education inspectors from the Board of Works or the School Board, and crusading journalists'.[2]

The personal altruism of George Bartley supplies one tiny example. The former South Kensington science examiner and lifelong education advocate was elected MP for North Islington in 1885. 'The district is a poor one', he described it to *The Times*, 'many of the streets very much so indeed; and although the North of London has not the sentimental sound of the East-end, yet it would not be difficult to find poverty and distress as great in the one part as in the other'. Bartley had achieved prominence ten years earlier in founding the National Penny Bank to encourage thrift by taking deposits of only 1*d.* at workplaces, schools and local branches across the country. Now, in 1886, he rented an unused hall in Islington, and spent £350 fitting it out as 'a small fine art and industrial exhibition', with loans from the Prince of Wales, Lord Ripon, the South Kensington Museum and other supporters. A small library was installed next door, with smoking and refreshments rooms where board games and tea were provided with a penny for admission.

> Each evening we have music, volunteer singing, instrumental music of all kinds, concerts, and lectures, given gratuitously by local and other talent from all classes of society. Those who help enjoy it as much as those who listen, so that the obligation is mutual, and we get the essential advantage of personal intercourse.[3]

A playroom for children was planned to cap it off, with a games area for skittles and swings, rooms for reading and music, and on the top floor a room 'for fathers who bring children, and who may like to stay and smoke and read the papers'. Bartley promised potential sponsors that

> the personal influence will be secured by my wife and other members of our family and friends, and those who are coming forward to devote, say, a day a month or even a day a year to reading aloud, telling stories, playing and singing, and otherwise leading the children to amuse themselves. This personal influence is the only way of bridging the class differences and raising us all.[4]

Such modest schemes at cultural provision for impoverished neighbourhoods have typically been regarded as isolated and eccentric. More substantial efforts like the Whitechapel Loan Exhibitions of Fine Art that commenced in 1881 and the People's Palace at Mile End from 1887 have attracted historians, but a great many others, like George Bartley's obscure little effort in Islington, have sunk from view. We might agree with Frances Borzello that 'it could never be claimed that taking pictures to the poor was a major movement. It takes a telescope to find it among the thousands of schemes to improve the lot of the poor in late Victorian England.'[5] Yet we are better off thinking of these efforts as the peaks of a many-tipped iceberg, apparently isolated but in fact merely discrete expressions of an underlying unity obscured beneath the surface.

Examples appear constantly when we read the pamphlets, public appeals, periodical articles and newspaper reports that documented late-Victorian social activism. When in 1884 a Rev. Dr MacLaren summarised the range of efforts 'to improve the condition of the lowest of our outcast population', it made an impressive survey. But alongside the preaching of abstinence, improvements in sanitation, education, temperance coffee-houses and bathing facilities, MacLaren saw a special role for moralising culture, 'the gracious influence of art and music, pictures and window gardening, and the like... [that] lend their aid to soften and refine'.[6] That same year, when the East End clergyman Harry Jones reviewed local social work for *Good Words*, he noted cultural philanthropic efforts such as fine art exhibitions, concerts and oratorios, and the Kyrle Society's 'desire to spread decorative refinement'; all provided, he felt, 'a vehicle...for the import of fresh and sweeter thoughts'.[7] The *Charity Organisation Reporter* captured alternative approaches to the 'social problem' through a fictional conversation in a railway carriage. Did the poor need bare subsistence, or something more refined and refining? One disputant concludes:

> I would...give the people not necessaries but luxuries. The first thing is to brighten their lives. Unless you have worked among the poor you have no idea of the absolute dullness of their surroundings. Everything about them is ugly, dingy and sordid, and the only bright bit of their lives is the public-house bar. Give them, if only a glimpse, of higher, nobler, purer enjoyment – a day in a garden or in a picture gallery, or good music.

> Give them a taste for these things and they will no longer be content with
> a sordid life...[8]

This emphasis on 'brightness', on 'higher, nobler, purer enjoyment' punctuated the everyday literature of social reformers. During its first year their
magazine *Eastward Ho!* promoted the concerts of the People's Entertainment
Society, the popular handicrafts encouraged by the Cottage Arts Association,
the attractions of the Bethnal Green Museum, and countless attempts to
improve popular taste in reading and literature. Contributors bemoaned the
lack of beautiful architecture in the East End, argued the necessity for reform
of popular amusements, and urged for the reservation of open spaces for
improving leisure.[9] 'No-one possessed of ordinary powers of observation',
wrote the scientist James Britten in 1889 in opening a discussion of 'Art and
the People', 'will deny that there has been, during the last few years, a great
advance in the direction of art; and that, side by side with this, has developed
the desire of "bringing beauty home to the people"'.[10]

Thus Borzello has a point, but if our purview extends beyond art exhibitions
to include concerts of fine music, reading groups and libraries, courses of
lectures, debates and *soirées*, we discover a rich crop of this kind of reformist
activism. Our evidence for these ephemeral philanthropic efforts comes from
newspaper reports, periodical articles, the social work journals and the occasional
appeals and pamphlets of the groups themselves. In the absence of comprehensive archival and primary sources, these obscure organisations and individuals
have been neglected by historical research, yet their motivations, strategies
and actions can nevertheless be recovered through this scattered source
material. In assembling it together we begin to see distinctive echoes in other
activities like the parish work of socially minded curates and vicars, the teas and
entertainments they and their wives organised to throw the net of 'civilising'
influence further afield than simple church attendance. We also encounter
reformers who were keen to foster special-interest clubs and reading groups as
forms of education, lecturers committed to university extension through local
classes in working-class neighbourhoods, and the first polytechnics that aimed
at higher education and improving recreation for working people. This chapter considers the cultural mission to the slums as part of this broader context,
and demonstrates how fundamentally embedded it was in the conceptions
and practices of late-Victorian social work. It was moralising and intrusive,
certainly, but it was also diffuse and enormously diverse.

* * *

Social reform through cultural provision in the visual arts was best exemplified by the Kyrle Society, founded by Miranda and Octavia Hill in 1875–7 to
'bring the refining and cheerful influences of natural and artistic beauty home
to the people'.[11] Arising out of Octavia Hill's pioneering work as a housing
reformer, and sparked by her determination to secure 'open air sitting rooms

for the poor', the new society commenced uncertainly under the title 'The Society for the Diffusion of Beauty'.[12] The two women grew up with three other sisters in a remarkable family of sturdy feminine independence and achievement, and by the mid-1870s were experienced social workers. Their mother, Caroline Southwood Hill, a writer and educationalist with progressive opinions, moved in Nonconformist intellectual circles as the daughter of Unitarian physician and health reformer Thomas Southwood Smith. The family fractured after the girls' father, the Owenite reformer James Hill, suffered a nervous breakdown and became estranged from them in the mid-1840s. After this time Mrs Hill and her five daughters were involved in the Ladies' Guild, a London craft workshop that trained underprivileged children in making toys, and from 1862 ran a school for girls in Nottingham Place, Marylebone.[13]

A long-term pupil of John Ruskin's, Octavia (see Figure 3.1) was invited by the social critic to manage a group of cottages in Marylebone for impoverished tenants in the mid-1860s.[14] Her system, first advertised in 1866 and the basis for her work thereafter, involved the purchase of dilapidated cottages that were then renovated and let to tenants at favourable rates under rigorous

Figure 3.1 Octavia Hill, 1877

supervision for cleanliness, punctuality in rental payments, and general good conduct.[15] A cheerful, bustling and intrusive landlord, determined to supply moralising assistance to the poor, Miss Hill 'organised entertainments, and outings for the tenants, started a playground, taught the neighbourhood children games and songs, planted trees, brought the tenants flowers, and, in many modest ways, attempted to bring beauty as well as order into her courts'[16], work that fed into the Kyrle Society a decade later. In the proposal that launched the new venture, written by Octavia's older sister Miranda as a paper read to the National Health Society, these initiatives united with Samuel Barnett's insight that 'it is not the poverty that is such a weight upon everybody in the East End, it is the ugliness' to become a clarion call for a new effort at urban amelioration, one street and one garden at a time, through improvements on a small – even miniature – and humane scale.[17] By December 1876 the society had taken the name of John Kyrle, the benefactor of Ross-on-Wye in Herefordshire who before his death in 1724 had endowed so many schemes for local benefit that he was immortalised as Alexander Pope's saintly 'Man of Ross' in his 1734 parable 'Of the Use of Riches'. It seems likely the Hills' latest endeavour was intended to answer Pope's lament 'And what? No monument, inscription, stone?'[18] The Kyrle Society was imagined by the Hill sisters as a latter day memorial to Pope's hero.

London supplied the new society's epicentre, but within five years local societies had been founded in Liverpool, Nottingham, Birmingham, Leicester and Glasgow. By 1893 its work had expanded to Cheltenham, Dublin and Edinburgh. Encouraged by royal patronage – Prince Leopold, the haemophiliac and favoured youngest son of the Queen, served as its president, and his sister Princess Louise as a vice-President – 'many another noble name distinguished in the world of art or in the world of philanthropy' gave their personal support.[19] Among them were the Duke of Westminster, the Earl of Meath and Lady Brabazon, the prominent artists Sir Frederick Leighton and G. F. Watts, the journalist George Sala, and the lawyer and commons preservation activist Robert Hunter. William Morris was an early supporter, and spoke heartily in its favour at a Kensington meeting of the Society in January 1881. The Kyrle Society shared in the great idealistic spirit of the age, he enthused, and

> how we look forward to the day when poverty shall be a name only for a dreadful phantasm of the past; when the brutality of the poor and the insolence of the rich shall have been slain by hope and pleasure shared by all; when the man of the most refined occupation, student, artist, physician, what not, shall be able to speak to him who does the roughest labour in a tongue that they both know, and to find no intricacy of his mind misunderstood – and when as a sign and symbol of all this, and the necessary outcome of it, this very London...shall have become a delightful abode of men, full of beauty, and guiltless of any spot of squalor.[20]

For its part the Kyrle Society preferred modest schemes that were small-scale, local and practical. As the ill-fated prince (he died in 1884, after a sharp fall) explained from the chair at the Society's third annual meeting, they hoped to make a difference 'by decorating Workmen's Clubs, Hospitals and Schools, by laying out gardens in waste ground, by encouraging the cultivation of plants...by giving concerts to the poor, and by securing open-air spaces for them'.[21] Its four departments supplied music, literature and the visual arts into impoverished neighbourhoods with a staunch moralising zeal. The Decorative Branch installed mosaics, painted murals and inscriptions in clubs, workhouses, schools, institutes, parish halls and hospital wards; 'any room used for social gatherings, without distinction of creed'.[22] They started with two wards in Westminster Hospital, where designs were supplied by Morris for the hospital's convalescent ward for women while Charles Harrison Townsend, an architect and secretary of the Branch, re-decorated the Bouverie Ward. Later projects followed at the Boys' Refuge, Whitechapel, the Working Boys' Home in Southwark and the College for Working Women in Fitzroy Street. Other efforts involved the loan of framed prints and photographs to clubs and institutes for up to six months, after which they were granted as a permanent gift. 'This has been found to be a most useful branch of the Society's work', commented the *Magazine of Art* in 1880, 'and the presence of interesting and nicely framed drawings or photographs on the walls often leads members to make efforts of their own to improve still further the general appearance of the room, and to feel a pride in making it look as pretty and bright as they can'.[23] The initiatives were on a small scale, humane and personal. The gift of six landscapes framed in stained oak and gilt to a Battersea working man's club were highlighted in 1890, along with a donation to the Young Women's Christian Association of decorative objects and pictures, and the decoration of an East London hospital ward with a series of twenty-two panels depicting English wild-flowers. The Society's efforts at the Anchor Mission Hall on Tooley Street, saw 'a complete transformation under the touch of the artist's brush', with walls panelled in pale primrose tones, highlighted with painted chrysanthemums and decorative selections from the Sermon on the Mount.[24] Four major decorative schemes were completed in 1893, including a landscape frieze of a coastal scene installed at a ward in the London Hospital alongside allegorical figures from the architect and designer Charles Voysey. Other projects included a new Japanese-inspired interior for a concert hall in Notting Hill, a design of foliage and heraldry for the ceiling of a Kensington parish hall, and illustrations of Schiller's 'Song of the Bell' at an Aged Women's Infirmary in Lambeth.[25]

The Society's Musical Branch, meanwhile, was initially directed by Malcolm Lawson, a popular composer of drawing-room songs credited with the arrangement for the 'Skye Boat Song' in the 1884 publication *Songs of the North*. It maintained a choir of seventy members and several concert bands 'with a view to provide recreation and amusement in poor districts'[26] in league with the entertainments provided by Lady Brabazon in hospitals and workhouses from around 1882 that later gave rise to the Workhouse Concert Society. The sacred oratorio *Elijah* was delivered by the Society's choir at St Peter's, London Docks, in Lambeth and at St Jude's Whitechapel in their initial season of 1877, a pattern that was repeated subsequently, as oratorios and recitals were performed with voluntary assistance from professional musicians and performers alongside amateurs.[27] Ballad concerts provided humbler fare: on those occasions, according to one enthusiast for the Kyrle Society's work, the novelist Lady Violet Greville, 'the music is as simple as possible and the words always English – nice, pleasant, or merry words – as little sentimental as possible'.[28] After one performance in Temple Gardens on the Victoria Embankment for the local poor, another supporter rhapsodised on the scene which 'pictures itself before us: the fragrant gardens in the gathering twilight; the gleam of the mighty river beyond; the musicians singing; the listening poor. No wonder the world at large called the scheme of the Kyrle Society romantic.'[29]

A Literature Branch was also busy supplying books, magazines and shorter tracts to workhouses, infirmaries, clubs and local libraries in poor districts. They published art pamphlets at low cost, and loaned decorative items such as flags and bunting for exhibitions and ceremonies. Emma Busk, the branch's Honorary Secretary in 1886, calling for donations of 'Just One Book' to various magazines, described the range of applicants to which they had supplied books, from solitary invalids to the 'vast infirmaries and hospitals which count their inmates by hundreds, through all the grades of Men's and Women's Institutes, Boys' and Girls' Clubs, Nurses' Libraries... seamen on long voyages, the blind, the East-End clubs, and village schools'.[30] Although donors were advised that works of religious controversy were not suitable, it seems the branch was happy to distribute a batch of 2,000 magazines sent by the Religious Tract Society in January 1886.[31] Finally, an Open Spaces Branch formed in May 1879 promoted recreational parks for the poor, re-laying burial grounds as public gardens and lobbying for the preservation of existing urban open spaces. It lobbied to secure nature reserves and urban parkland, and in collaborating with various 'commons preservation' societies helped precipitate the formation of the National Trust. This branch distributed flowers and plants in impoverished neighbourhoods, housing estates and institutions, but once again in a spirit of idealised transformation rather than simple sentimentality. In Morris's words, speaking in favour of the Kyrle Society's 'open spaces' work in early 1881,

> it is idle to talk about popularizing art, if you are not prepared to popularize reverence for nature also, both among the poor and the rich: can you expect the people to believe you to be in earnest in bidding them to love art and cultivate it, if [you]...take no heed of and pay no reverence to the greatest of all gifts to the world, the very source of art, the natural beauty of the Earth[?][32]

The Kyrle Society enjoyed the support of prominent sponsors and articulate advocates like Morris, a national organisation and several decades of conspicuous work, in some localities like Bristol right up until the 1940s. But it remained obscure even for contemporaries. 'The name by which the members have designated themselves', commented the *Art Journal* in 1881, 'and which few can pronounce correctly, and fewer still know the origin of, has materially helped to enshroud in obscurity the laudable objects for which they work'.[33] Its scattered records and publications have to date deterred any major historical assessment of its work and significance. But the tone and texture of the Kyrle Society's work, the motives and impulses that gave it shape and direction, and the responses it provoked from contemporaries, are amply documented in the commentary that its efforts inspired. It was easily satirised, as by *Punch* when it depicted a prim, aesthetic young lady offering a hungry worker a sunflower. 'But we would ask *Mr. Punch* himself', retorted the *Charity Organisation Review*, 'whether his own existence would be absolutely essential in a world that was entirely limited to the material wants of mankind'. This journal, the mouthpiece of the emerging profession of modern social work, fully endorsed the society's provision of 'natural and wholesome' tastes through moralising aesthetics:

> What the Kyrle [Society] really does aim at is to make these good, dull lives of honest men and women just a little brighter, to give them something to think and talk about, to show them that all pretty music and beautiful things do not belong to places where there is at least the temptation to evil ways....To the natural and wholesome taste that every man ought to possess for flowers, music, pictures, and books, and which are his safeguards from the alluring forms of vice presented as amusement, the Kyrle Society ministers to 'the utmost of its power'.[34]

Its work was inspired by convictions about the moralising potential of aesthetics in the social environment of British cities. As Octavia Hill explained to a young family friend, Sydney Cockerell, at a private meeting in December 1886, 'there is utter want of *reverence* amongst the poor'.[35] Instilling this moral sense through environmental influences was a touchstone of her housing improvements, which were never a matter of simply removing and replacing condemned buildings. Rather, as Anderson and Darling observe 'she sought to work within existing slums and transform patterns of inhabitation, producing model dwelling practices, rather than model dwellings. Reform was, then, enacted at the intersection of spiritual and moral improvements with material changes to environment.'[36] Improved dwellings for the poor, Hill insisted, 'was not so much a question of dealing with houses alone, as of dealing with houses in connection with their influence on the character and habits of people who inhabit them'.[37]

Accordingly, as decorative schemes to bring aesthetics and colour into the visual squalor of the urban everyday became the Kyrle Society's signature, moralising elements were ever-present. One of its earliest projects saw a poem, 'A Song of the City Sparrow', painted on zinc and mounted in the garden of one of Octavia Hill's Whitechapel housing projects in 1877. The lyric celebrated the modest virtues of the sparrow, resigned to its fate as a humble and unappreciated city-dweller in the midst of bleak winter when other birds had departed to more pleasant surroundings. The moral was clear: in the face of grim urbanity, there were still laws of nature, the turning of the seasons that dictated a designated place in the order of things, a reflection that might inculcate some of the 'reverence', an appreciation of larger matters of life and the spirit, that Miss Hill felt was absent. She asked:

> Is it not pleasant to think of the children having these words to read – painted in pretty colours, too – rather than looking at a blank wall? Sometimes I think we might even hope to carry with us the hearts of people by setting up for them deliberately very solemn and beautiful words indeed, coloured richly in lasting tiles.[38]

She suggested that the 'great, blank, dirty, dead side wall of a London church' could be decorated with a mosaic quotation from Charles Kingsley:

> Do noble things, not dream them all day long
> And so make life, death, and that vast for-ever,
> One grand, sweet song.

'The words are simple', she insisted, 'and would go home to the hearts of every passer-by; the bright colours, the look of expensive care bestowed on them, the fact that they are on the wall of a church, would give them a look of serious purpose...'[39] Another scheme of 1883 involved a colourful mosaic installed in a Lambeth churchyard, a cemetery re-made as a public garden, bearing the inscription '*All may have, if they dare try, a glorious life or grave.*' She hoped that the working man of South London 'might be reminded, as he read the words, that though his life was out of men's sight and seemed occupied with small things, seemed perhaps somewhat broken and wasted, there was a possibility of nobleness in it, if bravely and unselfishly carried on'.[40] She elaborated further on this theme in seeking contributions from the readers of the *Pall Mall Gazette*:

> It has been thought that these words would be appropriate to a church wall standing as this one does in a special way among the living and the dead, that a sermon in stones, thus placed, might go home to the hearts of some who pass quiet time sitting in the garden, or strike the eye of some one in that busy crowd hurrying over Waterloo Bridge from the station, presenting a sudden thought of a choice lying before them, a choice of living up to a noble ideal or standing by it till death. The words

are given in distinct characters, and the whole inscription will form, it is hoped, a gem of colour in that dreary neighbourhood.[41]

The environmental and aesthetic elements that were implicit to Octavia Hill's many projects occupied centre-stage in the Kyrle Society's work of moralising improvement: as one Society publication declared, 'all that tends to brighten, better, and beautify the lives of the poorer members of the community has the full sympathy of the Society'.[42]

* * *

A number of voluntary associations, now long-gone and largely forgotten, set out to supply fine music for working-class audiences in a similar spirit. A leading example was the People's Concert Society (PCS) that commenced in 1878, 'whose bright and pleasant entertainments', the *Musical News* commented twenty years later, 'for now so many seasons, have been the happy means of bringing some few hours' enjoyment into the grey drear [*sic*] lives of the poor folk of the East End, and other less favoured neighbourhoods'.[43] Florence Marshall, a capable composer and conductor of the South Hampstead Orchestra with its progressive mixing of male and female musicians, took a leading role in the society which enjoyed a high level of regard among professional musicians.[44] 'Songs are given, by way of variety', Marshall wrote in describing their concerts in 1880, 'but the main feature of the programmes is concerted chamber music, quartets and trios, such as are heard at the Monday Popular Concerts [in the West End]; with this difference, that only short portions of these works are performed at a time, so as not to tax too severely the attention of an untrained audience'.[45] The PCS mounted hundreds of classical chamber concerts in venues across London through the following decades, devoted to 'giving the audiences the best that art has produced' and helping pioneer the modern selective concert form. 'Notes of a biographical and explanatory kind are appended to the programme by way of helping inexperienced listeners to understand something as to the form of the music played', a PCS report explained in 1896, 'and the position of the various composers in the history of music'. In selecting vocal music, they aimed to 'represent the best of various types, including songs of the classical schools, old ballads, national songs, and the best things by composers of the day, and occasionally making vocal quartets and choral music a feature of the evening'.[46]

This type of moralising charity concert began as a philanthropic experiment, but it was sustained by a genuine surge in popular demand. The last decades of the nineteenth century witnessed an explosion in the popular consumption of music, visible in public performances of all kinds and assisted by advances in musical method and education. Active reformers saw a grand opportunity in all this. Marshall, for example, imagined music as a peculiarly democratic art form as she celebrated the rapid spread of popular concert events, singing classes, and musical tuition:

Music, the universal benefactress, knowing no respect of persons in the bestowal of her gifts; ignoring all restrictions of birth, of wealth, of sex, of nationality; ...music, the latest born of the arts, Heaven's especial gift to this town-ridden age, to the masses of mankind doomed by the march of civilisation to toil in cities, to people for whom the sights and sounds of Nature and the very feeling of God's fresh air for ever to be luxuries... Music, bless her! is not killed by crowds nor stifled by smoke.[47]

By the late 1890s there was ample evidence that these extravagant aspirations had, in some instances at least, been practically realised, as in the sequence of Sunday Evening Concerts of chamber music in 1899 hosted by the People's Concert Society in the Greenwich Lecture Hall. The concert committee, one report explained, contained 'Liberals, Conservatives, Socialists – all workers. Half the stewards were members of the Gas Workers' and General Labourers' Union....Many of these men are unskilled labourers, but one and all seemed to take the keenest pleasure in giving voluntary services.'[48]

Of course for many reformers and social workers musical performances often cloaked evangelical intentions, and many church services featured musical interludes and accompaniments to sweeten the doctrinal pill. The evangelism of social missions like the London Congregational Union, for example, included hymns sung to and by the homeless in their hostels and soup kitchens. '[T]here is something marvellous', commented one observer of their efforts, 'in the power of music over even these poor people. Perhaps it awakens some tender chord of recollection, perhaps it softens the soul, and the Gospel is sung into the heart; under its magic influence you will see a hard, defiant face here and there melt into tears, and a smothered sob shake the shrunken frame.'[49] The prominent clergyman Brooke Lambert called for free oratorios to be performed in ordinary parish churches as well as cathedrals. 'Any one who has attended an oratorio in a church, and has marked the faces of the people, especially those of the poorest, must have sighed over lost opportunities', he remarked.[50]

'Smoking Concerts', much less formal than oratorios or chamber recitals and less prone to stridently moralising, featured in the parochial social work of many parishes. As well as encouraging attendance and participation in parish life, these events were extolled as moralising influences that tended to encourage 'social sympathy' across the class divide. When the Church of England Working Men's Association secretary Charles Powell opened a concert for dock labourers in January 1886, for example, he rationalised the whole occasion as an opportunity for social reconciliation. In 'a few cheery words', the local newspaper reported,

he wished them all a happy New Year and better times than some of them had experienced lately, and pointed out to them the necessity of a better understanding between the denizens of the East and West End of the metropolis. When friends from the West had visited them they had found them not bad fellows after all, and they in their turn had found about what splendid fellows the East-enders were; what they wanted was greater knowledge of one another.[51]

One of the most successful voluntary groups to host musical concerts in poor neighbourhoods was the People's Entertainment Society (PES), formed by philanthropist Charles Bethune in 1878–9 to 'supply high class amusements among the poorer classes during the winter; to employ usefully the talents of those who have leisure, and are willing to devote a little time for the benefit of others; [and] to establish a better feeling between different classes'.[52] It began with a simple tea-party in a schoolroom in Lambeth in January 1879, when the personal hospitality of Mr Bethune, his sister and their 'cheery table' was extended to two dozen local residents, 'literally brought in out of the highways and gutters one cold and wintry Saturday evening' according to one account.

> There were flowers on the table, and tea and cake, for the benefit of some twenty-five poor creatures to whom flowers and cake were perhaps nearly as unfamiliar as olives and ortolans. There was a piano in the room, and, later on, the influence of music was brought to bear upon the guests, who, in their turn, were won over to contribute a song or narrate some char-acteristic personal experiences. Twenty-five poor souls, some of them well-known drunkards, were thus kept away from the public-house on Saturday night, the night when, apparently, the demon of drink is most on the rampage, because it is on Saturday that wages are paid, and the money that has been hardly earned lies in the palm, ready to be lightly spent.[53]

The experiment was repeated over subsequent weeks with enough success to warrant 'a series of Saturday-night "entertainments" in several of the worst and poorest localities in London'. A committee was formed with Bethune as secretary, and an annual subscription of ten shillings was set for supporters of the programme of work the new society had in mind: by the end of their first season in May 1879, sixty-six separate performances had been held across the metropolis.[54]

A nucleus of organised effort and motivation had thus emerged. With no religious affiliation, and seeking to 'cultivate a taste for good, high-class amusements, by giving instructive entertainments among the poor classes, in workmen's clubs, halls and institutes, in the hope of drawing them from lower places of resort', the PES prospered in the decade that followed.[55] It attracted significant support among well-placed philanthropists and public figures, while many professional musicians and artistes lent their support through practical assistance and performances.[56] There were considerable expenses to be covered in hiring venues, arranging for pianos and other instruments, printing and distributing programmes, and engaging professional accompanists. After the subscription scheme failed, donations and occasional fee-charging con-certs were introduced to fund the Society's seasons of free or heavily subsidised entertainments. PES 'penny concerts' continued throughout the 1880s at venues in Battersea, Clapham, Bermondsey, Rotherhithe, Kennington, Vauxhall, Westminster, Whitechapel and Holborn; the Society supplied numerous entertainments at Toynbee Hall and the People's Palace when these opened in 1884 and 1887 respectively. It seems audiences varied in size but usually numbered in the hundreds. PES supporter Ernest Hart estimated that 48 musical evenings had been given during 1884 in Bermondsey, Shoreditch and Stratford Town Halls and at Clerkenwell, and with an average attendance of around 500 had attracted some 25,000 people at threepence or sixpence a ticket.[57] Annual audience numbers approached 100,000 in the mid-1880s, it was claimed, when the society received annual donations totalling nearly £900.[58] As Viscount Folkestone explained to readers of the *Pall Mall Gazette*, the society was vigilant in distributing invitations and free tickets only through 'the principal inhabitants of the district and by the foremen of the different manufactories and workshops...in order to ensure that those only should gain admission for whose benefit and entertainment these concerts are given – namely that class of persons who cannot afford to obtain such recreation for themselves'.[59] This concern with the composition of audiences, together with a determination to police the gift of culture and so ensure its effectiveness, was an abiding theme in the late-Victorian cultural mission: if the politics of personal influence attracted conservatives like Folkestone and appealed to their sense of *noblesse oblige*, others felt that some vestige of personal connection was essential. According to Countess Cowper, another aristocratic philanthropist and one of the PES's most prominent advocates,

> how can personal influence begin better than by winning over the hearts of those we want to reach by our songs and our music? Once won you can say what you like, and do what you like, you have made them your friends, – and they resent nothing except neglect. To be among them constantly, to give them one's best and noblest thoughts, and to lead them to one's highest and purest aspirations – these are some of the means by which the people may be governed.[60]

PES events generally featured concert pieces by amateur performers assisted by paid professionals, intermingled with ballads and elements of light pantomime. The first programmes 'consisted chiefly of music, songs and ballads with English words being mostly chosen'; Lady Lindsay explained, 'but there were also readings, recitations, and duologues, both grave and gay, comic and pathetic'.[61] This mixed character endured, if we take her account of an 1884 PES concert supplied to *Eastward Ho!* readers as typical. The East End audience was composed partly of working men and women and partly 'of the humbler portion of the population, which we may, perhaps, term the very poor', attending for a penny fee. The evening of ballads, soloists, and light classical performances was punctuated by a novelty act intended to lighten the mood: a banjo band, without the customary blackened faces, 'composed of ladies and gentlemen all of gentle birth, and gifted with other and nobler musical qualities'. This interlude saw the aristocratic performers seated in a half-circle on the stage to play popular songs in the American 'negro minstrel' tradition, a spectacle that the Countess was convinced was offered and taken in a suitably edifying spirit. 'The whole thing is perfectly understood'; she insisted,

> and the East-End does not conceive for a moment, as the West-End might, that there can be anything derogatory or vulgar in the fact that ladies are playing upon instruments hitherto only used in music-halls or on racecourses; on the contrary, to their minds the instruments are ennobled by the players, and they say they love the sounds of the silver-mounted, silk string little instruments, which give their thoughts and minds a relaxation as it were, and enable them to take breath, before the severer music begins again.[62]

The popularity of these mixed programmes seemed to be confirmed by the audiences' appreciation for the chamber pieces that were the concerts' staple fare. 'When it is stated that these [PES] concerts are chiefly of chamber music', commented another enthusiast, the novelist Violet Greville, 'and that the pieces performed were by Beethoven, Mozart, Corelli, Brahms, Schubert, Haydn, Boccherini, &c., it will not be thought surprising that they could scarcely pay their expenses, but rather that large and appreciative audiences of the lower classes should greedily snatch at the grave musical and intellectual treat thus proffered them'.[63] PES evenings typically concluded with speeches, 'spoken with direct and simple earnestness...[with] a strong moral and elevating tendency, though no absolute mention of religion', and votes of thanks to the performers.[64]

The PES's success by the mid-1880s had convinced its aristocratic supporters that 'the working and wage-earning classes in the metropolis, when the opportunity is afforded them, show a great and very discriminating interest in high-class music'.[65] Not all observers, however, were convinced. George Sims, the slum journalist, doubted the value of such efforts:

> The well-meaning efforts of the societies which have endeavoured to attract the poor to hear countesses play the fiddle, and baronets sing comic songs in temperance halls, have not been crowned with anything like success for the simple reason that there is an air of charity and goody-goody about the scheme which the poor always regard with suspicion. They want their amusement as a right, not as a favour, and they decline to be patronized.[66]

* * *

Opportunities for sociability through clubs, societies and institutes was another important theme in late-Victorian social work. The encouragement of model social clubs for working-class men, women, boys and girls had been an enduring feature of 'rational recreation' efforts since the early 1850s, and even before then, as Beaven observes, 'most [British] towns and cities possessed societies that were designed to "improve" the working class. However, organisations such as the Useful Knowledge Society, the Mechanics Institutes, and the Mutual Improvement Society all shared an unwelcome feature: a near total rejection by both artisans and the rest of the working community'.[67] But with the introduction of refreshments and light entertainment the later clubs met with greater success, exemplified by Henry Solly's Working Men's Club and Institute Union (CIU) founded in 1862.[68] This body encapsulated the movement's philanthropic and reformist aspirations: aiming to provide a degree of supervision and regulation for affiliated clubs, it assisted with circulating libraries, lecturers, teaching apparatus, and periodic conferences and papers 'on subjects relating to the social, mental and moral well-being of working men generally'.[69] The number of clubs affiliated to the CIU grew from less than two dozen in 1862 to 245 in the mid-1880s, and to more than a thousand by 1904.[70] To begin with teetotalism and Bible classes were common features, but so too were refreshments, popular education, literary clubs and discussion groups, and the possibility of cross-class alliances of the kind previously associated with 'moral force' Chartism and the Christian Socialist movement. Just as 'Friendly Societies and Trades' Unions have done much to educate working men', the CIU proclaimed, 'and to raise them from a state of stupid improvidence and indifference, or of mere animal existence...so we may be well assured of the immense benefit that may accrue to working men from judicious and friendly organisation for worthy and elevating purposes'.[71] Beaven observes that Solly and others like him 'placed amusement at the centre of club activities in the belief that within a civilised environment working men would become attracted to the more elevating forms of leisure'.[72] Accordingly, penny readings, gymnastics, informal concerts and recitals, sporting contests and amateur theatricals were typical features of this burgeoning movement to actuate moralising influences on working people and families through sponsored clubs and institutes. As Price observes, through the example set by F. D. Maurice, his Working Men's College and other proponents of adult education and improved recreation, '[a]ny influence that tended to elevate and refine the habits, tastes and customs of the working classes could now find a place in the spectrum of improving institutions'.[73] Moralising influences through improved recreation and other 'civilising' pursuits took hold as a reaction against the stern paternalism of mid-century educational reformers concerned solely with 'useful knowledge' and artisanal self-help.

From the mid-1870s, however, many workingmen's clubs were shedding their reformist origins and developing a more autonomous character.[74] New clubs were formed on explicitly political grounds, while others were building larger facilities, halls and concert rooms, selling beer and spirits, and in some places hosting betting circles and other forms of gambling. They were emerging as important hubs of working-class life, small local epicentres of Stedman Jones' insular 'culture of consolation'. Not unexpectedly, many middle-class reformers were unsettled by the trend, and tended to imagine the worst. Charles Booth for instance classified the working-class clubs of East London as 'those which can be entered by a stranger and those which cannot'. The latter class he knew only by reputation as 'very bad', many being 'very disreputable indeed...a combination of gambling hell with the lowest type of dancing saloon. All alike maintain a jealous privacy.'[75]

Thus, to use another of Booth's classifications, reformers continued to sponsor rival 'superintended' clubs such as the Whitechapel Working Lads' Institute, founded by the city merchant and philanthropist Henry Hill in 1878 as a venue where young men 'may profitably spend their evenings, and so be saved from the temptations and snares of the streets, the public-houses, music-halls and low theatres'.[76] The factory girls' club established in the mid-1880s by social worker Basil Levett in Tabard Street, South London placed particular importance on outings and Bank Holiday excursions. 'No one', he wrote in an appeal for funds, 'has any conception of what the poorer parts of London are on a Bank Holiday; the only thing to do is to take the girls right away into the country'.[77] There is no way of estimating the number of these small, scattered and often short-lived ventures, but they were legion across 'Outcast London'. Whether large or small, substantial or insignificant, all these philanthropic clubs relied on well-to-do volunteers working alongside a committee drawn from the members, an arrangement that demonstrates their abiding faith in the possibility of cross-class 'friendships' as part of the clubs' corporate life. Indeed the potential for social reconciliation at clubs 'in which [working] men might meet together without running into temptation, and where those who are their well-wishers may meet them, not as patrons but as friends' was an important dimension for many advocates.[78] The sponsors of a new evening club for young working-class men and women in Marylebone, for example, advertised in late 1883 that 'a large staff of ladies and gentlemen will be needed to help in the work of superintendence and entertainment'.[79] A progress report on this effort nine months later captures for us the essential features of this and other philanthropic clubs:

> A committee of ladies and gentlemen and working men...[worked] to keep order, to take the names of new members, to give out books, to teach the members games, to play or to sing to them, and occasionally to give them a short interesting lecture, diversified by showing them sketches, photographs, or curiosities. A drawing class was started for the young men, and a crewel class for the young women. There were magic lantern entertainments, lectures on the microscope, a debating club, and gradually it is intended to give lessons in carving, modelling, knitting for the girls, and any minor arts which may give an outlet for their talents and energies. Smoking, cards, and gambling are strictly forbidden. There are recitations and readings from time to time, and once in three weeks a grand musical entertainment is given, at which the public are admitted at the charge of one penny.[80]

Much of this replicated the basic features of the 'self-managed' working-class clubs, which according to Booth featured 'entertainments on Saturday and Monday, and a concert or discussion, lecture, or some other attraction…on Sunday; and billiards, bagatelle, and whist are greatly played. Whether from the publican or from the club, these are the things demanded by the people – beer, music, games, and discussion.'[81] Inevitably the latter was often political, and in time the initial rules forbidding political affiliation and discussion in the organised workingmen's club movement were gradually relaxed. Hodgson Pratt, the co-operative advocate and CIU president from 1885 to the turn of the century, had no objection to frank political exchanges within the club environment. His annual address of 1886 underlined his desire 'to see them including men of all shades of political and social opinion'.[82] Smoking, discussion and debate, entertainment, games and refreshments were common aspects of the philanthropic clubs, too: the Anglican social reformer William Walsham How felt a refreshment bar was essential at any superintended club, with a gas stove for cooking sausages and eggs.[83]

But at one point or another the similarities ended. At the typical 'super-intended' social club, reformers imposed rules, policed behaviour and promoted models of social interaction, all of which distinguished them from the easy-going tolerance of the 'self-managed' workingmen's clubs. The moralising encouragement of temperance, thrift and self-help was always a feature. The Duke and Duchess of Westminster and other guests invited to the opening of the new Whitechapel Working Lads' Institute building in 1887 were told that members had already deposited nearly £80 in a provident society and savings bank.[84] Other virtues were encouraged in the improving club setting, including personal orderliness. 'If better manners are the first and most obvious result', wrote one commentator in endorsing clubs for factory girls, 'they are the sign of things more valuable – of interest in books, of kindness, unselfishness, modesty'.[85] By this time, by contrast, the CIU was very alert to 'moral patronage' in club life as a form of social intercourse. As Pratt warned in his 1886 address, even if affiliated clubs under the CIU banner needed 'special atten-tion' to the education of young apprentices 'in industrial, in technical, and in moral life', other forms of condescension (and especially the moralising strictures of their 'social betters') were to be carefully guarded against: 'patronage, no doubt, they [i.e. the club membership] would not tolerate', he insisted, as 'working men are no easier than other men under the depressing influence of moral patronage'.[86]

By the 1880s and 1890s the autonomous workingmen's clubs were increas-ingly commercial and businesslike in their outlook and management, providing 'more elaborate facilities for their members, the first of these being regular professional entertainment'.[87] Yet public lectures, musical interludes and recitals of various kinds remained standard fare. When Frederick Rogers, the Whitechapel bookbinder and educationalist, gave a lecture on English history at the Tower Hamlets Radical Club in mid-1883, his follow-presenter regaled their beery but good-natured audience with a literary recital from memory.

Rogers left with a nagging feeling: 'I could not help asking myself...what influence an association like that which I had just visited would have upon the character of its members if this was the highest it could offer them'.

> There was nothing coarse or low in the recital I had listened to. It was simply an average melodrama, such as may be seen on the stage of any minor theatre; but the conditions under which it was delivered were the reverse of elevating – the atmosphere reeking with the smoke of a hundred pipes, the tremendous consumption of beer, the 'beery' look that was gradually creeping over the faces of a large portion of the audience, the noise of pots and glasses, the unwashed and unshaven men – all combined to make a scene at once depressing and saddening.[88]

Rogers' disappointed tone, regretting the opportunities missed and 'higher natures' left unsatisfied, faithfully conveys the moralising hopes that sustained the superintended philanthropic clubs. By this time, as we see in the following chapters, a new generation of philanthropic clubs was coalescing in the settlements and polytechnics, in parish halls, lecture rooms and other centres of cultural philanthropy.

* * *

Although it tends to be treated as separate and distinct by historians, similar ideas about cultural influence, moral improvement and social conciliation permeated the work of the university extension movement from the mid-1870s. Arising in the momentum for reform and social service gathering at Oxford and Cambridge since mid-century, university extension attempted to disseminate higher education through peripatetic lectures into regional centres and cities. Its advocates were reformers determined to confront the insularity, college self-interest and clerical obstructionism of the universities: men like James Stuart at Cambridge, and Benjamin Jowett, Thomas Hill Green and Arnold Toynbee at Oxford were political Liberals seeking to recast the ancient universities as modern, responsive and genuinely national institutions. Like-minded reformers had earlier established a role for Oxbridge in supervising standards of school education, as in the Local Examinations pioneered at Oxford in 1857 that were quickly taken up by Cambridge examination committees and affiliated with the Committee of Council on Education.[89] Directly improving the quality of education for elementary and secondary school teachers was another early aspiration, along with meeting the swelling demand for women's higher education throughout the country.[90]

In this context, various proposals to improve popular access to university teaching matured in the late 1860s and early 1870s that confronted the prohibitive cost and social exclusiveness of Oxbridge's residential restrictions. Although, as Goldman shows,[91] more ambitious schemes for regional institutions were mooted, these proposals crystallised in the relatively modest

Cambridge 'Local Lectures' scheme trialled by James Stuart, a fellow of Trinity College, in 1873. The innovation was mirrored in the Oxford extension teaching organised by Arthur Acland after 1878. In both cases, locally managed courses were offered on a subsidised basis that nevertheless, as one of Stuart's colleagues, Canon Browne, later recalled, aimed to be 'of a University type', with genuine professional obligations: it was not simply 'a set of popular lectures, delivered by a lecturer or lecturer whose work ended when the last sentence of the lecture was spoken'.[92] Rather, they consisted of short certificate courses of study, typically of twelve weeks duration and consisting of lectures and tutorial classes, for students unable to contemplate prolonged study in the colleges of the old universities. In the decade that followed, Cambridge's Local Lectures concentrated on supplying academic courses of study in the industrial districts of the north, while Oxford's Local Examinations Committee tended to offer university extension studies of a more broadly civic character – economics, politics, history, literature – in partnership with local co-operative societies. They had broadly the same pedagogy, however: traditional university lectures and tutorials, with weekly essays, directed reading and personal interaction between lecturer and student. A syllabus and reading list was provided in advance, and students could take an optional final examination. 'The sort of work which was done in a college lecture-room was to be the type', Browne continued,

> that is to say, a lecture on some special point or points, and accompanied by some endeavour on the part of the lecturer to ascertain how far the class had followed him, and how far they had got hold of the point or points to which he had addressed himself. The audience were expected to work quite as hard as the lecturer.[93]

Individual 'People's Lectures' (as they were known in London), addressing a particular topic or to promote a new programme of lectures, were occasionally given by noted extension lecturers outside formal classes. But the personal connection was the hallmark, over time being taken as the key to extension's success. 'In ordinary popular lectures the lecturer treats his audience as a mass, throwing his information broadcast over it, ignorant as to where it may fall, and careless as to whether the seed falls on fertile soil or on stony places, where it can take no root', wrote another extension advocate.

> When the lecturer acts also as a tutor he looks upon his audience as individuals, he drills his seed into productive soil, taking care that the ground is prepared to receive it, and that each seed gets its proper proportion of food-giving manure. The minds of the teacher and the taught get into an intellectual grapple, and as the former should be the stronger man, he is enabled to drag the mind of the student from the dark holes in which it may lurk into the broad light of day.[94]

But even its most ardent advocates understood extension teaching had significant defects. To begin with it was uneven and desultory, the movement's
journal acknowledged in 1892: 'Local Committees seeking to supply the
somewhat varied wants of their audiences passed from Botany in one Term to
Shakespeare in the next, or from the French Revolution to Human Physiology'.[95] This remained a problem even as the course offerings matured and
strengthened in various localities: students might take a rich and challenging
course of study with a specialist lecturer over ten or twelve weeks, but if the
work was unrelated to other studies the ultimate educational benefit could
only be fragmentary. But if courses were to be popular and self-sustaining in
any given locality they needed to be interesting subjects taught by engaging
lecturers, and so a scattering of topics rather than mutually reinforcing fields of
study became the norm. In sum, this 'want of sufficient educational sequence in
the teaching', as a submission to the Gresham University Commission put it,
proved difficult to overcome.[96] Although numbers grew year upon year, and
peaked (for the Oxford extension lectures at least) at some 23,428 students in
1907–8, extension teaching under Stuart's model experienced only fitful and
stunted growth.[97]

For the teachers this work had a distinctive reformist character. From the
outset the supply of higher education into industrial districts and working-class
neighbourhoods was an essentially idealistic aspect of university extension
work, a commitment among extension lecturers that arose in many forms
from many sources. In tracing the 'call to university extension teaching',
Rowbotham sketches the main overlapping networks of college affiliations,
clubs and the personal circles of men like Arnold Toynbee, Edward Carpenter
and Michael Sadler from which the first generation of extension lecturers
were recruited. They tended to be liberals and radicals with shared concerns
about the universities' exclusiveness and a corresponding sense of social duty
for the wellbeing of the 'lower orders'. Carpenter, for one, remembered how
the idea 'had come on me with a great force that I would go and throw my lot
in with the mass-people and the manual workers. I took up the University
Extension work [in 1874] perhaps chiefly because it seemed to promise this
result'. Years of teaching astronomy in northern centres like Leeds, Halifax,
Nottingham, Barnsley, Hull and York followed. It seems young clergymen in
particular were drawn into extension work, and these men 'returned repeatedly
to the theme of class division, the need for social harmony' in their advocacy of
the extension idea, Rowbotham notes. 'They believed these could be overcome
by the personal act of communication of members of the upper classes and saw
the clergy as somehow neutral in the struggle and therefore well equipped to
be the messengers of class unity'.[98] But for Carpenter, at least, class unity
remained a distant dream, because 'as a matter of fact it merely brought me into
the life of the commercial classes; and for seven years I served – instead of the
Rachel of my heart's desire – a Leah to whom I was not greatly attached'.[99]

Various scholars have outlined the national picture as this late-Victorian
movement towards adult education took shape.[100] While Marriott and Welch

debate aspects of university extension's organisational evolution and responsibilities, Goldman develops a broader intellectual lineage of Oxford's contribution to adult education for over a century. In clarifying both its internal
rivalries and the diverse motives of its adherents, this scholarship highlights the
difficulty of conceiving university extension as a unitary movement: by the mid-
1880s, rather, it was a fragmented and highly localised phenomenon. Its funds
were raised locally, by local committees to pay the fees of visiting lecturers and
defray their expenses. This income might be topped up partially by grants
from the universities but was never (apart from a brief period of so-called
'whisky money' payments under the 1890 *Local Taxation Act*, and later still
after 1924) supplemented by an endowment or any public assistance.[101] In
London, our primary interest, the London Society for the Extension of University Teaching (LSEUT) developed as a 'vigorous voluntary body, full of
civic pride', nominally affiliated with Cambridge but infused by Oxford's
social mission towards the civic education of the 'new democracy'.[102] Taking
shape at discussions on the efficacy of the Cambridge Local Lectures at the
Royal Institution in May 1875, the Society was inaugurated at a Mansion
House meeting chaired by the Lord Mayor in June that year when leading
educational advocates like George Goschen (LSEUT President until 1885) and
Lord Lyttleton gave it their public endorsement. The Society's Council, formed
in 1875–6 and initially chaired by the same HRH Prince Leopold that we met
above, included representatives of nine leading London colleges – bodies like
the Working Men's College and the Birkbeck Institution, the pre-eminent
ones being University College and King's College – that together were
responsible for whatever higher education existed in the capital at this time.
Lectures and courses commenced the following year, and the first crop of
students enrolled in the seven courses offered at five separate centres. A young
H. H. Asquith, the future Prime Minister, offered courses in political economy at the London Institution and in Wimbledon, while the constitutional
historian F. W. Maitland offered a course on History and Political Philosophy
at the City of London College. Thereafter, the Society was a beacon of organisation, co-ordination and advocacy for local extension work in centres like
Whitechapel, Battersea, Croydon, Dulwich and Chelsea, as more systematic
courses of study than had previously been available took shape.

   The subsequent fortunes of the movement in London exemplifies the
importance of local conditions in that its branches, often set up independently
of formal colleges and institutes, rested entirely on local voluntary committees
and supporters. 'Organising university extension lectures became yet another
outlet for Victorian philanthropy', writes Burrows, 'with the important difference that, unlike other contemporary charities, the local organisers were also
keen members of the classes they organised.'[103] For this reason the class distinctions intrinsic to university extension work are not easy to plot: in many
cases its most ardent supporters were not necessarily middle-class reformers,
but rather self-improving artisans and working-class autodidacts keen to seize
the educational opportunities on offer, and willing to serve on committees and

raise funds to get them. Middle-class women and earnest young clerks on the model of E. M. Forster's Leonard Bast were other important constituencies. This local, voluntarist and socially diverse character had become the hallmark of the LSEUT and its work by the mid-1880s. After faltering early in the decade, Marriott regards its revival as due to a flexible, inevitably somewhat disjointed sets of lecture courses 'offered through widely scattered voluntary committees, which had no connection with a permanent institution of higher education, and at best only the vaguest hope of seeing one founded in their locality'.[104] By 1886 the work in London had attracted 5,084 students attending classes at thirty-two different centres administered by the Society. By this time university extension's major organiser in London, the LSEUT secretary Robert Roberts, could point with satisfaction to the disparate audiences that had attended some sixty-five separate courses given at centres across the metropolis. As he told the Royal Commission on a University for London in August 1888, extension classes 'included as a rule persons from all ranks of society, of all ages beyond the school age of 17 or 18, and of both sexes'.[105] By 1889 the attendance in London had climbed to 10,982, rising by 1901–02 to 15,407 enrolments in nearly sixty distinct local centres within the capital.[106]

Extension classes were extolled by their advocates as a genuine attempt at systematic adult education, and this is also how historians have tended to treat them, but we can readily see that as a mode of practical social reform they also shared much with cultural philanthropy. The extension idea captured university reformers keen to elevate the universities above their own parochial interests and serve the nation at large, and its driving mission and purpose was to supply liberal culture and intellectual opportunity to the population as a whole. Goldman points out that Arnold Toynbee, the impassioned Balliol tutor and idealist who pleaded for forgiveness and reconciliation in lectures to working men shortly before his untimely death in 1883, became the archetype, but he was not alone 'in his belief that university extension, by going out and showing the solidarity of the privileged with the underprivileged, would assist in unifying British society. Indeed, it was a standard assumption of all who took up the work in the later Victorian period.'[107] Extension lecturers 'should not only be able to instruct their audiences in the subjects of their Courses', Canon Browne declared at an 1894 discussion on how best to encourage working men in their higher education, 'but also get themselves into the hearts and souls of those whom they were teaching; when such a Lecturer had learnt to know a district, he should by all means be retained there, sympathy and mutual understanding being most essential to success in work of this kind'.[108] Striking this note in his 1891 outline of the movement's origins and prospects, Michael Sadler likewise captures for us how a high-toned idealism of social inclusion and reconciliation characterised university extension work amid the social anxieties of these late-Victorian decades. 'The poor students of England call upon culture to show its sympathy with their needs', he declared. 'The diffusion of intellectual interests, which gives to rich and poor the same

reserve of mental associations, is one of the only means by which we can hope
to bring about that solidarity of different classes which agitators vainly hope
to find in political equality.'[109] As Marriott writes, until 1900 this was

> the most characteristic defence of the new movement for higher adult
> education. The purpose was to leaven the lump, to alleviate the philistin-
> ism of provincial towns, the teaching profession, the functionaries of local
> government. In more dramatic terms it was to give the Democracy a
> sense of higher things, an antidote to anarchy and the mob-orator.[110]

Rowbotham agrees that despite their varying shades of political opinion, the
university extension lecturers of the 1880s and 1890s 'shared a great faith
in the power of ideas to overcome social and economic divisions and problems.
The generally stated purpose of university extension was to uplift all classes
through education….[and] culture was inseparable from ethical improvement.'[111] But this outlook and the social aspirations it embodied were not
confined to the movement's academic sponsors. The Whitechapel bookbinder
Frederick Rogers, after five years as secretary of the Tower Hamlets branch,
remained convinced of the supreme idealistic authority of the ancient universities. 'In looking back over what has been done in the past', he wrote in 1882,

> I cannot but feel that we are the pioneers in a great work: a work which
> must produce good fruit in the years to come. The English Universities,
> in spite of the exclusiveness which is all but inseparable from ancient
> institutions, have ever been the centre of all that is highest and best in the
> intellectual life of Englishmen; but until to-day they have been but for a
> favoured few. To me there is no grander or more inspiring thought than
> that which seems to lie behind this University Extension scheme. It bears
> within it the solution of many of the problems which vex the minds of
> those who are full of apprehension as to England's future.[112]

Seen in this broader context, university extension was framed as a moral
intervention for civic and individual spiritual renewal, a form of education
that aspired to social conciliation through personal connection and influence
across the class divide. In these respects it shared the moralising purposes
intrinsic to so many other forms of late-Victorian improving social work. As
Goldman surmises, Oxford's extension efforts 'grew out of internal university
reforms, the consequences of religious doubt, a sense of social obligation to
new and underprivileged classes, a fear of social disharmony, the development
of new "social liberalism", and philosophical idealism. We can be no more
precise than that…'[113] With the exception of the first factor, which was distinctive to the university setting, we see here motives that were equally intellectual, ideological, religious, and even psychological, and that were not
confined to extension advocates. The indistinct fusion of these elements that
sparked enthusiasm for university extension and what it might offer highlights

suggestive overlaps with contemporary efforts at moralising social improvement. As we see in the following chapters, the spread of local centres for
university extension classes in London from the mid-1870s, the cogency of
their promise to bring 'culture to the masses', and their evident success in
gaining and holding students were important dimensions of the late-Victorian
cultural mission.

* * *

All this suggests that the cultural mission was a late-Victorian philanthropic
undertaking of substance. Occasionally it stood out as a distinctive response,
clear and well-defined in the work of the Kyrle Society or the popular concerts; in other times and places it suffused a range of complementary and
overlapping social endeavours in parish, mission and local institutional work
and diffuse movements like university extension. What are the common elements of emphasis that help us to ground these diverse efforts as a mode of
social intervention?

Firstly, we have already noted that reformers' interventions were directly
moralising in that they aimed to alter the tastes and habits of working people
and the poor. They sought to penetrate into the inner sanctums of individual
lives, into the homes and communities of ordinary people, and re-make the
moral sensibilities that they felt were nurtured there for good or ill. These had
all been preoccupations of middle-class charity activism since the rise of the
evangelical 'social conscience', but they remained important to the social
work of the late-Victorian generation. Secondly, cultural reformers lamented
what they saw as the arid materialism of urban poverty, and hoped to
re-make it with colour, activity and life. 'The grey skies, the muddy streets,
the dingy houses, squalor, rags, and the dull tints of the people's dress have
absolutely killed the colour-sense among us', the novelist Violet Greville wrote
characteristically. The published prints and valentines pasted on the walls of
cramped houses were 'gaudy and hideous, vulgar and inartistic...while in the
streets there is nothing to be seen likely to attract admiration or create good
taste', she continued.[114] Amy Layard, a Mile End social worker with the
Windermere Lodge Girls' Club House, described how she decorated a former
jellied eel shop in preparation for a tea party for a group of factory girls to
transfigure the dreary setting:

> The windows were draped with 'Liberty' materials, in cheerful red; the
> fireplace was decorated...with an Indian shawl and vases of fine chry-
> santhemums; over it hangs a fine engraving from Holman Hunt's 'Light
> of the World;' and a little shed at the end, which is at ordinary times, a
> washhouse, was converted into an ornamental alcove, by the aid of a
> Japanese screen and a cottage piano.[115]

Reformers were also intent on overcoming what they saw as the insularity of
urban mass existence by encouraging fellowship and civility, a sense of social

participation that was more than sectional, beginning with an effort to transcend in some way the compelling social distinctions between classes, between 'rich' and 'poor'. Lady Lindsay captured this theme in her account of the first concerts hosted by the People's Entertainment Society in 1879. She imagined a 'great and warm sympathy', an all-embracing, sentimental connection that might transcend barriers and eliminate social distance. '[P]erhaps the greatest benefit to be derived from the entertainments', she surmised,

> the one that is most of all desired by those who take an interest in them, a benefit to be reaped alike by performers and by audience, is the strong new bond of a great and warm sympathy that is springing up around us. It is felt by those who help, and by those who are helped; it knits too often estranged classes together – the one responds to the appeal of the other. It is difficult to tell whether the rich and highly cultivated feel more pleasure in the evident delight of their listeners than the poor and weary workers evince in their appreciation of their entertainers' efforts.[116]

We see time and time again, in the social work of this generation of reformers, the notions that social redemption could be achieved by these 'bonds of sympathy' (in this older language), and that 'isolation' could be solved by 'connection' as the more contemporary terminology of social idealism phrased the issue. In both cases, personal character and inter-personal relationships were key to resolving the dislocations of the social problem. We may sincerely doubt this reformist diagnosis and the effectiveness of the solutions it implied, but our first step in comprehending this outlook historically is to listen to their voices and trace their thinking in action. In this way we might learn what they hoped to achieve, and what they contributed to the social activism of their day.

These aspirations – moral, environmental and social – lay at the heart of the late-Victorian cultural mission to the slums. As we have seen above, the scale of practical effort varied considerably, and many reformers pursued cultural philanthropic agendas individually or through small, short-lived associations and societies. Subsidised performances of fine music and occasions of polite sociability such as dinner parties and *conversaziones* were conducted to counter the lubricious attractions of pubs and music halls. Free libraries and lecture halls were established, hosting reading groups and evening classes. Exhibitions of fine art were mounted in temporary galleries and schoolrooms hung with bunting, while neighbourhoods and streets were dignified by instructive architecture, mosaics and decorative friezes.

These diffused efforts, that as we have seen were variously pursued through the obscure activities of minor associations and institutions, were made substantial and systematic at just a few epicentres of cultural provision and taken to a higher level of sophistication. 'All who have lived in East London', wrote the reformist clergyman James Adderley in 1887 as he contemplated the new and imposing edifice of the People's Palace, are agreed that the bulk of the people are in favour of concerts and entertainments of the first order, but very little has hitherto been done in this direction, except at isolated parish gatherings, at which West-End amateurs have performed here and there. But the Queen's Hall [at the People's Palace] is to be a great centre, where a continuous course of really good entertainments will be provided.[117]

At these 'great centres', the diffuse impulses and efforts of late-Victorian cultural philanthropy crystallised and were given institutional clarity. Describing the work of the Bermondsey Settlement in 1900, one commentator neatly captured the multivalent character of these epicentres of reformist effort when he imagined it to be simultaneously a mission, an educational institution and a charitable home.[118] We see in the next three chapters how these centres of social work emerged to exemplify and embody the late-Victorian mission to supply high culture to the slums. At Toynbee Hall in Whitechapel and the People's Palace in Mile End, and later at the Bermondsey Settlement south of the river, reformers sought to moralise, educate and improve, cultivate personal character and encourage fellowship and citizenship. In all these ways they set out to combat the isolation and fragmentation of urban modernity. Borzello comments that

> for all its quirkiness, [cultural philanthropy] sits comfortably among the ideas of its age, not just the ideas about art and society but among broader ones about philanthropy's role in improving the life of the poor. Far from a hopeful fantasy entertained by cultural philanthropists [alone], the goal of the individual's character improvement was basic to many of the more practical schemes to ameliorate the living conditions of the late-nineteenth-century poor.[119]

Developing this insight, the chapters that follow focus on these three centres of the cultural mission, and in exploring their foundation stories, their key aims and aspirations, we begin to re-position the seemingly far-fetched precepts of late-Victorian cultural philanthropy squarely into the mainstream of the period's moralising social work and urban reform.

Notes

1 M. Hamilton, 'Mission Women' *Nineteenth Century* 16 (December 1884), pp. 984–5; quoted in K. Woodroofe, *From Charity to Social Work in England and the United States* (London: Routledge and Kegan Paul, 1962), p. 61.
2 S. Joyce, *Capital Offenses: Geographies of Class and Crime in Victorian London* (Charlottesville: University of Virginia Press, 2003), p. 162.
3 'Recreation for the People' *The Times* 9 November 1886, p. 12.
4 'Recreation for the People', p. 12.
5 F. Borzello, *Civilising Caliban: The Misuse of Art 1875–1980* (London: Faber and Faber, 2014 [1987]), p. 38.

6   In G. W. McCree, *Sweet Herbs for the Bitter Cry* (London: National Temperance Publication Depot, 1884), p. 16.

7   H. Jones, 'Life and Work among the East-London Poor' *Good Words* (1884), p. 108.

8   'Luxuries and Necessaries' *Charity Organisation Reporter* 17 January 1884, p. 17.

9   See, for example, in the first six monthly issues of the periodical: B. Lambert, 'The Amusements of the People' *Eastward Ho!* 1:1 (May 1884), pp. 15–24; E. L. Jebb, 'Wood-carving Classes' *Eastward Ho!* 1:1 (May 1884), pp. 49–53; H. Fawcett, 'Bethnal Green Museum' *Eastward Ho!* 1:2 (June 1884), pp. 149–51; M. Hopkins, 'More about Amusements' *Eastward Ho!* 1:2 (June 1884), pp. 152–4; E. L. Jebb, 'Feasts of Ingathering: Hints for Recreation Classes' *Eastward Ho!* 1:3 (July 1884), pp. 173–8; F. Rogers, 'Working Men and their Amusements' *Eastward Ho!* 1:3 (July 1884), pp. 232–8; K. Cowper, 'People's Entertainment Society' *Eastward Ho!* 1:5 (September 1884), pp. 332–9; G. Layard, 'Open Spaces' *Eastward Ho!* 1:5 (September 1884), pp. 377–9; A. W. Balson, 'Music' *Eastward Ho!* 1:6 (October 1884), pp. 482–4.

10 J. Britten, 'Art and the People' *Dublin Review* 21:2 (April 1889), p. 377.

11 *Low's Handbook to the Charities of London* (London: Sampson, Low, Marston Searle & Rivington, 1888), p. 93.

12 See I. Fletcher, 'Some Aspects of Aestheticism' in O. M. Brack (ed.), *Twilight of the Dawn: Studies in English Literature in Transition* (Tuscon: University of Arizona Press, 1987), pp. 24–9; A. Anderson and E. Darling, 'The Hill Sisters: Cultural Philanthropy and the Embellishment of Lives in late-Nineteenth Century England', in E. Darling and L. Whitworth (eds), *Women and the Making of Built Space in England, 1870–1950* (Aldershot: Ashgate, 2007), pp. 51–68; D. Maltz, *British Aestheticism and the Urban Working Classes, 1870–1900: Beauty for the People* (Basingstoke: Palgrave Macmillan, 2006), esp. chapter 2, 'Octavia Hill and the Aesthetics of Victorian Tenement Reform'.

13 K. Gleadle, 'Hill, Caroline Southwood (1809–1902)', *Oxford Dictionary of National Biography* (Oxford: Oxford University Press, 2004) [www.oxforddnb.com/view/article/60328, accessed 15 January 2016].

14 For Octavia Hill, see G. Darley, *Octavia Hill: A Life* (London: Constable, 1990), E. M. Bell, *Octavia Hill* (London: Constable, 1942) and K. B. Beauman, *Women and the Settlement Movement* (London: Radcliffe Press, 1996), chapter 1.

15 O. Hill, 'Cottage Property in London' *Fortnightly Review* 6 (1866), pp. 681–7.

16 R. H. Bremner, '"An Iron Sceptre Twined with Roses": The Octavia Hill System of Housing Management' *Social Service Review* 39:2 (1965), p. 223.

17 Cited in Bell, *Octavia Hill*, p. 151.

18 See 'Who was John Kyrle?' *London Society* 39:232 (April 1881), pp. 392–7.

19 'The Kyrle Society' *Chambers's Journal* 3 June 1882, p. 352.

20 BL: Cockerell Papers, Add. Mss. 52722, f. 65, 'Speech of Mr William Morris at a meeting of the Kyrle Society Held in Kensington Vestry Hall'.

21 'Art Notes' *The Art Journal* (March 1881), p. 95. Prince Leopold's brief philanthropic career is summarised in Prochaska, *Royal Bounty*, pp. 118–19.

22 *Low's Handbook to the Charities of London*, p. 94.

23 'The Kyrle Society', *The Magazine of Art* (January 1880), p. 211.

24 F. E. Smiley, *The Evangelization of a Great City, or, The Churches' Answer to the Bitter Cry of Outcast London* (Philadelphia: Sunshine Publishing Company, 1890), p. 226–7.

25 Kyrle Society, *Report for 1893* (London, 1893), pp. 10–11.

26 Kyrle Society, *The Guide to the Italian Pictures at Hampton Court* (London: A. D. Innes and Co., 1894), n. p.

27 V. Greville, 'Social Reforms for the London Poor I – The Need of Recreation' *Fortnightly Review* 35 (1884), p. 26; R. Woods, 'The Social Awakening in London' *Scribner's Magazine* 11 (April 1892), p. 418.

28 Cited in Greville, 'Social Reforms for the London Poor', p. 26.
29 A. Corkran, 'The Kyrle Society' *Merry England* 3:15 (July 1884), p. 157.
30 E. Busk, 'The Kyrle Society' *The Spectator* 2 October 1886, p. 1308.
31 'The Kyrle Society' *Charity Organisation Review* 2 (February 1886), p. 70.
32 'Speech of Mr William Morris'.
33 'Art Notes' *The Art Journal* (March 1881), p. 95.
34 'The Kyrle Society', *Charity Organisation Review* 1 (December 1885), p. 506.
35 BL: Cockerell Papers, Add. Mss. 52623, f. 70, diary entry of 16 December 1886.
36 Anderson and Darling, 'The Hill Sisters', p. 40.
37 O. Hill, 'Blank Court: or, Landlords and Tenants', *Macmillan's Magazine* 24 (1871), p. 464, cited in A. S. Wohl, 'Octavia Hill and the Homes of the London Poor' *Journal of British Studies* 10:2 (1971), p. 113.
38 Published as 'Open Spaces' in her *Our Common Land (and Other Short Essays)* (London: Macmillan and Co., 1877), p. 145.
39 Hill, 'Open Spaces', p. 145.
40 O. Hill, 'Letter to my Fellow-Workers' (pamphlet) (London, 1883), p. 6.
41 'Occasional Notes' *PMG* 19 October 1883, p. 3.
42 Kyrle Society, *The Guide to the Italian Pictures at Hampton Court*, n. p.
43 'People's Concert Society' *Musical News* 19 March 1898, p. 294.
44 P. Gillett, 'Ambivalent Friendships: Music Lovers, Amateurs, and Professional Musicians in the Late Nineteenth Century' in C. Ashford and L. Langley (eds), *Music and British Culture, 1785–1914: Essays in Honour of Cyril Ehrlich* (Oxford: Oxford University Press, 2000), p. 333.
45 F. Marshall, 'Music and the People', *Nineteenth Century* 8:46 (December 1880), pp. 923–4.
46 'People's Concert Society', *Monthly Record* 2:1 (January 1896), pp. 10–11.
47 F. Marshall, 'Music for the Masses' *Nineteenth Century* 32 (July 1892), p. 68.
48 'Women's Settlements' *Hearth and Home: An Illustrated Weekly Journal for Gentlewomen* 435 (14 September 1899), p. 718.
49 [Anon.], *'Light and Shade': Pictures of London Life; a Sequel to 'The Bitter Cry of Outcast London'* (London: London Congregational Union, 1885), p. 59.
50 B. Lambert, 'The Amusements of the People' *Eastward Ho!* 1 (May 1884), p. 23.
51 'A Smoking Concert at the London Docks' *ELO* 9 January 1886, p. 7 (reprinted from *PMG*).
52 *Low's Handbook to the Charities of London*, p. 139.
53 Lady Lindsay, 'The People's Entertainment Society' *Time: A Monthly Miscellany of Interesting & Amusing Literature* 1 (1879), p. 467.
54 Lindsay, 'The People's Entertainment Society', p. 469.
55 Smiley, *The Evangelisation of a Great City*, p. 227.
56 A meeting of PES supporters at the Grosvenor Gallery in April 1881 was chaired by Sir Coutts Lindsay; attendees included the Earl of Shaftesbury, Viscount Folkestone, the founder Charles Bethune, Thomas Brassey M.P., Albert Grey M.P., Sir Julius Benedict, the Rev. Canon Erskine Clark and Signor Visetti. 'The People's Entertainment Society' *ELO* 9 April 1881, p. 6. See Lindsay, 'The People's Entertainment Society', p. 470 for a list of professional musicians involved in the PES's first year of performances. Gillet explores the tensions of professionalism and the amateur, often aristocratic, volunteers who performed at charity concerts in 'Ambivalent Friendships', pp. 333–9.
57 'Musical Education' *Magazine of Music* 1:8 (November 1884), p. 17.
58 *The Evangelization of a Great City*, p. 227.
59 'High-class Music for a Lower-class Public' *PMG* 25 January 1883, p. 2.
60 'Peoples' Entertainment Society' *Eastward Ho!* 1 (September 1884), p. 339.
61 Lindsay, 'The People's Entertainment Society', p. 470.
62 'Peoples' Entertainment Society' *Eastward Ho!* 1 (September 1884), pp. 333–4.

63 Greville, 'Social Reforms for the London Poor', p. 27.
64 Lindsay, 'The People's Entertainment Society', p. 472.
65 'High-class Music for a Lower-class Public' *PMG* 25 January 1883, p. 2.
66 G. Sims, *How the Poor Live, and Horrible London* (London: Chatto and Windus, 1889), p. 79.
67 B. Beaven, *Leisure, Citizenship and Working-class Men in Britain, 1850–1945* (Manchester: Manchester University Press, 2005), pp. 18–19.
68 See P. Bailey, *Leisure and Class in Victorian England: Rational Recreation and the Contest for Control, 1830–1885* (London: Routledge and Kegan Paul, 1978).
69 *The Conditions on which Local Societies will be Received into Membership with the Working Men's Club and Institute Union, and the Advantages to be thereby Obtained* (pamphlet) (London: Working Men's Club and Institute Union, 1863), p. 4.
70 Beaven, *Leisure, Citizenship and Working-class Men*, p. 25.
71 *The Conditions on which Local Societies will be Received*, p. 8.
72 Beaven, *Leisure, Citizenship and Working-class Men*, pp. 25–6.
73 R. N. Price, 'The Working Men's Club Movement and Victorian Social Reform Ideology' *Victorian Studies* 15 (1971), p. 119.
74 T. G. Ashplant, 'London Working Men's Clubs, 1875–1914' in E. and S. Yeo (eds), *Popular Culture and Class Conflict 1590–1914: Explorations in the History of Labour and Leisure* (Brighton: Harvester Press, 1981), p. 241.
75 C. Booth, *Life and Labour of the People in London* (First Series: Poverty Vol. 1) (London: Macmillan, 1902), pp. 94–5.
76 *The Times* 15 November 1883, p. 5.
77 'Factory-Girls' Club' *The Spectator* 12 May 1888, p. 655.
78 W. W. How, 'Working Men's Clubs' *English Illustrated Magazine* 87 (December 1890), p. 182.
79 'A Social Club for Young Men and Women' *PMG* 12 December 1883, p. 11.
80 'A Social Club for Young Men and Women' *Charity Organisation Reporter* 13 (September 1884), p. 304.
81 Booth, *Life and Labour* (First Series: Poverty Vol. 1), p. 96.
82 *The Spectator* (26 June 1886), p. 835.
83 How, 'Working Men's Clubs', p. 181.
84 'Whitechapel Working Lads' Institute' *ELA* 18 June 1887, p. 3.
85 'Working Girls' Clubs' *The Spectator* 1 February 1890, p. 172.
86 *The Spectator* 26 June 1886, p. 835.
87 Ashplant, 'London Working Men's Clubs', p. 249.
88 'A Sunday Morning at a Radical Club', *PMG* (1 June 1883), repr. in F. Rogers, *Labour, Life and Literature: Some Memories of Sixty Years* (London: Smith, Elder and Co., 1913), p. 98.
89 K. Künzel, 'The Missionary Dons – The Prelude to University Extension in England' *Studies in Adult Education* 7:1 (1975), p. 42.
90 See S. Marriott, 'The University Extension Movement and the Education of Teachers 1873–1906' *History of Education* 10:3 (1981), pp. 163–77. The interconnections between these movements are emphasised by S. Marriott, *Extramural Empires: Service and Self-Interest in English University Adult Education 1873–1983* (Nottingham: University of Nottingham Department of Adult Education, 1984), pp. 22–5.
91 L. Goldman, *Dons and Workers: Oxford and Adult Education since 1850* (Oxford: Clarendon Press, 1995), pp. 16–31.
92 Canon Browne, 'The Future of University Extension in London' in *Aspects of Modern Study: Being University Extension Addresses* (London: Macmillan and Co., 1894), p. 18.
93 Browne, 'The Future of University Extension in London', p. 18.

94   Lord Playfair, 'The Evolution of University Extension as a part of Popular Education' in *Aspects of Modern Study*, p. 7.
95   'The Education of the Citizen', *UEJ* 3:32 (November 1892), p. 111.
96   THLHL: 830.1, Toynbee Hall University Extension Scrapbook, *Memorial of the Council of the Universities' Settlement Association (Toynbee Hall) to the Gresham University Commission*, July 1892, n. p.
97   Goldman, *Dons and Workers*, p. 62.
98   S. Rowbotham, 'The Call to University Extension Teaching 1873–1900' *University of Birmingham Historical Journal* 12 (1969), p. 62.
99   E. Carpenter, *My Days and Dreams: Being Autobiographical Notes* (London: George Allen and Unwin, 1916), p. 79. See C. Tsuzuki, *Edward Carpenter 1844–1929: Prophet of Human Fellowship* (Cambridge: Cambridge University Press, 1980) esp. pp. 29–37.
100 See E. Welch, *The Peripatetic University: Cambridge Local Lectures, 1873–1973* (Cambridge: Cambridge University Press, 1973), Marriott, *Extramural Empires* and Goldman, *Dons and Workers*.
101 See Goldman, *Dons and Workers*, pp. 98–101.
102 Marriott, *Extramural Empires*, p. 34. The foundation of the LSEUT is treated in J. Burrows, *University Adult Education in London: A Century of Achievement* (London: University of London, 1976), pp.1–27, and briefly in Marriott, *Extramural Empires*, pp. 35–6. The University of London at this time was purely an examining body, and made no direct provision of teaching for extension purposes.
103 Burrows, *University Adult Education in London*, p. 7.
104 Marriott, *Extramural Empires*, p. 26.
105 Parlt. P., *Royal Commission on a University for London*, Minutes of Evidence XXXIX [c.5709-I] 1889, p. 189.
106 'Progress of the Work in London, 1876–1891', *UEJ* 3:30 (June 1892), p. 89, and Burrows, *University Adult Education in London*, p. 7.
107 Goldman, *Dons and Workers*, p. 48.
108 'Annual Meeting of the London Society: Conference on Working-men Centres' *UEJ* 5:51 (December 1894), p. 40.
109 M. Sadler, 'University Extension in England' *Quarterly Review* 172 (April 1891), p. 430.
110 Marriott, *Extramural Empires*, p. 27.
111 S. Rowbotham, 'Travellers in a Strange Country: Responses of Working Class Students to the University Extension Movement, 1873–1910' *History Workshop Journal* 10 (1981), p. 65.
112 F. Rogers, 'University Extension in East London: by a Local Secretary' *Cassell's Family Magazine* 8 (1882), p. 118.
113 Goldman, *Dons and Workers*, p. 56.
114 Greville, 'Social Reforms for the London Poor', p. 25.
115 A. Layard, 'A Tea-Party in Mile End' *Eastward Ho!* 4 (1886), p. 569.
116 Lindsay, 'The People's Entertainment Society', p. 472.
117 J. G. Adderley, 'What is the People's Palace Doing?' *Eastward Ho!* 7 (1887), p. 226.
118 W. Hunt, 'Some Aspects of Settlement Life' *The Wesleyan-Methodist Magazine* 123 (1900), p. 760.
119 Borzello, *Civilising Caliban*, p. 38.

4   One by one in Whitechapel

When the trailblazing university settlement Toynbee Hall was built in 1884 in Commercial Street, Whitechapel, it stood deliberately aloof from the grimy landscape of poverty surrounding it on all sides. Observers were struck by how 'the magnificent Gothic frontage of Toynbee Hall and its Balliol and Wadham Colleges stand in strange juxtaposition with the habitations of outcast humanity', as one put it in 1896 after more building work.[1] The settlement's neo-medieval cloisters and quadrangles were indeed a forthright statement in brick and stone of its founders' intentions in the misery-laced heart of 'Outcast London'. A surrogate home for several generations of educated, energetic young social workers, professional men and university graduates and an epi-centre of local charity work, its key personalities contributed to contemporary debates over the nature of poverty and its solution, including methods of social investigation from the late 1880s and models of regulation and state intervention in the first part of the twentieth century. Adult education, employment assistance, industrial regulation, pensions and national insurance were all part of the settlement's work, and progressive thinkers and architects of the welfare state like William Beveridge, R. H. Tawney and Clement Attlee all had formative experiences there.[2] As the settlement movement mush-roomed throughout Britain and internationally between the mid-1880s and the 1920s, the seminal influence of Toynbee Hall was widely acknowledged.[3] On this basis the settlement's foundation and subsequent fortunes have been well studied by historians.[4]

Here we re-visit the late-Victorian circumstances of Toynbee Hall's incep-tion, and review the climate of ideas and activism around this pioneering experiment to demonstrate the absolute centrality of the cultural mission to the settlement's practical social work. Toynbee Hall fused an intellectually informed Oxford social reformism with the practical parish activities of social workers in St Jude's, Whitechapel. It was as much the product of London parochial social work – of Broad Church community-building at the local level – as it was of the civic idealism nurtured at centres of 'New Liberalism' like Oxford's Balliol College. If the latter is personified by Arnold Toynbee, T. H. Green and Benjamin Jowett – all bit players in the story of the settlement's foundation, despite their allure for historians – the former is embodied in the experiences and convictions of Rev. Samuel Barnett, the originator and chief advocate of the settlement idea and Toynbee Hall's first warden (see Figure 4.1). Together with his wife Henrietta, and building on the experiences of ten year's residence as an Anglican clergyman in Whitechapel, Barnett took centre-stage as the settlement's decisive personality through its formative years.

* * *

The first concrete formulation of the settlement idea came in June 1883, when Barnett responded to an appeal from Cambridge undergraduates enthusiastic about social work but uninspired by the college missions then in vogue.[5] He agreed that evangelical missions offered little in the way of meaningful social improvement, and replied to the students urging them to undertake personal residence among the poor, adding that 'the English parish administration rests on the supposition that everywhere a set of cultured men should be at hand who were free to give their time, and these must be artificially placed in districts where they were wanted'.[6] Barnett's instinctive regard for 'university men' as active social workers had been bolstered by occasional visits, individually or in small groups, by Oxford undergraduates to work with him in Whitechapel from the late 1870s. A group of five (including Arnold Toynbee, whose fame later grew to eclipse his colleagues) had lodged in a former beer-shop from where they had contributed to university extension classes, charity administration and district visiting. It was modest in scale, but the essential idea of personal residence by educated men in impoverished neighbourhoods, to educate, moralise and improve by personal example and so build fellow-ship between rich and poor, remained key to the settlement proposal as it matured in 1883–4.

Samuel Barnett was nearly forty, mid-way through a career of incessant activity in a range of social reform causes.[7] Born in Bristol in 1844, the son of a wealthy bed manufacturer, he attended Wadham College, Oxford from 1862 and graduated with a second-class Honours degree in law and modern history. A period of travel in the United States in 1867 in the aftermath of the devastating civil war enlarged his social outlook considerably as he embraced a progressive liberalism. 'Born and nurtured in an atmosphere of Toryism', he was later to tell his fellow-workers, 'what I saw and heard [in the USA] knocked all the Toryism out of me'.[8] Back in England, he was ordained and assumed his first clerical position in late 1867 as W. H. Fremantle's curate at St Mary's, Bryanston Square, south of Marylebone, at a time when Fremantle (later Dean of Ripon) was first gaining his reputation as a progressive reformer. The parish was large, with around 28,000 residents, its prestigious houses and high street shops alongside rundown back streets and cul-de-sacs occupied by families of the labouring poor.

Here Barnett began his career under Fremantle's tutelage, delivering sermons once a fortnight, teaching in the parish school, occasionally conducting services and throwing himself into local charity and relief work. He brought personal qualities to the task – 'there was no one who was not struck by his obvious sincerity and earnestness', one colleague later recalled, 'and who did not admire his intense devotion to his work'[9] – but it is clear that Barnett's progressive churchmanship was ignited by the practical parish influences that Fremantle was trying to assemble in Marylebone. Liberal Broad Churchmen like Fremantle regarded the Anglican parish and its potential for community life as the great hope for a rejuvenated and genuinely national church and society. For them, 'the parish church had a two-fold function: to put the local people in touch with the larger national history and purpose, and to create a Christian community in microcosm which, when replicated throughout the land, would form a national Christian community'.[10] To these ends Fremantle innovated tirelessly, creating a lay council of thirty parishioners for church administration, opening the church itself for social activities, setting up clubs for working men and mothers and playgrounds for local children, and organising excursions, social evenings and light entertainments. In all this he had a willing and able assistant in Barnett, who took responsibility for a club room for working men in what had been a derelict house in Walmer Place near Marylebone Road. 'It held about twenty men and there were no conditions of membership', a fellow curate remembered.

> Subject to the limitations of space it was open to anyone every evening. Just a place where they could sit and talk, with a table or two for draughts, dominoes or chess if they liked to learn it. That was all, no cards, no drink. Here [Barnett] was to be found on the greater number of evenings every week, the centre of attraction to those who gathered there to hear him talk and to be drawn out by him.[11]

In this way Barnett contributed his own efforts – characteristically personal, sociable, and gently moralising – to Fremantle's busy ensemble of improving parish influences. 'We rarely, if at all, spoke of the politics of the day', Fremantle later remembered of his early relationship with Barnett, 'but I was very early convinced that the Church of England meant the whole nation uniting in all its parts as a Christian body, and that the attempts to narrow it must be combated. If this is Radicalism, then both he and I were Radicals to the core'.[12] In its plain essence, then, both men shared a progressive vision of urban inclusion and localised community connection through clerical leadership. 'My desire from the first was to make [in the parish] as near an approach as could be to the ideal of a Christian community', Fremantle later recalled.

> I hold that the vicinity of those living in a parish is in itself a bond of union....The parish is a divinely established microcosm, and though in a great city the larger unities of town and nation come more into view...yet many things combine to make the parish one family. We cannot, indeed, expect the parish church to be a spiritual home of all parishioners, but we can still make it a centre of good in which the rich may aid the poor, and

the school may become a nursery of the Christian family, and various institutions may arise for mutual good and for common interests beyond our own narrow boundaries.[13]

At St Mary's Barnett also encountered Octavia Hill and her Marylebone circle of London social workers and housing reformers. He joined with them in forming the first local committee of the Charity Organisation Society (COS), begun in 1869 to coordinate relief efforts and re-order local charity on rational principles, an approach that was perhaps more successful in Marylebone in the 1870s than anywhere else.[14] Described generously by Miss Hill at age twenty-six as 'a merry earnest boy, full of vigour and power of hearty enjoyment, with large and beautiful capacities, plenty of devotion and energy but young and with the world before him',[15] Barnett sat beside the vivacious, strong-willed Henrietta Rowling, one of Hill's younger protégés, at Octavia's birthday party in December 1870 and seems to have been capti- vated. Henrietta had been born into a wealthy, middle-class Clapham family in 1851, and following the early death of her mother was raised in an atmo- sphere of paternal affection and privilege. She was educated at a boarding school in Dover where both her compassion for the poor and independence of mind appear to have been encouraged, qualities that made her a bright and attractive personality in Octavia Hill's circle.[16] As the friendship deepened in the two years that followed, Samuel's thoughts turned to marriage. Although initially dismayed by the attentions of the awkward young curate, poorly dressed, with irritating mannerisms, 'small sensitive hands, a bald head, and shaggy beard',[17] Henrietta decided – on entirely rational grounds, her bio- grapher argues – to accept Barnett's proposal as the basis for a professional partnership in social reform.

They married in 1873, commencing a long and arduous career together. Henrietta recalled that in their shared endeavours, her husband was 'some- times the playwright and I the actor, while at other times I was the instigator and he was the organiser. On all matters we consulted and moulded each other's opinions or enlarged our respective outlooks.'[18] As the energetic, reforming vicar of St Jude's Whitechapel from 1873 to 1893, and then as Warden of Toynbee Hall from 1884 to 1906, Barnett became a distinguished figure in the late-Victorian social reformist *milieu*, an enterprising Broad Church Anglican and a liberal progressive on social problems. But Henrietta, as Koven recognises, 'was her husband's equal partner in all their celebrated initiatives', serving as a Poor Law guardian, school manager, charity worker and in countless other roles to the extent that Beatrice Webb called Henrietta 'the more masculine-minded of the two'.[19] Together they shed some of the shibboleths of Victorianism, growing ever more comfortable with public-spon- sored solutions to social problems and splitting with the COS hierarchy over direct municipal provision of welfare services, for example.[20] The Barnetts were in many ways transitional figures, insisting on a personal, moralising dimen- sion to social work even as their experiments helped lay the foundations of

Figure 4.1 Samuel and Henrietta Barnett, 1883

state-provided welfare in the early twentieth century. In an overdue promotion, Samuel was made a non-resident Canon of Bristol from 1893, and in 1906 took up a similar position at Westminster Abbey. By this time he had acquired confidence and presence, radiating sincerity, energy and practical conviction. 'A spare, slenderly-built man', a close friend and co-worker wrote in 1902, 'with scanty hair and a slight physique, and one whose apparel is seldom severely clerical, Mr Barnett will not strike the visitor at the outset as the man he is known to be'.

> He has not a fine pulpit presence, nor oratorical fervour, and he will tell you that he is 'not a literary man'. But in conversation, in the pulpit, and in his numerous contributions to the sociological literature of the time he stands out unquestionably as a man who thinks deeply, and speaks or writes because he has a message to deliver....He does not immediately fascinate men, but he compels them to listen to him, and somehow, through their reason rather than by appealing first to their heart, to fire them with the right sort of enthusiasm. The whole secret of his power lies in the earnestness and the severe but impressive logic of his convictions, in his freshness of thought, in the originality as well as the scientific economy of his methods, and in the deep and spiritual sympathy that actuates all he does and says.[21]

The Barnetts remained at Westminster as Samuel's health declined until his death in 1913. These years saw the germination of Henrietta's scheme for the Hampstead Garden Suburb, another pioneering initiative that focussed her public energies until her own death in 1936.[22]

* * *

But it was in Whitechapel between 1873 and 1906 that they found their life's work. Having refused a comfortable rural living in Oxfordshire in favour of this metropolitan parish of infamous squalor and misery, the newlyweds arrived at St Jude's in March 1873. There they found ample opportunities for social improvement: several acres of dense courts and alleys, bounded by the City of London to the west, and with Whitechapel High Street and its resident small shopkeepers to the south. As Henrietta later recalled, two or three main thoroughfares, their houses largely occupied by Jewish families, sliced though the dense courtyards of their parish. In these alleyways and courts 'the houses were three storeys high and hardly six feet apart, the sanitary accommodation being pits in the cellars; in other courts the houses were lower, wooden and dilapidated, a standpipe at the end providing the only water'.

> In these homes people lived in whom it was hard to see the likeness of the Divine. If the men worked at all it was as casual dock labourers....But usually they did not work; they stole or received stolen goods, they hawked, begged, cadged, lived on each other with generous indiscrimination, drank, gambled, fought, and when they became too well known to the police, moved to another neighbourhood.[23]

One later associate remembered a story, probably apocryphal, that 'the first act of welcome Canon Barnett met with from one of his future parishioners on entering Commercial Street to take possession of St Jude's vicarage was to be knocked down and have his watch stolen'.[24]

Whitechapel was already notorious as the grimmest, ghastliest quarter of 'Outcast London'. The setting for the gruesome 'Ripper' murders in the late summer of 1888, it had been stigmatised since the 1860s as the epicentre of East End misery, a 'nursery of destitute poverty and thriftless, demoralised pauperism...cast adrift from the salutary presence and leadership of men of wealth and culture', as Stedman Jones distils the reputation of the wider district.[25] This was heightened during the 1880s by a string of scandalous reports that dwelt on its dysfunction and misery a stone's throw from the City of London, the finance and mercantile heart of Britain's global wealth. The stark revelations of *The Bitter Cry of Outcast London* and *How the Poor Live* in 1883 and 1884 were widely taken to depict East End conditions, and prejudices against the district were further exacerbated by the repulsive exposés of East End child prostitution sensationally published in the *Pall Mall Gazette's* 'Maiden Tribute' campaign of 1885. The appalling conditions of

Whitechapel's sweatshops for the clothing trades were investigated by a House of Lords Select Committee, while other anxieties focussed on the volatile casual labourers of the East End docks, particularly during the period of aggravated unemployment and the Trafalgar Square disturbances of 1886 and 1887. The repetitive glare of such publicity etched a mental picture of the East End and its horrors deep into late Victorian imaginations, with Whitechapel its grotesque pinnacle.

But when he came to describe East End conditions in his sermons and lectures, however, Samuel Barnett stood against the lurid newspaper and pamphlet accounts. He delivered one sermon, 'East End Needs',[26] on several occasions in order to directly rebut the sensationalism of these accounts. 'The mention of East London always rouses interest', Barnett would begin. 'Some who have worn out their sensations on the horrors and ugliness of fiction look to find new excitement in the poverty of real life. They ply us with questions regarding the habits of the poor, ask to be shewn and offer to visit in the worst courts and seem disappointed that the inhabitants retain some marks of humanity.'[27] In another sermon he maintained that, despite the efforts of the publicists, 'the East is still unknown':

> Perhaps relying on sensational appeals you think it is haunted by starvation and vice; you picture men and women creeping from their hovels to eat the breakfast charity has provided, or children huddled in the corners seeking shelter and warmth; you think that respectable people need the company of a policeman, that it is [the] part of a wise man to leave his watch at home and of a wise woman to refuse to her daughter's permission to visit in a place so dangerous. This is an entirely wrong idea.[28]

The lurid accounts usually appeared during winter, he noted wryly, when press reporters deliberately sought out the narrow alleyways and overcrowded dwellings that confirmed their expectations of universal misery and hopeless poverty. The sort of room they arrived at was 'close and crowded, blocked with necessary furniture for eating and sleeping...[and] so fits in with expectations, with [the] mean exterior and the dingy crowds, that the one need of all East London seems to be relief, the means of livelihood'.[29]

Barnett was keen to supply an alternative picture, emphasising that the labyrinthine alleyways made notorious by the pamphleteers and press reports were exceptional even in Whitechapel, and that the general picture was much less grievous. 'The much talked of East London', he pointed out in a speech at Oxford to promote his university settlements idea, 'is made up of miles of mean streets, whose inhabitants are in no want of bread or even of better houses; here and there are the courts now made familiar by descriptions. They are few in number, and West End visitors who have come to visit their "neighbours" confess themselves...disappointed that the people don't look worse.'[30] In contrast to the impenetrable mysteries of the urban labyrinth summoned by the sensational authors, Barnett wanted his audience to imagine streets free of the taint of concealed depravity, with wide and open thoroughfares rather than the close alleys of popular prejudice:

[t]he East End of London is for the most part composed of streets; fairly paved, unusually wide and with brick one storeyed houses. These houses are inhabited by working people who have food enough and clothes enough, and whose lives if less full are certainly not more vicious than those lived in the West. These miles of streets tho', each like the other, are very depressing, offering to passers-by and inhabitants none of the refreshment of thought which variety calls out, suggesting to none thought outside their own narrow experience.[31]

It was the 'means of life' that East Londoners needed, Barnett suggested in a phrase that echoed F. D. Maurice, even more so than the material 'means of livelihood'. Attempting to describe the desolate lives endured in this landscape of urban monotony, he could only grope for negative statements. 'Trying to express that impression I say I am sensible of the dullness of the people, of their want of interest', he explained. 'Amusements, politics, religion are nothing to them. They have no union, no joy in society and membership, no rest in God'.[32] Social reformers, he urged, should 'work [so] that the poor may have first the means of life, that they may first feel the possibilities of being, their power to learn, enjoy and admire [the] use of books and leisure and beauty. We don't want the poor to repeat the follies of the rich, we want [them to] rise to live a higher life'.[33]

But the parish machinery to supply Whitechapel's social and religious needs was hopelessly unsuited to these high-minded aspirations. When he and Henrietta first arrived in 1873, 'the church and schools were derelict and the congregation non-existent', Barnett later told Charles Booth. 'The parish had been a scandal and the incumbent a mad man.'[34] They promptly issued a parish circular announcing a host of reforming schemes: a lay church council on Fremantle's example, experimental services to attract parishioners, and a new parish choir for women as well as men, because 'worship should be as social as possible'.[35] From that moment on, extending for over three decades of persistent effort, the Barnetts ushered a dizzying array of improving initiatives into life in Whitechapel during their protracted years of residence and social service there.

The reform of local poor relief along COS lines to combat pauperism and charity dependency was a priority, specifically the abolition of out-relief and indiscriminate almsgiving and the monitoring of welfare recipients as individual cases. With Octavia Hill they brought the provisions of the *Artisans' and Labourers' Dwellings Act* of 1875 to the neighbourhood in the form of model tenements run by charitable trusts. They built up a local branch for university extension courses, initiated the Children's Country Holidays Fund, and offered clubs and classes for trainee teachers in the new elementary schools. Mothers' meetings, social clubs and special interest societies were organised, alongside a welter of classes of all kinds. 'Before me lie handbills, brown with age', wrote Henrietta Barnett forty years later as she recalled the educational work of their busy Whitechapel years, advertising 'classes in singing, violin, literature, drawing, carpentering, modelling, French, German, shorthand, book-keeping for women, musical drill, Latin, arithmetic, and English composition', all taught by volunteers in the St Jude's schoolrooms.[36] From 1881 they organised the annual Whitechapel Loan Exhibition of Fine Art that precipitated a permanent successor, the Whitechapel Art Gallery, and were prime movers behind the establishment of the Whitechapel Public Library in the early 1890s. In total, the range and perseverance of the Barnetts' social and educational work is extraordinary, especially as most of these activities and causes were undertaken concurrently. Samuel's comment to their friend and ally, Philip Lyttelton Gell, in mid-1885 is testament to the range of his energies:

> There is a host encamped about me. Toynbee Hall its inmates and its finances. Church Reform, New Building for Exhibition. Whittington [club for boys] its management and educational development. University Extension its advertisement and guidance from frivolous influences. Schools their development in direction of technical teaching. Socialism and my position thereto. Christianity and the means of preaching it.[37]

In all these ways Barnett enlarged almost beyond recognition the traditional parochial duties of a mid-Victorian Anglican clergyman. As Meacham observes, 'Barnett's intention was to undertake to do at St Jude's what other clergymen were attempting elsewhere: to use the institutional machinery provided by a parish church to create a regenerated community'.[38] In the process he helped pioneer the characteristic 'social Christianity' of the period, diffusing a range of improving influences through parish work against local disadvantage.[39] Barnett had a large, perhaps limitless, conception of his role as a figure of local responsibility and social leadership. As he explained to his St Jude's parishioners in his first circular letter, 'I don't think that a clergyman belongs only to his congregation: every one in the parish has, I believe, a right to claim his counsel in difficulty, and his help to enable them to live the life and do the duty God has designed for them'.[40] Suiting actions to his words, he made his way around his new parish in old clothes and an ordinary hat, 'as unlike a parson as he could well appear' his wife remembered, talking to parishioners who often mistook him for an insurance agent.[41]

* * *

This effort of community renewal began with the fabric of their church itself, a grimy and unremarkable building of the mid-century Gothic revival. Unkempt, gloomy, chillingly cold, with clumsy galleries blocking the light and cluttering the central space, St Jude's church was, in Henrietta's estimation, 'a cheap structure, built by cheap thought and in cheap material', and they immediately set about its transformation. The galleries were removed, heaters installed for comfort, and panels of the chancel painted by artist friends with an emblematic frieze of corn and vines. When William Morris was approached for decorative advice, he suggested an apple green scheme stencilled in darker tones, with red and gold curtains and scarlet pillars. The walls above the main dado were cleaned and left in plain stone, with apple green highlights around the clerestory windows. 'It sounds gaudy', Henrietta conceded in her memoir, 'but it was not so when carried out, and on the scarlet pillars and the organ screen we placed fine photographs of Italian and Spanish masterpieces'.[42] 'The dull edifice [was] cleaned and repaired', wrote one of their co-workers, 'a dado of natural flowers painted round it, the organ rebuilt, and gradually but surely St Jude's came to be for many a centre of great spiritual refreshment'.[43]

The renovation embodied the Barnetts' progressive conviction that their parish church should be an attractive, well-used resource for the residents of the streets around. They hoped it would be a constant beacon of improving influences, and not just during conventional services for the faithful. The 'uselessness' of the building, given that it stood empty for most of the week, was 'a source of great pain' to Barnett, as he explained in a sermon three years after moving to Whitechapel. He wanted to throw it open 'as the resort of those who want quiet', and imagined 'how at midday and in the evenings it might be a centre of information or a place of common worship'. 'It seems hopeless', he continued, 'but this winter we propose every Wednesday evening to open [St Jude's] for musical services and lectures on subjects of common good'.[44] He reflected on these aspirations for the church and its local resonance during an 1884 speech to mark the latest renovations. 'The church', he hoped,

> should be the lecture hall, where, after a day's work, a man might learn facts through which he might look as through windows into the larger world; and the congregation formed of all classes, should be a body of neighbours united to recognise, amid their various works and callings, their common duty to men and to God. Then the church should be beautiful in the way in which houses are beautiful, and the hour of worship should be spent amid surroundings which are the common surroundings of daily life, and which will be raised by being associated with worship.[45]

As the walls and pillars were hung with prints, flower arrangements and photographs, artistic beauty and didactic explanation were harnessed together as an ensemble of improving influences. When one supporter, the artist and designer Henry Holiday, loaned a collection of paper drawings to hang in the church during 1889, each image had an explanatory description written out and hung below it. 'We shall hope to see many more people reading them', commented the parish magazine. 'Pictures should give thought as well as pleasure.'[46] Four prints by the contemporary Late Romantic artist G. F. Watts had been hung in the central aisle in 1887, and also offered spiritual lessons for contemplation. 'Love' and 'Death' as represented in the Watts pictures, Barnett explained in one sermon, were profound themes that deserved careful scrutiny. In the ordinary sense, human affection and mortality were 'familiar to the poor, but it has hardly dawned on them that the mysterious awful power which invades their homes and takes their strongest can be related to the love which makes weak women and poor men so kind to those who are weaker and poorer'. Another image, Watts' 'The Good Samaritan', taught 'man's duty to his brother man' in more orthodox biblical imagery.[47] Together the prints reinforced Barnett's repeated insistence from the pulpit that fine art had the power, just as religious truths did, to transfigure the commonplace experiences of the everyday. Both were potent demonstrations of his persistent theme that the sacred and ideal infused the secular and everyday.

Others were less convinced by the St Jude's decorations. The Barnetts' old friend and ally Octavia Hill, despite being a talented artist, founder of the Kyrle Society and an adviser in the St Jude's renovation,[48] had serious concerns. After Barnett had turned to her for advice about a decorative scheme for his church illustrating Bunyan's *Pilgrim's Progress*, specifically whether an idealised image of 'a true woman' in a mosaic would appropriately represent Bunyan's moral fable, he may have been surprised when Hill's sharp reply implied rebuke. 'Bunyan was thinking through all his personifications', she reminded him, 'not of exalting them. His eyes were set – are you going to try to set your people's – not on the glory of any human or earthly thing – but on Him through whom they do indeed receive a certain kind of glory, but whose presence first of all humbles them, till they are, as it were, nothing?'[49] For all her personal aesthetic taste, Octavia Hill had an old-fashioned dismay at representations of earthly, temporal themes in an explicitly religious setting like St Jude's. After visiting St Jude's for his religious influences survey in 1898, Charles Booth also found the 'aesthetic' touches made famous by the Barnetts (and maintained by his successor) rather unconvincing. 'It must be admitted that there is something too fanciful and a little ridiculous in the aesthetic decorations, pictures and photographs', he wrote, that to him seemed a faintly repellent 'affectation of Catholicity of feeling': 'A reproduction of some old masters, catholic picture[s] of the Virgin and Child, hung on every column. This effect was rather heightened by the intoning and chanting – ill done all of it. A kind of cheap copy of something good in its way but here out of place.'[50]

But others joined with the Barnetts in understanding the issue quite simply: fine art, where it was morally improving, complemented the spiritual practice of faith and worship to redeem the drab materialism of East End life. According to Barnett's East End colleague Rev. Harry Jones, 'true decoration is divine, and art which is really fine promotes culture...refinement may be kindled or prohibited, and thus, too, a vehicle is provided for the impact of fresh and sweeter thoughts'.[51] Henrietta Barnett argued in similar terms that school class-rooms needed light and decoration if they were to be a 'refining influence':

Beauty, to some extent, helps to refresh tired eyes....Prettily-coloured, picture-decorated rooms, flowers in the windows, banners in the hall, all help, while appropriate mottoes which face one at every turn in work-shop, dormitory, and school-room sow seeds of ideas which may perhaps bear their fruit in world-enriching action.[52]

Street posters in the autumn of 1881 advertised St Jude's latest innovation, a service for Sunday evenings devised by Mrs Barnett and known as the 'Worship Hour'. Providing a liberal mixture of hymns and private contempla-tion interspersed with literary readings and short performances by violins and the church organ, it was a semi-liturgical vehicle for the Barnetts' cultural mission to Whitechapel. Each week it captured the interfusion of spiritual, cultural and educational influences that was intrinsic to their parochial social work. Selections from oratorios by Handel and Mendelssohn were a parti-cular feature, both in the Worship Hour and ordinary evening services, that Barnett was often keen to explain in an accompanying sermon. Handel's *Messiah*, he commented in one, 'tells us as only music can of Judgement, sacrifice, sorrow, victory. Some of us have been caught by the sound, have forgotten our worries and our anxieties, the neighbours who offend and the happiness for which we seek.'[53] In another sermon he spoke of 'Music as the Spirit of Order', an antidote to unsettled passions and anxieties:

Music broods over such troubled hearts, and slowly forces its way; yield-ing to its power, proud passions sink back, our anger goes to its [proper] place, tender feelings retiring come forward, sleeping hopes fix themselves on things that are desirable, thoughts and hearts unite. Under the influ-ence of music there is order in our minds and peace: music is the spirit of God, ordering today as it has been ordering for millions of years.[54]

He imagined the harmonising, pacifying benefits of fine music as a palliative to human trouble and disaffection, speaking as it did of a higher order that transcended everyday strife. 'Listen to music as if it might be an echo of the unseen', he urged his congregation in January 1878.

Don't be content with pretty sounds, with the stirring of the senses, with its scientific wonder. Listen as you would listen to words from a lost friend, and know the unseen world. As you listen, you forget the dis-order, the disorder of our own lives, of the world which needs rich and poor.[55]

The young Sydney Cockerell, an ardent supporter of the Barnetts' cultural mission, attended Toynbee Hall in November 1890 to hear a lecture by Walter Pater on the poetry of Wordsworth, and afterwards stayed on solely to attend the Worship Hour in Barnett's church next door. He was 'rather impressed by the wise arrangement of the service – no tedious prayers – four anthems splendidly rendered, a reading from [Ewing's] *A Story of a Short Life* – and several hymns'.[56]

The Barnetts' renovation of St Jude's, and (more broadly) the contribution of beauty and moralising aesthetics to their services and parish activities, rejected the austere Evangelical tradition of ornamental simplicity in favour of something that came close to being a 'gospel of art'. But this was not something that can be called an 'aesthetic ideology', as Maltz argues, despite the cosmetic attractions of their church decorations. Rather it was a highly conventional, neo-Romantic evocation of fine art and idealised beauty, encapsulated in commonplace Broad Church Anglican terms as an embodiment of God's love for humanity. As Barnett's sermons explained, inspirational music and pictorial art were both to be welcomed as moralising influences in the grim landscape of metropolitan poverty because they evoked spiritual and transcendental realities amid quotidian materialism. Discussing the story of Orpheus in an evensong sermon (accompanied by a recital of a piece inspired by the Greek myth) during his first years at St Jude's, he asked

> does not God's voice come to us through music? As we listen don't we feel a power like that which drew the wife of Orpheus from the lower world upwards to the light? Has it not been so tonight – we turned into the church after a hard day's work. We have had little time for thinking. The streets seemed gloomy, work was dull, some of our fellow workers have shewn themselves to be mean, greedy people. Yet I am sure the music has struck something in our hearts; for a moment we have forgotten our cares and our wants, for a moment we have shared in higher thoughts and noble hopes. In that moment we heard God's call summoning us...[57]

Wrapped up in the parochial business of 'diffusive Christianity' which saw cultural, social, educational and civic improving influences all nestled comfortably together, Barnett's theology echoed Maurice and Kingsley in its evocation of beauty, art and truth as forms of Divine 'immanence' in the temporal sphere. In this tradition earthly beauty, itself a temporal manifestation of an eternal, ultimate beauty, was inherent to the 'Kingdom of God', and celebrating beauty was an act of gratitude to the heavenly Father. 'It is in giving thanks', Barnett stated in typical terms during a sermon of late 1880, 'that music has been written, the poetry sung and the picture painted which are now our joy'. This theme had important implications for his 'secular' social work:

> A thankful spirit is the source of the best art. It is because [of this] some are thankful that churches are decorated for the many. It is because [of this] some are thankful that the homes and ways of the sad and sick are brightened with flowers and beauty. The thankful spirit makes beauty, and beauty is the joy of the earth.[58]

The moralising benefits of culture and higher education, while not 'religious' in a narrow sense of the word, were entirely consistent with the task of moral and social amelioration that was essential to their Broad Church Anglican idealism. 'It is not just to please the eye or the ear that so much care is given by flowers and pictures to decorate the church and so much money spent on music', Barnett explained in one of his last parish reports in May 1892, 'it is rather because by their means the soul of the man sometimes becomes conscious of its own longings, and sometimes feels the glow of common worship'.[59] He and his wife were not aesthetes in any artistic sense of the term, but in their social ministry they extolled the fine arts as a revelatory and moralising force against a debilitating local environment of poverty, despair and demoralisation. Their moralising social idealism came into sharp relief as Samuel Barnett drew together his efforts in poor relief, entertainments, art exhibitions and country holidays in order to capture their common aspirations:

> In all [aspects], the object is to develop independence and goodwill, to bring out the resourcefulness of the poor and the taste of the ignorant, but always in such a way that the poor man, when he becomes rich, may not be greedy, nor the ignorant man intolerant when he gets knowledge....[If] our entertainments, our picture exhibitions, our country holidays, achieved their end, there would be a greater choice in pleasure, more evidence of individual taste on bank holidays, and more appreciation of 'the joys in widest commonalty spread'.[60]

* * *

In time, through Barnett's connections at Oxford, Balliol College and especially the latter's warden Benjamin Jowett, a handful of university men came to Whitechapel to assist them in their work. But there was a problem, as Barnett explained to Charles Booth in 1898, when these young men of culture and educated sensibility 'coming to live "in the East End" lodged here or there in the neighbourhood and became too much (it was thought) coloured by their surroundings – 'too dirty' Mrs Barnett said...' Their improving, ameliorating work amid the London poor demanded a certain level of social distance, it seems; and so 'joint quarters were provided for several in Hooper Square and this was really the beginning of Toynbee Hall'.[61]

This experience fresh in mind, Barnett's ideas for a new style of residential community to undertake social work in the East End began to coalesce. They were first sketched out in notes titled 'A Modern Monastery', a rough draft of the paper later presented at Oxford that appeared in the journal *Nineteenth Century* in February 1884.[62] The notes confirm Barnett's increasing disenchantment with the narrowly 'scientific' charity of 'those who by day sit in dreary offices, go in and out among the poor, plan methods of relief and bring to a focus the forces of charity...'[63] He now condemned the COS's limited vision of a life of dull respectability for the working poor. '[A] community of which the mass of the members would have the income and knowledge within the reach of the respectable workman is an ideal which a man would hardly sacrifice himself to promote',[64] he argued, offering instead an expansive vision of social transformation. 'It is not by wise refusals to give or even wise giving that the poor will be brought to that state of life to which they are called', Barnett insisted. 'Means must be found for spreading among the people the knowledge, the character, and the happiness which is God's gift to this age.' The lesson learnt by his time in Whitechapel was that legislation and 'scientific charity' would always fall short. He emphasised the need for active responsibility by 'a few whom sympathy has touched'; if such individuals would 'in each district form a vigilance committee and report weekly on foul drains, uncleansed rooms, and neglected ashpits more would be done for health and comfort' than by officials and legislation. The same, Barnett argued, applied to reformers who declaimed against the sweating system of the East London tailors, and 'talk wildly about the profits of the landlords': a personal responsibility and advocacy based on direct experience would be more likely to achieve genuine improvements.[65]

At this early stage, Barnett's ideas focused on the head of this small, tight-knit fellowship of active social workers. He seems to have coined a name for his experimental scheme in drafting the address, scratching out the words 'house connected with some well known college' and 'Hall' and writing instead 'university settlement'.[66] The leader of this new settlement, 'qualified by training to teach, qualified by character to command friendship and respect', would by his reputation and example draw like-minded men from the universities, ultimately working with 'not only the educated inhabitants of his new neighbourhood but also...people of all classes'. He would achieve an intuitive empathy with the condition of the people that impersonal charity and legislation both neglected:

> the same reputation would enable him to discover the work and the thought going on around him. He would become familiar with the teachers in the elementary and middle class schools, he would measure the work done by clergy and missionaries, he would be in touch with the 1000 and often miserable details of local politics...[he would] come into sympathy with the thought, the unknown thought, which is slowly moving in the masses.[67]

Much of this was conventional, not least its evocation of the conciliatory social idealism that, as we have seen, was such a defining feature of Barnett's parochial work. But the university connection supplied something innovative and distinctive. Barnett wrote of the 'strange charm which the old universities exercise; the Oxford or Cambridge man is still held to possess some peculiar knowledge'.[68] He imagined how their influence might be harnessed like a balm to effect social reform and reconciliation in the fractured modern city, and often used the biblical phrase (from Revelations 22:2) that 'the leaves of the tree were for the healing of the nations' to describe the social function of the old universities. 'The healing of outcast London', as one colleague surmised Barnett's position, 'would come from the establishment of a constant stream of the fresh young blood of the nation, year after year, from the Universities, to mingle with the populations that had been cut off by dire necessity from the main streams of thought and feeling'.[69] Animated by this idealist sense of social mission for the young men of Oxford and Cambridge that in his case bordered on the mystical, Barnett turned naturally to the universities to realise his settlement proposal.

In a celebrated paper delivered at St John's College, Oxford in late 1883,[70] Barnett further developed the themes sketched out in his notes for 'A Modern Monastery'. His address to the small gathering – Aitken described it as a society 'formed to bring its members into direct connection with the various social and intellectual movements which existed in the world outside'[71] – was very well received. Cosmo Gordon Lang, later Archbishop of York, was there, and 'well remember[ed] the effect of those words, or rather of his personality'.

> There was no gush, no exaggeration, no claim to provide a solution of the social problem. There was simply the quiet and earnest appeal of an Oxford man busy in the service of the people to other Oxford men to 'come and see', to learn the needs by sharing the life of that, to us, strange and dim outer world of East London.[72]

Barnett's proposal contrasted positively, just as the earlier letter to students at Cambridge had done, with the existing college missions, an older model of social work that saw individual clergymen supported by subscriptions from the sponsoring college with the sporadic assistance of like-minded volunteers. But such mission work, Barnett suggested, attempted nothing that could be called social reform, and provided little 'which will carry to the homes of the poor a share of the best gifts now enjoyed in the University'.[73] As such it was unworthy of the spirit of social idealism he saw afoot in the men of the universities, 'the idea which, like a new creative spirit, is brooding over the face of Society, and is making men conscious of their brotherhood': '[T]he desire was that as University men they should themselves bear the burdens of the poor – and the Mission requires of them little more than an annual guinea subscription'. The newly proposed 'university settlement' would not exist in opposition to the missions, 'but rather with a view to more fully cover their idea'.[74]

His quiet but compelling entreaty prompted further meetings to raise subscriptions as the practical business of implementing his settlement idea began. With more meetings at the two universities in early 1884, the Universities' Settlement in East London Association was a registered entity by the middle of the year, with an elected Council, registered members and defined fiduciary arrangements. Philip Lyttelton Gell and Barnett headed the list of initial subscribers, along with other worthies including the university extension advocate R. D. Roberts. The new association's primary objects were simply stated: 'to provide education and the means of recreation and enjoyment for the people in the poorer districts of London and other great cities; [and] to enquire into the condition of the poor and to consider and advance plans calculated to promote their welfare'.[75]

As donations and pledges for support came in from individuals, various colleges, and London-based philanthropic sponsors,[76] Barnett was not unexpectedly offered the wardenship of the settlement. He and his wife considered the matter during a Mediterranean holiday, making the decision 'solemnly', Henrietta later recalled, 'as we sat at the end of the quaint harbour pier at Mentone, the blue waves dancing at our feet, everything around scintillating with light and movement in contrast to the dull and dulling squalor of Whitechapel...'[77] After ten years of exhausting parish work the new venture offered a welcome change. 'The settlement will not add to the hardness of life', Samuel wrote to his brother in March, '[and] in every way it is likely to bring ease. We shall live in space, comfort and quiet – we shall give up the hard, wearing details of parish work to efficient curates. We shall have about us the salt of the earth in the shape of Oxford men, we shall have enough for their needs in our experience.'[78] A derelict Boys' Industrial School adjacent to St Jude's was purchased for £6,250 and demolished, to be replaced by a cluster of buildings by architect Elijah Hoole (see Figure 4.2) that comprised 'rooms for sixteen men, a class-room for 300 students, [a] large dining-room, conversation-room and drawing-room'.[79]

Construction was originally scheduled to be complete by mid-September, but poor weather, negotiations with contractors and alterations to the plan

Figure 4.2 Toynbee Hall and quadrangle, late-1880s

meant delays.[80] In early October the *Charity Organisation Reporter* visited the building site, and enthused how 'the prospect seen through an archway was... encouraging. Some red brick buildings were in process of erection; and a nearer look at them showed, even in their unfinished state, that they would have more affinity with the Chelsea Embankment than with the ordinary run of dull Whitechapel.'[81] With the construction of the settlement virtually completed in late November, Barnett 'took a party of neighbours', a group from a charity tenement building nearby, to visit the new settlement, and 'explained how they might take advantage of its resources'.[82] The Warden, his wife and the first settlement residents moved into Toynbee Hall on Christmas Eve, 1884, quite remarkably just a year after Barnett had first spoken publicly of 'modern monastery' in Whitechapel.

* * *

Barnett was undoubtedly a persuasive advocate, but what other factors and influences ensured his proposal fell on receptive ground? Contemporaries recognised that the new settlement owed its inception to many sources. Charles Booth, for one, shrewdly observed in 1898 that 'Toynbee [Hall] is really due to a "current of influences"...[including] the teachings of T. H. Green, the influence and personality of Jowett, Arnold Toynbee, the Bitter Cry; the general interest in slumming'.[83] The first three of these originated from Oxford and symbolised its intellectual climate; the last two invoked the practical environment of London social activism.

Both of these were vital and formative in framing the new settlement idea, but historians have weighed them up quite differently. Oxford's contribution has been celebrated, especially in the early accounts where the settlement was presented as the practical expression of a broad social conscience that had taken root at the universities, nurtured by impressionistic minds under the influence of Carlyle and Ruskin. Barnett's 1883 proposal was merely a 'suggestion that fell on fruitful soil prepared long before'.[84] The settlement's fiftieth anniversary was commemorated by a history that re-emphasised these origins, as Pimlott credited Barnett for turning Oxford's 'spirit of humility and contrition' epitomised by Arnold Toynbee to practical use in the settlement.[85] In more recent scholarly work, the influence of the great Victorian 'sages' has been relegated to the background but the contribution of Oxford to the Whitechapel settlement has still been regarded as definitive. The social philosophy associated with T. H. Green has been cited as the ultimate origin of the settlement's distinctive blend of education, social work and class reconciliation, and the allegedly 'Greenian' language of Barnett's proposal has been presented as evidence for this 'influence'.[86] This is ironic given that, for many in Oxford, Barnett's plainspoken appeal provided a refreshing contrast to the tortured syntax of the moral philosopher. The Toynbee Hall associate Henry Nevinson remembered attending Green's lectures persistently while at Oxford, 'though I never understood one single thought uttered by the simple, dark-browed, melancholic figure, who writhed and wrestled as he spoke, as though his thoughts were just beyond even his own power to grasp'.[87]

As Kadish points out, Green's influence on the origins of the university settlement was more a question of moral leadership than intellectual inspiration. His position as the sage-like Professor of Moral Philosophy, advocating a holistic view of social relations and a unity of ethics and politics, nurtured a sense of social responsibility in many idealistic undergraduates. Melvin Richter suggests that Green's remarkable intellectual influence was essentially due to the evangelical inheritance he shared with his students, and a shared dilemma rising from 'a crisis of faith precipitated by science and scholarship'.[88] 'Green's emphasis on the necessity for moral seriousness', agrees Timothy Gouldstone,

> even when it was seriousness that could no longer rest on doctrines concerning the Christian God, shows why he was able to capture the imaginations of many people despite his convoluted and difficult literary style. The questions asked by his philosophy were an articulation of the doubts and difficulties felt by a wide range of people, believers and otherwise, both in Oxford and elsewhere.[89]

Basic themes in Green's thought such as the notion of moral responsibility to the common good, civic duty and reciprocal social obligation translated readily into a case for practical action, and were adopted by undergraduates and university men determined to contribute to social reform.[90]

Arnold Toynbee was easily the most prominent of these.[91] A strikingly handsome, charismatic Oxford tutor and economic historian, Toynbee seemed to epitomise the socially active university men of his generation. He knew the Barnetts well; in addition to visiting them in Whitechapel, Henrietta Barnett recalled days at Oxford with Toynbee and his peers, and how 'in the evenings we used to drop quietly down the river with two or three earnest men, or sit long and late in our lodgings on the Turl, and discuss the mighty problems of poverty and the people'.[92] Despite chronic ill-health Toynbee was determined to pursue the cause of social reform in intellectual and practical life. After a strenuous series of lectures to working-class audiences on Henry George's *Progress and Poverty*, Toynbee suffered an untimely death in March 1883 and the university settlement movement had obtained its heroic martyr. Four days later, Barnett wrote to Toynbee's Oxford companion, Philip Lyttleton Gell:

> But now cannot some of us who loved him meet? Is there no upper chamber in which we may talk of him & see if his spirit won't come as a tongue of fire – will you meet here on a Sunday – you – Milner – Wise & any other – what think you? His work must not fall – no one can do it but together we may do something.[93]

Toynbee was subsequently memorialised in the name of the settlement.[94] Through active educationalists, reformers and social workers inspired by the likes of Green and Toynbee, so the argument runs, the liberal social ethics nurtured at Balliol spread to London social work. At Toynbee Hall, the torch was carried by Philip Lyttleton Gell, Alfred Milner, and others, all associates of Arnold Toynbee and students of Green's who participated in the establishment of the new settlement. According to Standish Meacham, Barnett's settlement proposal 'was the Balliol mode expressed as an exciting but apparently practical plan', and in the early years of the settlement, formally 'Idealist' notions of citizenship, the mutual responsibility of classes, and the importance of education were given effect as the 'Toynbee ethos' flowed from Balliol to Whitechapel.[95]

But a contrasting view of Toynbee Hall's origins and pedigree appear in two early memoirs of the settlement and its work,[96] where it was depicted as a direct outgrowth of the radical parish experiments that Samuel and Henrietta Barnett had initiated in Whitechapel from the 1870s. The Oxford men, although welcome visitors and valued social workers, were in reality mere assistants to a programme of social activism that was already well established. Revisionist arguments follow this emphasis to suggest that Toynbee Hall was 'rooted in...modest day-to-day pastoral work rather than in new concepts of social justice'.[97] By this argument, the settlement can be regarded as an expression of liberal Broad Church principles that endowed Anglicanism with a responsibility to foster national well-being through harmonious communities at the parish level. This outlook, as we have seen, had been nurtured during Barnett's experiences with Fremantle in Marylebone from 1867–73 and energised his efforts in Whitechapel.[98] The 'Balliol mode' and the formal philosophical Idealism of Green were tributary streams in the settlement's conception and development, this revisionist argument maintains: the basic tone of the settlement's activity sprang directly from this parish activism and its emphasis on community life and civic participation, educational opportunity and individual moral development. Thus the early years of the settlement should be seen, according to this argument, as 'largely the story of shifting organisation, manpower and sponsorship from parish to settlement'.[99]

In truth this debate rests on an artificial distinction, because given the underlying moral imagination of progressive social idealism manifested in both Greenian metaphysics and 'Broad Church' social liberalism, we can see that the experimental university settlement was a neat culmination of reforming energies arising from both of these sources. This is our best account of its remarkable success: Toynbee Hall sprouted in the fertile middle ground between formal ethics and Christian social activism, a *via media* demonstrated by Gouldstone's work on Anglican Idealism and Carter's insights on how Green sought to 'philosophise religion' while Anglicans like Holland and Gore sought to 'theologise idealism'.[100] Barnett was not in their league as a major theologian, but his practical idealism at Toynbee Hall demonstrated how proposals from this middle ground could rapidly harness support for concrete reformist schemes.

But even if the new settlement was in practical terms an extension of Barnett's practical 'Broad Church' experiments in Whitechapel, the universities made an important symbolic contribution to the new venture. 'It is the object of the Universities' Settlement', stated an early circular, 'to link the Universities with East London, and to direct the human sympathies, the energies, and the public spirit of Oxford and Cambridge to the actual conditions of town life',[101] and indeed in the early years of the Toynbee Hall the vast majority of its residents were 'university men'. Meacham traces the origins of 87 of the 102 men at Toynbee Hall between 1884 and 1900; of these fully 79 went there from either Oxford or Cambridge.[102] The significance of their relocation, not to the professions and privileges for which their education had qualified them, but to a life of social service in the East End, was commonly emphasised. In his address to the gathering at St John's College, Barnett had forcefully insisted that his eleven years' experience in East London had convinced him that 'none touches the root of the evil which does not *bring helper and helped into friendly relations*',[103] and on this basis he saw empathy and generosity of spirit as key ingredients. 'In the degraded quarters of the town', he assured listeners, 'in the wards of the workhouses, [the settlement residents] will find those to whom the friendship of the pure is strange, and who are to be saved only by the mercy which can be angry as well as pitiful'.[104] Residents would serve as district visitors and school managers, directing charity relief committees, 'and in these positions [will] form friendships, which to officials, weary of the full routine, will let in light, and to the poor, fearful of law, will give strength'. He felt sure that the everyday qualities of empathetic, educated gentlemen were needed as much as the exacting diligence of the social worker:

> Others who can spare time only in the evening will teach classes, join clubs, and assist in co-operative and friendly societies, and they will, perhaps, be surprised to find that they know so much that is useful when they see the interest their talk arouses. In one [working-man's] club I know, whist ceases to be attractive when the gentleman is not there to talk.[105]

The settlement thus begins to appear as much an expression of university extension principles as it was an expression of Green's social ethics or Broad Church Anglicanism. As we saw above, university extension had emerged in the 1870s as an important educational initiative to distribute the benefits of university learning and the personal influence of educated graduates among the broader urban population. Barnett was a great enthusiast, and had introduced his first university extension course in 1874 as an early initiative at St Jude's. 'The teachers would be men of knowledge and culture', he anticipated, and 'they would thus give their pupils something better worth having than mere information'.[106] After their inaugural efforts in 1874, when fifty students attended the first twelve-week course, a room in Cambridge Road was taken up for 1877's course on the physics of light. By 1878 the dissecting theatre at

London Hospital was the unlikely setting for courses on political economy, history, magnetism and physiology; the organising secretary Frederick Rogers remembered how 'skulls, bones and other things had to be got rid of before lectures on History or Political Economy began'.[107] From 1879, as an active supporter of the LSEUT, Barnett had chaired the Tower Hamlets committee that sponsored local extension courses; St Jude's School in that year, for example, hosted a *conversazione* for local extension students at which the LSEUT chairman, G. J. Goschen, voiced the movement's broadest aspirations. 'We must bring about the wider intercourse between those variously educated so that the best system might be recognised', Goschen suggested. 'If some common room in connection with the classes could be established, the intercourse would be more possible.' Henrietta Barnett later remarked that his words 'provided the seed from which sprang Toynbee Hall'.[108] At St Jude's, according to the parish magazine in 1889, 'we are very proud to think that the largest, and oldest established centre [of university extension in London] ...is the Whitechapel one – first at the London Hospital, then at St. Jude's Schools, now at Toynbee Hall'.

> Mahomet can't always go to the mountain, so the mountain goes to Mahomet. Only a very few people can become students *at* Oxford or Cambridge; so Oxford and Cambridge send some of their best scholars to teach those who must live at home or near their work, and have only their evenings in which to go on with their education.[109]

The importance of university extension to the new settlement is also underlined by its sponsors' desire to avoid being captured by Balliol or Oxford interests alone. Barnett and others on the Universities' Settlement Association were determined to avoid any exclusion of Cambridge. Tensions between the traditional rivals were perhaps inevitable, and became evident to Barnett after one of his supporters approached the Cambridge don and extension advocate J. R. Seeley in May 1884 and discovered the latter's impression that 'there is still a sense that Oxford does not want Cambridge [involved in the settlement scheme]'. 'That is how Seeley puts it', Barnett continued in conveying his concerns to Gell, 'and of course it means that Cambridge does not quite like following or getting helped by Oxford. You must show that Oxford has need of Cambridge, that without the latter, the Settlement cannot be such a marked success.' Any publicity for the settlement scheme should emphasise its relationship with the extension efforts of both universities, he advised. 'Hoist the University Extension flag', he urged. 'This belongs to the Universities, and University Extension cannot flourish [at the settlement] if only Oxford takes up the scheme. It is University Extension [that] will rouse Stuart and he will rouse the [Cambridge] undergraduates.'[110] In time there were many Cambridge supporters of the Universities' Settlements Association scheme, many no doubt sharing Sydney Vines' view (couched in Barnett's language) that the settlement's residents would 'take with them, as it were, a portion of our University life, transplant it there [in the East End], and start it, let us hope, in active and permanent growth'. It seemed a compelling appeal 'to give, as it were, an off-shoot of itself, a portion of its very life-blood to be transfused into the body of an apparently dying community'.[111]

All this underlines the intimate relationship between the university extension movement and Barnett's subsequent proposal to establish a university settlement in Whitechapel. The settlement idea had been around for some time, certainly since the example of Denison in the 1860s and in variations on Ruskin's guild idea.[112] But it prospered so verdantly in the mid-1880s not through Barnett's efforts alone or the receptive mood in Oxford, but also due to its direct compatibility with university extension that was gathering momentum at that time. As we noted above, the extension movement had been revitalised by de-centralised and voluntarist effort in the mid-1880s, a pattern of work nowhere better exemplified than by the efforts of Barnett and his co-workers in Whitechapel. Professor Stuart himself ascribed the success of the extension courses in London to the personal connections established, to the fact that the London system 'was altogether based on bringing the teacher into individual intercourse with his pupil'.[113] University settlements extended this idea, and proposed the creation of a community of graduates, beneficiaries of the best advantages the nation could provide, as emissaries of national culture and educated learning into the impoverished neighbourhoods of 'Outcast London'. From this perspective, the new settlement was the university extension idea writ large. As citizen 'settlers', conveying the tangible benefits of their social privileges to educate and empathise, settlement residents would be a powerful force for social amelioration and conciliation. 'I am afraid', Barnett concluded in the *Nineteenth Century,*

> that it is long before we can expect the rich and poor to live again as neighbours; for good or evil they have been divided, and other means must, for the present, be found for making common the property of knowledge. One such means is the University Settlement. Men who have knowledge may become friends of the poor and share that knowledge and its fruit as, day by day, they meet in their common rooms for talk or for instruction, for music or for play. The settlers…may share all their best with the poor, and in the highest sense make their property common.[114]

* * *

A letter by Barnett circulated at the universities in May 1884 called for applications from prospective residents for the new settlement. Their accommodation in Whitechapel would be comfortable, he promised, with a private study if required, all meals provided and 'ample facilities for social life. A large lecture room will be occupied by the Students of the University Extension Classes, among whom friends may be made. The dining room will be large enough to entertain many guests of all sorts and conditions. A drawing room and a smoking room will be for the common use of residents and their friends.'[115] The simple act of living among the poor was itself a valuable contribution to the aims of the settlement: 'those who are working for their livelihood and have but little time to spare for other objects', he assured applicants, 'may [at Toynbee Hall] pursue their work with the sense that by the mere act of residence they are doing something to draw classes together'.[116] Other circulars explained that the routine administration of local boards and committees to combat problems of sanitation, housing and public health would be everyday responsibilities. Francis Fletcher Vane, a soldier and minor aristocrat, discovered this when he spent his first month at the settlement in 1886 in various duties as a sanitation inspector, education administrator, committee member for youth clubs and rent collector. By such efforts the civic talents and responsibilities of residents were placed at the service of East London. But Vane's recollection that 'all of these enabled one to see the inner life of the poorest of the poor'[117] illustrates that the characteristic settlement emphasis on personal empathetic connections across social barriers was never far away.

In this way the role of the residents soon overtook the earlier emphasis on the settlement head as the conduit from Oxbridge to the East End. The dispiriting poverty of life in East London, Barnett contended, that had made its population 'careless of cleanliness, listless about the unhealthy condition of their workshops, and heedless of anything beyond the enjoyment of a moment's excitement', could be countered by 'sharing' the 'fuller lives and riper thoughts' of university men. 'Friendship', he continued, 'is the channel by which the knowledge – the joys – the faith – the hope which belongs to one class may pass to all classes'.[118] For the early resident Thomas Hancock Nunn, the men of Toynbee Hall lived 'without ostentation, either of poverty or of wealth…a mean of living as should enable them to draw together the classes divided by extremes; and, instead of living each by himself, they were to form themselves into a club and live together'. Sociability and fellowship were far more valuable, he felt, than any affectation of equality:

> Living alone men would not only cut themselves off from many of the nobler sources of enjoyment, but, in sharing the narrowness of the poor man's life, might lose the clue to its betterment. If they desired to deny themselves they were to do so not by making life smaller, but by making it larger, by living in a community of men who, with different religions and political views, were prepared to sink all minor differences for the sake of a great cause.[119]

Barnett agreed that the settlement was essentially 'a club-house in which men who had received the good things of the age might live and make friends, among those who had missed these good things'.[120]

Residents were not to deny their own class position, in other words, and the settlement was intended to support a comfortable, even elegant mode of life for them that befitted their education and status. Barnett always insisted that the residents would live just as they would otherwise, would simply 'live their own life…there must be no affectation of asceticism'[121] and in many ways retaining the camaraderie and comfort they had enjoyed at their university colleges. Promoting the scheme at Cambridge, Gell promised that life at the settlement would be 'along with all its hard work, a refined and civilizing life',[122] and indeed the Toynbee 'settlers' lived unambiguously as gentlemen in the unlikely setting of Whitechapel.

This broke with the pattern of most late-Victorian philanthropic schemes and charity ventures. Centres of social work in London's poor neighbourhoods were barren, functional places, where physical comforts were deliberately minimised. Oxford House, the rival university settlement in Bethnal Green, was regarded by Henry Nevinson as 'a more genuinely monastic establishment than Toynbee – quite free of pictures and tinsel decorations in the public rooms for one thing'.[123] As late as 1906, a note drafted by one Toynbee resident emphatically rejected claims that the settlers were 'a brave little band of "slummers"', 'cranks and faddists – "pleasant Toynbee youths who know nothing"', socialists and ascetics. Their intimate interaction with the life of the Whitechapel poor did not, he insisted, infer 'any lowering of our standards'.

> We are gentlemen, we have comfortable rooms, and a well-appointed table, to which we invite our neighbours (from the West End). We are waited upon by an admirable staff of servants, such as may be seen in the most refined of English homes. They know their place and keep it; we know our place also, and are for the most part, as befits gentlemen, unacquainted with their names.[124]

As we see in the following chapters, the busy everyday life of this 'club-house' for men of education and culture was imagined as an improving influence cast across the surrounding neighbourhood. Members of the settlement conducted classes and reading, organised music recitals, supervised clubs, helped run the Barnetts' annual art exhibition and entertained their new 'neighbours' to evenings of polite social intercourse. 'Thus, and with… occasional success', one recalled, 'we strove by music, plays, lectures, and classes on nearly all subjects, by Travellers' Clubs, by various games, by a good library, by boys' clubs, and many other devices to diffuse such happiness as knowledge or beauty or health may bring. "To make the best common", "to prevent useless knowledge", were among the watchwords of our band.'[125] These were phrases echoed time and time again by Samuel Barnett, the indefatigable cheerleader in everything Toynbee Hall did, who made sure that a personal motto, 'One by One', was stencilled in Gothic lettering high up in the settlement's drawing room. He recaptured the settlement's primary cultural mission in looking back on their first decade of work:

The establishment of Settlements is the work of those who believe that the gifts to modern times are good; that culture is gain, not loss; that cleanliness is better than dirt, beauty better than ugliness, knowledge better than ignorance....Settlements stand as an acknowledgment of the claims of all the citizens to a share in these good things, and as a protest against meeting those claims by the substitution of philanthropic machinery for human hands and personal knowledge. They express the desire on the part of those 'who have' to see, to know, and to serve those 'who have not'.[126]

* * *

A second defining feature of the new settlement was its trenchant masculinity, and recent scholars have been keen to interrogate the implications of its gender politics. Contemporaries occasionally called it a 'monastery', but this was intended as much to draw attention to its ideals of common life, social service and humility in confronting the needs of the poor as much it was a comment on its all-male character. If Lucinda Matthews-Jones over-states this theme in arguing that the Franciscan monastic ideal was key to the late-Victorian university settlements, her observation that the settlements made possible a masculine identity that 'allowed settlers to be active, social and public men who lived in a space that was neither straightforwardly domestic nor ascetic' is well made.[127] Seth Koven develops a more provocative reading, seeing the settlements on the Toynbee Hall model, like other expressions of the 'slumming' impulse, as vehicles for experimentation with sexual identities and subversive transgression. Philanthropy and eros entwined, he suggests, as sexual orthodoxies were challenged at the new settlements alongside conventional ideas about religion, social work, class relations and civic life. '"Comradeship" at Toynbee Hall', he writes, 'flirted dangerously on the boundaries between homosociability, homo-eroticism, and homosexuality'.[128] Some caution and balance is needed here, however, and the empirical objection that Koven's work 'privileges sexual motivations more strenuously than much of the surviving evidence warrants' carries some weight.[129]

The overt masculinity of Toynbee Hall is particularly striking when compared to the dozens of philanthropic bodies and voluntarist societies that were almost entirely administered by women. It seems a clear instance of a masculine encroachment through the development of professional vehicles for social work. Henrietta Barnett later presented the masculinity of Toynbee Hall as a deliberate strategy in her husband's formulation of the settlement idea.

[I]t must not be forgotten that...men, young men, intellectual men, had but recently joined the ranks of the philanthropists. The care of the poor, the children, and the handicapped had hitherto been left to women, or men of mature if not advanced years. Indeed, the novelty of Toynbee [Hall] was not so much that men chose to live among the poor, but that young and brilliant men had chosen to serve them in ways based on [critical] thought.

Consequently she was sure that it was not any innate assumptions about the capacities of men and women that underlay his decision to restrict residency at the settlement to men only, but rather his anxiety that the university men, 'still shy in their new role, would retire if the movement was captured by women'.[130] Beyond the body of residents themselves, even the settlement's Council and the external associations that supported its work from the universities were utterly masculine affairs, and a hearty 'club-room' atmosphere prevailed in the tobacco smoke and frock coats of Toynbee Hall's discussion groups and settlement dinners. When a social club for charity workers was established at Toynbee Hall in 1885, for example, it was soon forced to relocate, according to the COS journal: 'It was impossible that a club enjoying free access to a monastery should include women as its members, and a club of social workers without women was an absurd anachronism.'[131]

There was of course a single notable exception to this masculine club-room environment: the imposing, energetic and wilful figure of Mrs Barnett herself, who essentially managed the premises as chief housekeeper, supervising up to thirty cooks, cleaners, maids, and other servants.[132] Charles Ashbee, a Toynbee resident from mid-1886, jotted down his first impressions after an invitation to lunch. 'She is I think the Prior and Prioress of this place', he wrote, 'the working head. A fine noble bright-eyed vigorous woman she appears, and one that will have her own way and not be sparing of her own opinion. "I back my female curates against Samuel's any day", she cried – and I believe Samuel thought she was right. It is splendid to see a woman fired with a great idea and living up to it.'[133]

But did she chafe under the indignity of her ambiguous status in this 'modern monastery' that valorised university men as heroic social reformers? Given Henrietta Barnett's 'breezy self-confidence', the 'naïve self-assertion, sometimes to the borderline of bad manners'[134] that struck colleagues like Beatrice Webb, we might wonder how she managed without any formal title or position. Her frustrations seem to have come to a head in January 1887 over her exclusion from the settlement's Council, where titular supporters such as the Marquis of Ripon and E. N. Buxton, the former Liberal MP and chairman of the London School Board, had a role ahead of active insiders like herself.[135] Writing to P. L. Gell, the council chairman, the day these appointments were announced and without discussing the matter with her husband, Henrietta marked the second part of her letter 'Private' and asserted her own case in strong terms. Her first point was that the work of women should be tangibly recognised in progressive institutions such as the university settlement. She wanted a seat on the Council 'chiefly as a recognition of work for my sex's sake – recognition which would have been naturally given me for a tenth part of the work...if I had been a man – but which no one thinks of, as the work was done by a woman'. There were practical reasons as well, she went on to explain, because

> it is difficult as the [settlement] grows to guide the details and update the regulations, unless one knows all, as no repetition could teach one. Again and again it becomes my duty to learn the points by a word or a suggestion, and I cannot do this when I don't know the whole direction... Also I feel that there is a very distinct place for a woman as a woman on the Council. Servants, domestic government, women students, women officers all point to it, and are a very large part of the whole concern. I have spoken Gelly to you as a friend, and only to you. I feel that this ought to have come without asking...but women are again so ignored even among the best men, and so I tell you plainly what I have thought.[136]

'If you think me no gain do not hesitate to say so. I shall quite understand', she concluded diplomatically, 'and remember that the first reason is my strongest. It would do every whipper snapper who thinks he as a male is superior to women, good to know that big Toynbee [Hall] has asked a woman for her council – and it would make my very difficult (and miserably difficult) position in Toynbee much easier'. Gell appears to have been unable to accede to Henrietta's request, voicing his confusion about the recognition she had advocated for female social workers.[137] Although clearly disappointed, she accepted the rebuff with grace and sought to clarify her motives in a subsequent letter:

> what I meant by that word [recognition] was that a seat on the Council would be a testimony to the 1000s who now accept women's work as inferior, that a body of leading men thought it and the one who did it of sufficient value to be represented on and invited to their Councils about that work – but with that explanation of what I meant by the word let the matter drop. There will be many other opportunities in my life, I hope, when I can induce men to be just and fair to women...[138]

Few had cause to take issue, as did Henrietta on this small but significant occasion, with the implications of Toynbee Hall's gender politics in such a personal way.

* * *

Amid the idealism and activity powering the new settlement there were voices of criticism and dissent. Some came from within, and soon threatened splits and defections. The first and most significant of these saw factional tensions threaten the shaky Anglican consensus of the Universities' Settlement Association, as 'High Church' interests centred on a Keble College faction favoured a more doctrinal institution than the one proposed. The 'Keble people are...very vigorous and it will strain one's charity to be in spirit [with] these fellow workers', Barnett confided to his brother in March 1884. 'I must begin by quenching the desire to say what I think.'[139] With Barnett watching in quiet despair, the group soon split from the Association to found Oxford House at Bethnal Green.[140] Herbert Henson, a later warden of Oxford House, followed Barnett in imagining its residents as surrogates for the 'fugitive leaders' of East London, the 'cultured, leisured, educated individuals' who 'mingle in the local life and bring into it an element of unworldliness which in some measure modifies its unimaginative materialism'[141] But in time the two settlements took their separate paths. Henson later recalled that, in practice, many of the Oxford House residents were graduates preparing for ordination, with the result that the House acquired 'the atmosphere, and accumulate[d] the traditions, of a training school for parsons, and this was far from the intention with which it had been founded'.[142] As Henrietta Barnett recorded, the fact that fellow-Anglicans '[thought] it necessary to start another Settlement because Toynbee Hall was not in their opinion religious, was a deep, a very deep, pain to Mr Barnett'.[143]

Barnett's settlement had other critics, from across a wide spectrum. He told a gathering at the settlement in July 1889 that the place had been derided as 'too secular, too religious, socialistic and ecclesiastical...I have heard some say that it cares for nothing but culture and I have heard others declare that its chief function is teaching small boys to smoke'.[144] Many in the press detected 'an artlessness, not to say a temerity, about the proposal which savoured a little of the academic prig', and felt the fanciful social theories of undergraduates were best left at the universities. 'That the inhabitants of East London', opined *The Spectator*, 'who labour chiefly under the blank, immeasurable dullness of a restless but sordid life, were to be regenerated by the efforts of undergraduates and the sight of aesthetic furniture and Japanese fans, was a notion which appeared to be a preposterous, dull jest'.[145] Much commentary cheerfully mocked the 'Oxford man' in East London as a 'cherry-cheeked schoolboy', typical of the type who, according to *The Spectator* on another occasion, 'after a few years at the University, reappear triumphant as one of those missioners of society improving Mile End, – by what? Not by anything he had to teach, but "by contact" – with his sublime person as an Oxford man, bless the boy!'[146] Barnett's suggestion that the wealthy should be prepared to host the poor in their own homes seemed equally absurd. Such equality was impossible, wrote an Edward Green in a letter to *Eastward Ho!* after hearing Barnett speak in these terms in 1885. He countered that 'even if it were possible, for refinement and coarseness, cleanliness and dirt to mingle together', social reconciliation by cultural means was an impractical agenda for reform.

> Would many of the refined and cultured and clean be moved to such a sacrifice? A few bachelors and spinsters might, and a fewer number of childless married persons; but no father or mother would allow their boys

or girls to associate with the people of the streets. Why not? Because in practice the social fraternisation (except in schools) of extreme classes is impossible. The sooner the idea of such an artificial lifting up of the lower classes is given up, the better.[147]

Yet despite this kind of criticism the maintenance of a deliberately cultured life by educated young men at Toynbee Hall, in the midst of drab East London, remained intrinsic to the settlement's ethos for over twenty years. In 1893, nearly a decade after the settlement's foundation, Barnett explained how Toynbee Hall residents in East London, as 'unaffected' as only gentlemen could be, served to not only prove their 'common humanity', but to help dismantle established stereotypes of the wealthy that circulated among East Londoners. A resident's task, Barnett insisted, was 'to let himself be known, to live his own life without affectation of sacrifice or asceticism, to follow his own calling, do his own duty, take his own pleasure, and keep up his own standard of cleanliness and refinement'. In this way,

[A] few people who having received good things in their day are seen to be neither brutal, nor cruel, nor selfish, but human and friendly and dutiful, – do something to abate suspicion. They force their neighbours to enlarge their sympathies and include others than their own class in their social ideals. They do away with misunderstanding and make it more possible that united citizens may inhabit an improved city....East London needs to be familiar with the lives of those who have received the best to assure its people that the best is also for them and that goodwill is real.[148]

Many residents had their own reservations about the whole enterprise, and found these ideals difficult to sustain in practice. Although ostensibly a firm supporter, the writer Henry Nevinson, a shrewd observer and associate of the settlement who lodged nearby with his wife Margaret 'among bugs, fleas, old clothes, slippery cods' heads and other garbage', acknowledged that

in those early days it was the scene of some absurdity and some self-righteousness. Not so much among the inmates and other members themselves as among the solemn people who came down to encourage our 'noble enterprise', there was a lot of pompous chatter about 'shedding the light of University teaching among the dark places of the world'.[149]

'We all met in Whitechapel with some ill-defined notion of sharing what we had of knowledge, art, music and beauty with those who had so little'; Margaret Nevinson remembered, 'some had definite theories of social reform but on the whole few of us were prigs or self-righteous, [and] we were not above laughing at ourselves and our ideals'.[150] In a similar way the residents themselves brought a multiplicity of intentions – ideas and hopes that were not always clear and consistent – with them into their East End careers. When the young architect and craftsman Charles Ashbee arrived at Toynbee Hall in mid-1886, it was with mixed feelings, ambivalent intentions, and painfully unsure of his commitment. 'I arrived here last night', he wrote in his journal, 'my object to explore. I hope perhaps to live here later for a while, but rather as a sop to my own conscience, having now for three years talked philanthropy, I'm desirous of doing something. Yet I mistrust myself and this place also; myself for insincerity, Toynbee Hall for what seems at first a top hatty philanthropy'.[151] In time, Ashbee became a vocal internal critic of the settlement and its ethos. A social and sexual utopian in the mould of Edward Carpenter, keen to seek out homosocial connections in personal intimacy, it seems Ashbee 'saw life in the slums of Whitechapel as an escape from the political, social as well as sexual conventions of bourgeois respectability.... Toynbee Hall offered [him] a "chain of comrades" and ready access to the "rough boys" whose company he craved'.[152] His Ruskin classes at Toynbee Hall, which commenced in 1886–7 with three students studying *Fors Clavigera* and *The Crown of Wild Olive*[153] grew into a design class, and practical projects in painting, modelling, plasterwork, gilding and the study of heraldry followed[154] as it grew to around thirty young men, artisans and workers. Ashbee secured a workshop in a warehouse alongside the settlement where the group, now dubbed the Guild and School of Handicraft, settled in mid-1888 with Ashbee as its director. He explained their little hub of technical and art education as 'a co-operative society of workmen working for their livelihood in the day-time on the lines in which they teach in the evening'.[155] By May 1889, however, it had been decided 'in the interests of the future development of the School...[that] it should have an independent existence, and it will shortly be removed to more convenient premises'.[156] This was a significant rupture, as the group departed 'like old Greeks sailing away from the mother-city to found Hellenist colonies among the barbarians', in Nevinson's picturesque description.[157] Soon after, Ashbee's guild relocated to a permanent home at Essex House in Mile End, and severed the last of its ties to the settlement.[158] As he and his companions moved their Guild of Handicraft entirely out of Toynbee Hall's orbit, Ashbee fired his parting shot:

> Our object is not to create a *dilettante* and ephemeral school that shall be pretty and winning, and be supported on the passing charity of West End culture; its existence determined by the margin of spare time which we, and our friends, looking kindly on us, are enabled from the more earnest calls of life to yield it – *the School of a hobby*; our ideal is to create...a school...that shall be self-dependent and supported from within, not from without – *the School of a movement*.[159]

Arthur Laurie, a like-minded Toynbee resident who led another group of defectors into independent lodgings in Stepney Green at this time, was also clear that the high-minded social idealism and moralising politics of Barnett's settlement prompted the move. He did not blame the warden personally, but declared himself 'irritated' by the Toynbee atmosphere:

> We were supposed to be noble young men engaged in trying to do good to the poor. We did not feel noble and we had no desire to do good to anybody, and were quite incapable of doing so. We wished a closer contact with the people and lives of East London, and, more especially, the Labour leaders. As long as we lived in Toynbee Hall that was difficult.[160]

There had clearly been considerable internal tension and antagonism, but Barnett appears to have accepted these defections with a rueful resignation. As Ashbee and the others, a little 'swarm' of defectors, prepared to leave Toynbee Hall at Easter 1889, Barnett wrote to the settlement loyalist Gell that 'the principle of swarming is right, and the method may be right in this case but I am doubtful. These men are going to settle in Beaumont Square, and being "lawless" are going to do without a head – we shall see.'[161] For Ashbee's part, he felt the settlement had failed miserably in its primary ambitions:

> Its trouble was that it had no corporate life. It was neither a college, a convent nor a club; and there was never any leisure. Its members had no time to get together; they met in the evening for a rather perfunctory dinner, after which there was a rush of lectures, clubs, entertainments, and committees; and they met at a still hastier breakfast the next morning after which they all rushed off to their day's work in the West End.[162]

Privately he had come to detest Barnett's manner as a 'cold-blooded saintliness',[163] and vented this hostility towards his former mentor through the character Simeon Flux in his *The Building of Thelema*, a sharp satire of reformist hopes published in 1910. '[Y]outh needs dogma, directness, definiteness', Ashbee insisted as he reflected on the indifference of a fictional group of East End 'lads' towards the settlement's influence, 'and it was just the absence of this in the Rev. Simeon which made him the petted priest of a loosely-thinking, fashionable congregation, and that lost him the suffrage, he would no doubt dearly have kept, of these East London boys'.[164] Later still, in 1914, Stephen Hobhouse brought his Quaker social conscience to Toynbee Hall, 'but soon realised that it was much too comfortable for my present purposes, an "oasis" of Oxford and Cambridge academic life, whose doors shut one off from the drab poverty of most of the humble houses around'.[165] He soon relocated to a tenement in Hoxton and worked there for local organisations, serving on LCC committees and other forms of local social service.

* * *

Despite these voices of doubt and dissent, and the generational shift soon after the turn of the century, the original 'Toynbee ethos' of moralising personal influence persisted at the Whitechapel settlement under Barnett's leadership until he stepped down in 1906. Through that time, the settlement was imagined by its promoters as a fostering, empathetic hub of social work and improving influences to ameliorate the fractured, alienated urban community of the surrounding streets. It was an outpost which, to its supporters at least, promised to be 'a house of call for thinking men of all classes, drawn there by their work, their enquiries, and their friendships, or invited for the particular discussion of some definite social problem'. Associate membership was available to encourage this kind of participation.[166] The role of the permanent settlement residents, however, remained key as they personally enacted the settlement's social mission to East London. Samuel Barnett started one annual report with a rhetorical question: 'Is Toynbee Hall a college or a club?' His answer defined his experimental settlement as a fusion of both:

> It is a club in so far that the University men who make it their home live their own life, follow their own pursuits, and make their own friends; it is a college in so far that classes are held within its walls, and that students' residences flourish under its shadow. Whether the club will develop till through its members the influences gathered at the Universities affect the local government, the amusements, and the religion of East London; or whether the college will develop till all the buildings round Toynbee Hall be occupied by students under the direction of tutors and teachers, it is impossible to foretell.[167]

After two residential houses, named significantly after Oxford's Balliol and Wadham Colleges, were added for full-time students attending university extension classes, the settlement seemed well on the way to that final culmination. 'With St Jude's Church and the model tenement-houses included', commented Robert Woods, a visitor at the turn of the century, 'there is a community thus formed which is a fruitful and increasing source for the spread of intelligence, improved social life, and good citizenship, through Whitechapel and into the whole of East London'.[168]

But by this time a qualitative change in the settlement's character and activities was evident. If the middle years of the 1880s represented a time of high-minded experimentation, as the social idealism of Balliol and St Jude's fused together in its foundation, these streams drained away under a range of pressures. The convictions that sustained the settlement's moralising intervention in Whitechapel ebbed away (or, more positively, evolved) with experience and changing conditions, to be replaced by new concerns and commitments. The two decades before the turn of the century saw a high tide for the 'Toynbee ethos' and its notions of class reconciliation by personal residence among the poor, with the residents' redemptive presence supplying an almost mystical social leaven in 'Outcast London'. Thereafter, Toynbee Hall left these late-Victorian social idealist notions behind and instead sought to generate 'a new kind of elite, no longer to serve as disinterested mentors at the head of a local community but to assume instead positions of disinterested leadership within the expanding national bureaucracy'.[169] José Harris recognises that shortly after the turn of the century, 'an institution such as Toynbee Hall, with its emphasis on personal rather than collective action, began to look suspiciously irrelevant', as contemporary analysis moved towards impersonal and economic understanding of poverty. William Beveridge served as Barnett's sub-warden from 1903 to 1905 during these challenging times, striving to carve out a new purpose and direction for the settlement.[170] Thereafter, celebrated former Toynbee men made decisive contributions to social research, welfare policy and public administration: Beveridge to unemployment insurance, Cyril Jackson as Chief Inspector of the Board of Education, Clement Attlee and others.

But this influential latter-day history, shaping the evolving forms and practices of the modern welfare state in Britain, should not obscure the settlement's late-Victorian origins and initial character. Convictions about the power of gentlemanly empathy and the improving moral influence of this new breed of 'settler' resident drove Toynbee Hall's reforming programme from its foundation until the turn of the century. These impulses arose in the convictions of practical social workers like the Barnetts, expressing commonplace attitudes among practical social workers rather more than they did new directions in social theory or political philosophy. The neat correlation between these everyday ideals and the bold, new settlement proposal predicated on gentlemanly graduates working in 'Outcast London' along the lines suggested by university extension supplied the critical initial momentum to Toynbee Hall's cause.

Notes

1 H. Walker, *East London: Sketches of Christian Work and Workers* (London: The Religious Tract Society, 1896), p. 37. Wadham House and Balliol House were opened in 1887 and 1891 as residential quarters for students at the Toynbee Hall classes.

2 See R. A. Evans, 'The University and the City: The Educational Work of Toynbee Hall, 1884–1914' *History of Education* 11 (1982), pp. 113–125; A. Freeman, *Education Through Settlements* (London: George Allen and Unwin, 1920) and scholarly biographies such as J. Harris, *William Beveridge: A Biography* (Oxford: Clarendon Press, 1977) and L. Goldman, *The Life of R.H. Tawney: Socialism and History* (London: Bloomsbury, 2013).

3 An early overview is W. Picht, *Toynbee Hall and the English Settlement Movement* (London: G. Bell and Sons, 1914); a recent study is N. Scotland, *Squires in the Slums: Settlements and Missions in Late-Victorian London* (London: I. B. Tauris, 2007).

4 See J. A. R. Pimlott, *Toynbee Hall: Fifty Years of Social Progress 1884–1934* (London: J.M. Dent and Sons, 1935); A. Briggs and A. Macartney, *Toynbee Hall: The First One Hundred Years* (London: Routledge and Kegan Paul, 1984); S. Meacham, *Toynbee Hall and Social Reform 1880–1914: The Search for Community* (New Haven: Yale University Press, 1987). Unpublished dissertations

include S. Koven, 'Culture and Poverty: The London Settlement House Movement, 1870 to 1914' (Ph.D. thesis, Harvard University 1987); E. K. Abel, 'Canon Barnett and the First Thirty Years of Toynbee Hall' (Ph.D. thesis, University of London, 1969); L. Lagana, 'Toynbee Hall: Its Ideological Origins and Development' (Ph.D. thesis, City University of New York, 1980); J. R. Harrow, 'The Development of University Settlements in England, 1884–1939' (Ph.D. thesis, University of London, 1987), and L. Matthews-Jones, 'Centres of Brightness: The Spiritual Imagination of Toynbee Hall and Oxford House, 1880–1914' (Ph.D. thesis, University of Manchester, 2009).

5   H. Barnett, 'The Beginning of Toynbee Hall' in S. A. and H. O. Barnett, *Towards Social Reform* (London: T. Fisher Unwin, 1909), p. 246.

6   Cited in Picht, *Toynbee Hall and the English Settlement Movement*, p. 26.

7   H. Barnett, *Canon Barnett: His Life, Work, and Friends*, 2 vols (London: John Murray, 1918) is the unrivalled source, but see also Meacham, *Toynbee Hall and Social Reform*, pp. 24–8, and L. E. Nettleship, 'William Fremantle, Samuel Barnett and the Broad Church Origins of Toynbee Hall' *Journal of Ecclesiastical History* 33:4 (October 1982), pp. 564–79. Alison Creedon provides a thorough account of the Barnetts' marriage and joint career in *Only a Woman: Henrietta Barnett, Social Reformer and the Founder of Hampstead Garden Suburb* (Chichester: Phillimore, 2006).

8   Quoted in W. F. Aitken, *Canon Barnett, Warden of Toynbee Hall: His Mission and its Relation to Social Movements* (London: S.W. Partridge, 1902), p. 25.

9   A. S. W. Young, cited in Barnett, *Canon Barnett*, vol. 1, p. 29.

10 Nettleship, 'William Fremantle, Samuel Barnett and the Broad Church Origins of Toynbee Hall', p. 568.

11 A. S. W. Young, cited in Barnett, *Canon Barnett*, vol. 1, p. 27.

12 W. H. Fremantle, cited in Barnett, *Canon Barnett*, vol. 1, p. 22.

13 W. H. Draper (ed.), *Recollections of Dean Fremantle* (London: Cassell, 1921), pp. 82–3.

14 J. Lewis, *The Voluntary Sector, the State and Social Work in Britain* (Aldershot: Edward Elgar, 1995), p. 50.

15 LMA: Barnett Papers, F/BAR/460; copied by Henrietta Barnett from a letter to May Harris dated November 1870.

16 See Creedon, *Only a Woman* and K.B. Beauman, *Women and the Settlement Movement* (London: Radcliffe Press, 1996), pp. 4–16.

17 Barnett, *Canon Barnett*, vol. 1, p. 37.

18 H. Barnett, *Matters that Matter* (London: John Murray, 1930), p. vi. The Barnetts' remarkable partnership was acknowledged in an early study (Aitken, *Canon Barnett, Warden of Toynbee Hall*, p. 6), but was routinely overlooked until S. Koven, 'Henrietta Barnett 1851–1936: The (Auto)biography of a late Victorian Marriage' in S. Pedersen and P. Mandler (eds), *After the Victorians* (New York: Routledge, 1993), pp. 31–53.

19 S. Koven, 'Barnett, Dame Henrietta Octavia Weston (1851–1936)', *Oxford Dictionary of National Biography* (Oxford: Oxford University Press, 2004); online edition, September 2013 [www.oxforddnb.com/view/article/30610?docPos=2, accessed 14 Jan 2016]. Webb is cited in Meacham, *Toynbee Hall and Social Reform*, p. 36.

20 See Abel, 'Canon Barnett and the First Thirty Years of Toynbee Hall', pp. 34–46.

21 Aitken, *Canon Barnett*, pp. 161–2.

22 See Creedon, *Only a Woman* and Barnett, *Canon Barnett*, vol. 2, pp. 312–24.

23 Barnett, *Canon Barnett*, vol. 1, pp. 73–4.

24 T. Okey, *A Basketful of Memories* (London: J.M. Dent, 1930), p. 56.

25 G. Stedman Jones, *Outcast London: A Study in the Relationship between Classes in Victorian Society* (London: Penguin, 1992 [1971]), pp. 15–16.

26 LMA: Barnett Papers, F/BAR/504 Sermon Notebooks, 'East End Needs', n. p.

27 'East End Needs', n. p.

28 LMA: Barnett Papers, F/BAR/498 Sermon Notebooks, ff. 25–7; sermon delivered 17 September 1877 and repeated 29 September 1878 (f. 33).

29 'East End Needs', n. p.

30 S. A. Barnett, *Settlements of University Men in Great Towns* (Oxford, 1884); repr. in Pimlott, *Toynbee Hall*, p. 271.

31 LMA: Barnett Papers, F/BAR/498 Sermon Notebooks, f. 25.

32 'East End Needs', n. p.

33 'East End Needs', n. p.

34 BLPES: Booth Collection, B/227 f. 241, interview with Samuel Barnett, 16 March 1898.

35 LMA: Barnett Papers, F/BAR/466, printed letter of 7 March 1873.

36 Barnett, *Canon Barnett*, vol. 1, p. 326.

37 DRO: Gell Papers, D3287/B2, letter to P. L. Gell from S. A. Barnett, 2 August 1885.

38 Meacham, *Toynbee Hall and Social Reform*, p. 29.

39 See J. Cox, *The English Churches in a Secular Society: Lambeth, 1870–1930* (Oxford: Oxford University Press, 1982), esp. chapter 4.

40 LMA: Barnett Papers, F/BAR/466, printed letter of 7 March 1873.

41 Barnett, *Canon Barnett*, vol. 1, p. 82.

42 Barnett, *Canon Barnett*, vol. 1, pp. 78, 218.

43 Aitken, *Canon Barnett*, p. 76. Lucinda Matthews-Jones considers this theme of spiritual renewal and urban 'sanctification' in her 2009 thesis 'Centres of Brightness', and explores the renovation of St Jude's, Whitechapel in 'Sanctifying the Street: Urban Space, Material Christianity, and the G. F. Watts Mosaic in London, 1883 to the Present Day', in T. W. Jones and L. Matthews-Jones (eds), *Material Religion in Modern Britain: The Spirit of Things* (Basingstoke: Palgrave Macmillan, 2015), pp. 62–3.

44 LMA: Barnett Papers, F/BAR/497, sermon at St Jude's on Sunday 1 October 1876.

45 Cited in Aitken, *Canon Barnett*, p. 138.

46 'The Church', *St Jude's*, 1:3 (March 1889), p. 25.

47 S. A. Barnett, *Fifteenth Pastoral Address and Report of Parish Work* (London, 1888), p. 9.

48 She suggested to Henrietta, for example, in early 1879 that they go together to the National Gallery to choose an appropriate picture to be copied for St Jude's. BLPES: Coll. Misc. 512, f. 26, letter of Octavia Hill to Henrietta Barnett of 26 January 1879.

49 BLPES: Coll. Misc. 512, f. 122.

50 BLPES: Booth Collection, B/387, f. 11, notes by Charles Booth of 6 February 1898.

51 H. Jones, 'Life and work among the East London Poor' *Good Words* 25 (1884), p. 108.

52 H. Barnett, 'How to Develop Individual Character in the Children Collected Together in Large Pauper Schools' in *Practicable Socialism: Essays on Social Reform* (London: Longmans Green and Co., 1895), p. 118 (pamphlet orig. publ. 1886).

53 LMA: F/BAR/509, undated St Jude's sermon.

54 LMA: F/BAR/514, Wednesday Evensong sermon, St Jude's, 7 March 1877.

55 LMA: F/BAR/515, sermon of January 1878, entitled 'Music the Echo of the Unseen World.'

56 BL: Cockerell Papers, Add. Mss. 52627, f. 63, diary entry of 23 November 1890. *The Story of a Short Life* (1885) by the children's writer Juliana Horatia Ewing was a celebrated homily on the moral fortitude of disabled children.
57 LMA: F/BAR/496, sermon for Wednesday Evensong, 16 February 1876, ff. 31–3.
58 LMA: F/BAR/503, sermon entitled 'Law of Growth' delivered at St Botolph-without-Bishopsgate 10 October 1880 and at St Jude's 16 October 1881.
59 St Jude's Whitechapel [S.A. Barnett], *Nineteenth Pastoral Address, Report of the Parish Work, and Accounts for the Year 1891–1892* (London 1892), p. 9.
60 *Nineteenth Pastoral Address*, p. 9. The last phrase is from Wordsworth's *The Recluse*, l. 771.
61 BLPES: Booth Collection, B/227, ff. 241–2.
62 Surviving fragments of which are in the Barnett Papers, Lambeth Palace Library: MS 1466 ff. 34–41. See Koven, 'Culture and Poverty', pp. 49–54.
63 LPL: Barnett Papers, MS 1466, 'A Modern Monastery', f. 35.
64 'A Modern Monastery', f. 35.
65 'A Modern Monastery', f. 39.
66 'A Modern Monastery', f. 40.
67 'A Modern Monastery', f. 40.
68 'A Modern Monastery', f. 40.
69 *Thomas Hancock Nunn: The Life and Work of a Social Reformer* (London: Baines and Scarsbrook, 1942), p. 36; reprint of an article 'One and All' dated August 1913.
70 This was later published in different versions, including as 'University Colonies in Great Towns' in the *Oxford Chronicle* (and reprinted as a pamphlet by the Chronicle Company, Oxford, 1884), followed by 'The Universities and the Poor' in *Nineteenth Century* 15 (February 1884), pp. 255–61 and later reprinted as 'University Settlements' in *Practicable Socialism*, pp. 165–74.
71 Aitken, *Canon Barnett*, p. 118.
72 *Stepney Welfare* (July 1913); cited in Barnett, *Canon Barnett*, vol. 1, p. 310.
73 Barnett, 'The Universities and the Poor', p. 257.
74 Barnett, 'The Universities and the Poor', pp. 257–8.
75 Universities' Settlement in East London, 'Memorandum and Articles of Association' (Oxford, 1886), p. 3.
76 Briggs and Macartney, *Toynbee Hall: The First One Hundred Years*, p. 8.
77 Barnett, *Canon Barnett*, vol. 1, p. 311.
78 LMA: F/BAR/2, letter of 1 March 1884.
79 LMA: F/BAR/2, letter of 1 March 1884. The fabric of the new settlement is discussed below in chapter 7.
80 In late May 1884, Barnett wrote to Gell, who was approving expenditure for the construction on behalf of the Universities' Settlement Association: 'I greatly fear we may not be ready by September. It will be a blow to us if we have no rooms, and they will take some time to dry and [be] fit for habitation. Urge Hoole by all your powers.' DRO: Gell Papers D3287/B2, letter of 26 May 1884.
81 'L.E.S.', 'Toynbee Hall' *Charity Organisation Reporter* 13 (October 1884), p. 333.
82 LMA: F/BAR/20, letter to F. G. Barnett of 26 November 1884.
83 BLPES: Booth Collection, B/227, f. 201. These notes were made after an interview with Ernest Aves at Toynbee Hall in mid-1898.
84 W. Picht, *Toynbee Hall and the English Settlement Movement*, p. 27. This argument is revived in S. Eagles, *After Ruskin: The Social and Political Legacies of a Victorian Prophet, 1870–1920* (Oxford: Oxford University Press, 2011), pp. 114–33.
85 Pimlott, *Toynbee Hall*, p. 43.
86 P. Gordon and J. White, *Philosophers as Educational Reformers: The Influence of Idealism on British Educational Thought and Practice* (London: Routledge and Kegan Paul, 1979), p. 104.

87 H. W. Nevinson, *Changes and Chances* (London: Nesbit and Co., 1923), pp. 39–40.
88 M. Richter, *The Politics of Conscience: T. H. Green and his Age* (London: Weidenfield and Nicholson, 1964), p. 15.
89 T. Gouldstone, *The Rise and Decline of Anglican Idealism in the Nineteenth Century* (Basingstoke: Palgrave Macmillan, 2005), p. 49.
90 A. Kadish, *Apostle Arnold: The Life and Death of Arnold Toynbee, 1852–1883* (Durham: Duke University Press, 1986), pp. 40–1.
91 The world historian Arnold Toynbee (b. 1889) was the son of Toynbee's brother, named in his late uncle's memory. F. Millar, 'Toynbee, Arnold Joseph (1889–1975)', *Oxford Dictionary of National Biography*, (Oxford: Oxford University Press, 2004); online edition, January 2008 [http://www.oxforddnb.com/view/article/31769, accessed 20 June 2016].
92 Barnett, 'The Beginning of Toynbee Hall', p. 245.
93 DRO: Gell Papers D3287/B2, letter of 14 March 1883.
94 See Kadish, *Apostle Arnold*, pp. 223–31 for Toynbee's various official memorials.
95 This view is most fully developed in Meacham, *Toynbee Hall and Social Reform*, but see also Gordon and White, *Philosophers as Educational Reformers*, pp. 103–7, and Evans, 'The University and the City', pp. 114–15.
96 Aitken, *Canon Barnett*, and Barnett, *Canon Barnett*.
97 Nettleship, 'William Fremantle, Samuel Barnett and the Broad Church Origins of Toynbee Hall', pp. 564–5. For Anglican Idealism in this context, see Gouldstone, *The Rise and Decline of Anglican Idealism*; for Maurician theology see E. Norman, *The Victorian Christian Socialists* (Cambridge: Cambridge University Press, 1987), chapter 2, and C. Walsh, 'The Incarnation and the Christian Socialist Conscience in the Victorian Church of England' *Journal of British Studies* 34 (1995), pp. 351–74.
98 Nettleship, 'William Fremantle, Samuel Barnett and the Broad Church Origins of Toynbee Hall', pp. 572–4.
99 D. B. McIlhiney, 'A Gentleman in Every Slum: Church of England Missions in East London, 1837–1914' (Ph.D. thesis, Princeton University, 1976), p. 288.
100 M. Carter, *T. H. Green and the Development of Ethical Socialism* (Exeter: Imprint Academic, 2003), p. 106. See also Gouldstone, *The Rise and Decline of Anglican Idealism*, and A. P. F. Sell, *Philosophical Idealism and Christian Belief* (New York: St Martin's Press, 1995).
101 Universities' Settlement Association, *The Universities' Settlement in East London* (Oxford, 1884), p. 3.
102 Meacham, *Toynbee Hall and Social Reform*, p. 44.
103 'Settlements of University Men in Great Towns', p. 272 (original emphasis).
104 'Settlements of University Men in Great Towns', p. 269.
105 'Settlements of University Men in Great Towns', p. 269.
106 Cited in Barnett, *Canon Barnett*, vol. 1, p. 332.
107 Rogers, *Labour, Life and Literature*, p. 80.
108 Barnett, *Canon Barnett* vol. 1, p. 332–3.
109 *St Jude's*, 1:1 (January 1889), p. 6.
110 DRO: Gell Papers, D3287/B2, letter to P. L. Gell of 22 May 1884. Barnett continued to emphasise the theme three months later, writing to Gell on 9 August: 'Money matters seem still to hang, and I hope you did manage to put some ginger upon Cambridge. We want both men and money thence. Either would bring the other.'
111 Universities' Settlement Association, *Work for University Men in Great Towns* (pamphlet) (Cambridge, 1884), p. 24.
112 Eagles, *After Ruskin*, chapter 2.
113 'Extension of University Teaching' *The Times* 26 April 1883, p. 8.
114 Barnett, 'The Universities and the Poor', p. 261.

115   LMA: A/TOY/5, 'Universities' Settlement in East London: Toynbee Hall', printed circular.
116   LMA: A/TOY/5, printed letter of Samuel Barnett, May 1884.
117   *Agin the Governments: Memories and Adventures* (London: Sampson, Low, Marston and Co., 1929), p. 58.
118   LMA: A/TOY/5, S. Barnett, 'Universities Settlements in East London' printed open letter, n. d.
119   Cited in Aitken, *Canon Barnett*, pp. 124–5.
120   Toynbee Hall, *Ninth Annual Report* (London, 1893), p. 13.
121   S. Barnett, 'Twenty-one Years of Settlements', *University Review* (June 1905), cited in Barnett, *Canon Barnett*, vol. 1, p. 312.
122   *Work for University Men in East London* (pamphlet) (Cambridge, 1884) p. 14; proceedings of a meeting held at Cambridge Guildhall, 24 May 1884.
123   Bod. L: Nevinson Papers, MSS. Eng. Misc. e.610/1, f. 16, journal (1893) entry of 11 February.
124   LMA: Toynbee Papers, A/TOY/22/3/6, 'What Toynbee Hall Does for East London'. This ms. note, attributed in a pencil annotation to C. M. Lloyd, appears to be personal correspondence or a draft letter to the press.
125   H. W. Nevinson, *Changes and Chances* (London: Nesbit and Co., 1923), p. 81.
126   S. A. Barnett, 'A Retrospect of Toynbee Hall' in S. A. and H. O. Barnett, *Towards Social Reform*, pp. 259–60 (orig. publ. 1895).
127   L. Matthews-Jones, 'St Francis of Assisi and the Making of Settlement Masculinity, 1883–1914' in J. H. Arnold and S. Brady (eds), *What is Masculinity? Historical Dynamics from Antiquity to the Contemporary World* (London: Palgrave Macmillan, 2011), p. 298.
128   S. Koven, *Slumming: Sexual and Social Politics in Victorian London* (Princeton: Princeton University Press, 2004), p. 263.
129   R. C. Windscheffel, [review of *Slumming*] *English Historical Review* 122:495 (2007), p. 274.
130   Barnett, *Canon Barnett*, vol. 2, p. 51.
131   'The Denison Club' *Charity Organisation Review* 3 (November 1887), pp. 408–9.
132   Barnett, *Canon Barnett*, vol. 1, p. 318.
133   KCAC: Ashbee Papers, CRA/A/1/2, f. 216.
134   B. Webb, *My Apprenticeship* (Harmondsworth: Penguin Books, 1938), vol. 1, p. 239.
135   *The Times*, 22 January 1887, p. 7..
136   DRO: Gell Papers, D3287/B2, letter from Henrietta Barnett of 22 January 1887. She concluded: 'I shall however abide by your decision, and shall speak to no-one – not even SAB – on my thoughts or my letter'.
137   The basis for Gell's refusal is not known; his response was not retained in the Barnetts' personal papers.
138   DRO: Gell Papers, D3287/B2, letter from Henrietta Barnett of 9 February 1887.
139   LMA: F/BAR/2, letter of 1 March 1884.
140   See Koven, 'Culture and Poverty', esp. pp. 75–96, and L. Matthews-Jones, 'Centres of Brightness' for assessments of the relationship between the two settlements.
141   H. H. Henson, 'University Settlements in the East End' in H. Jones (ed.), *Some Urgent Questions in Christian Lights* (London: Rivington's, 1889), p. 257.
142   H. H. Henson, *Retrospect of an Unimportant Life* (London: Oxford University Press, 1942), p. 29.
143   Barnett, *Canon Barnett*, vol. 2, p. 29.
144   LPL: Barnett Papers MS1466, f. 54, address by Samuel Barnett at Toynbee Hall, 2 July 1889.
145   *The Spectator* 17 January 1885, p. 79.
146   'A Commentary in an Easy-Chair' *The Spectator* 16 August 1890, p. 210.

147 Letter printed in 'Notes and Notices' *Eastward Ho!* 3 (May 1885), p. 94.
148 S. Barnett, 'Introduction by the Warden', in Toynbee Hall, *Ninth Annual Report* (London: 1893), pp. 15–16.
149 Nevinson, *Changes and Chances*, pp. 78–9.
150 M. W. Nevinson, *Life's Fitful Fever: A Volume of Memories* (London: A. and C. Black, 1926), p. 79.
151 KCAC: Ashbee Papers, CRA/A/1/2, f. 210.
152 S. Koven, 'From Rough Lads to Hooligans: Boy Life, National Culture and Social Reform' in A. Parker, M. Russo, D. Sommer and P. Yaeger (eds), *Nationalisms and Sexualities* (New York: Routledge, 1992), p. 370.
153 Toynbee Hall, *Third Annual Report* (Oxford, 1887), p. 15 lists Ruskin's *Time and Tide* and *Fors Clavigera* as the set texts for Ashbee's class. This reading circle was one of several in the category of 'Language, Literature and Morals', and operated independently of the class for technical instruction in carpentry, wood-carving and modelling.
154 Including the decoration of the Toynbee Hall dining room 'which has comprised the painting of a design in free-hand on the wall, modelling in carton pierre and gilding, and the making of a frieze of shields that have been worked in the clay, cast in plaster and then painted and gilded'. THLHL: C. R. Ashbee, 'Proposal for the Establishment of a Technical and Art School for East London' (printed memorandum, n. d.).
155 [C. R. Ashbee], *The School and Guild of Handicraft at Toynbee Hall* (London, 1889) and C. R. Ashbee, *School and Guild of Handicraft: Statement of its Nature and Purpose* (London, 1888).
156 *First Annual Report of the School of Handicraft* (London, 1889), p. 1.
157 Nevinson, *Changes and Chances*, p. 91.
158 For a statement of the Guild and School's Ruskinian programme, see C. R. Ashbee, *An Endeavour Towards the Teaching of John Ruskin and William Morris* (London: Edward Arnold, 1901), pp. 1–10.
159 C. R. Ashbee, *A Short History of the Guild & School of Handicraft* (London, 1890), p. 9.
160 A. Laurie, *Pictures and Politics: A Book of Reminiscences* (London: International Publishing Company, 1934), pp. 73–4.
161 DRO: Gell Papers, D3287/B2, letter from S. A. Barnett of 1 April 1889.
162 VAM: Ashbee Memoirs (typescript), vol. 1, f. 8.
163 VAM: Ashbee Memoirs (typescript), vol. 1, f. 51, entry of 30 December 1888.
164 C. R. Ashbee, *The Building of Thelema* (London: J. M. Dent and Sons, 1910), p. 175.
165 S. Hobhouse, *Forty Years and An Epilogue: An Autobiography (1881–1951)* (London: James Clarke and Co., 1951), p. 133.
166 Toynbee Hall, *Second Annual Report* (London, 1886), p. 7.
167 S. Barnett, 'Introductory Note', in Toynbee Hall, *Fifth Annual Report* (London, 1889), p. 4.
168 R. A. Woods, *English Social Movements* (London: Swan Sonnenschein and Co., 1892), p. 96.
169 Meacham, *Toynbee Hall and Social Reform*, xi.
170 Harris, *William Beveridge*, pp. 47–8.

5   An impossible story in Mile End

In the years Toynbee Hall was founded, another East End philanthropic experiment took shape further out on the Mile End Road. The Beaumont Trust's extravagant plan to build a 'Palace of Delight' was London's most flamboyant charitable venture of the 1880s, and although its style contrasted in many ways with the Whitechapel settlement the two drew on common impulses. Announcing their scheme in June 1885, the Beaumont Trustees expressed their desire 'to place before the city of wealth and culture, the city of light and luxury, a scheme…whence, as from a centre, the influences that make for a higher life may be diffused through the neighbouring city of toil and poverty'.[1] Imagined as a majestic edifice for art, music, books, leisure, learning and recreation, humming with fellowship and cultural opportunity through clubs, classes, concerts and exhibitions, the People's Palace drew on the same currents of late-Victorian cultural philanthropy, the same underlying liberal humanism and moralising social idealism, that we have seen animating Barnett's scheme. Its public persona, however, was markedly different: from its literary conception in the pages of a best-selling novel to the royal fanfare of its lavish opening celebrations, the People's Palace was a *tour de force* of charitable effort, manifested in a remarkable public subscription of 1884–7 that raised over £100,000 in donations large and small to realise the Trustees' scheme.

Maintaining the novel institution, however, proved a more difficult task. By 1890 the Beaumont Trust's shambolic finances were close to collapse, and an audit confirmed that debts at the Palace exceeded assets by over £36,000. This was 'partly due to the undertaking of more than the Palace could afford, partly also to the system of ordering goods for the institution and paying and checking accounts being very defective'.[2] Ironically, given the Palace's mission to benefit East London, the chief victims of this mismanagement were some 500 local tradesmen, each owed between £2 and £10 in unpaid bills. Far from a benefaction, to many in Mile End the People's Palace must now have seemed a pompous folly. Thereafter, and largely as a result of these financial problems, its administration gradually passed to its major sponsor, the Worshipful Company of Drapers, one of the grand livery companies of the City of London. As the emphasis shifted from moralising culture to technical education, the prosaic title East London Technical College was favoured for the educational component as the main hall became a commercial entertainment venue.

Despite this compelling late-Victorian narrative of 'boom and bust' philanthropy, few historians have paid sustained attention to the People's Palace, the circumstances of its foundation and larger significance.[3] It is typically presented as something unique and fantastic, the improbable flowering of a novelist's fanciful vision in the unpromising soil of Mile End; confused, unrealistic and doomed to fail. In Simon Joyce's view, for example, 'its history offers an instructive case study of what happens when imaginative projects are actualised in a real-world economy, and when social reform is undertaken on the basis of a literary blueprint'.[4] This chapter disputes this verdict by clarifying the Palace scheme's character and purposes, which despite eccentricities belonged squarely in the mainstream of late-Victorian progressive social liberalism. It shared enough with other centres of philanthropy and education to appear to contemporaries as a bold but intrinsically coherent proposal, one that rapidly gained credibility and momentum.

* * *

The imposing new People's Palace of 1887 rose on much older foundations. Opened in November 1840 by J. T. Barber Beaumont, a Unitarian financier and philanthropist with lucrative interests in insurance, the Beaumont Philosophical Institution aimed to provide education and recreation to the working men of the streets around Beaumont Square, Mile End. Its hall seated around 1,500 people for lectures and performances; downstairs on a lower level were class-rooms, a library and a museum for scientific displays. After its founder's death in 1841 the Institution was sustained by £13,000 conferred by his will 'for the purposes of affording [the residents of the area] intellectual improvement and rational recreation and amusement, by means of libraries, access to reading the newspapers, and journals, lectures and other means for the diffusion of useful and entertaining knowledge'.[5] An annual guinea subscription was paid by around 250–300 working men, clerks and artisans by 1851. 'The founder required the delivery of *moral* lectures every *Sunday* morning', explained one account of London's institutes at this time, 'but his son and executor has altered the time of delivery of these lectures to week-day evenings....There are a few members attending the French, drawing and discussion classes, and the large funds at the disposal of the society are expended in giving expensive concerts'.[6] A later account described the old Beaumont Philosophical Institution as a place 'where men might meet in order to facilitate the knowledge of scientific truths, and for encouraging the disposition to cheerful social recreation, as well as to afford some of the usual advantages of a Literary Society...'[7] The Institution had a distinct ethical dimension; a Unitarian magazine later felt that with more rigorous doctrinal teaching 'there might possibly have survived, amid the failure of the rest of the scheme, a well-established Unitarian congregation'.[8]

By 1879 the Institution was moribund, gaining notoriety as a cheap entertainment venue, its class rooms unused and the library closed up, its Board of Trustees defunct and inactive. The building closed and its lease was surrendered. As local efforts arose to put the original endowment to better effect, two separate applications were made to the Charity Commission for use of the Beaumont funds in 1879–81. One was from the Tower Hamlets university extension committee chaired by Samuel Barnett to finance their local lectures, re-open the Philosophical Institution in Beaumont Square, and so expand their provision of higher education in the East End. The other was from an East London businessman and philanthropist Sir Edmund Hay Currie (see Figure 5.1), who together with the Rector of Stepney, Rev. George Coker, proposed the endowment of a new institution with the fund, a measure that would require the reconstitution of the original charitable scheme and the appointment of new Trustees. After some deliberation and despite the legal complexities involved the Commission favoured the latter application.[9]

Sir Edmund Hay Currie (1834–1913) came from an affluent Tunbridge Wells family, with a career in the family company, the Bromley malt distillers John Currie and Co., a share of which he inherited from his father and which later merged into Tanqueray Gordon and Co. Currie's philanthropic work saw him chairman of the London Hospital, an active supporter of the Metropolitan Hospital Sunday Fund for some forty years, and vice-chairman of the London School Board in 1873–6 after being elected the Tower Hamlets representative in 1870 (he continued to serve in 1882–5 and 1888–90). He was instrumental in the adult education work of the Bow and Bromley Institute from the early 1870s, and stood unsuccessfully as a Liberal candidate for Tower Hamlets in 1874, his only foray into representative politics. At the London School Board, an epicentre of educational reforming effort, Currie was active on the Works Committee, and oversaw the construction of new schools and the appointment of E. R. Robson as the Board's chief architect. By the end of that decade he was an experienced fund-raiser and philanthropist, by his own admission 'a very successful beggar' who had raised over £120,000 to support the hospital.[10] Married to the daughter of a clergyman, and knighted for his philanthropic endeavours in 1876, Currie's biography represents the conventional progress of a prosperous mid-Victorian businessman into the upper echelons of London philanthropy. A diligent, worthy but essentially unremarkable man, we get little sense of his personality or character in the extant sources.[11]

By 1881 he was increasingly active in advocating a new scheme of management for the moribund Beaumont Trust, adding his name to a second memorial to the Charity Commission urging its renewal through a new Board of Trustees. At this time, Chapman concludes, 'the Memorialists [including Currie] desired that a large measure of discretion to act be left to the trustees in deciding the future plans for the trust',[12] and although their basic

Figure 5.1 Sir Edmund Hay Currie, 1887

intentions were clear – to put the existing fund of £12,000 to some educational use involving recreation and improving cultural opportunities in a new building for the revived Beaumont Institution – they had not resolved on a concrete proposal. The re-drafting of the Beaumont Trust's charter was finalised by March 1882, and the new trustees under Currie's leadership began to sketch out the new scheme. Despite being rebuffed on his university extension plans for the old Institution, Samuel Barnett agreed to serve as a trustee, remaining adamant that 'such a college or collegiate institution as is contemplated is greatly needed in this district'.[13] A Mansion House meeting followed on 21 June, chaired by the Lord Mayor, when Currie's vision for the renewal of Beaumont's legacy was first aired. Maintaining the endowment's original intention to promote 'the intellectual improvement and rational recreation and amusement' of local inhabitants, the trustees imagined a new institution would 'not only provide for the East-end the educational advantages conferred by the City of London colleges or by the evening classes at King's College, but also would furnish a good library and reading room, together with other means of recreation and opportunity for social intercourse'.[14] There was little else in the way of concrete detail at this stage. As Currie explained in equally vaporous language at a Charity Commission meeting shortly afterwards, there was 'about half a million of poor population in the East End without any place of resort for those who wish to read books or papers, or to meet for "rational recreation and amusement"'.[15] He asked for £5,000 to be released from the original endowment to purchase a new site as fundraising for the renewal of the Philosophical Institution got underway.

* * *

All this work of 1882 coincided with the tremendous popular success of a serialised novel of East End philanthropy. Walter Besant's *All Sorts and Conditions of Men: An Impossible Story* centred on a fictional 'Palace of Delight' for the East End poor, built by two philanthropists to supply the district with every form of refining cultural opportunity: fine art, music, books, classes, clubs and social occasions. Its spirit tallied closely with the Beaumont Trust's nebulous scheme, prompting the Trustees to co-opt the remarkable publicity power of Besant's novelistic vision to their own proposals. Besant's papers were destroyed at his death, Currie's are not extant; and as the Beaumont Trust archive is incomplete in this respect we have little documentary evidence to illuminate the development of their relationship. Harry Jones, the East End clergyman and member of the expanded Board of Trustees, remembered his 'strenuous insistence' that the Trust embraced Besant's fictional blueprint: 'I was full of *All Sorts and Conditions of Men*', Jones recalled, '[and] I proposed Mr Walter Besant as a trustee'.[16] This seems to have happened in late 1882 or early 1883, and thereafter the Trust drew freely upon the features of the 'Palace of Delight' as depicted in Besant's novel for their own revived and re-imagined institution. They unveiled their full scheme in May 1885, calling for subscriptions to complement the original fund and so erect a vast centre of popular recreation and education, expensively outfitted and providing a plethora of entertainments, activities and educational opportunities for the East London poor.

Its Besantian title, the 'People's Palace for East London' was a publicity masterstroke, capturing as it did a sense of heady romance rarely seen in the prosaic world of charity and adult education. As he observed omnibuses marked 'People's Palace' travelling along the Holborn Viaduct, one writer considered it 'an age of miracle when the title of a chapter from a popular novel is transferred to a placard on a 'bus'.[17] The success of the scheme seemed a parable for the times for the late-century chronicler T. H. S. Escott:

A popular novelist gave a fancy sketch of a palace in which art, pleasure, and instruction should meet together to gladden the lives of the London poor. Almost as soon as could have been done by the genius of Aladdin's Lamp, the People's Palace shoots up in the Mile End Road.[18]

Thus, in the contemporary view, the Trust scheme was a direct realisation in actuality of Besant's fanciful 'Palace of Delight'. The novelist later claimed *All Sorts and Conditions of Men* was the 'text-book' for the whole scheme,[19] and in 1912 the *Dictionary of National Biography* described the Beaumont scheme as 'Besant's People's Palace', recording how subscriptions were 'collected under the direction of Sir Edmund Hay Currie, with Besant's active co-operation, for the foundation of an institution on the lines which Besant had laid down'.[20] To many, this celebrated instance of a 'social problem' novel generating practical results belied the charge that writers could do little more than describe social evils and prick the public conscience. As final preparations were made for the opening of the Palace in Mile End, *The Spectator* was pleased that East London owed its grand new facility to the 'wild fancy' of the novelist, a 'lasting monument to the wise and impartial exponent [i.e. Besant] of the working people to many hearers who would never learn any-thing about them in any other way...'[21]

Born in 1836, the bookish son of a Portsmouth wine merchant, Besant (see Figure 5.2) spent an unhappy year at King's College, London in 1854–5 before finding solace at Christ's College, Cambridge where he graduated B.A. in 1859.[22] Among his associates was the liberal historian John Seeley, who introduced him to the work of Coleridge, Carlyle and Maurice. After strug-gling to find work in journalism and a sojourn teaching at the Royal College, Mauritius, in 1867 Besant returned to London and a literary career sustained by his position as secretary to the Palestine Exploration Fund. His partner-ship with *Once a Week* editor James Rice after 1872 generated nearly a dozen novels – moralising adventure tales and historical romances for the most part, although one curious novel of 1878, *The Monks of Thelema*, developed a satire on Oxford social liberalism that signalled an interest in larger reforming themes – until Rice's death from cancer in 1882. An unusual partnership, it seems Besant 'did most of the actual writing, while Rice was chiefly respon-sible for plot construction and handling all business arrangements with pub-lishers'.[23] Thereafter, writing alone and with the benefit of an established reputation, Besant turned to novels on social themes and antiquarian studies.

His social novel *All Sorts and Conditions of Men,* serialised in *Belgravia* and published as a 'three-decker' in October 1882, placed Besant 'in the front rank of the most popular writers of the day'.[24] A philanthropic romance, depicting an East End 'Palace of Delight' of culture, art and general gaiety to ameliorate an urban landscape of dull mediocrity, the novel was a spectacular commercial success, selling 250,000 copies by 1914 and inspiring a feature film as late as 1921. Emboldened by his new status as a social reformer, Besant joined Charles Leland in 1884 in forming the Home Arts and

Figure 5.2 Walter Besant, 1888

Industries Association sponsoring evening schools for handicrafts, woodwork, weaving and embroidery, lending his name to causes as diverse as the Ragged School movement, female education and employment, free public libraries and the Salvation Army's farm colonies. A founding member of the Society of Authors, he was highly active in promoting literary copyright, organising the Society's first management committee and editing its periodical *The Author* after 1890. Described by an interviewer as 'short, sturdy, pleasant-faced and pleasant-voiced...full of sympathy and common sense, with a brisk, bright, business-like manner, which puts one at ease immediately',[25] Besant was naturally liberal in temperament, 'a highly clubbable man, an energetic organizer, and an instinctive reformer'.[26] His professional status saw him comment on public issues with a tone of robust common-sense that echoed the authorial voice of his fiction.

This phlegmatic public persona contrasted with the more rarefied intellectual sensibilities of Besant's literary contemporaries. As the populist foil for

Henry James' stance in the so-called 'Art of Fiction' exchange of 1884, for example, Besant advocated plain, 'truthful' storytelling that was typical of his 'tone of honest, uncomplicated common-sense', even if James' rejoinder exposed the ambiguities and inconsistencies of his position.[27] Accordingly, George Gissing's comment that Besant was 'first and foremost a man of business...Culture, in my sense of the word, he does not possess' typifies the verdict both of Besant's literary peers and modern scholarship.[28] After an 1893 dinner at the Authors' Club Gissing went further, dismissing Besant in a diary note as 'commonplace to the last degree; a respectable draper'.[29] Nevertheless Besant was knighted in 1895, some six years before his death, as much to recognise his acclaimed public conscience and civic spirit as for any literary merit. The essential mediocrity of his style, the formulaic superficiality of his portraits and plots recognised by later critics,[30] were overlooked or forgiven by contemporaries. As *The Spectator* gushed at the height of his fame and influence,

> Mr. Besant does not belong to any school or class of novelists; he is unique. If there be persons who do not care about his works...[they] will be found among the empty-headed, the cold-hearted, and the vulgar-minded, with all those to whom his purity would be mawkish, and his 'deep-veined humanity' unintelligible.[31]

But as 'purity' and 'deep-veined humanity' came in the crisis-ridden, critical twentieth century to seem little more than Victorian moralism and sentimentality, Besant's reputation evaporated, 'one of the most precipitous [declines] in the history of British fiction', in the years after his death in 1901.[32]

Yet novels like Besant's, as one critic argues, 'should be interesting to us precisely *because* they are less "literary" – less sophisticated about their strategic displacements, silences and suppressions, more open about their propaganda content, not so conversant with the art of abstraction'.[33] We see this in Besant's fictional depiction of East London, which he claimed owed little to his own imagination. When asked by a popular magazine about the material for his East End novels, he professed to have little to say: 'I simply walked about the East-end, and wrote down almost exactly what I saw and heard'.[34] He remembered that his second East London novel, *Children of Gibeon*, was 'as truthful as a long and patient investigation could make it. I knew every street in Hoxton; I knew also every street in Ratcliffe; I had been about among the people day after day and week after week – neglecting almost everything else'.[35] For all its direct reportage, however, Besant's depiction of East London was a carefully crafted urban toponymy loaded with authorial interpretation. All the conventional civic features of city life were absent from his purgatorial East London, despite the two million men, women and children living there. 'They have no institutions of their own to speak of', he told his readers in *All Sorts and Conditions of Men*, 'no public buildings of any importance, no municipality, no gentry, no carriages, no soldiers, no picture-galleries, no theatres, no opera – they have nothing'. The novel offered a landscape uniquely abandoned and neglected, paradoxically spectacular in its absolute want of interest. 'Probably there is no such spectacle in the whole world as that of this immense, neglected, forgotten great city of East London', Besant continued. East Londoners were denied a sense of history, pageantry and civic heritage in this landscape of pitiless obscurity:

> They are Londoners, it is true, but they have no part or share of London; its wealth, its splendours, its honours exist not for them....They are beyond the wards, and cannot become aldermen; the rich London merchants go north and south and west; but they go not east. Nobody goes east, no one wants to see the place; no one is curious about the way of life in the east. Books on London pass it over; it has little or no history; great men are not buried in its churchyards, which are not even ancient, and crowded by citizens as obscure as those who now breathe the upper airs about them. If anything happens in the east, people at the other end have to stop and think before they can remember where the place may be.[36]

In Besant's account this obscurity infused and vitiated even the physical streetscape of East London. The streets of his 'Joyless City' were 'mean and without individuality or beauty; at no season and under no conditions can they ever be picturesque; one can tell, without inquiring, that the lives led in those houses are all after the same model, and that the inhabitants have no pleasures'.[37] The old spectre of public lawlessness had been largely banished: Whitechapel Road had previously been notorious, for example, but now Besant felt 'the road is not worthy of this reputation: it has of late years become orderly; its present condition is dull and law-abiding'.[38] His East London was a repetitive vista of urban monotony, a visual repetition of two-storied terraces to the horizon, and 'all furnished alike; in each ground floorfront there are the red curtains and the white blind of respectability, with the little table bearing something...to mark the gentility of the family'. The conclusions to be drawn about the moral, civic and social life of this population echoed Samuel Barnett's verdict on the more impoverished quarters around Whitechapel. It was the 'means of life', and not the 'means of livelihood', that were absent.

> Now, the really sad thing about this district is that the residents are not the starving class, or the vicious class, or the drinking class; they are a well-to-do and thriving people, yet they desire no happiness, they do not feel the lack of joy, they live in meanness and are contented therewith. So that it is emphatically a representative quarter, and a type of the East End generally, which is for the most part respectable and wholly dull, and perfectly contented never to know what pleasant strolling and resting-places, what delightful interests, what varied occupations, what sweet diversions there are *in life*.[39]

Pointedly subtitled 'An Impossible Story' as if to pique a philanthropic response, Besant's novel followed Angela Messenger,[40] a Cambridge-educated 'New Woman' and heiress to a brewing fortune, who lives *incognito* as a humble dressmaker in the dismal neighbourhoods of East London to learn of its inhabitants and better understand their social circumstances. She meets Harry Goslett, an adopted scion of the aristocracy seeking his proletarian roots as a cabinetmaker. The two come together as partners in social reform (and, inevitably, in marriage at the novel's close) to bestow a vast 'Palace of Delight' upon the disadvantaged East End population as Harry's ideas combined with Angela's riches. A place of leisure and recreation to convert 'this dismal suburb into a home for refined and cultivated people', their Palace offered the 'accomplishments and graces' of dancing, singing, music, 'skating, bicycling, lawn tennis, racquets, fives, and all kinds of games; rowing, billiards, archery, rifle shooting'; acting, recitation, gardening, cookery and 'the laws of beauty in costume'. Importantly, they conceive their 'Palace of Delight' as a place of public spectacle in the tradition of the 1851 Great Exhibition and Crystal Palace, entirely devoted to 'sweet and pleasant things' and untainted by utilitarian matters of education or technical training. Even formal literary study would be spurned in favour of classes 'in letter-writing, especially love-letter writing, versifying, novel-writing, and essay-writing; that is to say on the more delightful forms of literature – so that poets and novelists should arise, and the East End, hitherto a barren desert, should blossom with flowers'. Angela imagines hall after hall at their Palace, for concerts, theatre, dancing, a skating rink, public lectures, 'a permanent exhibition of our small Arts', and a picture gallery.[41]

Besant's businesslike narrative style had little place for abstract reflection on the ultimate benefits of this philanthropic benefaction. These seemed to the novelist to be self-evident, and he spent little effort exploring the larger implications of moralising cultural provision. But at one point his characters imagine a Morrisian surge of creativity among the apathetic masses of East London:

> 'There shall be no house in the East End', cried the girl, 'that shall not have its panels painted by one member of the family; its wood-work carved by another, its furniture designed by a third, its windows planted with flowers by another.' Her eyes glowed, her lips trembled.[42]

Elsewhere Besant's heroine imagines how her gifts would instigate a moral transformation in more conventional terms. By giving the refined pleasures enjoyed by the wealthy to the residents of the 'grim and sombre streets' of this 'purgatory', to be enjoyed freely by the local population regardless of their economic means, Angela imagines a new 'civilised' spirit emerging among a blighted, brutish population.

> She would awake in dull and lethargic brains a new sense, the sense of pleasure; she would give them a craving for things of which they as yet know nothing....They should cultivate a noble discontent; they should

gradually learn to be critical…they should cease to look on life as a daily uprising and a down-sitting, a daily mechanical toil, a daily rest. To cultivate the sense of pleasure is to civilise.[43]

Scholars have snorted derisively at Besant's 'conscience-stricken upper-class philanthropists, acting out their bizarre slum pastoral',[44] or marvelled at this 'refreshingly different solution',[45] but in fact the philanthropy enacted in the novel commended itself in its day by invoking familiar and acceptable possibilities of social reform. It delivered tangible social improvement without ambiguity: as another critic shrewdly observes, Besant's text provides 'the problem, defined in easy terms, and [also] the solution, blessedly free of scruples or complications. Therein, surely, lies the secret of [the novel's] astonishing, and otherwise inexplicable, success'.[46] Far from any bizarre or fantastical quality, an artless simplicity was part of the Palace's appeal to Besant's readers and later to the charity-giving public. Not only was the diagnosis of the East End's ills that accompanied the scheme reassuring and unsensational, with its emphasis on monotony rather than squalor and boredom over criminality and vice, but the cure that was proposed seemed to respond directly to the need. The novel's romantic idealism charmed a Victorian public that sentimentalised charity relief and preferred heroic personal action to the rational, utilitarian impersonality of the New Poor Law and the COS's 'scientific charity'. As an early critic of Besant's novel recognised, it is significant that Angela 'violates every canon of the science of political economy' in her philanthropic work.[47] Besant dramatised personal conscience put into action, a materialised idealism that was lauded by experienced East End social workers like his fellow-trustee Harry Jones:

> I am sure…that an individual exercise of generosity on a large scale, however Quixotic it might be esteemed, would produce genuinely wholesome results. We do not sufficiently appreciate the excellence of eccentricity. It is a pity that Mr. Besant called his charming book 'All Sorts and Conditions of Men' an 'Impossible Story.' Virtually it is not impossible. It indicates a need which could be met.[48]

Besant's 'Palace of Delight' was sufficiently grand and idealised to transcend the ordinary procedures and routine of charity administration, promising something wondrous and transformative. Yet as a piece of liberal reformism the fanciful scheme made no promise to fundamentally alter existing social and economic realities. On the contrary, it optimistically asserted the viability of existing social arrangements and the essential co-humanity of rich and poor. 'The rich' were imagined as generous and compassionate, alert to the deprivation and suffering of the disadvantaged, 'the poor' as moral agents capable of self-improvement and responsive to the compassionate attention of the wealthy. '[S]tructured around the hope that nonviolent modes of democratic social transformation were possible – to leave things exactly as they were, only better', *All Sorts and Conditions of Men* manifested social idealism as a literary mode.[49] As Harry

Goslett explains to his 'fellow' East Enders in a speech to mark the opening of their Palace, the socialist and Radical agitators who had attempted to mobilise working-class resentment had failed to supply any genuine and lasting benefit. This was in contrast to the Palace, where ordinary East Londoners could enjoy 'all the things which make the lives of the rich happy', ensuring a common enjoyment of cultured pleasures that would mitigate existing divisions of class and wealth. Goslett's speech continues in phrases that evoke for us the social idealism that underpinned cultural philanthropy at large:

> 'It is not by setting poor against rich, or by hardening the heart of rich against poor, that you will succeed: it is by independence and by knowledge. All sorts and conditions of men are alike. As are the vices of the rich, so are your own; as are your virtues, so are theirs. But, hitherto, the rich have had things which you could not get. Now all that is altered: in the Palace of Delight we are equal to the richest: there is nothing which we, too, cannot have...[50]

* * *

As the Beaumont Trust scheme gathered momentum in the years that followed, its beguiling 'Besantian' qualities saw the novelist hailed as the originator of the essential concept. A decorated banner on the route for the royal procession to open the People's Palace in May 1887 announced, under the heading 'All Sorts and Conditions of Men',

> The people possess, as well as the Queen,
> A Palace they claim as their own;
> May Beaumonts and Besants in numbers be seen,
> To add further grace to the Throne.[51]

Other commentators routinely overlooked the Trust's contribution to the scheme altogether. *The Spectator* regarded Besant as the most effective modern novelist since 'we know of no other who has induced mankind to subscribe £100,000 for an unselfish object'.[52] Better-informed observers understood it as a shared achievement; in Charles Booth's words, it was 'the idea of Mr Besant and the work of Sir Edmund Currie',[53] but most contemporary observers neglected the latter's role altogether. Historians have also tended to overlook this joint responsibility for the People's Palace scheme.[54] An exclusive attention to Besant's 'blueprint' obscures the extent to which the final scheme was an amalgam of ideas emerging from a coalition of pragmatic reformers, rather than the 'Impossible Story' of the novelist alone. In early July 1887, shortly after the new Palace had opened, the Beaumont Trust's chairman sought to correct the contemporary misconception that the Palace was all Besant's idea. While acknowledging Besant's contribution in raising public awareness of the Palace scheme, Currie forcefully claimed 'absolutely for the Trustees the initiative of this great work; that no-one had anything to do with it in 1879, except the then Rector of Stepney... and myself...'[55]

As we have seen, under a re-organisation of the Trust approved by the Charity Commission in 1882, the seven original trustees were joined by twelve more to create a new Board under Currie's leadership to begin fund-raising and apply the endowment to a new building. Along with Currie and members of the Beaumont family, the Trustees now included prominent East London figures such as clergymen Samuel Barnett and Harry Jones, the parliamentarians James Bryce and C. T. Ritchie (Currie's opponent in Tower Hamlets in the 1874 election), and local business figures such as Spencer Charrington, Hugh Hoare and George Crowder. As a new Trustee, for his part Barnett hoped 'to be able to do a little towards establishing that East London College or Athenaeum which was in our thoughts when, ten years ago, my wife and I came to live here [in Whitechapel], and began to realise the needs of our new neighbours'.[56] Plans for the new scheme were discussed by this body, and refined through public meetings held at the Mansion House. The initial model, favoured by the Trust until mid-1882, was simply to provide lectures and evening classes, with 'other means of recreation and opportunity for social intercourse' clearly subordinate to the main educational objectives. The Trustees, commented the *East London Observer* in an early reference to the scheme, 'are taking the bold course of seeking public aid for the erection of a large building, which shall contain lecture-rooms and a library, and be available both for the purposes of instruction and entertainment'.[57]

In November 1882, the new Board of Trustees considered a more detailed proposal for their new institute 'for the instruction and recreation, the improvement and pleasure of the inhabitants of the East of London, to be called ———.' Its name remained a suggestively blank space on the page. Although the Besantian title 'People's Palace' had not yet been adopted, the multi-faceted character of the revitalised institution was already clearly established. 'The scheme should embrace', they agreed, 'the best points of a college, and of a German Concert Garden...it should be available for the people all year round. In various degrees it should possess the attractions of the Library; the Public Reading-room; the Science, Art and Literature classes; the Gymnasium; and the Public Garden'.[58] In all these aspects, the blueprint for the reformed Beaumont Institution was highly complementary to the ideas proposed in Besant's novel of that year, but had arisen among the Trustees entirely separately. This juncture, or shortly afterwards, seems to have been the moment that Besant was invited to join the Trust. Harry Jones' recollection that he made the introduction is partly contradicted, it should be noted, by the Palace librarian's memory that it was one of Currie's assistants, Arthur Brownlow, who first 'came to [Currie] after reading [Besant's] the "Impossible Story", saying "That's our work, Currie, that's the object for which we must aim", and thenceforth the new venture of the Beaumont Trustees was known by the name of "The People's Palace"'.[59]

The broad objects and institutional framework may have been complementary, but the two schemes did not match each other precisely. At odds with the novelist's 'Palace of Delight' was the Trust's pragmatic emphasis on utilitarian technical education that even at this early stage was central to their thinking. 'The young should have opportunities of instruction and amusement', they noted, 'for development and training of mind and body. The former should be of a kind to fit them for the various trades carried on in East London, and should aim at embracing the best technical education'.[60] Far from being a later idea that was crudely grafted onto Besant's 'Palace of Delight', as was maintained by the novelist and some of his contemporaries, the provision of technical education was central to the Beaumont Trust's proposal from the outset. Accordingly, an application was made to the Drapers' Company for financial support in January 1884, and its Court of Assistants voted £20,000 from existing corporate funds 'towards the cost of building and equipping technical schools, to form part of the proposed institution, the vote being conditional on funds to establish other portions of the work being subscribed'.[61] They also granted the Mile End site for the proposed scheme.[62] Technical education was an early theme that grew ever more prominent in the Palace's subsequent development.

On this basis we see that the People's Palace did not emerge butterfly-like from the novelist's 'fancy' alone. The defining connection between moralising recreation and technical instruction in the Beaumont Trust's scheme predated their endorsement of the Besantian 'Palace of Delight', an embrace that now seems due to the promotional advantages it offered rather than its status as an authentic 'blueprint'. Thereafter, the actual realisation of the scheme rested on the energies of Currie above all others: a fact generously recognised by Besant when he spoke at a dinner to recognise the chairman's achievements in early 1891. 'Who designed it?' the novelist asked. 'Sir Edmund. Who drew the plan? Sir Edmund. Who supplied the technical schools, the bath, the gymnasium, and fathered the great scheme as a whole? Sir Edmund.'[63] Whatever the debt to his fictional 'Palace of Delight', Besant applauded the realisation of the Trust's scheme as a monumental achievement. Currie skilfully hitched the sentimental charm of Besant's fictional vision to a raft of pre-existing practical proposals, bringing improving recreation and cultural opportunities together with technical education in a flamboyant way to capture the public imagination. As the donations and subscriptions mounted, and the Palace's grand edifice began to rise over Mile End Road, Besant and Currie could share equal credit.

But as we see below the hybrid itself contained little that was truly original; on the contrary the Palace was an educational model very much in vogue at the time. Just as Samuel Barnett's proposal for a university settlement in Whitechapel gained traction through related movements (namely, university extension and Broad Church parish activism), so too did the People's Palace scheme prosper alongside contemporary movements for technical education and moralising recreation.

* * *

Thus the Beaumont Trust's 1885–6 public appeals for their scheme outlined something more than a literary fantasy.[64] They delineated, rather, a highly practical institution with two clearly defined aspects. Under one roof they promised to draw the cultural amenities and opportunities depicted in Besant's 'Palace of Delight' together with a highly pragmatic, utilitarian system of technical instruction. If the identification of Besant, the leading philanthropic novelist of the day, with the scheme invested it with prestige and imaginative vigour, the sober pragmatism of its facilities for technical education offered a balancing counterweight. The scheme flourished because there was no confusing attempt to blend the two in operational terms; rather, both were presented as the separate and complementary basic elements of a twin-faceted scheme.

From the first public advertisements in mid-1885 the Trustees promised that technical schools, 'furnished with every necessary for trades of every description',[65] would be integral to the scheme, and to this end the Drapers' Company and technical education featured prominently in the publicity campaign thereafter. Pupils leaving the local elementary schools, the Trust asserted, 'unwisely aim at being clerks, rather than following trades, and the object of the trustees is…to place technical schools within an easy reach of every East End lad, and to instil into his mind the idea that to have a trade at his back is better than to become a clerk'.[66] Technical education gave Currie the opportunity to emphasise its practicality, and the Trust went so far as to insist that the 'nucleus of the whole project is the educational department, on whose foundation the system of recreation will be raised'.[67] The Beaumont Trustees envisaged a *de facto* university for East London; a 'University of Rational Recreation and Technical Education' as Currie grandly described it. Thus the fund had

> for its object not only the relief of the architectural dullness of East London by the erection of a suitable palace for the recreation and relaxation of the poor, but also the advancement of their material and moral well-being in the shape of technical schools and workshops where their education might be continued and completed.[68]

Besant himself, an active Trustee for several years by this time, applauded this element explicitly. Referring to the young men of East London lacking gainful occupation, he promised that the Palace would 'take that boy out of the streets….Once master of a trade his future is assured.'[69] The emphasis corresponded to prevailing anxieties that Britain's system of technical instruction suffered by international comparison. The country's 'rough-and-tumble system [of technical education] is no longer adequate', *The Spectator* commented in 1885: 'Germany and Switzerland, on the Continent, but, above all, the United States of America – the only rivals whom we need really fear in industrial competition – have already made rapid strides to the front under the influence of universal education'.[70] An exacting Royal Commission on Technical Instruction between 1881 and 1884 had compared local practices with the international scene, but little had been done to assuage concerns that organised foreign systems were far more effective than the disorganised trade schools and apprenticeships found at home. By responding to these concerns the Palace scheme achieved a large measure of its credibility. By uniting two different realms of public anxiety, the improvement of the condition of the urban poor and the maintenance of Britain's industrial supremacy, it promised to address both in a single ambitious centre of social improvement in the capital's industrial heartland.

At the same time, its 'Besantian' flavour allowed the Trust to capitalise on the extraordinary success of *All Sorts and Conditions of Men*, as when the diagnosis of East End monotony offered in the novel was replicated in the Trust appeals. 'We have, at last, begun to realise', explained one, 'the heritage of dullness and dreariness, of unlovely and monotonous existence, which is the portion of the multitudes who are the basis of our commercial greatness, the condition of our pleasure and leisure'.[71] Catch-phrases from Besant's novel that had entered popular usage re-appeared in publicity material for the Palace, imagined as 'large and rotund, with welcoming doors, inviting 'all sorts and conditions of men' to enter and assemble themselves together'.[72] The actual workings of the new institution, moreover, directly evoked the romanticism of Besant's 'Palace of Delight'. Majestic in scale and luxuriously ornamented, the Trust's Palace would be a sumptuous setting for fine art, literature, musical concerts, dances and exhibitions in the vast and ornate Queen's Hall at its centre. As the Trust's architect, Currie's old London School Board colleague E. R. Robson, started work on the scheme in 1884, he seems to have started with the central Hall and added one thing after another to it, just as Angela Messenger had done in fiction: a glass-framed 'Winter Garden' of tropical plants, 'gymnasia for both sexes, together with swimming baths, racquet and tennis courts, bicycle tracks and running grounds, and indoor games and amusements of every description, including billiards and chess, …[and] reading rooms and libraries on the model of those at the British Museum'.[73]

Alternating between utility and fancy, practicality and vision, between cultural opportunities in art, music, literature and social intercourse and the utilitarian benefits of technical instruction, the Palace's promoters set out to seize public attention with their multivalent scheme. 'The English language still wants a precise term to describe the Institution which it is proposed to found', the Trust announced, urging that while 'a hasty judge might say that [the scheme] was at once too sweeping and too elaborate in its aims…such is not the case. The enterprise is highly organised, but not over organised; each part, however distinct in its functions from the rest, is necessary to the healthy working of the whole'.[74] 'It will be seen at once', agreed *The Standard,* 'that the undertaking is not modelled on the lines of anything that already exists, but will combine in itself the advantages presented by a number of agencies that, as a rule, operate apart'.[75] The multivalence of the enterprise, the collection of diverse improving influences it collected under one roof, was widely applauded. 'It is proposed', observed the *East End News*, 'to provide public halls for lectures and exhibitions, promenades for bands and entertainments, rooms for clubs and classes, to found a library, and to build swimming baths. The scheme, in fact, aims to embrace the best points of a college and a German concert garden...'[76] The *Jewish World* spoke for many when it recognised in the Palace 'an institution combining the advantages of a Crystal Palace, a Birkbeck Institution, a Toynbee Hall, and a *Turnverein*....We are inclined to found high hopes on this grandiose scheme'.[77] 'We can only express a fervent hope', wrote reformist clergyman J. G. Adderley in *Eastward Ho!* in mid-1887 as the grand edifice neared completion, 'that the Beaumont Trustees will never depart from their original intentions....Thus will the great Palace in Mile End Road be at once the drawing-room, the library, the concert-hall, the school, the picture-gallery, and the home of the people of East London, who have so real and great a need of all and each of these great blessings.'[78] In all this, as a sermon preached in Westminster Abbey by the chaplain to the Bishop of London claimed, the Palace scheme partook of the 'undying spirit of Christianity'. Notwithstanding its provision of secular amusement, the Palace's concern for 'righteousness', he felt, reflected 'that element in man that touches on the ideal, the eternal, the divine, and it is therefore concerned with all that refines and elevates and purifies. Whole populations among us are dragged down by dulness, by the mere absence of healthy interests and inspiring emotions. Is it not the duty of the Church to attack this cause of moral deterioration?'[79] Letters of support from the Archbishop of Canterbury, the Bishop of London and the energetic Bishop of Bedford, William Walsham How, likewise refuted accusations that the Palace was merely a secular endeavour. The latter believed there were 'still greater gifts of God' than those on offer at the Palace, 'but ease and refined enjoyment, and the power of understanding what is delightful and elevating, are God's very precious gifts too, and it is part of Christian duty and of the law of Charity on the part of those who value them to make it possible for their brethren to enjoy them'.[80] A romantic language of traditional philanthropy, extolling wise and benevolent 'gifts' from the wealthy to the poor, was also being mobilised. The Trustees 'appeal[ed] to those whose life is graced and enlarged by all the gifts of nature and art to communicate the means of a true education – technical, literary, artistic, physical – of ordered amusement and recreation, and to clear the way for a higher estimate of comfort and of the meaning and possibilities of life'.[81] The grandson of J. T. Barber Beaumont approved the new direction Currie had taken with his family's endowment. The Palace scheme, he felt, furthered his grandfather's wish 'that the working classes should possess now a culture more refining and refined than that whereunto they were admitted in his day'. He asked:

> Can we believe that there is in them want of will and power to receive such culture? None who visit the National Gallery, the British Museum – none who visited Northumberland and Zion Houses, lately thrown open to all by the liberality of their noble owner, a man indeed large of heart – can doubt that beneath the...unassuming garb of our humblest artisans, are found souls capable of appreciating the highest work of art, and, could they be brought into action, talents capable of imitating them.[82]

Harry Jones, who remained an ardent and vocal supporter of the Trust scheme, agreed that such 'great gifts...would no more "pauperise" the recipients than the British Museum does Bloomsbury Square, or Kensington Gardens do the regions around them'.[83]

Thus the provision of cultural opportunity and improving sociability at the Palace met with warm endorsement in many quarters. The parliamentarian W. S. Robson declared to a Poplar Town Hall meeting to support the scheme in early 1886 that 'statesmen and philanthropists had given far too little attention to the pleasures of the people. It was a striking and alarming incident of English life that there was so little social intercourse. It was by this intercourse that refinement and gentleness of nature were cultivated.'[84] The Trustees invited other cultural philanthropic efforts such as university extension, picture exhibitions, the Kyrle Society choir and other musical societies to work with them, venturing to suggest that 'for all of [these] and many other agencies now at work the scheme will provide a centre and a local habitation'.[85] Press commentary applauded their wisdom. 'Its grounds and buildings will furnish an excellent site', observed *The Spectator* when the full proposal was unveiled in May 1885,

> for the many agencies that are now at work for the benefit of working-men or for those that would probably grow up among working-men themselves when they were secure of a local habitation. There is an excellent Society which gives good music at a merely nominal cost...there would probably be little difficulty in organising plays as well as concerts; and what has hitherto seemed the impossible problem of providing places in which young men and women can dance without risk of impropriety, may at last be solved here.[86]

A spectacular royal procession and ceremony to lay the foundation stone on 28 June 1886 set out to capture these high-minded sentiments as a didactic public ritual. The occasion cost the Beaumont Trust nearly £1,900, much of it spent on decorations for the Prince and Princess of Wales' procession through the heart of the East End, along the great thoroughfare from Aldgate to Mile End that seemed to burst into life for the occasion.[87] Newspaper observers saw in the spectacle a 'panorama of public jubilation, blazoned on house-fronts, reflected in the faces of the multitude' that had gathered to 'welcome their future King and Queen'. 'All Whitechapel and Mile-end seemed to have emptied their teeming population – old and young – into the main road', went one account, 'and every householder appeared to take a personal interest in the visit, and to have determined to give as hearty a welcome to the visitors as was in his power'.[88] Three triumphal arches were erected along the route that, together with a massive floral trophy at Mile End Gate, pennants, streamers and messages of welcome, formed 'a prodigality of decoration [that] was of itself something wonderful to behold' according to the *Daily Telegraph*. The royal carriage was preceded by the Lord Mayor's civic procession, with

military and volunteer escorts, but the East End was not unrepresented: a pha-
lanx of 'ragged boys' from the local Barnardo's Home were in the vanguard,
followed by the 'Pride of the East' brass band together with a thousand
delegates from East London's trade unions, temperance associations and
friendly societies.[89] Whether by their representative presence in the formal
procession, or in the avid crowds along the route, the enthusiastic response of
the East End population inspired confidence. 'The East-enders may be unre-
servedly congratulated', thrilled the *Morning Chronicle*, 'on having so unmis-
takably honoured themselves by honouring those whom they were privileged
to welcome in their midst'.[90] The appreciation on display encouraged optimism
about the likely effects of the Trust's philanthropic gift:

> All along the route...the mass of spectators was solid and enthusiastic,
> and included numberless representatives of the 'horny-handed sons of
> toil', who clapped their hands to some purpose. The welcome was, in
> fact, a people's welcome, and one which only those who are commonly
> called the 'lower classes' know how to give. 'Let us thank and encourage
> him', which formed one of the numerous inscriptions along the route, was
> the keynote of the greeting, and shows that the people of the East-end
> know how to appreciate any movement designed for their welfare.[91]

* * *

Not everyone was persuaded by the scheme, of course, and the Trustees'
insistence that their improving 'Palace of Delight' would be open every day
was an inevitable provocation to sabbatarian opinion. In an appeal directed at
the working families of the district, the Working Men's Lord's Day Rest
Association summarised the Beaumont Trust proposal:

> *News Rooms* for the Study on Sundays of the Betting, Sporting, and all
> the sensational News of the day, from 2 till 10 o'clock at night. Organ
> recitals on Sundays, not for worship mark you, but for *Amusement*. The
> Sunday has hitherto been preserved as a day of *rest* and *worship*. The
> Trustees of the People's Palace want to make it a day for *amusement*.[92]

A 'People's League against the Sunday Opening of the People's Palace' was
formed, led by the Rev. Thomas Richardson of St Benet's, Stepney, immediately adjacent to the Palace site, who sought to conscript local opinion to his
view that the Palace was a secularizing influence and a frivolous distraction
from Sunday worship. In the other corner, supporters of the scheme and liberal-minded clergy rallied to the Trust's insistence on Sunday opening. One
commented to Currie: 'I understand that the People's Palace will supply a
drawing-room to the poor, and it seems to me most churlish and narrow-
minded to talk of closing a drawing room on Sundays'.[93] Temperance cam-
paigners were also quick to raise objections, Bishop Wilberforce asking in a

letter to *The Times* whether the proposed Palace would be conducted on temperance lines. Currie deferred the issue until after the Palace had been built, but Besant stepped up with a forceful statement that 'the palace is built for the use of the people....I trust sincerely that it will be managed by working men on working men's pay, offered by them, policed by them, and conducted by them for themselves, in accordance with their own views as to the interpretation of the founder's intention'. He took the opportunity to underscore the tone of liberal emancipation that he hoped would be embodied there:

> For my own part, I should say that the London working man, if he is to look upon this palace as entirely his own, his place of recreation as well as of instruction, will insist upon being treated as a free and rational being, able to run alone and fettered by no grandmotherly legislation. Otherwise it is easy to foretell what the future of this palace will be. The working man is not a child, and he will not be treated as a child.[94]

Other objections went beyond predictable temperance or sabbatarian misgivings. As the refusals to subscribe retained in the Trust's correspondence files indicate, many potential donors preferred to support less-flamboyant measures than an extravagant 'People's Palace'. I. J. Booth, a director of the local Romford Brewery, doubted that 'Walter Besant has really gauged the wants and wishes of East London', and thus preferred to support the classes at the existing Bow and Bromley Institute. It was better, he felt, 'to develope [*sic*] a plant of natural growth than build up the wild scheme of a novelist's dream, and then look for customers afterwards'.[95] Other refusals were more idiosyncratic. A J. H. Faulkner of Newgate Street E.C., for one, felt 'that great majority of those out of work are so because they will only work at extortionate wages and what is still worse do only half an honest day's work after all. I am persuaded that those that won't work "neither shall they eat" – nor even have Palaces to lounge in or their schooling paid for'.[96] 'Surely the Country which pours its hundreds and thousands into the East End should be called upon to subscribe to their well-being', suggested another correspondent, while others felt that it was the middle classes that deserved philanthropic aid. 'Spend the cash in hand as the founder [of the Beaumont Trust] intended it should be spent', urged a Mr F. Bartlett of Croydon, '[not to] swell the notions of the workers with vain ideas of their own importance by providing them with increase of luxuries paid for by many who can ill afford the means'.[97] Some potential supporters attracted to the essence of proposal were dismayed by its lavish scale: 'the way to serve the poor people', wrote one, 'would be to have meeting rooms and reading rooms and talking rooms in all parts of the East End, instead of having the £100,000 building concentrated in one place, far removed from the homes of most....I think the whole thing a folly, even though you have got rich fools to promote the "People's Palace"'. The letter was signed 'A possible subscriber, but not for the The People's Palace'.[98]

Other refusals deplored the patronising terms under which the Palace was being bestowed upon the East End poor. 'The appeal would not be so absurd if there was not so much real want existing', declared one respondent. Others dissented in more eccentric and aggressive terms. 'Will have nothing to do with such wicked rubbish', scrawled one recipient across the appeal form.

> Give them work first & improve their minds afterwards. Happiness is only to be found in contentment & rich wicked persons as yourselves for your own ends pretend to have the welfare of these ½ starved animals at heart – you teach them to be miserable & you encourage them in envy hatred and malice of the better born and higher class persons. You admit you cannot bread [*sic*] a race horse from a Norfolk donkey then why try to bread a man from the lowest of Gods animals – the beastly poor.[99]

More temperate voices were unsure that education and recreation were in fact compatible in the way the Beaumont Trust proposed. The *East London Advertiser* worried that 'one would subordinate the other…human nature is so strong in favour of deferring mental improvement and technical training to a more convenient occasion, that…the cheap concert, the well-fitted gymnasium, the attractive winter garden, and other such attractions would empty the class-rooms, or, at least, reduce their influence and power to do good'.[100] Some scepticism about the scheme was inevitable, parliamentarian Henry Green told a Poplar meeting of early 1886 to promote the fund, because 'education and recreation had almost come to be considered antagonistic to each other, since they were only to be obtained at different places'.

> Hitherto, if they wished for education, they had to go to the night-school or the mechanics' institute; if they wished for pleasure, and were not content with the mild dissipation of the concert or the tea meeting, they must be ready to run some risks, and take their wives and sweethearts to some place which was under the guardian angelship of the Middlesex magistrates. (Laughter.)[101]

In the event, the fact that the educational components were substantially funded by the Drapers' Company provided a convenient villain as the Palace struggled with its finances. Disappointed supporters imagined the Palace's educational aspects as mere appendages, that had spoiled the appeal and prospects of the 'Palace of Delight'. Harry Jones likened the Palace's later shift to a more explicit program of technical instruction as 'the coming of a cloud over Mr Besant's delightful dream'.[102] Besant's disingenuous claim, made in his autobiography, that 'a polytechnic was tacked on to it; the original idea of a place of recreation was mixed up with a place of education', can be regarded as the most emotive of these: 'alas! alas!' he continued theatrically, 'what might not the Palace have done for the people if the original design had been carried out, if no educational side had been attached, and if the Drapers' Company had never touched it?'[103]

This was a brazen misrepresentation of what had actually transpired. As we have seen, technical instruction was a cornerstone of the Beaumont Trust People's Palace scheme from the outset. As the proposal matured, the Trustees had collectively re-conceived the Philosophical Institution as bold amalgam of instruction and recreation, of 'practicality' and 'delight'. The latter aspect was more fanciful and noteworthy, capturing both the imagination of commentators and the derision of sceptics alike, and so came to dominate public perceptions of the scheme. Yet at every point the Trustees took great pains to emphasise the practicality and viability of the proposal, principally by its close association with pragmatic technical education.

* * *

Although notable for its scale and high public profile, the People's Palace was far from being the only late-Victorian institution of its kind. On the contrary, the model of education and recreation it embodied was highly favoured by contemporary advocates of reformed technical education as the term 'polytechnic', borrowed from continental Europe much earlier in the century, began to enjoy greater currency.

In London, the creation of the City Parochial Foundation in 1891 following the Liberal government's 1883 *City of London Parochial Charities Act* provided the major impetus for the establishment of polytechnic institutions. After lengthy resistance by vested interests, James Bryce's reforming legislation had swept away the 'dead hand' of parochial endowments in the depopulated City of London parishes, opening a floodgate on vast sums of money for charitable purposes.[104] In the decade that followed, inquiries by the Charity Commission and various parliamentary bodies considered the most suitable projects for expenditure. Open spaces, popular education and cultural amenities had long been favoured: as early as 1881, Bryce had addressed a COS conference on preferred uses for City Parochial Charities funds, and suggested 'the promotion of secondary education...the provision of museums, free libraries, art collections, recreation grounds, open spaces, etc.'[105] However a final decision to fund a substantial network of metropolitan polytechnics (and in doing so laying out the subsequent pattern of London's centres of higher education) was taken after the Charity Commissioners had been convinced by two pioneering experiments in recreative education. These were Quintin Hogg's efforts at the Regent Street Polytechnic, and the Beaumont Trust's People's Palace in East London.[106] Both struck contemporaries as eminently worthy ventures, which responded directly and effectively to the problems and needs of the day.

The Regent Street Polytechnic dated back to the late 1830s and had been known for popular lectures, technical displays and amusements, 'a place where children of the upper classes were taken to hear popular-science lectures, to see showy chemical experiments, and to be amused with all sorts of novel and astonishing things', as a later account put it with only a little exaggeration.[107] In early 1882 the premises were purchased by Hogg, a wealthy city merchant and philanthropist, to expand his Young Men's Christian Institute at Long Acre, a club for education and improving recreation he started as part of a day school for the poor in the 1860s. 'What we wanted to develop our institute into', Hogg wrote, 'was a place which should recognise that God had given man more than one side to his character, and where we could gratify any reasonable taste, whether athletic, intellectual, spiritual or social'.[108] In its new guise the Polytechnic offered secondary schooling and trades instruction for boys during the day and more formal technical education for young men in the evenings, along with ample opportunities for improving leisure. Students or other members paying a modest subscription fee could use the Polytechnic's sports grounds, join its sporting teams, clubs and debating societies, attend evening concerts and lectures, and take up opportunities for educational travel.[109] By 1883 enrolments had reached 6,800, rising to 11,000 by 1888. Sir Philip Magnus, the leading advocate of reformed technical education at this time, described Hogg's model approvingly as 'both a school and a club; and whilst the scope of the school is narrowed by a distinct bias towards bread-winning pursuits, the objects of the club are widened so as to include many forms of amusement which are foreign to club life, as understood by the frequenters of Pall Mall and St James's Street'.[110]

We are not surprised, then, that the still-nebulous People's Palace drew directly on Hogg's experience and model. Robert Mitchell, Hogg's secretary in Regent Street, advised the Beaumont Trust directly on suitable educational arrangements at the nascent Palace, ensuring that the Polytechnic's lead was closely followed: the age limits (young men and women aged 16–25), membership and class fees, the emphasis on clubs and a members' institute for social activities were all features taken from Hogg's experiment and applied in Mile End.[111] During the subscription effort the Palace's architect, E. R. Robson, invited the sugar grandee Henry Tate, a potential donor who later endowed the Tate Gallery, to dine with himself and Sir Edmund Hay Currie, 'afterwards to proceed to the old Polytechnic in Regent Street which Mr. Q. Hogg has made such a success of in a spirit and manner such as we want at the East End'.[112] Certainly contemporaries regarded them as cut from the same cloth, and after visiting Regent Street and Mile End during 1887, the economist and Assistant Charity Commissioner Henry Cunynghame wrote a persuasive memorandum extolling the virtues of both institutions.[113] His paper drew together many concerns about the nation's economic and social condition: increasing dependence upon machinery (particularly by younger artisans, who thereby failed to learn a trade), the decline of small manufacturing, the increase in foreign competition and the concentration of industry amid urban over-population. The latter induced anxieties about the 'semi-independent life of the factory [which] has a tendency to destroy home instincts, and to create a population of nomads without a sense of the pleasures, duties, and responsibilities of a settled position'. Cunynghame was especially concerned by the 'quite extraordinary' extent of migratory labour in London:

> It is not too much to say that a large portion of the population of London is consequently changing its habitation. This has a most unsettling effect on the character. Men and women become as it were lost in the crowd. They form few friendships, and are isolated, and hence there is no body of public opinion that can be brought to bear upon them to keep them from actions of which they would be ashamed.[114]

As a result, the schemes of education he favoured involved associations and activities to form moral habits and reinforce strength of 'character'. His enthusiastic endorsement of Hogg's exemplary Polytechnic echoed the plethora of recreational opportunities that were such a feature at the People's Palace. 'There is no compulsion here', Cunynghame reported of Hogg's institution,

> it would be impossible; but gymnasia, swimming baths, and reading-rooms are provided. Facilities are given, which are eagerly embraced, for the formation of rowing clubs, walking clubs, cricket clubs, football clubs, botanical and antiquarian societies, all of which are managed by the boys and are self-supporting...[115]

Cunynghame's detailed report, which concluded with an outline of a model polytechnic, supplied a compelling rationale for the network of educational and recreational institutions across London that were then built or nurtured by City Parochial trust funds during the following decade.[116] After signalling their interest in the polytechnic schemes during 1888, the Commissioners declared in their 1889 *Report* that 'the experience of the past year has shown that the plan of combining technical and industrial training with physical and mental recreation', which had been initiated at the Regent Street Polytechnic

> and which has since, under the sympathetic and able direction of Sir Edmund Currie, adopted at the People's Palace, Mile End, was not one which depended for its success on circumstances peculiar to the older institution, but was capable of being applied to other Institutions [that are] similar in their general character.[117]

Thereafter, in a process that Owen and Belcher have traced in detail, quite phenomenal sums of money released by the 1883 reforms were dedicated to the various polytechnic experiments. As well as building on current ideas about technical education, the polytechnics founded in the 1880s and 1890s were imprinted by a contemporaneous set of preoccupations about the reform of popular recreation. As Belcher writes,

They promoted the intellectual, moral and spiritual improvement of the working classes, they could aspire to be centres of civilization, 'people's palaces', in their neighbourhoods, and, just as importantly, they required a positive effort of will on the part of those who participated in their benefits. They fostered those very qualities of self-help and independence which distinguished the deserving from the undeserving poor.[118]

Thus the Beaumont Trust's proposal for a 'People's Palace' in Mile End, rather than being an eccentric creature of fancy, spawned from a novelist's imagination, should instead be viewed as an expression of a much broader impulse. Through Cunynghame, the Charity Commission was convinced that great centres of improved recreation, moralising entertainment and practical education would assist the social wellbeing of the working populations of urban districts. The balancing of recreational opportunities and technical education in the one local facility, in centres that became known as 'polytechnics' after Hogg's institute rather than Besantian 'palaces', was in fact a highly credible response by philanthropic interests to problems of urban disadvantage as conceived in the mid-1880s.

A memorial proposal mooted during 1885 to commemorate the life and work of the Earl of Shaftesbury further supports this contention. Lord Mount-Temple, the retired Whig politician and member of the Mansion House Committee appointed to honour the great humanitarian, suggested a 'Memorial Hall' in Shaftesbury's name to be erected in the East End for London's working population. Rooms at the Memorial Hall were envisaged 'for the occupations that are most conducive to the civilization and moral and religious development of working people – such as a Library, newspaper reading room, coffee room, conversation room, opportunities for games of skill'. The governing principle of the scheme, as Mount-Temple explained to Samuel Barnett in asking for advice, was to provide a venue where the working population might obtain 'society and amusement independently of the Public House and the Music Hall'. This was an aspiration shared with the Royal Victoria Hall in Lambeth, where Mount-Temple had been an active supporter to the extent that he underwrote its early debts.[119] 'Your experience of Toynbee Hall', he beseeched Barnett in 1885, 'might enable you to suggest something which doesn't occur to people who are not actively engaged in trying to influence and help the people of the East End'.[120] His proposal, independently conceived, shared the key ambitions of the People's Palace, Hogg's Polytechnic and other schemes for large centres of adult education and improving recreation. Through Barnett, Mount-Temple came into contact with the Beaumont Trust scheme for the first time and found it 'strongly confirmed the ideas I had formed'.[121]

The level of consultation after that is unclear, but the prospectus for an 'East London University' that was subsequently presented to the Mansion House committee suggested the Beaumont fund might be integrated into the scheme to bolster its finances. Although it acknowledged a conceptual debt to the Regent Street Polytechnic, the prospectus also borrowed a number of features from the Beaumont scheme, especially its broad appeal to the whole East London population, not just young people and students, and its systematic balancing of educational and recreative functions. Much as was envisaged with the People's Palace, the proposed centre would act as a point of co-operation between existing recreational societies and associations. With an Executive Committee to govern 'with the people for the people', harmoniously preventing 'moral degeneration' by 'the co-operation of all for the good of each', the Shaftesbury Memorial University was imagined as an idealised community of learning and leisure, with responsible citizenship as its active principle. Like the People's Palace, it rested on the notion that sociability, civic interaction and the ameliorative power of culture were integral to the social improvement of the urban poor. It would introduce 'the most ennobling works of the great composers' and 'a home for true artistic instruction' to the East Londoner. The benefit of 'mutual knowledge' through social intercourse to overcome the 'isolation' of life among the masses saw an emphasis upon the importance of 'Association'. The task of social regeneration by dismantling the 'anonymity' of life among the mass was made explicit:

> Perhaps the worst obstacle to true views of citizenship in East London is that want of mutual knowledge, that isolation which gives point to the commonplace that there no man knows his next-door neighbour. A true spiritual life is thus rendered more difficult than ever.[122]

Ultimately, although Mount-Temple attempted 'to open a wider vista of usefulness for the object of subscriptions', the committee preferred to fund a convalescent home for poor children as a fitting tribute to Lord Shaftesbury's life and work.[123]

* * *

Each of these embryonic institutions – the People's Palace, Hogg's 'Young Men's Christian Institute' and later Polytechnic, and the abortive vision of a 'Shaftesbury Memorial University' – responded to a key issue in the late-Victorian technical education debate, namely whether large institutions should offer general liberal education or specialised occupational training. In the words of the scientist Thomas Huxley, perhaps the period's most influential voice for improved industrial education,

> [T]he education which precedes that of the workshop should be entirely devoted to the strengthening of the body, the elevation of the moral faculties, and the cultivation of the intelligence; and especially... imbuing the mind with a broad and clear view of the laws of that natural world with the components of which the handicraftsman will have to deal.

The earlier this happened the better, Huxley urged, because the younger the artisan, 'the more important is it that he should devote the precious hours of preliminary education to things of the mind, which have no direct and immediate bearing on his branch of industry, though they lie at the foundation of all realities.'[124] Institutions like the polytechnics and the People's Palace shared these aspirations but resolved the balance differently. Rather than offering a liberal education *prior* to occupational training, they made physical, moral and intellectual education available to artisans and labourers *alongside* the workshop and technical school. In this context, the scale and splendour of the People's Palace, its deliberately experimental combination of recreation and technical instruction, and its poly-thematic provision of amenities under one roof seemed a highly effective remedy. It promised to enhance moral character and mental capacities among working people, and especially the young, but without neglecting the pragmatic realities of industrial training. The basic nature of the People's Palace could thus be enunciated to the subscribing public in terms that made clear sense: as a centralised, 'polytechnic' institution that offered improving opportunities in recreation and trade skills, but that simultaneously was a grand embodiment of the potential for social conciliation as the wealthy acted on their obligations to the poor. In all these ways it was a carefully calibrated experiment that was inevitably persuasive to many.

More potent symbolism was on show on 14 May 1887 when another royal procession, this time graced by HM the Queen herself, made its stately progress into the heart of 'Outcast London' to declare the Palace open. It was an irresistible embodiment of the social conciliation of the 'Two Nations', especially poignant given that the Golden Jubilee of 1887 was a moment of national reflection as well as celebration. Victoria's parade into the East End seemed to embody the social progress of her age. 'The Queen passes today from a palace to a palace – silently establishing by such an act the close approach which has taken place during the last fifty years between the upper and the lower ranks of the State', the *Daily Telegraph* enthused. 'No commemoration of the Jubilee year could be more charged with meaning than this, which is so plain a sign of the concord existing between the Throne and the People'.[125] The full procession commenced at Paddington Station, from where five royal carriages, escorted by the 2nd Life Guards and met periodically by detachments of troops and military bands, made their way down Oxford Street, to Aldgate and into Whitechapel Road. The Queen's passage into the East End (for the first time in her reign, it was generally, though erroneously, believed) carried immense significance.[126] East London's transformation for the occasion seemed, once again, to anticipate the vivifying benefits promised by the Palace. 'Aldgate and Bow, Whitechapel and Limehouse have blossomed forth', proclaimed the *Telegraph*, 'with Venetian masts, emblazoned shields and trophies, and festoons of flags, the very lamp-posts having become temporarily aesthetic with the aid of crimson cloth and evergreens'.[127] The raw industrial character of the district had itself been cast off, the *Evening Standard* fancied:

> Even the dirty and prosaic railway arches that span the road were for the nonce converted into something approaching 'things of beauty', their

dinginess being hidden under a lavish display of coloured cloths and flags; Stepney Station giving a hint of its utility by the words 'Commerce' and 'Industry' on either side of the words 'God save the Queen'...[128]

But for all its high hopes, momentum and prestige in the mid-1880s, the People's Palace quickly faltered. All the Trust's efforts in 1882–7 had been concentrated on fund-raising and construction rather than supporting the Palace's expensive activities into the future. The lack of a recurrent funding base (apart from the technical schools) was a fatal flaw, something that Currie acknowledged blithely in the management scheme he developed for the Palace's first year of operation. 'Looking to the future and to the fact that at present our only income is derived from the interest of £12,000, producing £370 per annum', he announced, 'any work we start for this year must be paid for out of the capital. At the same time it is *of the greatest importance that we should at ONCE start our scheme*'.[129] It was a disastrous mistake, leading to chaotic finances within just a few years. In the face of uncontrolled expenditure, financial disarray and spiralling debt, the Charity Commission was obliged to intervene, appointing Henry Cunynghame as external auditor in March 1890. His report of July 1890 – received a month after Currie, surely anticipating its findings, announced his resignation – found that the practice of 'borrowing from capital funds in order to meet current expenditure' had been 'a fertile source of confusion'.[130] Considerable reductions were imposed on the staffing establishment and expenditure during 1890–1. The Drapers' Company was the only source of sizeable ongoing income, and assumed in return an ever-increasing responsibility for its operations, starting with an annual grant of £7,000 to run the Technical School under a new arrangement in 1892 while the Palace's cultural philanthropy was wound back. The distinct functions of education and recreation were increasingly estranged, and fully separated governing bodies were established for each in 1890–2.[131] The Queen's Hall and the Winter Garden continued to host concerts, gala occasions, lectures and social gatherings, but no longer with the lavish style and moralising intentions that marked the People's Palace as a philanthropic experiment. The grand unitary vision that had stoked public interest in the 1884–7 subscription campaign was wound down as vocational instruction came increasingly to the fore.

By 1901, the shift in the attitude and morale of the Palace's staff was palpable. When in July that year the Toynbee Hall resident Ernest Aves, working for Charles Booth's survey, asked the Palace's secretary directly whether the Palace work interested him, the answer left little room for idealism. 'He said it did not', Aves reported, 'by which...he meant that he felt no particular interest in or sympathy for the people he found around him. Socially his attitude may be almost said to be antipathetic, and this was especially noticeable when he referred to the Jews and the "rough"'.[132] The People's Palace Day School for young apprentice artisans continued, alongside evening classes in mathematics, physics, chemistry, technical drawing, geometry and so on, as part of an adult Technical College. The Queen's Hall was let out commercially for Saturday evening concerts and Sunday organ recitals, and during holiday periods 'entertainments are given, such as costume recitals, performances by military and other bands, ventriloquists, etc.' During winter it was hired out about twice a week 'for concerts, bazaars, charitable teas, dog shows, etc., and occasionally for meetings and lectures', but there was little in the way of close operational oversight. 'The programme and class of entertainment is submitted for the approval of the governors, and the clerk or some other member of the staff attends from time to time to see that order is maintained and that the entertainments are of an unobjectionable character'.[133]

It was a hollow remnant of the grand philanthropic vision of the mid-1880s. By 1907, and with its absorption into the University of London as the East London Technical College, the animating spirit of Besant's 'Palace of Delight' and Currie's more nuanced polytechnic experiment had both evaporated, leaving only a shell behind.

Notes

1   Beaumont Trust, 'A People's Palace in East London' (London, 1885), reproduced in W. S. Beaumont, *A Brief Account of the Beaumont Trust and its Founder J. T. Barber Beaumont* (London: Charles and Edward Layton, 1887), p. 41.
2   QMUL: QMC/PP/6/4, H. Cunynghame, 'Assistant Commissioner's Financial Report', 29 July 1890, p. 3.
3   Along with G. P. Moss and M. V. Saville, *From Palace to College: An Illustrated History of Queen Mary College* (London: Queen Mary College, 1985), see A. Chapman, 'The People's Palace for East London: A Study of Victorian Philanthropy' (M.Phil. thesis, University of Hull, 1978) and P. M. Brading, 'A Brief History of the People's Palace Library' (M.A. thesis, University of Sheffield, 1976); D. Weiner, *Architecture and Social Reform in Late-Victorian London* (Manchester: Manchester University Press, 1994) and her 'The People's Palace: An Image for East London in the 1880s' in D. Feldman and G. Stedman Jones (eds), *Metropolis London: Histories and Representations since 1800* (London: Routledge, 1989), pp. 40–55; S. Joyce, 'Castles in the Air: the People's Palace, Cultural Reformism, and the East End Working Class' *Victorian Studies* 39:4 (1996), pp. 513–38.
4   Joyce, 'Castles in the Air', p. 515.
5   TNA: Charity Commission, CHAR7/5 Beaumont Institution, 'The Philosophical Institution' [copy of legal memorandum, *c.* 1866], f. 99.
6   J. W. Hudson, *The History of Adult Education, in which is comprised a Full and Complete History of the Mechanics' and Literary Institutions* (London: Longman, Brown, Green & Longmans, 1851), p. 173.
7   Beaumont, *A Brief Account of the Beaumont Trust*, p. iii.
8   *The Christian Life: A Unitarian Journal* 3 July 1886.
9   See Chapman, 'The People's Palace for East London', pp. 104–10 and TNA: Charity Commission CHAR 7/5 (Beaumont Trust).
10 TNA: Charity Commission, CHAR 7/5, 'Interview Memorandum' dated 24 July 1882.
11 See his obituary in *The Times*, 14 May 1913, p. 9 and Chapman, 'The People's Palace for East London', pp. 102–4.
12 Chapman, 'The People's Palace for East London', p. 107.
13 TNA: Charity Commission, CHAR 7/5, 'Extract from letter dated January 26 1881'.

An impossible story in Mile End   137

14 LMA: A/BPP/2/1 Beaumont Trust, 'Preliminary Statement' (June 1882) n. p.
15 *The Times*, 22 June 1882; TNA: Charity Commission, CHAR7/5 Beaumont Institution, correspondence from Beaumont Trustees dated 19 July 1882 and 'Interview Memorandum' of 24 July 1882.
16 *Fifty Years, or Dead Leaves and Living Seeds* (London: Smith, Elder and Co, 1895), p. 94.
17 J. Tunis, 'The People's Palace: A Palace of Joy' *Lend a Hand: A Record of Progress* 8:3 (1892), p. 151.
18 *Social Transformations of the Victorian Age: A Survey of Court and Country* (London: Seeley and Co., 1897), p. 362.
19 *The Autobiography of Sir Walter Besant* (London: Hutchinson and Co., 1902), p. 245.
20 *Dictionary of National Biography* (Second Supplement, Vol. 1) (London: Smith, Elder and Co, 1912), p. 154.
21 *The Spectator* 22 January 1887, p. 114.
22 See S. Eliot, 'Besant, Sir Walter' *Oxford Dictionary of National Biography* (Vol. 5) (Oxford: Oxford University Press, 2004), pp. 507–9; C. Machann, 'Sir Walter Besant', in *Dictionary of Literary Biography* vol. 135, (Detroit: Gale Research, 1994), p. 41; and Besant, *Autobiography*. The celebrated theosophist Annie Besant was the estranged wife of Besant's younger brother, Frank.
23 *Dictionary of National Biography* (Second Supplement, Vol. 1) (London: Smith, Elder and Co., 1912), p. 154.
24 L. Melville [Lewis Saul Benjamin], *Victorian Novelists* (London: Archibald Constable and Co., 1906), p. 292.
25 'Mr Walter Besant and the East-enders', *Cassell's Family Magazine* (1893), p. 66.
26 Eliot, 'Besant, Sir Walter', p. 509.
27 See M. Spika, 'Henry James and Walter Besant: "The Art of Fiction" Controversy' *Novel* 6 (1973), pp. 101–19; J. Goode, 'The Art of Fiction: Walter Besant and Henry James' in D. Howard, J. Lucas and J. Goode (eds), *Tradition and Tolerance in Nineteenth-century Fiction* (London: Routledge and Kegan Paul, 1966), pp. 243–81; S. Eliot, '"His Generation Read His Stories": Walter Besant, Chatto and Windus and *All Sorts and Conditions of Men*' *Publishing History* 21 (1987), pp. 52–3.
28 P. Mattheisen *et al.* (eds), *The Collected Letters of George Gissing: Volume Three: 1886–1888* (Athens: Ohio University Press, 1992), p. 199: letter to Algernon Gissing of 8 April 1888. Neetens comments: 'In criticism we find Besant produced as a Philistine but amiable populist, a deluded and outdated optimist...' W. Neetens, 'Problems of a "Democratic Text": Walter Besant's Impossible Story', *Novel* 23 (1990), p. 248.
29 P. Coustillas (ed.), *London and the Life of Literature in Late Victorian England: The Diary of George Gissing, Novelist* (Hassocks: The Harvester Press, 1978), p. 354: entry of 19 November 1893. He and Besant jostled for public attention as prominent contributors to the 'social question': see 'Two Philanthropic Novelists: Mr Walter Besant and Mr George Gissing' *Murray's Magazine* (April 1888), pp. 506–18.
30 'The style of *All Sorts and Conditions of Men* is undistinguished, and there is a marked tendency to indulge in trite observations and a wealth of unnecessary detail; the atmosphere is artificial; the characters are not men and women but types...and the purpose is always so much in evidence that the illusion essential to an artistic work is not produced.' Melville, *Victorian Novelists*, p. 307. According to Bindoff, poor characterization was the novel's chief flaw, 'for hardly one of its figures can be said to live: all are types, caricatures, or cardboard shapes, not one real person'. 'East End Delight' *East London Papers* 3:1 (1961), p. 34.
31 *The Spectator*, 22 January 1887, p. 114.

32 Machann, 'Sir Walter Besant', p. 41.
33 Neetens, 'Problems of a "Democratic Text"', p. 249.
34 R. Blathwayt, 'Mr Walter Besant and the East-enders', *Cassell's Family Maga-zine* (1893), p. 65.
35 Besant, *Autobiography*, p. 248.
36 W. Besant, *All Sorts and Conditions of Men: An Impossible Story* (London: Chatto and Windus, 1894 [1882]), p. 18.
37 *All Sorts and Conditions of Men*, p. 132.
38 *All Sorts and Conditions of Men*, p. 61.
39 *All Sorts and Conditions of Men*, pp. 132–3, emphasis added.
40 Literally intended as a 'messenger angel'. Chapman ('The People's Palace for East London', p. 101) suggests the character owed much to the prominent heiress and philanthropist Angela Burdett-Coutts.
41 *All Sorts and Conditions of Men*, pp. 52–4.
42 *All Sorts and Conditions of Men*, p. 54.
43 *All Sorts and Conditions of Men*, p. 184.
44 'Fact and Fiction in the East End' in H. J. Dyos and M. Wolff (eds), *The Victorian City: Images and Realities* (London: Routledge and Kegan Paul, 1973), Vol. 2, p. 598.
45 Eliot, 'His Generation Read His Stories', p. 36.
46 Bindoff, 'East End Delight', p. 39.
47 Melville, *Victorian Novelists*, p. 304.
48 H. Jones, 'Life and Work among the East-London Poor', *Good Words* 25 (1884), p. 51.
49 Neetens, 'Problems of a "Democratic Text"', p. 248.
50 *All Sorts and Conditions of Men*, pp. 329–30.
51 *The Times* 16 May 1887.
52 'The Gospel of Amusement', *The Spectator* 26 October 1889, p. 547.
53 C. Booth, *Life and Labour of the Poor in London* (First Series, Vol. 1) p. 118; Chapman, 'The People's Palace for East London', pp. 109–12.
54 Chapman's unpublished thesis is an exception, and remains the most detailed and accurate account of the Palace's early development.
55 LMA: A/BPP/2, 'Memo. to Beaumont Trustees' 8 July 1887.
56 Cited in H. Barnett, *Canon Barnett: His Life, Work and Friends* (London: John Murray, 1918), Vol. 1, p. 340.
57 'The Beaumont Institution', *ELO* 8 July 1882, p. 5.
58 LMA: A/BPP/2/1, Beaumont Trust, '[Statement] For Final Consideration on Tuesday November 6 at 11 a.m.', n. p.
59 M. S. R. James, *Sketch of the People's Palace and its Library* (London: John Bale and Sons, 1893), p. 4.
60 Beaumont Trust, '[Statement] For Final Consideration', n. p.
61 DCA: Court of Assistants Minute Book MB 58 (1890–93) f. 65, report dated 12 June 1890. 'In January, 1884, an application was laid before the Company from the Beaumont Trustees, for assistance in carrying into effect a wide expansion of their trust, by establishing an institution for the promotion on a large scale, of social recreative and educational objects, among the population of East London.'
62 Occupied since 1728 by the Bancroft almshouses and school, this site became available as the Company prepared to re-locate the establishment to Woodford Green, Essex. Chapman, 'The People's Palace for East London', pp. 117–18.
63 'Presentation to Sir Edmund Hay Currie' *Palace Journal* 7 (February 1891), p. 99.
64 These proposals were Beaumont Trust, *A People's Palace in East London* (pamphlet) (London, 1885); *The Beaumont Trust Scheme for the People's Palace in East London* (pamphlet) (London, n. d. [1885]); E. H. Currie, *The Beaumont*

Trust: Extract of an Appeal, issued through the medium of the Press (pamphlet) (London, 1885); Beaumont Trust, *A People's Palace in East London* (pamphlet) (London, 1886) (QMUL: QMC/PP/2/1-2).

65 This wording featured in a circular sent to all the major daily newspapers and published on Wednesday 27 May 1885.

66 *The Beaumont Trust Scheme for the People's Palace in East London* (London, 1885), n. p.

67 Beaumont Trust, *A People's Palace in East London* (pamphlet) (London, 1885), p. 42.

68 *The Times* 11 June 1886, p. 10.

69 W. Besant, 'The People's Palace', *Contemporary Review* 51 (February 1887), pp. 231–2.

70 'Technical Education', *The Spectator* 11 April 1885, p. 489.

71 Beaumont Trust, *A People's Palace in East London* (London, 1885), p. 41.

72 Beaumont Trust, *Handbook to the People's Palace: General Description of the Building, and Statements of the Hopes of The Founders* (London, 1887), p. 3.

73 *The Times* 11 June 1886, p. 10.

74 QMUL: QMC/PP/2/2.

75 *The Standard* 27 May 1885.

76 'A Visit from the Prince and Princess of Wales', *East End News* 15 July 1884.

77 *Jewish World* 12 February 1886. The *Turnverein* gymnastic clubs had been popular among German immigrant communities in the United States since mid-century.

78 J. G. Adderley, 'What is the People's Palace Doing?' *Eastward Ho!* 7 (August 1887), p. 227.

79 Beaumont Trust, *A Sermon preached by the Rev. J. M. Wilson, M.A. at Westminster Abbey on The Church and the Labouring Classes with especial reference to the Beaumont Trust Scheme for the People's Palace in East London* (pamphlet) (London: Maclure and MacDonald, 1886), p. 4.

80 Beaumont Trust, *A Sermon preached by the Rev. J. M. Wilson*, p. 10.

81 Beaumont Trust, *A People's Palace in East London* (pamphlet) (London, 1885).

82 Beaumont, *A Brief Account of the Beaumont Trust*, p. 21.

83 H. Jones, 'Life and Work among the East-London Poor', *Good Words* (1884), p. 51.

84 *The Times* 19 January 1886, p. 6.

85 Beaumont Trust, *A People's Palace in East London* (pamphlet) (London, 1885), p. 42.

86 *The Spectator* 30 May 1885, p. 701–2.

87 LMA: A/BPP/2/1, 'Statement of Account'; W. S. Beaumont's copy. The bills tendered to the Trust by 16 December amounted to £1866–19–17.

88 QMUL: QMC/PP/17/1: Beaumont Trust scrapbook, unreferenced newspaper clipping.

89 *Daily Telegraph* 29 June 1886.

90 *Morning Chronicle* 29 June 1886.

91 QMUL: QMC/PP/17/1: Beaumont Trust scrapbook, unreferenced newspaper clipping.

92 Working Men's Lord's Day Rest Association, *Extraordinary Conduct of the Trustees of the People's Palace* (pamphlet) (London, 1888), n. p. (emphasis in original). Other pamphlets issued against by the Association against the Beaumont Trust proposal include *Important Objections to the Sunday Opening of Public Libraries, News Rooms, Museums, Etc.* (London, 1888); *The People's League against the Sunday Opening of the People's Palace* (London, 1888). See LMA: A/BPP/2/1.

93 QMUL: QMC/PP/4/1, letter from J. Spencer Curwen of 26 July 1886.

94 QMUL: QMC/PP/17/1: Beaumont Trust scrapbook, undated clipping from *Church Times* (February 1886).

95   QMUL: QMC/PP/2/13, letter of 1 February 1886.
96   QMUL: QMC/PP/2/12, undated letter.
97   QMUL: QMC/PP/2/12, undated ms. note and letter of 19 January 1886.
98   QMUL: QMC/PP/2/12, anonymous letter, dated 'West London, 14 Decr. 1885'.
99   QMUL: QMC/PP/2/12, undated and anonymous response to 'One Pound' appeal.
100 'The East End Palace of Delight' *ELA* 30 January 1886, p. 7.
101 'The People's Palace for East London: What will it be?' *ELO* 23 January 1886, p. 7.
102 Jones, *Fifty Years*, p. 95.
103 Besant, *Autobiography*, pp. 245, 247.
104 See D. E. Owen, 'The City Parochial Charities: The "Dead Hand" in Late Victorian London' *Journal of British Studies* 1 (1961–2), pp. 115–35.
105 H. Bosanquet, *Social Work in London 1869–1912: A History of the Charity Organisation Society* (London: John Murray, 1914), p. 376.
106 Like the Beaumont People's Palace, there has been little sustained historical scrutiny of Hogg's Regent Street Polytechnic; it remains, one historian writes, 'all but hidden from history'. M. Strong, 'Class Trips and the Meaning of British Citizenship: Travel, Educational Reform, and the Regent Street Polytechnic at Home and Abroad, 1871–1903' *Journal of British Studies* 51 (2012), p. 106.
107 A. Shaw, 'London Polytechnics and People's Palaces' *Century Magazine* 40 (June 1890), p. 166.
108 'Extract from Mr Quintin Hogg's Account of How the Regent Street Polytechnic was founded', in C. Booth, *Life and Labour of the People in London* (Third Series: Religious Influences) Vol. 7 (London: Macmillan, 1902), p. 393.
109 Strong, 'Class Trips and the Meaning of British Citizenship', p. 109.
110 P. Magnus, 'The New Polytechnic Institutes' *Good Words* 30 (December 1889), p. 622.
111 See Chapman, 'The People's Palace for East London', p. 168, and A. Shaw, 'London Polytechnics and People's Palaces', pp. 163–82.
112 QMUL: QMC/PP/2/13, copy of letter from E. R. Robson, 17 December 1885.
113 'Memorandum upon the Social, Physical, and Intellectual Improvement of the Poorer Classes of London', especially in relation to Institutions that unite Recreation with Education' dated 3 December 1887. Parlt. P.: *Return of certain Memoranda and Reports by Charity Commissioners or their Assistant Commissioners on Technical Instruction, on Institutions combining Recreation with Education and on Free Libraries* 1890 (142) LV, pp. 112–216.
114 'Memorandum upon the Social, Physical, and Intellectual Improvement of the Poorer Classes of London', p. 116.
115 'Memorandum upon the Social, Physical, and Intellectual Improvement of the Poorer Classes of London', pp. 125–6.
116 V. Belcher, *The City Parochial Foundation 1891–1991: A Trust for the Poor of London* (Aldershot: Scolar Press, 1991), *passim*.
117 Parlt. P.: *Thirty-Sixth Report of the Charity Commissioners for England and Wales* 1889 [c.5685], p. 36.
118 Belcher, *The City Parochial Foundation*, p. 73.
119 A. Geddes Poole, *Philanthropy and the Construction of Victorian Women's Citizenship: Lady Frederick Cavendish and Miss Emma Cons* (Toronto: University of Toronto Press, 2014), pp. 111–12.
120 QMUL: QMC/PP/16/2, letter to Barnett of 26 October 1885.
121 QMUL: QMC/PP/16/2, letter to Barnett of 29 October 1885.
122 QMUL: QMC/PP/16/2.
123 QMUL: QMC/PP/16/2, letter to Currie of 29 October 1885.
124 T. H. Huxley, 'Technical Education' *Fortnightly Review* 29 (January 1878), p. 52.
125 *Daily Telegraph* 14 May 1887.

126 The Queen had in fact opened a new wing of the London Hospital, Whitechapel High Street, in March 1876. See F. Prochaska, *Royal Bounty: The Making of a Welfare Monarchy* (New Haven: Yale University Press, 1995), p. 111.
127 *Daily Telegraph* 14 May 1887.
128 'Special Edition: The People's Palace: Opening by the Queen' *Evening Standard* 14 May 1887.
129 LMA: A/BPP/2, *People's Palace for East London (Beaumont Trust)* [scheme of management], (London, 1887), n. p., emphasis in original.
130 QMUL: QMC/PP/6/4, f. 3.
131 TNA: Charity Commission, CHAR7/5 Beaumont Institution, printed report 'The People's Palace, including the Bow and Bromley Institute', n. d. [*c.* 1903], p. 454; H. Farmar, 'The Drapers' Company and East London' *East End Papers* 1:3 (1960), p. 8.
132 BLPES: Booth Collection, A56 f. 54, interview at the People's Palace for a 'Report on Polytechnics', dated 19 July 1901.
133 TNA: Charity Commission, CHAR7/5, 'The People's Palace, including the Bow and Bromley Institute' (printed report, dated *c.*1903), p. 454.

6   Social duty in South London

The cultural mission as a mode of moralising social work reached something of an apotheosis in the two East End examples considered so far. As we have seen, in their own ways Toynbee Hall and the People's Palace were pioneering experiments, each the culmination of developmental factors pertinent to their own specific situation. But there was much that was shared, too: both began as nebulous proposals, grounded in a shared diagnosis of urban *anomie* and tedium rather than lurid slum depravity, that took shape in response to various contextual realities. Despite cosmetic differences of scale, publicity and religious affiliation, they shared a tone of romantic errantry, a social idealism manifested in themes of obligation, duty, moralising improvement and social uplift that helped to capture attention. But they were also grounded in practical schemes of educational provision (namely, university extension and the polytechnic idea) that gave them credibility as part of the reformist mainstream. The cultural mission to the poor crystallised in these distinctive East London 'centres of light' as each coalesced and gathered momentum.

Elsewhere we find equivalent ideas and aspirations permeating other attempts to induce the urban poor into self-improvement through moralising cultural influences. Neither entirely 'secular' nor avowedly 'religious', much like Toynbee Hall and the People's Palace, these more obscure efforts are also 'practices and moments in which transitions, overlaps and contradictions of religious and secular occur'.[1] Turning our attention south of the river, to the other metropolitan landscape of urban poverty that attracted reformist attention in the last decades of the century, we see a crop of pertinent examples that also demand closer scrutiny.

Emma Cons was busy supervising model housing for poor tenants in Lambeth from the late 1870s. Cons was a capable woman of humble background, the daughter of a London piano craftsman, and had herself worked as an engraver and stained glass artist. She had met Octavia Hill at the Ladies' Guild run by Octavia's mother, and then later joined her friend as a paid rent collector and building manager for the South London Dwellings Company. She was soon an active and prominent housing philanthropist in her own right.[2] With assistance from Caroline Martineau, the scientist and cousin of the prominent Unitarian theologian James Martineau, Cons secured the lease on a decrepit and notoriously unruly music hall, the Victoria Theatre, on the corner of Waterloo Road and New Cut in 1879.[3] Re-decorated and freshly outfitted the following year (once more under a scheme by Elijah Hoole) and re-titled the Royal Victoria Hall, it was managed by the Coffee and Music Halls Company as a temperance venue with variety entertainments. These tried to attract popular audiences without indulging in the bawdy insinuation that typically prevailed in commercial music halls. In this they trod a careful line: 'we do not attempt to exclude *mere* vulgarity', a member of the management committee explained in 1886, 'so long as it is free from what is actually wrong, and those who like rouge and golden wigs may enjoy them to their heart's content at the "Vic." on a Saturday night'.[4] Ventriloquists, panoramas, dissolving views, clog dancers and comical cats: the vivid posters that survive from the early 1880s suggest a lively venue with genuinely populist attractions.[5]

But the original hopes that it would soon be financially self-supporting were disappointed. 'All expectation of a dividend was given up at the end of a few months', one of the managers acknowledged, as losses mounted to £2,800 by August 1881. Thereafter the venue was run by a committee chaired by Liberal MP Samuel Morley and with Miss Cons as secretary, 'which, being convinced that the thing was a moral success though a financial failure, raised subscriptions to meet the difference between the receipts and the expenditure'.[6] Thus the company was wound up and its assets vested in trustees who purchased the lease so it could operate on a rent-free basis. Ballad concerts, orchestral recitals, performances from a prim *corps de ballet*, lectures, conferences and social meetings – all calculated to be more 'improving' than the usual run of variety entertainments – became the regular fare. A weekly programme of penny science lectures began at 'The Vic' in 1883, delivered by noteworthy scientists and public educators to large audiences of 500–900 by various estimates.[7] When the naval officer, explorer and anti-slavery campaigner Verney Lovett Cameron described his epic 1873–5 journey across Africa by foot, the crowd swelled to over two thousand, matching the throngs that heard Professor Malvern describe the Egyptian war in September 1882.[8] In 1885 these educational elements were consolidated in three rooms as a working men's club and institute, available to local subscribers. As a library, clubhouse, gymnasium, drill room and learning centre, it combined all the classic elements of improving recreation and adult education:

[One room] is supplied with all the leading morning and evening daily papers, and the principal weekly periodicals; and here billiards, bagatelle, chess and draughts may be played. In a lower room fencing, boxing and other athletic exercises may be practised under the direction of a military instructor; while in another department debating and other educational classes are held. It may also be used as a reading room by those who wish to be quiet, and out of the tobacco smoke, which is allowed in both the other rooms. Here too, 'talks' on such subjects as 'Robert Burns, the Poet of Democracy', and 'Thomas Carlyle and Hero-Worship' are given to as many members as care to listen. The 'talks' are followed by a discussion, in which all present are invited to join.[9]

In September 1889, the institute was formally constituted as the Morley Memorial College for Working Men and Women, and from that time served as one of South London's centres of adult education, evening classes, and university extension lectures: in Charles Booth's words, becoming 'what is in effect a minor polytechnic'.[10] As Geddes Poole shows, despite the moralising strictures of the original 'temperance music hall' these efforts shared the liberal impulses of other centres of adult education as a form of social work. Jeffrey Cox comments that 'the Old Vic, with its temperance lectures, improving concerts, temperance cafe, adult vocational classes, gymnasium and library, was distinguishable only in its scale from any number of church- and chapel-related institutions that had grown out of settlement and parochial and mission hall activity – prompted by precisely the same improving motives which had led Miss Cons to Lambeth in the first place'.[11]

Another and somewhat more eccentric example is St Winifred's Hall on Lower Road, Rotherhithe. Here an independent mission centre and institute took shape from 1888 that continued to thrive, in its small way, through to the turn of the century, blending a more overt missionary evangelicalism with cultural and recreational endeavours.[12] Its founder, Henry Morriss, was a senior clerk in the City merchant firm Stedman and Crowther when he established the St Winifred's Youth Institute and Mission in his home neighbourhood of Rotherhithe in 1888. His little centre of improving influences was named after the school in one of F. W. Farrar's popular stories for young readers, and evolved from an informal botany class Morriss had started to share his interest in the subject. His intentions, as he later put it, were 'to help a few boys in the neighbourhood by keeping them off the street, and helping them to learn various subjects, and spend happy evenings with mutual friends – but above all to help them to live as true disciples of the Lord Jesus Christ'.[13] By 1890 he had taken over an old hall, cleaned and furnished for use as a gymnasium, which as his membership grew relocated to a railway arch the following year. This was cramped and leaked in wet weather, and so a larger hall in Lower Road opposite the Rotherhithe Public Library was leased from February 1892. An overtly evangelical enterprise, St Winifred's offered services, bible classes and lay sermons interspersed with lectures, clubs, choir performances and other improving entertainments. It had a particular emphasis on youth work, according to an outline of his scope of activity in a local newspaper, with

> children's special services, Bible classes for young men and women, little girls' physical drill, young women's mutual improvement class, and gymnastic society; parliamentary and literary society, minstrel society, boys' mutual improvement class, band of hope, young men's gymnastic society,

pleasant Saturday evening entertainments for the people, and a slate club for men.[14]

In this way Morriss proselytised local working men and women in what Cox calls a pattern of 'diffusive Christianity', as Christian exhortation, literary and scientific study, clubs and associations, music and sociability were rolled together. An autodidact like his students, Morriss enjoyed collecting, popular science and antiquarianism: by the mid-1890s, his personal collection of botanical and geological specimens had grown to some two thousand curiosities, displayed as a small museum in the former stables at the rear of his home in Lower Road. 'His individuality is marked', commented a local newspaper approvingly, 'and it has made its mark upon those who surround him. He believes in rational recreation and physical improvement being linked with spiritual Christianity. Such men are urgently needed.'[15] Ernest Aves drew his own conclusions after visiting Morriss and his little institute in 1900: 'a quick-witted, ingenious man', he surmised, 'with a mind full of pigeon-holes, all labelled, and a life made coherent by a very practical Christianity'. Morriss had his qualities, he felt sure, yet was 'consistently in danger of appearing a monstrous prig, but he always saves himself, and comes out as a genuine Christian man, working hard at a cause for which it is not an exaggeration to say that he has devoted his life. He is safe, but the danger is perhaps that he may be making prigs.' This in itself was not necessarily a bad thing, Aves reasoned. 'They would however be good prigs', he continued, 'and stand a good chance of keeping straight in life'. He noted that more than a hundred boys from St Winifred's had been placed in clerical and office positions in the City, and 'practically all are doing well'.[16]

Revealingly, Morriss took pains to embed his own life story into a written account of his mission to the self-improving young clerks of Rotherhithe, a hint of solipsism that suggests the work was freighted with self-identification. He surely found its successes and his own prominence, even if on a modest and local scale, immensely gratifying; with further evidence of this kind we might follow Koven in attempting to re-construct the psychological charge Morriss likely drew from this kind of sustained youth work.[17] But there are anomalies as well: Morriss was self-taught, like his students, and like Miss Cons was no fashionable interloping 'slummer', being a long-term resident of Rotherhithe and just as familiar with its needs and circumstances as were his institute members. His underlying purpose, it seems, was to advance his recruits through education into coveted positions as clerks and office assistants.

* * *

The South London urban setting where Emma Cons and Henry Morriss settled down for their life's work may have been less notorious than its East London counterparts across the river, but for social workers and reform-

minded commentators it demanded its own ameliorative effort. South of the
Thames was a typical nineteenth-century sprawl of low-level housing, shops
and factories, with a pronounced strip of industry along the river, cut through
by railways and major roadways. The wharves of the old riverside districts –
Lambeth, Southwark, Bermondsey downstream to Rotherhithe – had been
sustained by trade and shipping for centuries, generating dense neighbourhoods of warehouses, narrow streets and courts housing dock labourers, bar-
gemen and carters. The river's edge downstream from London Bridge and
The Pool witnessed massive investment and dock development, especially the
great expanse of the Surrey Commercial Docks opposite Limehouse Reach
and the Isle of Dogs, but even as late as the 1850s there were open fields and
undeveloped allotments relatively close by. The daily necessity of traffic and
movement shaped South London's urban form, in shipping and the docks,
and more pertinently as the century wore on in the main roads to the cross-
river bridges. Railway routes fractured the streetscape with elevated embank-
ments and bricked arches. With their produce supplied by rail or river barges,
factories for jam, pickles and biscuits, breweries, tanneries and leather-works
joined the older maritime industries of the riverside district as the century
progressed; a surge of residential development saw the undeveloped pockets
of land south of the river rapidly filled in to house these workforces. Inner
South London remained primarily industrial, criss-crossed by highways and
railways, as the residential suburbs beyond mushroomed with population
growth. Suburban railways took the wealthy and respectable to new housing
on the urban fringe, but riverside London in general 'remained the site of
such major employers of unskilled labour as the docks, markets and railway
termini, as well as many gas works; of the "sweated trades" of tailoring, boot-
making and furniture-making; and of the more specialised trades with surviving systems of apprenticeship, such as printing, bookbinding and
coopering'.[18]

Descriptions of the locality favoured during this period reflected contemporaries' dismay at the drab and formless character of South London's
suburban growth. As early as the 1860s local voices deplored the fact that
South Londoners had no major libraries, public museums or galleries, and
very few formal centres of education or improving recreation. 'We cannot
boast of mechanics' institutes, or of museums, or of a free library, or of a
chamber of commerce, or of a market hall or of one building suitable to the
needs of the people', wrote a correspondent from Lambeth to the new local
newspaper in January 1865.[19] But as Draper explains, local newspapers might
have lamented the civic shortcomings of South London but could do little to
rectify them. Late-century social explorers and social workers, clergymen and
crusading urban journalists re-worked these modes of urban representation,
emphasising alienation, sterile monotony, shapelessness and torpor as the
defining features of late-Victorian London as it sprawled out south of the
Thames. The new Bishop of Southwark, Edward Talbot, for example, when
his diocese was created in 1906 in an attempt to rectify the problem,

wondered aloud: 'What is there to stir one's pulses in this strange shapeless district, without visible unity or coherence, without common municipal institutions, such as bind into unity the great provincial cities, this dull and drab mass of grimy town?'[20]

Like contemporary depictions of the East End, South London was considered 'abandoned', lacking local leadership, dull, tedious and materialistic. 'I am convinced that the south of London needs more help than any other part', wrote Octavia Hill to her supporters and co-workers in 1877, 'it is specially difficult to send [social] workers of the kind I think it wants because we have no good leaders or centres there. The East [End] is far richer in them.'[21] Charles Booth began his survey of the religious life of the district in characteristic style with an evocation of the streetscape that carefully presented a distinct social and moral diagnosis:

> To a stranger the first impression is that of a net-work of wide thoroughfares starting from the bridges and meeting to form again fresh centres of radiation....The second impression, resulting from more intimate knowledge, is that of a maze of small streets and courts crowded in many parts with low-living population. These streets, set at every conceivable angle to each other, appear on our map like the stitches of embroidery filling in the groundwork of the pattern made by the crossing of the main thoroughfares. And a terrible embroidery it proves to be, as we look closer and closer into it: of poverty, dirt and sin.[22]

The parishes of central Southwark around the Borough High Street supplied ample evidence of the latter as Booth's survey progressed into its 'Religious Influences' phase in the late 1890s. Much of it was quiet desperation rather than brazen depravity, at least if we go by the cameos noted by Booth's researchers. In Maypole Alley off Borough High Street, for example, George Duckworth encountered a middle aged woman 'pulling fur at her open window [with the] air full of fluff and herself covered with it'. She spoke to him in a 'shaky, husky voice'; 'must do it to live, you know'.[23] The cramped streets in the 'The Grotto' district nearby struck him as utterly miserable, inhabited by carmen and waterside labourers and their families, with Lower Grotto Place as 'the worst of the lot in appearance' when he visited it in May 1899. Here a sign advertised two rooms for 5/6 per week, with no washhouse but a yard behind, the sort of detail that appealed to Booth's investigators. Duckworth noted 'many children, all well fed but dirty, and with sores on [their] faces; clothes ragged, too large or too small, windows broken and patched'.[24] But when he spoke of the district to the residents of the Women's Settlement in nearby Nelson Square, however, he was surprised when they disputed his impressions. 'Of the Grotto District they did not know much but what they knew of it was in its favour: "very respectable, only very poor"', he noted.[25] When it came to the area around Birdcage Alley and Marshalsea Road, he suggested the whole should be marked in black on their poverty map:

the inhabitants of the houses and [common] lodging houses are prosti-
tutes and ponces and thieves, those in St George's buildings are waterside
labourers and market porters (no gutter merchants). Youths and middle
aged men of the lowest casual class loafing; undergrown men; women
laughing with draggled skirts; hatless but hidden under long shawls; a
deformed boy with naked half formed leg turned in the wrong direction
made up the scene.[26]

Active social workers had similar habits of diagnosis and interpretation to the
poverty investigators, being keenly alert to these impressionistic signifiers of
social geography in the streets of impoverished neighbourhoods. An important part of their moralising effort, alongside their attention to behaviour,
social standing and character of local people, was tied up in the remodelling
of the urban environment itself. Octavia Hill's experimental rebuilding of part
of Red Cross Street, Southwark as a reformed community hub amidst what
was regarded as the worst slum in South London captures this preoccupation – and the pattern of intervention that came with it – for us.

As her fame as a housing reformer and practical social worker grew, Hill
began managing a number of run-down properties in Southwark for the
Ecclesiastical Commissioners, the body charged with managing the property
assets of the Church of England, in mid-1884. In her characteristically busy
style, Hill took the initiative in 1886 in negotiating a long-term lease with the
Commission on a disused site in Red Cross Street, disfigured by a derelict,
burnt-out paper factory. The neighbourhood around was notorious for its
dense courts of unmitigated poverty. 'Revisiting them after an interval of ten
years', Charles Booth wrote in 1899, 'I brought away the same black picture,
the same depression of soul, as on the first occasion; the only relief being due
to the destruction of some [of the courts], and the only hope the prospective
destruction of the rest'.[27] For Hill and her co-workers, though, the setting
seemed ripe not for demolition but rather for improving intervention on their
characteristically small and personal scale. She had always favoured small,
homely accommodation, preparing and managing cottage dwellings rather
than large tenement blocks, seeing better potential for domestic virtue and
closer relations between tenant and landlord, neighbour with neighbour. She
and her Southwark social workers – sixteen lady visitors and rent collectors,
with other occasional volunteers – also wanted to initiate an equally characteristic range of cultural and social influences. 'We want space for carving
and mosaic classes', she wrote in her annual 'Letter' to her supporters in
1886, 'for musical drill, for winter parties, and lectures and concerts, for
dances and acting. We have a good workmen's club there [in Southwark], and
a hall will be an important adjunct to it.'[28] In Red Cross Street she had the
opportunity to implement these ideas in earnest.

Announcing her latest project – 'being by far the largest real gifts for the
people I ever had, or dreamed of'[29] – in a letter to *The Times* in March 1887,
Hill outlined plans to re-make the derelict site as a decorative garden, edged

by a group of cottages and communal hall; a model for improved community life replete with moralising cultural influences. 'If I secure the hall', she explained, 'I shall be able to use it in summer in connection with the garden for music, flower shows, reading room and library, and it will be available in winter for our various concerts, entertainments, musical drill, lectures, and parties'.[30] The young Sydney Cockerell, a family friend and avid supporter of Hill's efforts, started working for her at this time as secretary to the Red Cross Hall fund, and recalled that £2,105 was subscribed that day, rising to £2,500 by the end of the month.[31] He visited the 'Promised Land' of the Southwark site (as he described it sardonically in his diary) for the first time on 24 March, finding it a 'desolate and dreary wilderness at present', filled with rubbish and sodden paper, with warehouses and a high block of tenement housing encircling it on three sides.[32]

As the promised funds materialised, the warehouses were demolished and the debris burnt in bonfires over six weeks. 'The ashes were good for the soil in the garden', reported the ever-practical Miss Hill, 'and we were saved the whole cost of carting the paper away'.[33] Through the second half of 1887 the site was re-made as a traditional village common and formal garden edged by cottages and a communal hall (see Figure 6.1). But the covered playground

NEW HALL, GARDEN, AND COTTAGES, RED CROSS STREET, SOUTHWARK
Recently Built and Thrown Open for the Use of the Poor through the Exertions of Miss Octavia Hill

Figure 6.1 Red Cross Hall and Garden, Southwark

hinted at the contemporary practicality of the scheme: built from salvaged timbers, it ran down the length of one boundary and as well as permitting children to play in wet weather served as a terraced viewing platform for the whole area. Lady Ducie supplied funds to lay out the garden, with a band-stand, pond and footbridge, 'walks winding between lawns and flower-beds, planted with crocuses and other bulbs', the whole being later described by Charles Booth as 'charmingly fantastic'.[34] The commons preservation cam-paigner Robert Hunter, a trustee in the scheme, donated ornamental goldfish for the pond.[35] It is easy to overlook the novelty of a formal, public garden laid out in ornamental fashion in an inner city neighbourhoods at this time, because as Hill's biographer later observed, 'the *kind* of garden too was new. There were not then many amateurs [establishing gardens]. A garden was something formal and expensive implying a paid staff.'[36] Another wealthy sponsor, Lady Jane Dundas, financed the cottages that fronted the garden, ten gabled and red-tiled homes designed by the architect Elijah Hoole who worked on Octavia Hill's schemes for over forty years. Each cottage had four rooms and its own washhouse, with 'a scrap of garden in front and its own little garden at the back....The front rooms all looked over the flower garden.'[37] The scheme was completed by the erection of Red Cross Hall at one end of the site, funded by a donation of £2,000 from the former parlia-mentarian Henry Cowper. This was a solid mock-Tudor structure in red brick also designed by Hoole, with a timber hammer-beam ceiling and detailing that the architect later remembered fondly as a 'romance in bricks and mortar'.[38] Declared open by the Archbishop of Canterbury in early June 1888, the Hall was a simple structure for all its grand historical associations, opening at one end onto the garden and with committee and club rooms at the other. It was open every Sunday for lectures and music recitals, with facilities for a cadet corps and gymnastics, men's club and reading room.[39] 'The day of the opening was a lovely one, could not have been more beauti-ful'; Miss Hill reported as she announced the long-awaited redemption of Red Cross Street:

> [K]ind friends from far off sent us the most lovely flowers and green boughs in plenty; a group of friends undertook the decorating, under Miss Astley's direction, and they put on one of the great bare warehouse walls, not yet overgrown by the young creepers, which we hope will one day clothe them, a large inscription, red letters on white ground, framed with garlands 'The wilderness shall rejoice and blossom as the rose'; the Kyrle Choir came and sang for us...all gave a solemn sense of gladness to the great gathering of fellow-workers, rich and poor, which will long live in our memories as crowning a time of very full blessing.[40]

Cockerell, not yet twenty years old, was thrilled with the opening spectacle, describing the event as 'very successful, [the] place gay with a multitude of flowers...and a concourse of grandees and Southwarkians'.[41] An illustration in *The Graphic* captured the idealised community life that reformers hoped the setting would encourage: children play, families rest on park benches, a sprightly gardener tends the newly planted shrubs.[42]

Inside the hall visitors encountered a series of life-sized frescoes on plaster, paid for by public subscriptions after another appeal in *The Times*. These were executed by the Kyrle Society after designs by Walter Crane, and commemorated the 'Heroic Deeds of the Poor', such as Alice Ayres, a young nurse who died in a Gravel Lane fire in 1885 while saving three children in her care. The panels foreshadowed the ceramic plaques designed and installed by the eminent artist G. F. Watts at Postman's Park beside St Botolphs-without-Aldersgate in 1900. These plaques were joined by another fifty up until 1930, today known collectively as the 'Watts Memorial to Heroic Self-Sacrifice'.[43] A decade and a half earlier the same aspirations supplied suitably moralising visual texts for the Red Cross Hall and cottages scheme. Contemplating the Alice Ayres panel, Emilie Barrington, an ardent supporter of the Kyrle Society and its work, captured its moralising intent exactly:

> The idea of memorialising the heroic deeds of the poor, carries us much further into the hearts of the poor than could any scheme for merely beautifying, however artistically, any of their dwellings or public rooms. It expresses, not so much the desire to give something to the poor, and share with them the delights of art and culture, as the acknowledging, by commemorating the heroism of their deeds, that we have got something from the poor which we can appreciate, and which we delight to honour.[44]

Once Red Cross Hall was built and its garden and cottages complete, we have few clues as to how its earnest moralising agenda fared in practice. Miss Hill and men like the Rev. Ingham Brooke, an associate of the Barnetts in Whitechapel, remained heavily involved, so we might assume that the original tone of moralising self-improvement continued to hold sway. At the same time, though, the promoters were keen to encourage participation from local residents. After a meeting at Red Cross Hall on 20 July 1888 Cockerell recorded 'the election of three working men on [to] the Committee of Management. Miss Hill, Miss Ironside, Miss Johnson, etc. there'.[45] A range of social events, evening lectures, dances and performances were held at the venue, all beholden to the committee over which hovered the watchful scrutiny of reformers like Brooke and Miss Hill. When Cockerell forwarded an application from a local group to conduct a dance in Red Cross Hall in its first year, for example, Octavia Hill deferred the issue to the management committee but only after passing her own verdict. 'They have the Christmas and St Patrick's Day dances', she surmised, 'and I feel as if two a year were perhaps enough. You see they sell tickets to everyone, and it is less like an annual meeting of friends than a means of raising money if it becomes frequent.'[46] From this we surmise that social events, if they were to qualify as an 'occasion' suitable for Miss Hill's philanthropic encouragement, required a certain moralising intent, with commercialism and triviality to be watchfully resisted. For his part Cockerell (as we see on pp. 256–7) hoped that the dances and musical concerts at Red Cross Hall would be lively and stimulating, but often recorded disappointment in this regard. He regretted that a musical performance there in January 1890 was 'rather a dull concert, too sacred'; later that week he was back at Red Cross Hall for a tableaux performance of *Sleeping Beauty* which also proved 'rather dull altogether, but [with] a very crowded and excitable audience of children, which needed a good deal of controlling'.[47] Beyond such fragments, sadly, few sources exist to suggest for us either the terms under which Red Cross Hall was managed, or how its facilities were used by the 'Southwarkians' themselves. We can be confident, however, that a prevailing tone of earnest moralising self-improvement remained a keynote of reformist effort there for as long as the indomitable Octavia Hill was involved.

* * *

Bermondsey was another riverside locality of South London that seized and held the attention of social workers and poverty investigators. Here in our period some 140,000 working people squeezed into around 1,500 acres of single-storied housing, tenement blocks, railways, docks, wharves, warehouses and factories. Apart from the riverside of Bermondsey Wall and Rotherhithe Street, where men queued daily in their hundreds for the scarce casual work on the docks, the street markets and tanneries, Bermondsey's major local employers were large food factories: Peek, Frean and Company made biscuits alongside Jacob's crackers, Hartley's fruit jams, Crosse and Blackwell for pickles and relishes, the Courage brewery and the Anchor butter factory. 'In no district perhaps can the prevailing industries be so readily detected by their smells as here', Booth wrote in describing the district. 'In one street straw-berry jam is borne in on you in whiffs, hot and strong; in another, raw hides and tanning; in another, glue; while in some streets the nose encounters an unhappy combination of all three'.[48] Menial, low paid and insecure work could be found sack-making, in the local leather-work shops, the tanneries and, most obnoxiously, the glue-yards. Hop-picking in Kent remained an annual relief for many: one Catholic priest in Bermondsey estimated in 1900 that fully a third of the children and adolescents and many of the adults in his congregation made this annual excursion in the warmer months.[49] But in Bermondsey work was hard, repetitive, poorly paid and unreliable. Irish dock labourers made up the most visible section of the local population, many gathering daily at local landmarks such as Nutkin's Corner on George Row in the hope of obtaining casual work. Women went to the jam factories, did charing work or sack-making, hawked goods at the market or eked out a miserable living at home pulling fur from carcasses. 'The lowest class of woman who works [locally] shells peas in the market', the Booth inquiry was told by social workers at the Women's Settlement in Nelson Square, 'above them are box makers. Girls go out to work as soon as they leave school: for the first year or two they work intermittently, but afterwards settle into regular factory work.'[50] In the opinion of local minister Thomas Richardson, 'the girls and young people generally tend to better themselves and take better positions than their parents; especially is this the case when they rub shoulders with those better off than themselves'. He gave the example of a young girl, the daughter of a doorman, who had learnt shorthand and typing and had secured a clerical position earning fifteen shillings a week.[51]

The whole panorama had for reformers a dreary and dispiriting character. 'I know no set of people in London who look quite so poor as those who do their marketing in Bermondsey New Road on Sunday morning', Charles Booth asserted in 1902. 'I know no district of equal extent so depressing to the spirit as that which lies between Long Lane and Great Dover Street'.[52] But if it was poor, Bermondsey was no social wilderness of decay and neglect. Much of the pressure for affordable housing came from extensive building work, with a new generation of larger warehouses being built, reducing the number of local dwellings and causing rents to rise. Altogether these decades saw Bermondsey's residents endure a high degree of social and spatial mobility, and rarely by choice. Railway extensions had resulted in many streets being pulled down; by 1900, one local Congregationalist minister commented ruefully that 'Bermondsey will soon become a network of railway arches'.[53] Rambling tenement blocks like Wolseley Buildings, known colloquially as 'Father Brown's buildings' after an active local Roman Catholic priest who ministered to the mainly Irish population there, evoked the changing character of the district. Evictions and re-locations were a constant feature of life in and around these tenements: 'you constantly see the piles of furniture with children crying by them or minding them', the Booth inquiry was told in January 1900. With slum clearances and rent hikes, many families were being squeezed out of the district altogether or forced into crowded accommodation. 'Nor do the [improved] dwellings afford relief as rents are high and the restrictions make them too expensive for men with large families', a local dissenting minister observed. In one of the new tenements, Hanover Dwellings, three rooms cost as much as 8/6 a week and were well beyond the stretch of those without secure employment.[54] For another Bermondsey minister, H. A. Burleigh, pastor at the Drummond Road Baptist Church, the neighbourhood was 'very depressing and is becoming poorer. Shopkeepers and working people who can afford it go to the suburbs. Young people also go, e.g. those who are in lodgings. Bermondsey has a bad name and they do not like to say that they live there.'[55]

Despite the uniform prevalence of visible poverty, general conditions of public health were considered reasonable by informed observers. Thomas Richardson at Rotherhithe put it down to the large open spaces in the district, especially the docks themselves, the river and the park.[56] Public drunkenness was rare. Burleigh had 'witnessed more drunken people on one Saturday night in Glasgow than in 8½ years in Bermondsey and their immediate neighbourhood. All the people drink but they don't get drunk', he assured the Booth inquiry, and indeed the 'only time when you see them drunk is on Bank Holiday, then you see the young fellows and girls'.[57] William Hunt, a settlement advocate with experience of Bermondsey, knew how to pique interest by confounding the slum stereotypes. The district 'was one of the most uninteresting and least known in all London', he insisted in 1900.

> Somebody has described it as a sandbank on the side of the Thames. It is a corner, on the road to nowhere, and has little within its borders to attract the curious outsider. We cannot boast even the picturesque blackguardism which has drawn so many descriptive pens and pencils to that other and better known East End on the north side of the Thames. There is plenty of ignorance, misery, and sin, but little of what the law calls crime....It is simply a closely packed gathering-ground of the hopeless, helpless, more or less honest poor; not nearly so interesting, perhaps, as a place where lawlessness abounds, but surely as deserving.[58]

* * *

These same impressions helped draw one of the most vitally energised Nonconformist ministers of the day – a man later eulogised as the most important Methodist since Wesley – to the drab streets of Bermondsey in 1891 to begin the work of spiritual and educational uplift that continued at his death nearly sixty years later. Born in Lewisham in 1854, the son of a shipowner and businessman, John Scott Lidgett (see Figure 6.2) was brought up in a devout Blackheath Methodist family in the imposing shadow of his maternal grandfather, the prominent Wesleyan educationalist John Scott.[59] Scott had been the founding principal of the Westminster Teacher Training College in 1851 to supply qualified teachers to Methodist schools, one of the first in Britain, and served twice as president of the Wesleyan Methodist Conference. He cut a tremendously imposing figure to his impressionable grandson, who remembered him 'endowed with deep devotion, great dignity of character and remarkable sagacity'.[60] Accordingly Lidgett was drawn almost inevitably to the ministry, with a strong emphasis on social welfare and popular education: the text of an 1862 address by his grandfather that he took with him through life, for example, made a strident case for working-class entitlement to a genuine liberal education. When his father's early death propelled him into employment, Lidgett spent an unrewarding two years working in a City insurance and shipping firm followed, in 1873–5, by studies at University College, London in logic and philosophy. Upon graduating he immediately joined the Wesleyan Methodist ministry, serving on circuits based in the Staffordshire pottery town of Tunstall, then at Southport, Cardiff and Wolverhampton.[61]

In September 1887 Lidgett landed in Cambridge, barrel-chested, energetic, recently married, and fired with notions of social service. He had considerable

REV. JOHN SCOTT LIDGETT M.A.
President of the Wesleyan Methodist Conference, York 1908
and Editor of "The Methodist Times."

Figure 6.2 John Scott Lidget, 1908

practical experience of educational and social work from his earlier circuit appointments, and a sharp sense of the social estrangement that typified the industrial centres of Britain. 'I had learnt much of the economic conditions which then prevailed', he later wrote in his autobiography *My Guided Life*, and had attempted

> a good deal of pioneer effort in various educational and recreative enterprises, upon which my excellent Superintendents looked askance. I had become deeply concerned about the growing separation, and the consequent estrangement, of the different social classes, which led not only to

political and economic strife, but to a class-consciousness and self-enclosed narrowness which was as gravely injurious to the more prosperous classes, to say the least of it, as it was to those whom they employed.[62]

He was encouraged to take a leading role in the university's Wesley Society by his Cambridge mentor, Dr William Moulton, a biblical scholar and head-master of the Leys School, a boarding school for boys from Methodist families where Lidgett often preached. Through the Wesley Society Lidgett had weekly contact with a brilliant group of students that included a number of wranglers, sharp intellects who had placed highly in the Mathematical Tripos, and other young scholars of theology and philosophy, the classics and natural sciences. 'I spent my Sunday evenings, after service, with these men and with a growing number of undergraduates, discussing papers on a wide number of outstanding subjects and occasionally contributing philosophical papers myself', he later remembered. 'On Monday evenings I met them for spiritual fellowship and gave them guidance and advice to the best of my power. On Fridays my wife and I entertained them in groups at my house.'[63]

Lidgett clearly relished this company, and Cambridge's atmosphere of high-minded duties and higher aspirations. *My Guided Life* dwells on one occasion, Temperance Sunday in late November 1887, when he preached to the Leys School boys and 'a fair sprinkling of undergraduates' and all his social, moral and religious concerns seemed to fall together as one grand project. Rather than decrying drunkenness as an individual moral failing as the occasion seemed to demand, his sermon discussed social fractures and environmental influences, namely 'the effect that the spiritual, intellectual and physical conditions had on those who were overcrowded in cities and the spiritual loss sustained by those out of contact with its industrial masses'.[64] Citing I Corinthians 12.26, and the phrase 'and whether one member suffereth, all the members suffer with it', Lidgett invoked Christian metaphors for community and mutual fellowship that might inspire and sustain ethical citizenship as the means to meaningful social welfare. 'Deeply moved by my subject', as he later remembered,

> I endeavoured to describe the spiritual, intellectual, and physical conditions which did so much to strengthen the temptations to intemperance in crowded cities, and dealt, in a way that has since become familiar, with the wholeness of society, and with the spiritual loss sustained by the well-to-do, educated and leisured from their failure to share their advantages and to co-operate with the industrial classes in remedying these adverse and demoralizing conditions.[65]

The 'wholeness of society', 'spiritual loss' and the need to 'share advantages': here again, we see the raw elements of social idealism manifested in plain everyday convictions. For Lidgett their implications of these convictions for his own career were clear and irresistible. In a moment of charged emotion a week later, feeling certain this clarity of insight was a divine calling, he stopped by the roadside at night when returning from a service in the village of Quy, four miles northeast of Cambridge. Looking up devoutly to a moonlit, tempestuous sky, Lidgett resolved that whatever influence he could muster would be directed 'to creating relationships of "sharing" between all classes, and by personal service, extending beyond the limits of the ordinary Church work to embrace all the interests of the community, on the part of the well-to-do, educated, and leisured'.[66] Dramatised in this way as a personal vow to God, his search for the means of social and civic redemption came to rest on the idea of a Methodist settlement in inner London. 'It seemed to me that I must endeavour to plant a colony', he recalled, 'somewhat on the lines of Toynbee Hall, in one of the poorest districts of London, to be carried on in a distinctively evangelical spirit, but with the broadest possible educational and social aims, and free from all merely sectarian or sectional ends'.[67]

This moment of psychological drama inaugurated months and years of dogged, persistent hard work. After investigating suitable neighbourhoods for his scheme and settling on Bermondsey, Lidgett raised money from Methodist schools and organisations across the country, and directed the establishment of the settlement itself. Thereafter, from the opening of the Bermondsey Settlement in early 1892, he had a base from which to project his ferocious reforming energies into South London and the larger sphere of metropolitan social work. He served as a poor-law guardian from 1892 to 1906, and was a member of the London School Board from 1897 and the London County Council's education committee for nearly a quarter-century, from 1905 to 1928. Elected to the LCC as an alderman in 1905, he soon spearheaded the Progressive Party (the municipal Liberals) in that political arena, at first informally and then as party leader from 1918–28. In Bermondsey he remained warden of the settlement until 1949, a remarkable figure, still delivering sermons and chairing committees into his nineties. When he died in June 1953, he was remembered as more than simply a great Methodist, the natural successor to Hugh Price Hughes and the 'most potent voice in the councils of his Church' for over three decades. 'He took up and carried on', the *Manchester Guardian* declared in its obituary, 'the good work begun by Hughes of breaking down the self-satisfied isolation in which the Methodism of two generations ago was so often content to live'.[68]

The reference to Hugh Price Hughes is apposite, as Lidgett stood alongside that revered exponent of 'social Christianity' as a key radical presence in late-Victorian Dissent. Historians have tried to capture the larger historical moment in which both men participated, as the pious, doctrinal Nonconformity of Hilton's 'Age of Atonement' expanded into something larger, more socially inclusive and fixed on general social welfare rather than narrow evangelism and individual salvation. 'Two changes of emphasis were fundamental for the emergence of the social Gospel', writes David Thompson. 'One was a broader concept of the State and its purposes; the other was a broader concept of the redemption wrought by Christ'.[69] 'The punitive God of old gave way for the kind father who understood and made allowances'; observes James Obelkevich. 'Christ became a Hero, Brother and Guide. Inward experience of sin and conversion faded; everyone [now] had their spark of the divine spirit'.[70] For Jeffrey Cox it was a matter of self-identification as Nonconformist communities and key thinkers came in from the margins:

> No longer sectarians on the fringes of society, Nonconformists found that sectarian theories of society no longer made sense. They were no longer withdrawn from the world, but participants in the world. Their political activities took on a religious significance, society became a kind of church, government became an agency of God's work in the world.[71]

Lidgett embodied these shifts and aspirations, both in his desire to reconfigure Christ's redemptive presence for humanity and in his convictions about the necessity for untiring political activism. As Turberfield demonstrates, Lidgett embraced the social gospel as a deep intellectual and moral commitment, one that had a systematic theological dimension. Against the traditional nonconformist view that treated Christ's death as atonement for humanity's sins to a wrathful God, radicals like Lidgett turned their attention to Christ's 'manward' relationship with humanity itself. This was a more liberal and humane emphasis 'which stressed the moral transformation the Cross produced in the individual'.[72] As Cox puts it, the progressive Nonconformist Liberals were developing a new sense of social work, using terms like '"preventative philanthropy" or "constructive philanthropy" to distinguish them from the old "merely remedial" philanthropy. This concept...fit in with the liberal Nonconformist notion that God did not work exclusively through supernatural intervention, but also through the ordinary structures of politics and philanthropy.'[73] 'If we would fill the Churches we must go outside them', Lidgett explained in an early statement of his work in Bermondsey, where he fitted actions to his words by cutting short his ordinary chapel services to deliver Sunday morning open-air lectures on religious themes in Southwark Park, followed by clubroom talks on Christian history on Sunday evenings.

> We must set forth the whole Gospel in all its spiritual and ethical splendour. And we must remember that the working people have minds, are exercised about the perplexing mysteries of the world, and must be talked to as men, not indeed controversially, but plainly, sympathetically, and with competent knowledge.[74]

In practical terms this kind of mission centred on comprehensive, co-ordinated social work. In a Sunday afternoon lecture in early 1897 at the Bermondsey Town Hall on the shortcomings of religious work in the neighbourhood, Lidgett dwelt on the lack of co-ordination between church bodies and agencies, the introspection and complacency that often marked missionary endeavour, and the need for personal energy. But the real essence, he emphasised was 'a broader and bolder philanthropy', one that involved social conciliation and the overcoming of narrow selfish interests. 'In this matter of philanthropy', he declared,

> a heavy weight of responsibility rested with those leisured dwellers in pleasant surroundings, whose lives were spent entirely on themselves. They needed a new crusade, which would bring young ladies from their tennis and their dances to help the children of the slums, and the factory girls, who after the long hours of fatiguing work had no resource except in the rebound to the rowdyism of the streets. They needed men who would devote themselves to the service of workers bowed down by casual labour, by narrow wages, and depressing conditions of life.[75]

* * *

What attracted him to Bermondsey in particular, and what did he hope to achieve there? In Lidgett's account, he and Moulton – president of the Wesleyan Conference at this time, and a vocal advocate for the scheme among influential Methodists – cast about for an impoverished London district beyond the reach of existing social agencies. Bermondsey was poor but not utterly destitute, lacking the kind of sensational poverty, criminality and public misery that drew attention to neighbourhoods like Whitechapel and Southwark. For Lidgett and his co-workers, Bermondsey suffered a drab industrialism, an everyday tedium and alienation, where ordinary lives were asphyxiated by dreary work routines lacking any inspiration or stimulation. 'The evidence went to show', he later remembered, 'that Bermondsey was almost unhelped at that time by personal service from outside. 'Here in south-east London', wrote a young man, "we have nothing between heaven and hell, the church and the public-house".'[76] This was precisely the kind of district he was after, the very image of a socially 'outcast' neighbourhood and population, sorely lacking what Barnett and Maurice called 'the means of life' rather than 'the means of livelihood'. 'Here is a great population of artisans and labourers', Lidgett appealed to fellow-Methodists, 'with scantier religious accommodation than any other part of London, and similarly behind-hand in all philanthropic and educational work'.[77] A sense of Bermondsey's 'emptiness' as far as cultural and educational amenities were concerned energised his moralising, improving mission to the district. 'The dullness of South London life is a deadly spiritual foe', he declaimed in the settlement's second report in 1893.

> How sadly wanting in imagination, in energy, in enjoyment, of life, in power victoriously to face new conditions, our Londoner becomes after a few years' work under our present industrial and social conditions! Our task is to back the man against the machine in all who come to us.[78]

Similar statements of purpose in the settlement's early reports show how Lidgett's whole enterprise was grounded in an urban imagination, a disquiet at the *anomie* and alienation evident in impoverished city neighbourhoods, rather than any sensationalised crisis of personal misery and vice. Lidgett put it plainly in his third report: 'All that we are, for the present, striving for is that poorer London should come to have the same advantages as provincial towns of moderate size', he wrote. He conjured a vision of a more harmonious and integrated urban community, where amenities and opportunities might be more widely shared. In these towns, he wrote, 'wealth and poverty are neighbours' to mutual benefit. 'Institutions – educational, medical, charitable – spring up from the generosity of wealthy and enlightened citizens. Generation after generation, their families contribute to the administration of public affairs and philanthropic undertakings which only education, leisure, riches and highly-trained Christian character can give. And hence the solidarity, the *esprit de corps*, the local pride which such towns display.' This pointed to the fatal flaw of metropolitan life:

> How different is South London, with its churches starved because members and money have removed, almost entirely unblessed by the benefactions of the rich, with scarcely any young people, of education and leisure, to minister to the people...and yet what multitudes there are around us in the prosperous suburbs, who could change all this were but their hearts moved by a generous enthusiasm for God and the people!...To us who live down here and see the multitudes of helpless poor along the river-side, and know how much a handful of devoted men and women could effect, the wish becomes habitual that we could make our young and privileged friends come and see these things for themselves, for then surely they would say, 'Here am I, send me!'[79]

These ideas – widely shared in the reformist 'moral imagination' and far from idiosyncratic – remained integral to the Bermondsey Settlement enterprise, just as they had helped spur comparable work in the East End discussed above. As Lidgett explained to a meeting there nearly twenty years later, reflecting on the settlement's origins, Bermondsey's needs 'could not be dealt with by indiscriminate charity, not by the purely religious work of churches and mission halls'. A larger and more generous social impulse was needed, as 'those more richly endowed both as regards mental qualities and fortune, and, at the same time, imbued with the Christian principle of self-sacrifice, should come back and live among the poor, to help them in every possible way to realise that they were not forgotten by those more richly dowered with fortune'.[80]

Lidgett's new settlement in Bermondsey was directly modelled on Barnett's Whitechapel experiment, and when the local newspaper described how 'the building will include an institute, containing lecture hall, library, and gymnasium, a residence for about 20 men, and a warden's house', it was describing a type of residential community for social workers that was now becoming familiar to the public.[81] He and Barnett both looked with dismay on drab city streets filled with toiling industrial workers and disadvantaged families, and hoped to redeem them as harmonious communities through local leadership, improving influences and encouragements to citizenship. It was possible for Lidgett – as it had not been for Toynbee Hall's sponsors seven years earlier, or the group that founded Oxford House in Bethnal Green – to propose a 'settlement', a centre for civic community, popular education and social work in Bermondsey in terms that were familiar enough to rouse potential supporters. But if the model essentially replicated Toynbee Hall, it needed to be executed from scratch, as there was no parish machinery or local institutions for Lidgett to work with in Bermondsey as had been the case with the Universities' Settlement Association, or an existing charitable trust as had been the case in Mile End with the People's Palace. As he later recalled, the 'main object of the Settlement was to bring a force of educated workers to give help to all the higher interests of the neighbourhood, religious, educational, social and administrative', a scheme that, by his own admission 'had to be plunged complete on the neighbourhood instead of springing from small beginnings'.[82]

In early 1889 he aired his proposal to meetings of the university Wesley Societies at Oxford and Cambridge on successive nights, and enthusiastic resolutions of support were passed. Other meetings at the universities of London and Edinburgh followed, and once it had been endorsed by the Wesleyan Methodist Conference that year the serious business of fundraising began. 'I often felt like a mendicant', Lidgett remembered, 'hawking his patent in the hope of its being eventually taken up'.[83] Funds were raised by appeals to philanthropic trusts and Methodist schools around the country, and a guarantee fund of £500 per year established, towards a total figure of around £14,000 for the settlement buildings and establishment costs. A site in Farncombe Street, running off the main Jamaica Road, was secured and with half the funds raised a design was commissioned from Elijah Hoole, the architect of choice for the settlement movement given his work at Toynbee Hall.

When the foundation stone was laid in July 1891 – Farncombe Street gaily decorated with bunting and colourful quilts, filled with people and a military band, and graced with worthies including the Lord Mayor in regalia attended by his sword and mace bearers, parliamentarians and other luminaries – Lidgett seized his chance to reiterate the primary ambitions of his scheme. He offered a vision of their liberal and progressive local educational centre, dedicated to self-culture through university extension courses and popular lectures, 'choral and orchestral societies, and classes in various branches of science, literature, and art. All these classes will be open, unless the contrary is stated, to both sexes....The fees for membership will be low, so that there may be no financial difficulty in the way of those who seek our help.'[84] Some bible classes and devotional gatherings were envisaged, but 'secular' education, recreation and sociability supplied the fundamental tone for the improving activities of the new settlement. Reading circles in science, history and literature would be formed, 'so that a taste for home reading may be developed', alongside a host of other improving measures and opportunities. 'Those who join any of our classes and societies will have the right to use our library and gymnasium', Lidgett assured his listeners crowded into the street as he enlarged his vision of civic and social integration,

> and to become members of the athletic clubs and recreative societies which we purpose [*sic*] to organize. We hope to arrange conferences from time to time for the discussion of subjects of social, economic, educational, moral, and spiritual importance. We shall also endeavour to bring together exhibitions of works of art and other objects of interest. Our workers desire to take such part as may be permitted in the general philanthropic and administrative work of the neighbourhood. Once more we wish it to be known that we shall always be glad to welcome in our buildings, so far as possible, any charitable or trade societies desiring accommodation.[85]

As building continued for the rest of the year he was busy raising funds, recruiting residents and enlisting partners such as the London Society for the Extension of University Teaching, the Recreative Schools Association and the Home Reading Union for the new settlement's activities. By late 1891 the tall, red-brick settlement building was finished (see Figure 6.3), and was declared open by Sir John Lubbock amid a chilly crowd of well-wishers on 6 January. Hailed as 'practically another Toynbee Hall', the fledgling settlement was welcomed by the *University Extension Journal* as a new centre of extension teaching in South London, starting with a course on 'The Chemistry of

BERMONDSEY SETTLEMENT.

Figure 6.3 Bermondsey Settlement, 1895

Everyday Life, illustrated by experiments' by Professor Lewes and a Saturday evening lecture on Shakespeare's *Macbeth*.[86]

* * *

Among the settlement's first group of residents in 1892–3 were 'university men' like T. T. Brunyate and T. P. Kent, graduates of Christ Church, Oxford, and Henry Mundahl who had read mathematics at St John's College, Cambridge before going to the bar. G. M. Hanks had attended Sidney College, Cambridge and J. B. Ronald was an Edinburgh graduate. Their co-residents T. E. Webb, J. M. Rippon, J. E. Heath, Oswald Passmore and E. E. Roberts, however, did not advertise a university affiliation. Dormitory accommodation was available with meals for 21 shillings a week; men in shared rooms paid three shillings more and others could opt for private rooms of their own.[87] It was altogether more frugal and restrained than Barnett's showier settlement across in Whitechapel. As to their daily duties, the brief career of Oswald Passmore, who spent two years at the settlement before an untimely death in September 1894, captures the range of work undertaken by residents. A Sunday School teacher, Passmore also contributed as an officer of the settlement's company of the Boys' Brigade, conducting drill and church parades, organising football matches and swimming competitions. He was clerk of the settlement's Parliamentary Debating Society, organised entertainments for students and helped with the St George's Social Club.[88] Other residents worked as managers for the London School Board (eight filling this role in 1893), having oversight of school governance and appointments to teaching positions.[89] Others like Brunyate used their expertise to supply free legal advice to local cases, and virtually all of them taught classes, supervised clubs and hosted social events. 'In social work', one of the settlement workers wrote in 1898, 'the Warden...leads the way as a member of the London School Board and guardian of the poor for St Olave's Union, and the rest of us follow according to our several vocations as guardians, school managers, Girls' Club and Guild of Play organisers, workhouse visitors, and so forth'.[90] Other volunteers and settlement workers came for perhaps a day or an evening per week; one estimate in 1895 put this number at around fifty.[91]

But the Bermondsey work was far from an entirely masculine affair. In an early sign of things to come, a cadre of women workers had taken up lodgings and started work even before the Settlement's official opening ceremony. In this way women made an essential and esteemed contribution to the Settlement's work from the outset. The first of the women's settlements had appeared earlier with the Women's University Settlement in Southwark in 1887, followed in the 1890s by the 'Time and Talents' settlement in Bermondsey and the Lady Margaret Hall Settlement in Lambeth.[92] If the first two university settlements in Whitechapel and Bethnal Green were in a sense professionalising incursions by male graduates into the female-dominated world of parish meetings, home visiting, rent collecting, nursing, school-teaching and general poor relief, Lidgett's new centre helped correct the balance by valuing the professional contribution of female social workers in an entirely public way.

Permanent lodgings for the female residents were established at 149 Lower Road, Rotherhithe, about a mile east of Farncombe Street. This was occupied in November 1891 with the rental and furnishings supplied by an external supporter, a Miss Barlow, of Edgeworth near Bolton in Lancashire. The 'Women's House' of the settlement, as it became known, filled a large terraced house facing Southwark Park and the local dockyards 'with their piles of Norway timber and the tall masts that bring visions of far away lands, to look out upon behind'.[93] In the first year it was led by Shirley Richardson, who resigned due to family troubles and was succeeded in late 1892 by the highly capable Mary Simmons. During the 1890s around eight to ten women typically lived at the Rotherhithe house at any one time, the earliest recorded residents being Miss Thompson, who took on COS casework, and a Miss Adelaide Richardson. They were joined by a Miss Wratten, a graduate of the Jubilee Institute for Nurses whose work in 1892–3 as the only trained nurse in Rotherhithe was supported by donations from girls' schools, fund-raising and charity sales of second-hand clothing. These permitted her to handle around 150 local cases, consisting of more than 2,000 visits per year, as well as offering a course in home nursing among the settlement's evening classes. In this way the nurse's presence was as much a question of moral and educational influence as it was simply medical: 'it is not only in the direct saving of life and health that the nurse's work tells'; Mary Simmons wrote in 1897, 'its general influence on the side of household sanitation, of cleanliness, and of a higher moral tone is considerable'.[94]

Significantly, the Rotherhithe 'Women's House' was self-managed, running independently of the main Settlement Committee as an independent 'Ladies Association', but participating fully in the many activities of the settlement as a whole. There was an element of resolute self-sufficiency as these progressive women stepped up to work alongside their male colleagues. As Mary Simmons put it in 1897, 'believing as we do, that in a world composed of men and women, any advance must be most efficiently carried on by their combined powers and energies, it is a vital characteristic of our Settlement ideal, that the work should be mixed in this way'.[95] 'It is impossible to separate a statement of the doings of the Ladies Association from the general account of our progress', Lidgett agreed, 'because they have taken part in all our activities; but wherever work for women and girls is mentioned in this Report it will be understood that it is to this Association that the credit must be given'.[96] Alongside nursing, health and sanitary inspection, COS casework, visiting the elderly and infirm and running social clubs, the settlement women assisted local children through the Children's Country Holidays Fund and the Invalid Children's Aid Association. Many were teachers, by training or by inclination, and in 1896–7, for example, in addition to needlework and domestic economy, the women workers and external volunteers taught classes in drawing, woodwork, grammar and literature, modern and classical languages, arithmetic and algebra.[97] The classwork had a social dimension, as when the settlement women hosted meetings of the Southwark Pupil Teachers Association for young female teachers employed by the London School Board, bringing some fifty to Farncombe Street for gymnastics on Saturdays followed by afternoon tea. 'Those who appreciate the immense responsibilities, not only intellectual but moral, which await these young people will feel how important it is to strengthen the elevating personal influences which should mould the life and character of elementary teachers', Lidgett commented shortly after this work began.[98]

With the Rotherhithe accommodation fully occupied, the settlement's female workers soon overflowed into various addresses in the neighbourhood. One was begun by Ethel Emuss and another worker on the corner of Farncombe Street and Jamaica Road, and two others took up a three-roomed flat in the Russell-Scott Buildings, a block of charitable dwellings near Mill Pond Bridge, in December 1895. One of these, Grace Hannam, was a remarkable woman blessed with a magnetic personality, energy and great self-conviction. Originally from Lewes in Sussex, Hannam had been a Wesleyan sister at Hugh Price Hughes' West London Methodist Mission, theologically conservative but socially radical in its urgent, evangelising response to metropolitan poverty. There in 1894 she had founded what became the 'Guild of the Brave Poor Things' for local disabled children and the elderly, many of them from impoverished families or experiencing social isolation. To begin with, as Koven observes, the Guild 'merely provided a weekly venue…for farthing teas, games, and fanciful costumes, but it launched Sister Grace's career as one of the most innovative and forceful advocates for the disabled in twentieth-century Britain'.[99] Bringing her energies to Lidgett's settlement in Bermondsey from late 1895 until 1902, Hannam styled herself the 'Children's Resident' and (as we see on pp. 225–8) expanded this work alongside a 'Guild of Play' for able-bodied children. She later returned to Sussex to establish the Chailey Heritage Craft School and Hospital, a pioneering welfare and support centre that taught disabled children craft skills, sewing and domestic economy.

* * *

Despite the ardent Christianity of many of its residents, the Bermondsey Settlement was not a centre of direct religious instruction or worship and shared little with conventional missions. Its first annual reports described some evangelical work at neighbouring chapels through services and Sunday School classes, but proselytizing the poor through preaching and doctrine was never a feature of its everyday activities. Even if the first of its published aims announced a general desire 'to bring additional force and attractiveness to Christian work', in truth this was a way of encapsulating the motives of the residents and supporters, rather than capturing their explicit objectives. Lidgett had spoken directly to this issue at the foundation stone ceremony:

The reasons which have led us to build this institute and house are not sectarian. We are urged by Christian motives to do what in us lies to bring together classes too much separated by distance, by apparently conflicting interests, and by misunderstanding; to promote a fuller co-operation of all those who care for the condition of the people; to pro-claim the duty which all privileges impose on those who enjoy them to serve the common weal, and to help those who are gaining the blessings of shorter hours of toil and better wages to obtain a growing share in the highest goods of life. For us everything that tends to perfect the spiritual, mental, and physical powers of men and women, and to bring about improved social relationships, is a good in itself, and part of the redeem-ing will of God.[100]

Importantly, the purpose-built settlement did not have a chapel of its own, Lidgett choosing instead to deliver sermons and conduct services each week at the nearby Silver Street and Southwark Park chapels, both at arm's length from the main building. He could not be faulted for want of missionary zeal, in other words, but the separation meant that the settlement's work had a Christian but deliberately non-sectarian and non-missionary character. 'There is no very intimate connexion between the Chapels and the Settlement', Ernest Aves concluded after visiting Lidgett's pastor, R. T. Ritson, at the Silver Street and Southwark Park chapels in early 1900, 'in spite of the dual position held by Mr Lidgett'. Ritson himself felt that the Settlement did not contribute very much, and certainly less than he hoped for, to his mission work at the two chapels. 'For the most part Religion is kept outside of the Settlement work', Aves concluded, 'and if it were obtruded [Ritson thought] that a large proportion of the people who use the settlement would leave it. There appears to be a certain incompatibility between denominational and settlement work.'[101]

When discussing the inter-connections of the social and religious work at the Bermondsey Settlement, therefore, Lidgett maintained the same delicate balance that faced Samuel and Henrietta Barnett in Whitechapel. He never doubted the settlement's religious character for an instant, but always insisted that its objectives were holistic and social even if tied up with individual moral amelioration. His first report on their evangelistic work in Bermondsey, for example, struck a cautious note: 'Much may be done by the efforts of popular evangelism', he allowed, in deference to the conventional expecta-tions of many of his donors. 'But they must be aided by a large and generous plan of social action for the improvement of the material, intellectual and moral condition of the people.'[102] His eyes were fixed on these broader concerns, rather than narrower considerations of individual salvation and self-help. 'The cause of personal redemption in all its aspects – religious, moral, educational' was how he typically encapsulated the settlement's objects to the press.[103] The last of the settlement's 'general aims' at its commencement in 1892, which insisted that through all aspects of its work 'it shall be perfectly clear that no mere sectarian advantage is sought, but that it shall be possible for all good men to associate themselves with our work', exposed the settlement to criticism from more evangelically minded Nonconformists.[104] Neighbours like the Free Church minister Pastor Thomas Richardson preferred to consider it as primarily an educational centre: even if it taught bible classes, he did not consider it a centre of 'Aggressive Unsectarian Christian Work', the terms in which he promoted his own mission services in Rotherhithe.[105] In response, Lidgett could only insist (as he did in the settlement's first report) that 'our whole aim is profoundly Christian', in language that captured the doctrinal essence of the late-century 'social Gospel'. 'Our guiding principle is, that everything is sacred which tends to the perfecting of any faculty implanted by God', he maintained, 'to the more efficient performance of daily duty, to the deepening of reverent interest in the world in which God has placed us, and especially to the promotion of those relationships which should exist between all those who have been redeemed as Sons of one Heavenly Father.'[106]

This Maurician 'Immanence' theology gave him one corner to fight from, but a characteristically late-Victorian urban imagination provided him with another. These relationships and the difficulties raised by their absence had particular resonance in the arid tedium of everyday Bermondsey, where like other liberal reformers he was convinced civic integration and citizenly participation were essential first steps to social welfare. 'The pulse of common life has but a feeble throb in London, the civic and social spirit is greatly wanting, and thereby the dullness and monotony of our lives, and the dreariness of our surroundings are much increased', he wrote in the settlement magazine in 1895.

> The ideal of the Settlement is to challenge especially the younger men and women of Bermondsey and Rotherhithe to change all this; as they may do by the intelligent and brotherly use of their narrow leisure, and by the formation of friendly associations in study, recreation and public duty. These will by and bye [*sic*] help to raise the standard of public life, and to improve the means for common action to secure that larger light, liberty and co-operation, for which the best among us are looking as the remedy, with God's blessing, for the evils which afflict both individuals and the general life in crowded neighbourhoods like this.[107]

The themes of social conciliation to heal a fractured city, joined with moralising uplift for its working population – the innate social idealism that animated Toynbee Hall and the People's Palace – were thus equally present in Lidgett's Bermondsey labours, plainly codified in the settlement's published aspiration 'to become a centre of social life, where all classes may meet together on equal terms for healthful intercourse and recreation'.[108] Moral amelioration through culture and civic association were intrinsic to this goal, assisted by 'facilities for the study of Literature, History, Science and Art', and a desire 'to bring men together to discuss general and special social evils and to seek for their remedy'. 'We need to arouse the sense of social duty, the civic spirit', Lidgett urged readers of his second annual report in 1893, 'the will to co-operate with unselfish bent for the common good'.[109] 'It is of the highest importance that this spirit of co-operation and mutual service shall be felt in every class and society of the Settlement', he urged elsewhere in repeating his sense of their ultimate purpose.

> All students should feel that they belong to the Settlement, and in a cer-
> tain sense that the Settlement belongs to them. They should recognise a
> personal responsibility for making it as social and helpful a place as it
> can possibly be. We should try to make every student feel at home; every
> student should be on the look out to make acquaintance with others and
> gradually form friendships thereby; and every student should seek to
> develop the social side of our work with intent....Chess, bicycling, the
> gymnasium, the friendly concert in which all take part, are [all] means of
> strengthening the social spirit.[110]

The moralising work of the settlement aimed to strengthen this spirit among students and local residents through participation, mutuality and fellowship. A pithy motto, 'One and All' was adopted as its stated ideal of 'social union and social service' echoed through all its activities. When the first issue of the *Monthly Record* appeared in early 1895, for example, Lidgett saw the magazine as 'a bond of fellowship, and a means of intercourse, between us all. Those who seldom meet may speak to one another through its columns, and feel that they belong to one body, having common ideals and aims.'[111]

* * *

In practice, these liberal ideals were given credible substance in the settlement's educational work. It combined the polytechnic and university extension models for technical and adult education, conceived in fact as 'a connecting link between the Goldsmiths' Institute at New Cross and the Polytechnic in the Borough Road' during the fund-raising effort.[112] Students paid a membership fee of a shilling per term, or 2/6 for the year, permitting them to use its library and join its social clubs. They were then charged a shilling for their first enrolment and a reduced rate of sixpence for any additional courses taken. Some were individual classes, while the major courses could be taken towards a larger programme of study. In the first full year, 1892–3, some 800 students enrolled in nearly fifty separate courses of study at the settlement's 'Working Men and Women's College', ranging from 174 in the large university extension course on 'Physiology and its application to Hygiene' offered by Dr Haycraft, to very small groups of four to six students in fields such as biology, mechanics, principles of sound, light and heat, and political economy. Commercial courses in book-keeping, shorthand and typewriting were also popular, attracting around 220 enrolments altogether in the first year, as were practical courses in cookery, dressmaking, ambulance and home nursing.

It is unclear whether it was the course content, the skills of the lecturer, or the intrinsic lustre of extension classes that attracted students to the physiology class, but the success of Dr Haycraft's initial course was a hearty local endorsement of the LSEUT teaching programme, and inaugurated a close relationship between Bermondsey and the university extension movement during the 1890s. One of the first settlement residents, the lawyer Henry Mundahl, was later distinguished as the country's leading extension lecturer on political economy, and the author of the major syllabus on that subject.[113] In time, though, the relationship with university extension was best exemplified by Dr Charles Kimmins, who took up residence in late 1894 just as he was appointed secretary of the LSEUT.[114] Kimmins was an experienced extension lecturer for the Cambridge syndicate, with particular success over several years training teachers in Norfolk, and a popular lecturer on scientific topics. An entertaining public speaker, Kimmins delivered a series of stirring free lectures with practical experiments and demonstrations on light, fire and colour in Bermondsey Town Hall in January 1895, culminating in the dazzling appearance of Lidgett's ten-year old son on the stage, bathed in rainbow light 'like another Joseph' with the help of a spectroscope.[115] Kimmins settled into his work in Bermondsey with equal aplomb, teaching classes, serving on committees and running clubs. An avid music-lover and frustrated violinist, he helped organise a minstrel troupe and could be relied upon to sing popular songs at settlement gatherings. Developing the interests in education and child psychology for which he was later noted, Kimmins met Grace Hannam when helping manage her Guild of Play, and the two married in 1898.

The Bermondsey classes were not all popular spectacle and practical skills, however. Language classes were well supported by enrolments, with over 100 students studying advanced and introductory French, but there was lower demand for History, Latin, Shakespeare and Church History. Nevertheless, as Lidgett commented in his second annual report, the list of courses 'shows that we are striving after greater completeness in the courses open to our students, and are giving prominence to liberal culture side by side with "bread and butter" subjects'.[116] Two years later more than fifty separate classes were still being offered weekly in the Settlement during term time, the majority run by volunteers and in small class groups, something that was extolled as essential to the intimate, humane and personal character of the Settlement itself. 'It is, in its way, equally pleasing to find one pupil in a Resident's private room being coached in some special subject as it is to go into a crowded class-room'; Lidgett wrote, 'for it shows that we are carrying out our ideal of being a colony of friendly men and women, who will count no trouble too great to help anyone upward in the path of knowledge and higher life'. But he admitted 'a thrill of no small pleasure' as he surveyed the range of lectures, classes and other improving activities offered on a typical evening, from an Athletic Club practising gymnastic exercises in our fine Gymnasium to the Lecture Hall, where our Musical Society is rehearsing an Oratorio, and thence to a crowded Shorthand Class, on to a large Physiology Class taught by a Cambridge graduate, to rooms occupied for Shakespeare or Arithmetic or Grammar, ending with our busy Workshop, where Wood-carving is going on, and reflect[ing] that, shorthand, arithmetic and grammar being left out, none of these people could have these advantages were it not for the Settlement.[117]

Thus the formal classes of the settlement, held at Farncombe Street or at the Bermondsey Town Hall for the more popular lectures, aimed to supply something more than plain educational instruction. As was the case at Toynbee Hall and other settlements, a moralising aspiration towards personal connection and social conciliation was paramount. As Lidgett explained it, 'the fact that so much of our teaching is voluntary and is given by those who, on the highest grounds, are anxious to share the advantages of their own knowledge with others, tends to impart a human interest and sympathy to the work which it otherwise could not have'.[118]

Outside these classes, a host of activities were launched on a more sociable and fraternal basis, part of the settlement's effort 'to lift the students above the monotony and drudgery of their life by giving them the opportunity for wider culture, for healthy recreation, and for social intercourse'.[119] The end result was a barrage of reforming, moralising, refining and improving educational influences, in clubs, classes, concerts and social gatherings. Music, literature and the arts were all prominent. 'I notice that in language and literature alone there are fifteen different classes during the week'; one visitor wrote in 1898,

> while in the musical section, besides the choral society, orchestra, lectures on music, sight singing and solo singing, there are lessons on the violin, viola, 'cello, flute, clarionet, cornet and mandoline; and if any of my readers happen to be able to play the dulcimer, the sacbut, or the psaltery, I would counsel them to keep it secret, or Mr. Lidgett will very surely impress them to come and teach at the Bermondsey Settlement.[120]

The settlement's musical clubs and ensembles thrived under the directorship of John Borland, with the Choral Society maintaining a membership around 100 strong, and the Popular Musical Society offering violin classes at the settlement that attracted around 80 students. Together with the settlement's orchestra these musicians had performed their first major piece, Handel's *Judas Maccabaeus*, at the Bermondsey Town Hall in April 1892.

These large collective efforts were important, because reformers insisted that the cultural and social opportunities on offer at the Settlement were not to be isolated or solitary activities. As we see on pp. 221–5, virtually every aspect of the settlement's work generated a social club, foremost among them the St George's Social Club established in a former public house on West Lane, a narrow street running down to the river's edge at Cherry Garden Stairs, in 1894. For Lidgett it was 'the working-man's drawing room, the place where he meets his friend and can enjoy social intercourse and recreation. Its general condition will be an index to the moral and intellectual tone of its members, just as other people's drawing-rooms are.'[121] A Working Girls' Club had begun earlier, in October 1893, meeting three times a week under the direction of Mary Simmons and Miss Barrs. It attracted around sixty young women employed locally in various trades who paid a penny each per month as a membership fee.

* * *

This progressive social idealism sustained Lidgett and a succession of co-workers for decades, well beyond the active lifetime of the other centres of late-Victorian cultural philanthropy we have encountered. Constant donations were needed to offset an annual debt on operating costs that within a few years was running at around a £115 shortfall, a figure that had tripled by early 1896.[122] Some annual grants were received around the turn of the century from the City Parochial Foundation, but when recurrent funds were sought from the London County Council in early 1907 the normal annual deficit for the settlement, after taking into account the income received from students' fees, was still estimated at between £300 and £500.[123] A meeting in November the following year to resolve the debt problem was told that the settlement owed some £3,650 including a capital account debt of £2,500 and £300 arising from the ongoing expenses of the Women's House.[124] Voluntary donations to a commemorative fund to retire the debt were forthcoming, but the longer-term problem of managing its parlous finances continued all the way through to the end of Lidgett's term in 1949. The building continued to be used as a rest and respite centre during the Second World War despite bomb damage, teaching local children as an impromptu day school when the local schools were flattened in September 1940. With Lidgett's departure the tone of Methodist social work in Bermondsey inevitably changed, leading to the eventual closure and demolition of the settlement in 1968.

Lidgett was convinced that his settlement offered a sense of membership to students and visitors that would in turn impart social and civic cohesion to the local neighbourhood. 'We are teaching many to improve their gifts and then to use them for others', he wrote on this theme in the settlement's second report.

> Thus they are finding a higher temper and a wider range of interests. For the young artisan, shop assistant, or clerk, to be called upon to assist in establishing University Extension Lectures, or in providing good music for his neighbours, to make a parish see how important it is that women should act as guardians of the poor, to enforce sanitary interests…what is this but to supply a liberal education in the practical duties of a Christian citizen? This is the supreme end of our educational work.[125]

But for all its Methodist affiliations and earnest endeavours, the Bermondsey Settlement in the 1890s was nevertheless a lively and high-spirited place, whether at gatherings of the Guild of Play or the recitals and band practices, evening classes with magic lantern illumination and extemporised, often highly anecdotal lectures. When we read of an impromptu cricket match in the lecture hall, involving the warden and one of the residents, played with a ball of wool and a poker from the fireplace as other volunteers were counting the takings from a jumble sale to aid the Nursing Fund in January 1897, we catch a sense of the good humour that infused their outwardly earnest social work.[126]

Such glimpses of informal moments at these centres of moralising social work are rare but illuminating. In the chapters that follow, which treat our 'centres of light' as a group, we cross the threshold and peer inside to the extent that our sources allow, in order to investigate the places and spaces reformers created within, the audiences they were able to attract, and the occasions and encounters they hosted.

Notes

1   J. Seed, '"Secular" and "Religious": Historical Perspectives' *Social History* 39:1 (2014), p. 10.
2   See A. Geddes Poole, *Philanthropy and the Construction of Victorian Women's Citizenship: Lady Frederick Cavendish and Miss Emma Cons* (Toronto: University of Toronto Press, 2014), chapter 3.
3   See 'The Royal Victoria Hall – "The Old Vic"' *Survey of London* (Vol. 23: Lambeth: South Bank and Vauxhall) (London: London County Council, 1951), pp. 37–9.
4   'The Royal Victoria Hall' *Charity Organisation Review* 2 (November 1886), p. 400. See *The Graphic* 20 August 1881, p. 196.
5   See the British Library's Henry Evans collection of theatrical ephemera: 'Evanion Catalogue' [http://www.bl.uk/catalogues/evanion/About.aspx, accessed 30 July 2015].
6   'The Royal Victoria Hall: its work and its want' *Charity Organisation Review* 2:21 (September 1886), p. 318. 'The "Victoria", New Cut' [correspondence], *The Spectator* 19 May 1888, p. 684.
7   'The "Victoria," New Cut', *The Spectator* 19 May 1888, p. 685.
8   N. Hellis, 'The Royal Victoria Hall and Coffee Tavern' *Leisure Hour* 400 (April 1885), p. 280.
9   Hellis, 'The Royal Victoria Hall', p. 280.
10 C. Booth, *Life and Labour of the People in London: Third Series: Religious Influences* (Vol. 4: Inner South London) (London: Macmillan, 1902), p. 27. See Geddes Poole, *Philanthropy and the Construction of Victorian Women's Citizenship*, chapter 5 and the Morley College 125th anniversary history, published in 2015.
11 J. Cox, *The English Churches in a Secular Society: Lambeth, 1870–1930* (Oxford: Oxford University Press, 1982), p. 88.
12 Cox notes St Winifred's briefly in *The English Churches in a Secular Society*, p. 88.
13 H. F. Morriss, *The Story of a Mission by Its Founder* (London, n. d. [c.1898]), p. 2.
14 *Southwark Recorder* 4 July 1896, extracted in Morriss, *The Story of a Mission*, p. 14.
15 *Southwark Recorder* 4 July 1896.
16 BLPES: Booth Collection, B280, interview with Henry Fuller Morriss, 3 February 1900, f. 201.

17 See S. Koven, *Slumming: Sexual and Social Politics in Victorian London* (Princeton: Princeton University Press, 2004), especially chapter 1, pp. 1–22.

18 H. McLeod, *Class and Religion in the Late Victorian City* (London: Croom Helm, 1974), p. 6.

19 Cited in N. Draper, '"Across the Bridges": Representations of Victorian South London', *London Journal* 29:1 (2004), p. 31.

20 'Introduction' to Southwark Diocese and South London Church Fund, *The Diocese of Southwark, being a Short Account of the History, Character and Needs of South London and other Parts of the Diocese* (London, 1906) cited in Draper, 'Across the Bridges', p. 38.

21 O. Hill, *Letter to My Fellow-Workers* (pamphlet) (London, 1877), p. 10.

22 C. Booth, *Life and Labour of the People in London: Third Series: Religious Influences* (Vol. 4: Inner South London), pp. 4–7.

23 BLPES: Booth Collection, B/363, f. 151.

24 BLPES: Booth Collection, B/363, f. 133, f. 140.

25 BLPES: Booth Collection, B/363, f. 213.

26 BLPES: Booth Collection, B/363, ff. 145–7.

27 C. Booth, *Life and Labour of the People in London: Third Series: Religious Influences* (Vol. 4: Inner South London), p. 8.

28 O. Hill, *Letter to My Fellow-Workers* (pamphlet) (London, 1886), p. 7.

29 O. Hill, *Letter to My Fellow-Workers* (1886), p. 8.

30 O. Hill, 'Public Garden and Hall for Southwark' *The Times* 14 March 1887, p. 7.

31 WAC: Octavia Hill Papers, D. Misc. 84/2, f. 2.

32 BL: Cockerell Papers, Add. Mss. 52624, f. 35, diary entry of 24 March 1887. See also E. M. Bell, *Octavia Hill* (London: Constable, 1942), p. 120.

33 O. Hill, *Letter to My Fellow-Workers* (pamphlet) (London, 1887), p. 4.

34 W. T. Hill, *Octavia Hill: Pioneer of the National Trust and Housing Reformer* (London: Hutchinson, 1956), p. 121; C. Booth, *Life and Labour of the People in London: Third Series: Religious Influences* (Vol. 4: Inner South London), p. 27.

35 J. Price, *Everyday Heroism: Victorian Constructions of the Heroic Civilian* (London: Bloomsbury, 2014), p. 67.

36 Bell, *Octavia Hill*, p. 121.

37 Bell, *Octavia Hill*, p. 121.

38 Bell, *Octavia Hill*, p. 122.

39 [E. Barrington], 'The Red Cross Hall' *English Illustrated Magazine* 117 (June 1893), p. 611.

40 O. Hill, *Letter to My Fellow-Workers* (pamphlet) (London, 1888), pp. 5–6.

41 BL: Cockerell Papers, Add. Mss. 52625, f. 40, diary entry of 2 June 1888.

42 *The Graphic*, 30 June 1888.

43 See J. Price, *Heroes of Postman's Park: Heroic Self-Sacrifice in Victorian London* (London: History Press, 2015).

44 [Barrington], 'The Red Cross Hall', p. 616.

45 BL: Cockerell Papers, Add. Mss. 52625, f. 47, entry of 20 July 1888.

46 BL: Cockerell Papers, Add. Mss. 52722, f. 178, undated postcard.

47 BL: Cockerell Papers, Add. Mss. 52627, ff. 18–19, diary entries of 19 and 23 January 1890.

48 C. Booth, *Life and Labour of the People in London: Third Series: Religious Influences* (Vol. 4: Inner South London), pp. 120–1.

49 BLPES: Booth Collection, B280, interview with Rev. Father Murnane and others, Church of the Most Holy Trinity, Parker's Row, 22 February 1900, f. 248.

50 BLPES: Booth Collection, B/363, f. 219.

51 BLPES: Booth Collection, B280, interview with Thomas Richardson, Rotherhithe Free Church, 16 January 1900, f. 33.

52   C. Booth, *Life and Labour of the People in London: Third Series: Religious Influences* (Vol. 4: Inner South London), pp. 101–2.
53   BLPES: Booth Collection, B280, interview with Rev. H. Rosier, Jamaica Road Congregational Church, 16 February 1900, f. 151.
54   BLPES: Booth Collection, B280, interview with Pastor J. T. Figg, Abbey Street Baptist Church, January 1900, ff. 123–5.
55   BLPES: Booth Collection, B280, interview with Rev. H. A. Burleigh, Drummond Road Baptist Church, 22 February 1900, f. 171.
56   BLPES: Booth Collection, B280, interview with Thomas Richardson, Rotherhithe Free Church, 16 January 1900, f. 49.
57   BLPES: Booth Collection, B280, interview with Rev. H. A. Burleigh, Drummond Road Baptist Church, 22 February 1900, f. 179.
58   W. Hunt, 'Some Aspects of Settlement Life' *The Wesleyan-Methodist Magazine* 123 (1900), p. 678.
59   The major biography is A. Turberfield, *John Scott Lidgett: Archbishop of British Methodism?* (Peterborough: Epworth Press, 2003). See also E. Baker (ed.), *John Scott Lidgett: A Symposium* (London: Epworth Press, 1957).
60   Lidgett, *My Guided Life* (London: Methuen, 1936), cited in B. Frost, 'God Cares Also for Minds: John Scott Lidgett, the Bermondsey Settlement and Methodist Educationalists' in his *Pioneers of Social Passion: London's Cosmopolitan Methodism* (Peterborough: Epworth Press, 2006), p. 45. Lidgett is an under-researched figure in the history of Methodism and 'social Christianity' more broadly: J. T. Smith, 'Methodism and Education', in *The Ashgate Research Companion to World Methodism* (London: Ashgate, 2013), p. 417.
61   See Turberfield, *John Scott Lidgett*, chapter 1.
62   J. S. Lidgett, *My Guided Life* (London: Methuen, 1936), p. 59.
63   Lidgett, *My Guided Life*, pp. 61–2.
64   Frost, 'God Cares Also For Minds', p. 47.
65   Lidgett, *My Guided Life*, p. 62.
66   Lidgett, *My Guided Life*, p. 60.
67   Lidgett, *My Guided Life*, p. 63.
68   'Dr John Scott Lidgett', *Manchester Guardian* 18 June 1953, p. 3.
69   D. M. Thompson, 'The Nonconformist Social Gospel' in K. Robbins (ed.), *Protestant Evangelicalism: Britain, Ireland, Germany and America c.1750 – c.1950* (Oxford: Basil Blackwell, 1990), pp. 262–3.
70   J. Obelkevich, 'Religion' in F. M. L. Thompson (ed,), *The Cambridge Social History of Britain: Volume 3: Social Agencies and Institutions* (Cambridge: Cambridge University Press, 1990), pp. 334–5.
71   Cox, *The English Churches in a Secular Society*, p. 174.
72   Turberfield, *John Scott Lidgett*, p. 49.
73   Cox, *The English Churches in a Secular Society*, pp. 169–70.
74   Bermondsey Settlement, *Second Annual Report* (London 1893), p. 12. 'I did my best to make the teaching simple and popular, sympathetic and positive, but not controversial', he reported. For Lidgett's lectures see Bermondsey Settlement, *Third Annual Report* (London, 1894), pp. 15–16.
75   J. S. Lidgett, 'Religion in South East London' *Monthly Record* 3:3 (March 1897), p. 34.
76   J. S. Lidgett, *Reminiscences* (London: Epworth Press, 1928), p. 28.
77   J. S. Lidgett, 'The Proposed Settlement for Religious, Social and Educational Work in South-East London' *The Wesleyan-Methodist Magazine* 14 (January 1890), p. 75.
78   Bermondsey Settlement, *Second Annual Report*, p. 19.
79   Bermondsey Settlement, *Third Annual Report*, p. 8.
80   'Bermondsey Settlement', *South London Press* 20 November 1908.

81 'The Lord Mayor in Bermondsey' *South London Press* 18 July 1891.
82 Lidgett, *Reminiscences*, pp. 29–30.
83 Lidgett, *Reminiscences*, p. 29.
84 'The Lord Mayor in Bermondsey', *South London Press* 18 July 1891.
85 'The Lord Mayor in Bermondsey', *South London Press* 18 July 1891.
86 'Notes and News', *UEJ* 3 (15 January 1892), p. 3; 'The Bermondsey Settlement', *Southwark and Bermondsey Recorder* 14 November 1891.
87 Bermondsey Settlement, *First Annual Report* (London, 1892), p. 12.
88 Bermondsey Settlement, *Third Annual Report*, p. 10.
89 Bermondsey Settlement, *Second Annual Report*, p. 24.
90 'Mission Work at the Bermondsey Settlement' *At Home and Abroad* 11 (November 1898), p. 215.
91 T. C. Collings, 'The London Settlements: Bermondsey' *Leisure Hour* (September 1895), p. 742.
92 See K. B. Beaumont, *Women and the Settlement Movement* (London: Radcliffe Press, 1996), esp. chapters 5–7.
93 M. Simmons, *Report of the Bermondsey Settlement: Some Account of the Women's Work* (London, 1897), p. 8.
94 Simmons, *Report of the Bermondsey Settlement*, p. 31.
95 Simmons, *Report of the Bermondsey Settlement*, n. p.
96 Bermondsey Settlement, *First Annual Report*, p. 12.
97 Simmons, *Report of the Bermondsey Settlement*, p. 33.
98 Bermondsey Settlement, *Second Annual Report*, p. 21.
99 S. Koven, 'Kimmins , Dame Grace Thyrza (1870–1954)', *Oxford Dictionary of National Biography* (Oxford: Oxford University Press, 2004); online edition, May 2006 [www.oxforddnb.com//view/article/34315, accessed 13 January 2016]. See also Kimmins' obituary, *The Times* 4 March 1954, p. 10.
100 'The Lord Mayor in Bermondsey' *South London Press* 18 July 1891.
101 BLPES: Booth Collection, B280, interview with T. N. Ritson of the Bermondsey Settlement Circuit, 17 January 1900, ff. 89–91.
102 Bermondsey Settlement, *First Annual Report*, p. 11.
103 'Women's Settlements' *Hearth and Home: An Illustrated Weekly Journal for Gentlewomen* 435 (14 September 1899), p. 717.
104 Bermondsey Settlement, *First Annual Report*, p. 9.
105 BLPES: Booth Collection, B280, interview with Thomas Richardson, Rotherhithe Free Church, 16 January 1900, f. 43; Rotherhithe Free Church, *Annual Report of an Aggressive Unsectarian Christian Work in South-East London* (London, 1899), enclosed in B280, f. 37.
106 Bermondsey Settlement, *First Annual Report*, p. 10.
107 J. S. Lidgett, 'The New Session', *Monthly Record* 1:7 (October 1895), p. 73.
108 Bermondsey Settlement, *First Annual Report*, n. p.
109 Bermondsey Settlement, *Second Annual Report*, p. 19.
110 J. S. Lidgett, 'Ideals of the Settlement and How to Realise Them', *Monthly Record* 1:8 (November 1895), p. 85.
111 'A Watchword', *Monthly Record* 1:1 (January 1895), p. 4.
112 'The Bermondsey Settlement' *Southwark and Bermondsey Recorder* 18 November 1891.
113 See A. Kadish, 'The Teaching of Political Economy in the Extension Movement', in A. Kadish and K. Tribe (eds), *The Market for Political Economy: The Advent of Economics in British University Culture, 1850–1905* (London: Routledge, 1993).
114 'Notes and News' *UEJ* 5:51 (December 1894), p. 34; 'Bermondsey Settlement Free Lectures' *Monthly Record* 1:1 (January 1895) p. 3.
115 'Free Lectures for the People' *Monthly Record* 1:2 (February 1895), pp. 19–20.
116 Bermondsey Settlement, *Second Annual Report*, p. 18.

117   Bermondsey Settlement, *Third Annual Report*, p. 19.
118   'The Bermondsey Settlement' *London* 9 January 1896.
119   Bermondsey Settlement, *Second Annual Report*, p. 19, echoed in Collings, 'The London Settlements', p. 740.
120   'Mission Work at the Bermondsey Settlement', p. 215.
121   'The Bermondsey Settlement' *London* 9 January 1896.
122   'The Bermondsey Settlement' *London* 9 January 1896; *The Times* 13 January 1897.
123   SLHL: clipping file 360–76, 'Bermondsey Settlement Educational Institute' LCC minutes, 19 February 1907.
124   'Bermondsey Settlement' *South London Press* 20 November 1908.
125   Bermondsey Settlement, *Second Annual Report*, p. 19.
126   'A Carnival and Sale of Work' *Monthly Record* 3:2 (February 1897), p. 20.

7   Places, spaces, audiences

As we have seen, Samuel Barnett, Walter Besant and John Scott Lidgett all played their part in actively resisting the sensational visions that spiced the late-Victorian 'Outcast London' debate. In conceptualising and promoting their schemes of cultural uplift, they painted a very different picture of London's poor neighbourhoods. They characterised urban poverty not as a matter of acute distress, criminality and sensational squalor, but rather as perpetual monotony, the weary routine of bleak, everyday tedium eked out daily by countless thousands in the vast impersonal metropolis. Without denying the real existence of squalor, crime and misery, they concentrated their larger concern on the spiritual poverty of life 'in the mass', on the dour humdrum of industrial urbanism. In their efforts we see cultural philanthropy gaining traction, not as a set of abstract ideas (whether 'Arnoldian', 'Ruskinian', 'Greenian', Broad Church Anglicanism or Maurice's 'Immanence') but rather as a lucid, persuasive response to the slow crisis of nineteenth-century urbanism when seen in this way. It was an intervention into urban landscapes and communities seen as afflicted by uniformity, dull and mechanical routines, a visual and social monotony that in their eyes denied the vital potential of life itself. Their disquiet at the absence of libraries, galleries, concert halls, associations and educational opportunities in these drab suburbs of dull respectability and workaday labour was part of their dismay at the absence of influences that might encourage citizenship, fellowship and individual potential.

Turning now to the spatial and physical dimensions of their work, we are struck by how each of these reforming efforts involved highly didactic attempts to create meaningful niches for their interventions into this broader urban landscape. In this chapter we consider how the cultural mission to impoverished neighbourhoods manifested in physical architecture and built space. The Oxbridge references of Toynbee Hall's quadrangle and creeper-covered walls, the instructive statuary of Queen's Hall at the People's Palace, and the elevated height and steep roofs of the Bermondsey Settlement were all tangible expressions of the moralising intentions underlying the late-Victorian cultural mission.

University charm and domestic elegance in Whitechapel

As a physical statement, Toynbee Hall presented a forceful contrast to the surrounding neighbourhood, supplying (like the other settlements that followed its pattern) 'the "theatre" for an on-going drama which constantly reaffirmed the mutual roles of the participants'.[1] A deliberate echo in brick of the colleges of Oxford and Cambridge, an attempt to conjure up some of their atmosphere as a place in which to live, visit and study, the buildings erected on Commercial Road in 1884 made a valiant attempt to implant the architectural heritage of the old universities in a landscape of metropolitan poverty.

As Barnett's proposal rapidly evolved in the first months of 1884, the London School Board architect Elijah Hoole was engaged to prepare drawings and by the end of March he could see how a 'university settlement' might look in bricks and mortar. Barnett was delighted by Hoole's scheme, calling it 'a manorial residence in Whitechapel' in an enthusiastic letter to his brother.[2] We have little sense of how the design developed and what kind of input Barnett or others had, as plans and correspondence are only fragmentary. But it is significant that stylistic variations suggested by the architect were resisted by Barnett as 'Queen Anne interference with our House'.[3] These would have been features like a higher, more imposing façade, steeper roof-lines, Flemish gables and a multitude of windows. Like others in the settlement movement Barnett's architectural tastes were conservative, tending to the homely romanticism of the Gothic Revival that during the 1880s was increasingly considered old-fashioned and it seems he needed to insist upon these preferences to counter his more adventurous architect. Whatever the circumstances of its design, the completed building had a powerful – indeed theatrical, as Deborah Weiner suggests – symbolic presence in Whitechapel, but one that needs to be carefully interpreted. It is a simplistic caricature to depict Toynbee Hall's architecture, as Weiner does, as the outcome of 'a deeply self-conscious movement which tried to recreate a feudal world in the urban slum'. Certainly, its 'Old English' styling, drawing loosely on Gothic, Tudor and Elizabethan architectural models, gave the settlement the time-honoured, enduring solidity of an 'English manor house, with heavy chimney stacks, stone dressing and [traditional] brick'.[4] But this was no wistful echo of a vanished social order, as Weiner and other critics of the settlement ethos have implied, nor was it an embodiment of a modern 'reflective monasticism' as suggested by Matthews-Jones.[5]

Rather, Toynbee Hall was a physical expression in brick and stone of the liberal conception of the university college as a surrogate home, a welcoming and mutually supportive community of scholars and students.[6] Behind its 'gatehouse' entry complete with oriel window onto Commercial Road, it had all the iconic elements of Oxbridge colleges in miniature, so to speak, to suit the cramped site and limited finances: a common room, drawing room, tennis court and enclosed quadrangle, which evoked, rather plaintively, the historic dignity of university life amid grim East End streets. Entering Toynbee Hall's quadrangle, one visitor reported, 'you might think yourself in an Oxford collegiate edifice, only there are no surroundings of gardens and waters, and a tall factory chimney does not aid the illusion'.[7] Visiting the building site in October 1884, the *Charity Organisation Reporter* had been impressed:

> the windows of all the large living-rooms look out upon a recessed and quiet court, or quad, about to be laid out as a garden; for the promoters of this settlement seem fully to understand that, unless the pleasantness, and recreations, and refreshments of life are well looked after…few of their friends will habitually come and see them, and so the enterprise will stagnate.[8]

The American Robert Woods described how

> [e]ntering a narrow arch from one of the noisiest streets, and passing through to the rear of a large warehouse you find yourself in a court, or 'quad', so dear always to the heart of a university man. The windows, roof, and tower strengthen the impression. Vines grow on the walls, and there are window-boxes full of flowers.…These surroundings serve to keep fresh the reminiscences of the residents, and, on the other hand, to bring the working people into something of the classic university atmosphere.[9]

Around the carefully orchestrated space of the quadrangle, the brickwork and detailing in doorways and windows was intended to leave an indelible impression on the visitor entering this 'transplant of university life in Whitechapel':

> The quadrangle, the gables, the diamond-paned windows, the large general rooms, especially the dining-room with its brilliant frieze of college shields, all make the place seem not so distant from the dreamy walks by the Isis or the Cam. But these things are not so much for the sake of the university men as of their neighbours, that they may breathe a little of the charmed atmosphere.[10]

The building was neither a reclusive monastery nor a self-assured, exclusive country manor. It was rather a figurative 'gift' from the university to the slum, from intellectual wealth to ignorance and poverty, that made explicit the altruistic philanthropy and the redemptive aspirations of the settlement's sponsors and the first generation of 'university men' who arrived there to live and work in Whitechapel. Some fancied that the cluster of buildings at Toynbee Hall ripened with age, gathering hoary associations the way historic colleges had done at the old universities. One of the Barnetts' most loyal co-workers, W. F. Aitken, maintained at the end of the warden's tenure in 1906 that

> at Toynbee Hall are represented all the old foundations of our two great Universities. Like the grand old colleges whence its residents came, it bears its silent records in picture, panel, and brickwork, not only of the

practical results of the teaching given within its walls, but also of the worth
of those who have given of their best to the cause it exists to serve...'[11]

In this Barnett and his fellow university settlers echoed the enthusiasts for
university extension, who also revelled in the venerable architectural heritage
of the ancient universities, the tangible manifestation (as they saw it) of the
spirit of liberal culture nurtured around the 'dreaming spires'. Under ordinary
circumstances the inspirational university townscape was of course denied to
the young clerks, artisans and women taking up university studies through
extension lectures and classes elsewhere. 'We cannot bring to London', the
Liberal MP John Morley observed in relation to university extension efforts
in the metropolis, 'the indefinable charm that haunts the grey and venerable
quadrangles of Oxford and Cambridge'.

> We cannot take you into the stately halls, the silent and venerable libraries,
> the solemn chapels, the studious old-world gardens. We cannot surround
> you with all those elevated memorials and sanctifying associations of
> scholars and poets, of saints and sages, that march in glorious procession
> through the ages, and make of Oxford and Cambridge a dream of music
> for the inward ear and of delight for the contemplative eye.[12]

But this was precisely what Barnett and his co-workers set out to achieve in
their elaborate and ambitious effort to settle university graduates and their
influences in the dull and grimy streets of Whitechapel, where the 'sanctifying
associations' of Whitechapel's *faux* university supplied a touchstone for their
improving social mission. In 1886, as a new residential college for extension
students, named Wadham House to honour Barnett's own Oxford connections,
was being added to the settlement and local opinion wondered what these new
'student chambers' would contribute, the *Toynbee Journal* was sure the edifying uplift of the original scheme would continue. 'The plans have been got
out by Mr Hoole', it assured readers, 'who has shown his sympathy with
humanity, which is the same in the poor and in the rich, by making the dwellings something more than barracks. They will have a beauty and character of
their own.'[13] The university associations remained paramount, the very essence
of the settlement's mission to redeem the slum neighbourhoods around through
education and culture. 'In the midst of this charming scene', wrote one visitor
at Toynbee Hall's party to open a session of extension classes in late 1895, 'one
might have imagined oneself far away in some old university town; but only
in imagination, for the dismal realities of the poor East-end were ever-present
in the hoarse cries of the traffickers in Wentworth-street and the distant hum
of the multitude who on Saturday night crowd Whitechapel's highways.'[14]

Just as the settlement's architectural presence tried to harness the inspirational heritage of Oxbridge to the task of London social work, so too were
the decorative aesthetics that had been part of the Barnetts' parish work at St
Jude's now given free rein in its interiors. The task fell to a brisk domestic

superintendent in Henrietta Barnett, who ensured that 'in all rooms neutral drabs were abolished: Whitechapel needed lovely colours'. A particular effort was made in the public areas such as the large reception room (see Figure 7.1), where she recalled 'we finally decided to make it exactly like a West-end drawing room, erring, if at all, on the side of gorgeousness'.[15] 'This is really a magnificent room', commented one visitor, 'and might belong to the master's-lodge of some Oxford or Cambridge colleges, but we have seen drawing-rooms in such places which are by no means so impressive'.[16] Wallpaper, curtains, and carpets were chosen in fashionable fabrics and patterns – aesthetic, certainly, but also very conventional by this time – producing a mood described by one resident as 'very greenery yellowy'.[17] In a satirical reflection written two decades later, the craftsman, architect and utopian socialist Charles Ashbee described the settlement's drawing room from the perspective of a visiting East Ender. The depiction was coloured by his own bittersweet emotions about Barnett's mission to the slums, now seen in sarcastic hindsight:

It was painted a sallow green, and furnished with photographs and antimacassars, and it contained a large assortment of cheap and ladylike chairs of the choicest Tottenham Court Road shapes and sizes, and of the fashion of the 'eighties – a 'jolly art room' Charley called it. At the end of the room was a large fireplace, on which was painted in great Gothic letters the motto, 'One by one.' 'That shows 'e's got method', Charley flung in as an aside.[18]

If the art and furniture of the drawing room made an explicit statement about beauty and social work, the settlement's university associations were invoked by a modelled frieze of gilded college shields installed in the dining room by Charles Ashbee's own handicrafts class during 1888.[19] In the library, as one extension student described it, portraits of Browning, Tennyson and Ruskin 'brighten the walls, and the busts of Homer and of Marcus Aurelius look down upon the scene',[20] and the public rooms and corridors were liberally hung with portraits and landscapes that had been donated or loaned. It was an impressive collection, and the young Sydney Cockerell recorded his visit to the settlement in November 1889 purely in terms of the artworks on display. 'Went to tea at Toynbee Hall' he wrote that night, '[and] saw Watts' portraits of Matthew Arnold, Browning, Lord Shaftesbury, his "Esau", Britomart and Soul's Prism, Miss Harris' (and Mrs Morgan's) very beautiful "Madonna and Child" and a picture or two by Holman Hunt.'[21]

Cockerell was young, impressionable and a budding art critic; more experienced or sceptical visitors were not always so enamoured of the settlement's sumptuous interior. Herbert Henson, the head of the rival Oxford House in Bethnal Green, for instance, found all this modish aestheticism a little overwhelming. After one visit in 1888 he noted that the settlement's drawing room 'was exceedingly pretty and tasteful: but far too luxurious for my taste (fancy S. Paul on that Sofa, contemplating that statuette: & drinking afternoon tea out of those cups!)'.[22] Another Oxford House man, the young

Figure 7.1 Toynbee Hall Drawing Room, 1892

aristocrat David Lindsay, Lord Balcarres (later Earl Crawford), visited Toynbee Hall in July 1892 and despite a basic sympathy with its endeavours came away 'rather disgusted with the place', largely for its lavish fittings and the liberal secularism of its social programmes. Like Henson he felt a more frugal and utilitarian tone was needed for East End social work. 'I rejoice in my heart that my lot had not fallen to Toynbee [Hall]', Lindsay wrote with uncharacteristic vehemence in his diary. '[O]ur new Oxford House which I had been condemning as too luxurious, compares with Barnett's palazzo as would a pawnbroker's shop to the Papacy'.[23] His overall impression was of a pampered island of insular comfort:

> The saloon is filled with luxurious armchairs[,] sitting in which we watched and envied the residents who were drinking choice teas and

mouthing well-baked breads. The dining-room is sumptuous, the lecture-room superb. The passages are like a photography showroom and the library rivals our Bodleian. The Quadrangles are festooned with Japanese creepers and comforted with cosy seats: behind the house is a very fine tennis court, and I shuddered to think of the little back yard [at Oxford House] where we had just been playing squash fives.[24]

'Toynbee [Hall] is a palace', he snorted indignantly, '[where] art and culture take precedence of teaching the elements of morality'.

Observers seem to have divided into separate camps, some feeling like Lindsay that decorative beauty and artistic sophistication had gone too far in the new settlement while others remained convinced with the Barnetts that its rarefied interior faithfully ministered to their work of spiritual uplift. For his part, Barnett stressed that residents maintained 'the environment of a cultured life. There is no affectation of equality with neighbours by the adoption of mean or dirty habits. There is no appearance of sacrifice.'[25] The settlement's sponsors were determined to infuse the new building with the ambience of Oxbridge's liberal humanism, now brought dramatically into social action to redeem the spiritual poverty of 'Outcast London'. The settlement's ambience, they felt, permitted a contemplative peace and companionship for residents and visitors alike, sustained by the calm, 'cloistered' hush that they wanted to prevail there. According to one observer, 'During the day, only a distant rumble is heard from the streets. In the evening the place is delightfully quiet.'[26] Another felt that 'with the music of the violins floating out through the drawing-room windows...the roar of London was all unheard'.[27] Like the educational opportunities it offered, the influences of beauty, culture and intellectual fellowship it made possible, and the 'university men' whose kindly, encouraging friendship could be discovered there, the calming and inspirational qualities of the settlement were imagined as a gift to the settlement's East End 'neighbours'. Henrietta Barnett's extraordinary drawing-room, an artistic parlour the like of which could not be found for miles around and the dominant public space within the settlement, was emblematic of all this. Far from being a quasi-monastic retreat, a contemplative haven for tired social workers at the end of their day's labours, the drawing-room was, as one visitor observed, 'mainly intended for the use of the poor. The idea is that the poor should see something of the life of the cultured and wealthy classes, of the rest and refinement and art and ornamentation of good homes.'[28] As we see in the following chapters, here in the Barnetts' remarkable drawing-room Toynbee Hall's mission of moralising social conciliation was most vividly put into effect.

Palatial nobility in Mile End

The new People's Palace that Queen Victoria declared open in May 1887 was also rich with material symbolism. A grand physical gesture of philanthropic generosity, the imposing new edifice faithfully captured the improving vision of its promoters in brick, stone and glass. Regrettably for Currie and the Trustees, an incomplete façade dampened the mood on this otherwise splendid occasion. In contrast to the effusive decorations along the route of the royal procession, the tarpaulin-shrouded Palace appeared a little forlorn:

> At the Palace itself there was not a great deal of outside ornamentation. The huge brick building of the Queen's Hall stands, it must be confessed, a gaunt-looking structure, though after the ceremony of to-day the work of hiding it from sight in the splendid architectural design for the entire block of buildings which has been approved, and for which the money has been subscribed, will go on without any delay.[29]

The architectural historian Deborah Weiner takes this shortfall to be very significant in our assessment of the Beaumont Trust scheme. A major conceptual impasse, she argues, had stopped the building work in its tracks and prevented the completion of the building's façade until 1890–91: 'The difficulty in completing the scheme, particularly its main façade along Mile End Road, indicated an inability to define the nature of a People's Palace, its purpose, its direction, its role in the community.'[30] But this view arises from a simplistic understanding of the Palace's origins and trajectory. In Weiner's account, the Palace originated in the imagination of the novelist, was hurriedly constructed by the Trust amid the 'crisis years' of the mid-1880s when ambitious social solutions were in vogue, and was then finally converted to the 'more austere vision'[31] of the Drapers' Company as its Technical College. Saddled with Besant's romantic and 'implausible' blueprint, she argues, the promoters of the Palace scheme lacked a clear idea of its purpose and as a consequence their proposal was fatally ill-defined.

As we have seen above, this view is untenable given the Trust's clear endorsement of the polytechnic model prior to their adoption of the Besantian title 'the People's Palace' for essentially promotional reasons. Moreover Weiner's interpretation of these events, and the evidence she cites in support, are largely visual rather than documentary. The Beaumont Trust vacillated, she argues, over an appropriate material 'face' for the building that had been sketched out – implausibly, in her view – in Besant's fiction. Given the absence of a description of the Palace's exterior in *All Sorts and Conditions of Men*, she feels that the sponsors of the new institution faced a problem: 'What would a People's Palace look like? How would it relate to its surroundings? What message was to be conveyed and to whom on Mile End Road? How would the building accommodate the disparate functions that would take place under one roof?'[32] These uncertainties, it is suggested, explain the apparent inability of the Trust's architect to erect the novelist's vision as a material building. Weiner stresses the significance of the building's changing 'face' in the Trust's appeal literature; from a structure in cast iron and glass that echoed the Crystal Palace, to a building that expressed more forcefully the romantic, 'Besantian' qualities of a 'Palace of Delight', to a realised façade that was austere and restrained.

In fact, the surviving correspondence in which architectural work for the Palace is addressed establishes that the early sketches for their publicity pamphlets had very little design significance at all. Far from being the considered proposal of the Trustees and their architect, these drawings were only intended to attract attention by invoking the scale and grandeur of the project. E. R. Robson, the School Board architect engaged for the Palace scheme, refused an initial request for a drawing in early June 1885, stating 'I very much doubt if we can make a reasonably good drawing which could be permanently placed at the head of a subscription list until the general scheme has been rather further advanced with plan.'[33] Understandably, he was reluctant to advertise any proposed building in detail when in fact he had barely commenced the design. Two weeks earlier, in mid-May, he had only made a general sketch of the plan and 'the roughest possible suggestion of cost', and matters appeared to have progressed little further by early June. Trust Secretary Brownlow reassured the architect that 'any details of the sketch would of course be quite unnecessary', and emphasised that the Trustees only sought an attractive water-coloured image in the manner of a Christmas card. 'The suggestion I made to the Beaumont Trustees', he wrote, 'was that we should get out an Appeal to every house in London and the suburbs, and as an ordinary circular would be likely to be in 9 cases out of 10 cast aside, I suggested that the Appeal should be specially attractive...'[34] Robson remained obdurate, insisting 'that at the present moment there really is not even a sketch of the proposed Building, and therefore it is not possible to place one at the head of your proposed appeal'.[35] It was only after a personal visit from Currie the next day that Robson promised to furnish an 'attractive sketch' for the appeal.

The resulting image (see Figure 7.2) of a standard Victorian public building, complete with neo-classical ornamentation and a glass pediment and dome evidently inspired by Paxton's Crystal Palace, graced the Trust's first public appeal in mid-1885. It was not intended by either architect or Trust to represent anything but the most general impression of the scheme. Robson hoped that the rushed sketch was suitable for the purpose, but reiterated that '[T]he building looks too little like the dream it is at present...'[36] Even this relatively prosaic design sparked hostility; one appeal form was returned to the Trust with an opinion angrily scrawled in red ink across Robson's sketch:

> If such a style of architecture as this is followed, it is only another instance of the way in which (publicly) subscribed money is foolishly expended – Do you think the extra money to be spent in ornamentation will profit the poor people one jot! No – it will the Builder etc etc – After this I shall not subscribe, but I should like to see your account of your stewardship.[37]

After Robson commenced proper design work in late 1885,[38] an alternative sketch (see Figure 7.3) of the proposed building was ready for the pamphlets

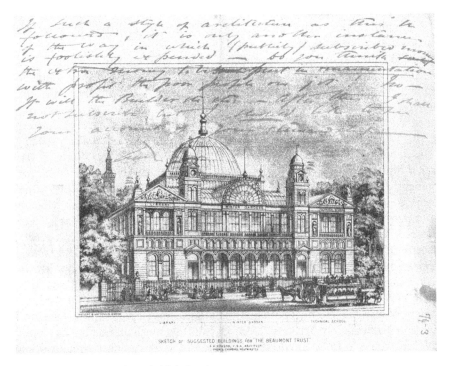

Figure 7.2 People's Palace, initial sketch

Figure 7.3 People's Palace, as depicted

issued at the foundation stone ceremony in June 1886. The new design was grander in scope than the earlier illustration, and its colonnaded entrance, fanciful minarets and dome roundly evoked Besant's romantic 'dream', especially when presented fancifully in sylvan isolation in the Trust's publicity leaflets. Press comment was overwhelmingly favourable. The *Pall Mall Gazette*, for example, noted approvingly that the 'face of the edifice towards the main road will be distinguished by a semi-circular portico, carried on columns, of a long, bold sweeping range, that vastly adds to the imposing effect of the finely-proportioned design'.[39] The *Daily News* commented that Robson had produced 'a very striking design, with towers, arcades, and a crystal dome, a terrace and garden for open-air promenades, a fine concert-hall, with several minor halls, and a suite of workshops in the rear'.[40] The domed entranceway served a practical purpose, moreover: heating arrangements would be installed, the *East London Observer* was pleased to see, 'and it is intended to serve as a playground for children in the daytime throughout the year, while in the evening it is to serve as a sort of common-room in which those who choose may sit and chat and smoke their pipes'.[41] Earlier, Robson had advised the Trust 'the principal entrance will be a room certainly well calculated for children'.[42] He had abandoned the 'enormous Railway Station of a Hall' proposed in earlier designs, 'in which nobody's voice could be heard, and in which no music, except the din of a band in the centre, would be possible', and instead proposed an outer room, the main hall, and the adjacent palm-house as the main elements in the design proposal.[43] This division remained integral to the final scheme.

On this evidence we see that Weiner's hasty verdict overlooks several key matters entirely. In the first place, the initial pamphlets were only illustrative sketches, not schematic designs, and were never intended to be realised in the building itself. Secondly, the difficulty in completing the building contract was due to the increasingly shambolic nature of the Trust's financial affairs, which impaired progress far more instrumentally than any conceptual shortcomings might have done.[44] Keystone elements such as the Queen's Hall, the Palace Library and the Winter Garden were erected unchanged and precisely according to the original proposals, and only the south front, among all the major features of the Palace scheme, received any extensive modification when the funds dried up (see Figure 7.4). Finally, and most pertinently, the tremendous success of the Trustees' subscription campaign tends to contradict the notion that the Palace scheme was ill-defined or uncertain. The Drapers' Company were important sponsors, but also acknowledged the 'considerable public support' for the Palace scheme that had resulted in 'about £70,000 being subscribed within a comparatively short period of time' during the main subscription of 1885–7.[45] This reflected the Beaumont Trust's skilful campaign to encourage donations for the scheme, as they seized the potential of Besant's striking vision and filled it out with their own practical proposals, resulting in a feasible and achievable scheme that still retained a romantic, 'Besantian' flavour. A fine line between romance and practicality was

Figure 7.4 People's Palace, realised scheme

successfully navigated, both in the proposal itself and the strategies that engendered public confidence and ensured success in the subscription campaign.

The Palace's vast concert hall and magnificent library completed in 1887–8 were thus triumphant realisations of the trustees' grand vision (see Figures 7.5 and 7.6). Erected at a cost of over £25,000, fully a quarter of the original Palace fund, the Queen's Hall was acclaimed as the East End counterpart to other landmarks like South Kensington's Albert Hall and the relocated Crystal Palace at Sydenham. Stretching 130 feet long, with a width of 75 feet and 60 feet from floor to ceiling at the centre, it provided seating for audiences of several thousand amid luxurious decorative splendour. Its gigantic scale was emphasised in the promotional literature,[46] and observers marvelled at the elaborate ornamentation:

> The great music or concert hall is a vast room accommodating some 4000 people, with a fine coffered ceiling and lofty windows. A succession of short, circular galleries run in a wavy line around the great hall, each one borne up by a carved female figure, while a course of caryatides supports the arches of the roof. The whole is brilliantly decorated in pale gold and white.[47]

'Upon the design and embellishment of this room', Currie asserted at the official opening, 'the architect has concentrated all his ability, and the Trustees hope that its intrinsic beauty may be a permanent source of pleasure to all who use it'.[48] The vast concert hall and ballroom was encrusted with a stained-glass ceiling, decorated columns and gilded balconies; a luxury of ornamentation that observers found stunning. The *Illustrated London News* thrilled that neither the House of Lords nor Henry VII's chapel at Westminster were 'nobler in design, or more graceful in detail' than the new facility for the poor of East London.[49] 'Elaborately adorned and shining in gold and colour', commented *The Times* after the opening ceremony, '[the Queen's Hall] presented a fit interior for a State display'.[50] After attending a concert there the correspondent for the *Musical Times* described it as 'eminently beautiful, and happily its beauty is not of a sombre kind, but of a character so bright and cheerful as to raise the spirits of a visitor escaping from dull habitations and dreary thoroughfares'.[51]

The Hall's symbolism was sufficiently important to be carefully explained in the official handbook prepared for the opening ceremony, where particular attention was paid to the ensemble of statues running down either side of its length.[52] Marble figures of twenty-two queens stood in alcoves on either side of the vast hall, crowned by an imposing, life-sized figure of Victoria herself in the centre of the rear wall. The *Handbook* carefully explained this instructive tableaux of inspiring femininity, in that the assembled queens were 'representatives of many noble, if humble and unknown women, whose pulses have beat in sympathy with high aims, or whose strength has been spent in labour for the welfare of their country or people',[53] monuments to feminine compassion personified in the maternal figure of the queenly sovereign. Like the grand effigy of Victoria herself at one end of the concert hall, the collection of statues reminded visitors (as one wrote) 'of all the great and good queens who have laboured and sympathised with the people'.[54] This moralising purpose was allied with an opportunity, well suited to Victoria's Jubilee year, for anecdotal history and popular monarchism. The *Daily Telegraph* saluted the spirit of the decorations: 'Day-labourers will come and go in sight of ESTHER and BOADICEA, of HELENA of Rome and CLOTILDA of France, with all the other crowned and renowned ladies whose fair faces are there turned to the statue of her Majesty seated at their head.'[55]

The descriptions of the queens' virtues in the appendix to the *Handbook* did not, however, generally salute their statecraft.[56] Most illustrated domestic virtues, replicating the widespread late-Victorian perception of Victoria herself, as Richards observes, as a 'domesticated monarch whose public image resided not in the trappings of the upper class but in the middle-class ethos of frugality, self-denial, hard work, and civic responsibility'.[57] Eleanor of England, for example, was described in the *Handbook* as 'a tender mother, a loving wife, and an unselfish woman', and Queen Anne was distinguished as 'almost the first Sovereign of England who had no desire for despotic powers, being more remarkable for her domestic virtues than for her skill in governing'. Others were distinguished by their devotion to their menfolk, such as Queen Margaret who 'spent her life in the struggle to maintain the rights of her husband and son'. Matilda of Germany was 'like a better angel to her husband, always exhorting him to do what was right, and restraining his anger'. The reified female virtues of compassion, benevolence and modesty

THE QUEEN'S VISIT TO THE EAST END
THE OPENING CEREMONY IN THE QUEEN'S HALL OF THE PEOPLE'S PALACE

Figure 7.5 Queen's Hall, People's Palace, 1887

were illustrated by several figures including Zenobia of Palmyra, an 'Arabian Princess' who, after being defeated by Rome, 'showed her real greatness by living quietly and contentedly as a private person till her death'. Feminine gentility was personified by Margaret of Scotland 'whose character and influence purified the rough nobles among whom she lived'. Only a few, most notably Victoria herself and her predecessor in an earlier 'golden age', Elizabeth I, represented epochs of national glory, when, in the case of the latter, 'the nation was brimming over with life and energy, and the Queen was worthy to be its head'.

When the sumptuous venue was not being used for concerts, the *Handbook* explained, it would be thrown open as 'a general reading and social room, where families and friends will be able to sit and chat. The Queen's Hall will then be a drawing-room for those to whom high rents forbid the luxury of a drawing-room at home.'[58] It would be an arena for polite sociability, they hoped, but also for public discussion and lectures, in 'meetings either formal or informal on the social questions which stir all hearts, and about which people of all classes should confer together'.[59] Initially, as we see in the chapter that follows, this kind of discussion was organised in didactic terms as 'Popular Lectures for the People' and the Hall was not available for commercial rental at all, but when this was relaxed in the 1890s applications to hold meetings and lectures to air more dissenting radical views were invariably denied. The limited administrative records that survive for the Queen's Hall (dating from 1893–5 only) indicate that a request from the Social Democratic Federation for the anarchist intellectual Prince Pyotr Kropotkin to deliver a lecture at the People's Palace in June 1894 was declined, for example, as was a more benign application from a candidate for the School Board election. In May 1895, an application from a M. D. Talleman for a lecture on 'The Supply of Food to the Working Classes' was similarly declined.[60]

Perhaps inevitably, the moralising atmosphere of the Queen's Hall proved a liability in the longer term. Embellished in the florid taste of its period as a token of class generosity, moralising improvement and the possibilities of social reconciliation, the efficacy of the People's Palace as a centre for the leisure and education of future generations of East Londoners was fatally compromised. Nearly fifty years later, neglected and aesthetically moribund, the Queen's Hall was destroyed by fire in the early hours of 25 February 1931 to the ill-concealed relief of most locals.[61] Arthur Laurie, a former Toynbee Hall resident and lifelong social worker, remembered it as 'a concert hall which had little merit outside, and inside was the most hideous and revolting example of internal decoration in London'; he was gladdened by its destruction.[62]

The expense and attention to detail that characterised the Queen's Hall was mirrored at the People's Palace Library, an architectural gem erected to the rear of the Palace site and originally scheduled to be opened in June 1888. Following the death of Kaiser Wilhelm, the royal ceremony was postponed to August that year as the centrepiece of the Palace's Autumn Fête. The Library cost fully £10,000 to build, 'a truly noble building' in Besant's estimation. 'There are already some who think that the architect has done even better in this splendid room than in the Queen's Hall', wrote the Palace librarian.[63] Octagonal in plan, modelled on the famous Dean's Kitchen in Durham Cathedral with Queen Anne modifications, its high skylight and narrow windows accentuated the perpendicular design.[64] Each pier supporting the dome was surmounted by a bust by the memorial sculptor Francis Verheyden of a literary notable (Shakespeare, Milton, Scott, Wordsworth), providing a gallery of didactic sculptures which, ranged high above the readers, echoed the queenly figures in the concert hall. A portrait of Currie was hung from the main balcony, and higher still were the names of classical philosophers in ornamental panels around the octagonal skylight. The library's ambitious shelving space made provision for some 250,000 volumes in the galleries between the main piers, surrounding readers up to the upper windows. 'Though we do not hope to fill all the shelves for many years to come', Besant explained to possible donors, 'we look forward confidently to making, before long, a collection complete for ordinary students in every branch of learning as well as a library of recreative literature for those – naturally the majority of our readers – who come in the evening for a comfortable place where they may sit in warmth and light over a pleasant book.'[65] Sadly, relying

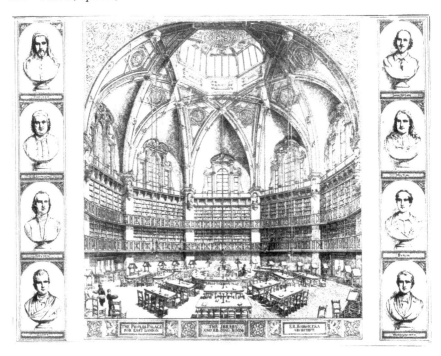

Figure 7.6 People's Palace Library, *c.* 1887

as it did on donations or ongoing funding that never materialised, the collection never surpassed one-twentieth of that figure.[66]

'A centre of bright and pleasant social life' in Bermondsey

John Scott Lidgett's settlement across the river in Bermondsey (see Figure 6.3) boasted little of this expensive decorative finery, but its architectural presence was just as didactic as its East End counterparts. The tall building erected in Farncombe Street in 1891 was also designed by Elijah Hoole who was married to one of Lidgett's aunts, drawing on advice from the Barnetts.[67] A central tower, crowned by battlements and a flagstaff, faced the tennis court and evoked a rather combative Elizabethanism: visitors arrived at the base of the tower and entered through a graceful arch surmounted by an oriel window. But alongside these elements were fashionable 'Queen Anne' features – the tall façade, bright red brick, flat pedimented gables, steep roofs and bay windows – that Barnett had restrained in Hoole's initial scheme for Toynbee Hall. Here they were given full play: with its high, multiple chimney-stacks in brick, dressings and mullions in stone, and rows of lozenge-paned windows to let in the light, the bold new settlement building cheerfully mixed up a whole range of historical references in a way that typified this mannered and distinctive late-century style.

For this reason Weiner's one-dimensional account of the Bermondsey Settlement as a reactionary throwback to a fantasy of pre-industrial 'Merrie England' is rather stretched, not to say misleading. The architecture of Lidgett's new building in Farncombe Street was no simple, un-ambiguous statement of 'Old England', part of what Weiner rather simplistically views as the 'self-consciously paternalistic architecture' favoured by the settlements 'which tallied with the movement's nostalgic view of history'.[68] Rather, its visual language was altogether more contemporary and progressive. From the commencement, local opinion saw it as a thriving centre of higher learning and adult education in a modern industrial city, as when the *South London Press* observed that '[w]hen complete, the entire building will present somewhat the appearance of a college, and though necessarily plain and without elaboration, will have a character appropriate to its purpose'. The newspaper went on to explain how it was being constructed, not by a commercial builder 'but by a co-operative association of workmen, who obtained the contract in competition with a number of building contractors of good standing'.[69] If this complicates Weiner's picture somewhat, a closer look at the building's 'Queen Anne' elements demonstrates that the building was rather more than a paternalistic sermon in brick. As Girouard points out, the 'Queen Anne' style was resolutely modern, leavened by progressive idealism, whimsically eclectic historical references and a light stylistic touch. For architects, designers and their fashionable clients, beginning with the Rossetti–Webb–Morris circles where it had originated in the 1860s, it embodied the union of art and enlightenment, free of the heavy-handed religious moralism of neo-Gothic. It was a precise architectural expression of the fusion of art and liberal social reform, embodying the idea of 'sweetness and light' – beauty, art, culture – harnessed in moralising social intervention against the grim, everyday materialism of the modern city. Girouard describes how, after the style coalesced into a definite identity by the mid-1870s, it thereafter surged in popularity with an appealing essence that could be readily grasped: despite its name, 'Queen Anne' architects did not set out to faithfully reproduce the style of the early eighteenth century. It was, rather, highly flexible and adaptable and spoke directly to progressive aspirations. Patriotic in its local red brick, with a relaxed asymmetry and vernacular modelling, and a 'delicate exaggeration of period' (in Girouard's neat phrase), the new style supplied a positivity and restrained English exuberance missing from the staid mid-century architectural orthodoxies that it challenged. Accordingly, it suited the public mood and became one of the touchstone architectural aesthetics of the last quarter of the century, especially once the new London Board Schools built in this style in the mid-1870s 'captured the imagination of the public as impressive and immediately recognisable symbols of enlightenment...[identifying] "Queen Anne" as the style of the moment and the style of progress'.[70] Most importantly for us, this eclectic, progressive mixture of elements supplied an ideal architectural language for the period's cultural philanthropy. Girouard captures its character and appeal precisely when he describes how, for younger architects, the light and airy new style 'gave them everything they had been looking for':

> Those who were bored by or sceptical about religion, took to 'Queen Anne' because it was emphatically secular. To those in reaction against contemporary values 'Queen Anne' seemed deliciously old-fashioned. It was gentlemanly but not aristocratic, middle-class but not bourgeois, eclectic but not uncouth, pretty but not frivolous, unassertive but chic, reminiscent of the country but adaptable for the town. They took to its sweetness, and used it for the spreading of light.[71]

The archives of the Bermondsey Settlement do not survive, and there are no architectural plans extant either; we have nothing like the richness of sources and documents produced by either Toynbee Hall or the People's Palace to develop a better sense of its architectural character. The settlement's public appeal, mainly directed to Methodist benefactors rather than general philanthropy, did not have the expansive promotional reach of the Beaumont Trust's fund-raising efforts, for example, and there were relatively fewer academic and intellectual visitors than came to Toynbee Hall, and correspondingly fewer descriptions and memoirs. But we know with certainty how it looked, and we can recapture – once we recognise the Queen Anne features for what they are – the didactic, progressive intentions of its founders. Some descriptions help us to reconstruct its internal elements and features, which, if they were less ostentatious than the other centres of cultural uplift in Whitechapel and Mile End, shared in their moralising, interventionist spirit. A local newspaper supplied one of the few descriptions now extant of its internal arrangements:

> Entering under the central tower by the arched doorway, and passing through the lofty vestibule…a wide corridor will be reached, giving access to the dining-hall, and separated from [it] by a panelled screen. To the right of the dining hall will be a spacious drawing-room, where the dwellers in Bermondsey will meet visitors from more favoured parts of London. To the left will be the lecture hall, with accommodation for 400 persons. Beneath the lecture hall will be a gymnasium of ample dimensions, approached by separate staircases from [the] court in front of the settlement buildings [and] the garden, which will be laid out in their rear. The remainder of the basement will be occupied by the kitchen and offices, communicating with the dining hall by a lift. On the first floor will be a spacious library, sets of rooms for residents, and class-rooms for various subjects of study, while the laboratory, workshop, and residents' rooms will occupy the upper floors. The entire building may be regarded as consisting of three sections – first, the central portion, which is chiefly residential; secondly, the left wing, which will be largely educational; and, thirdly, the right wing, consisting of the warden's house, which, for want of funds, will be at present omitted.[72]

So like both Toynbee Hall and the People's Palace, albeit on a more modest scale than both, the public spaces of Lidgett's settlement included a large hall for public gatherings, lecture rooms for class discussion, lecturing and applied science, spaces for gymnastics and physical activity, club rooms and a library. It was practical and modern in these respects; all were essential amenities for large-scale and effective adult education in the university extension mode. Given that face-to-face, personal contact was important to the settlement ethos, Bermondsey would also now have a large, comfortable sitting-room much like Toynbee Hall. Its library was under-stated by comparison with those across the river and was usually described as a 'Reading Room'. But it was nevertheless a similarly contemplative and companionate space, as captured in Lidgett's description of its homely atmosphere when 'full of members of the Settlement studying, reading magazines and newspapers, or quietly playing games of chess or draughts, with the picture of the Good Shepherd looking down upon us to remind us what is to be the spirit of the place. Here friendships are built up and social intercourse provided for under the best conditions.'[73] The settlement's upper floor had another dining-room, 'with bed-sitting facilities for 15–20 resident men who had their own common room....There was also a caretaker's quarters and a warden's flat, where the Lidgetts lived in somewhat sparse conditions.'[74] A welcoming atmosphere of domesticity and homely comfort was all-pervasive, something that its advocates felt was essential to its character as a surrogate community supporting its residents, the students and club members that would be drawn to its activities. As Lidgett explained in 1896,

> the Settlement being the home of many of us, there is a comfort and home-likeness about it that no public institution could have, as is seen at once by those who visit us and see the classes which are held almost every night in our dining-room and drawing-room; and we are enabled to give an amount of individual attention to many of our students which would be otherwise impossible.[75]

But traces of the moralising aesthetics that were in profuse over-abundance at Toynbee Hall and the People's Palace were also evident, as residents and supporters decorated the rooms and corridors with pictures, flowers and ornaments. Beseeching external supporters to help in practical ways, Mary Simmons felt

> we could make the Settlement much more a centre of bright and pleasant social life than it is, if we had outside friends who could make it their business to supply us with good engravings and pictures...plants, bulbs, flowers and beautiful things. We cannot afford to buy these things, but I have been in numbers of houses each of which might fill one of our class or club rooms with beauty and yet have plenty for itself. And cut flowers or better still bulbs and plants, we sorely need in regular supply.[76]

This extended to public art in the drawing room, where prints of Edward Burne-Jones' lush and languid series *The Briar Rose* were hung, illustrating the Perrault fairy story with images of sleepers entwined in thorns and briars, the knight and sleeping princess at either ends of the visual sequence. The story was re-told for reader's of the settlement's magazine, and as we see on p. 263 the originals were exhibited in the Settlement's first loan exhibition of fine art in 1896.[77]

Illuminating the 'Centres of Light'

The intrinsic symbolism of light and illumination offered the essential metaphor for this work of supplying culture, art, learning and education to London's working poor. Much as Sherlock Holmes celebrated the new Board Schools as 'Lighthouses...Beacons of the future!' standing over the low, 'lead coloured sea' of South London in Conan Doyle's fiction, so too did cultural reformers use the idea of an external illumination of dark places and spaces to encapsulate their redemptive cultural mission against urban poverty.[78] Metaphors of radiance and enlightenment were invoked endlessly in descriptions of the settlements that, one by one, followed on Toynbee Hall's model, as when Walter Besant called them 'lamps in a dark place'. '[T]he lamp of the Settlement', he wrote, 'the more widely its light penetrates, the further the darkness recedes; the deeper is the gloom, the more brightly shines the light of this lamp so set and so illuminated and so maintained'.[79] From sites such as Toynbee Hall, *The Times* observed in promoting the People's Palace scheme, 'where voluntary workers carry out their praiseworthy schemes, there beam forth rays of cheering and ennobling light...while for the remainder of the eastern half of the Metropolis...it would be difficult to call to mind any centre whatever affording relief to the "dull monotony" which renders existence so flat, and joyless, and mean'.[80]

In this way, the redemptive, improving 'light' of self-culture and education was imagined beaming into the gloomy, benighted life of urban poverty and ignorance. We see it in Besant's fiction at the moment when his 'Palace of Delight' is unveiled with a brilliant flash of electricity. Contrasting dramatically with the shabby gloom of the street outside, it flashes miraculously like a divine intervention before turning out to be an entirely modern technology:

> Presently she stopped before a great building. It was not lit up, and seemed quite dark and empty. Outside, the planks were not yet removed, and they were covered with gaudy advertisements, but it was too dark to see them. There was a broad porch above the entrance, with a generously ample set of steps like unto those of St Paul's Cathedral. Angela rang a bell and the door was opened....
>
> 'Patience', Angela whispered. 'Part of the mystery is going to be cleared up.'

'Light up, Bill', said one of the men. Then the whole placed passed suddenly into daylight, for it was lit by the electric globes.[81]

Angela Messenger's real-life counterparts likewise turned to the symbolism of light in the practical illumination of their new philanthropic centres amid urban poverty and disadvantage. The Beaumont Trustees were especially determined to showcase their new palace of culture and learning for the people in a literally brilliant way. During daylight, the vaulted stained-glass roof of the Queen's Hall admitted the morning sunshine 'with a subdued and softened light, tinting and painting all around us with a glory all its own',[82] but the original lights proved insufficient by night. Electric lighting, at that time a technological novelty rarely found in East London, was installed throughout the Palace in late 1892 at an extravagant cost, given their difficult finances, of £5,000.[83] The installation made an important contribution to the Palace's projected identity. Thirty brilliant arc lamps, each of 2,000 candle power, were installed along with a thousand incandescent lamps throughout the Palace. Arc lighting had emerged in industrialised cities from the 1870s, principally in large-scale public settings suited to its uniquely brilliant quality of light. 'Arc lighting was the first artificial [light] source', comments the critic Wolfgang Schivelbusch, 'that produced too much light for many purposes. Unlike all earlier innovations which had been metaphorically compared to the sun, arc lighting really did resemble sunlight, as spectrum analysis shows. As bright as daylight, arc-light overwhelmed people when they saw it for the first time.'[84] It was precisely this effect that the Palace administrators sought: the initial gas lighting system in the Palace Library (donated by a benefactor at a cost of £200) was replaced within three years by four powerful electric arc lamps. As they shone out, flooding the dim gas-lamps of the streets and dwellings around, these radiant fixtures announced the Palace's mission to the East End in the clearest possible terms.[85]

The elevating social mission at the social settlements on Toynbee Hall's model was also projected through artificial lighting. But in contrast to the expensive, brash lighting of the Palace's electrical fixtures, the discreet ambience of the Whitechapel settlement's drawing-room and quadrangle was evoked by shaded lamps and gaslights, enhanced on special occasions by delicate 'fairy lights' and oriental paper lanterns. An account of a university extension party in September 1895 captures for us the tonal ambience of the settlement when fitted out for social entertainment:

The quadrangle was artistically hung with fairy-lights and coloured lanterns, which glowed softly among the Virginia creepers which trail along the old brick walls; the lights gleamed out from the lattice windows, over which the gables rose against the stars; around the quaint dove-cote opposite the clock the pigeons sleepily clustered; while above all, with the tower of St Jude standing out darkly, the moon rose through a ripple of white clouds.[86]

The description turns the mind's eye upwards, as if an appreciation of the scene directly encouraged contemplation of higher things. The points of light generated by the settlement 'glowed softly' or 'gleamed', in contrast to the 'flaring lamps' of the 'crowded streets hard by' mentioned later in the account. Schivelbusch suggests that, as artificial lighting became more common, shaded lamps and muslin curtains enjoyed a parallel rise in popularity through the nineteenth century 'to dampen and diffuse light that was regarded as too intense, hard and aggressive' for home life.[87] Tempered light became characteristic of the domestic realm, and perpetuated the homely qualities of traditional light sources such as the candle and the fireplace. The lights came into their own during open-air concerts and recitals in the warmer months of the year: '"The prettiest little corner in East London", as someone called the Toynbee Quad the other day, has well deserved the praise when week after week the neighbours have gathered to enjoy the lights and music.'[88] The lighting and the atmosphere it engendered seemed to draw visitors into an embrace of warmth and illumination during the settlement's 'At Homes'. 'Always a centre of light and leading in Darkest London, Toynbee Hall was, on Saturday night, brilliant with myriads of lamps and radiant with the presence of a thousand interested guests', ran one characteristic report. 'Festoons of lamps cast a warm light over all the surroundings, forming a striking contrast to the gloomy model dwellings which tower on every hand and abut on the Toynbee residences.'[89] Again we see an imagined intervention of artificial light – in this case homely, intimate and inviting – cast through the efforts of social reformers into the gloomy obscurity of urban poverty. The *London* correspondent well understood the metaphorical conventions: 'The working class occupants of these dwellings were interested spectators of the scene, and enjoyed the reflected brilliance of Toynbee, whose aim is to introduce a little more light into the lives of such people.'

The ubiquity of this language underlines for us how the settlements' cultural mission was announced just as clearly in their lighting arrangements as occurred at the People's Palace. If the flamboyant new venture in Mile End was announced in light as an expensive, progressive venue for mass recreation and improving education, so too were the transplanted university colleges in 'Outcast London' marked out by their lanterns and shades as a surrogate 'home' for the labouring poor, as welcoming communities of culture, education and sociability.

All sorts and conditions?

What kind of audience did reformers imagine would gather in these rarefied, didactic, carefully illuminated settings? Dockers, labourers, tradesmen and apprentices, seamstresses, factory girls, the invalid elderly and unwashed children, respectable trade unionists and homeless paupers: in principle at least, all were the objects of the cultural philanthropists' social work. But who actually crossed the threshold to attend concerts, classes, lectures, reading groups and club meetings once each 'centre of light' was ready to welcome them inside? The question has preoccupied modern historians as much as it did contemporary observers. The consensus now (as it was then) is that the optimistic rhetoric captured in phrases like 'all sorts and conditions of men' and 'the best for the lowest' fell short in practice, and that in a basic sense cultural philanthropy failed to attract the audience for which it was intended. The issue deserves close consideration, unless we are satisfied to regard this apparent disconnection between aspiration and reality as simply 'the gulf between democratic aspirations in theory and elitist sensibilities in practice'.[90]

In the first place, it seems clear that despite the universalist rhetoric of their fund-raising and establishment, the 'lowest' strata of the casual labourers and 'outcast poor' were never considered a genuine constituency for the cultural mission. The exclusion was implied in the urban representations we saw in the chapters above, depicting as they did the repetitive lives of working people in regular wage employment, with meagre incomes and pinched homes, rather than the threatening, demoralised 'submerged tenth' of the sensationalist accounts. Perceptive observers like Henry Cunynghame well understood the implications for practical philanthropy. 'Complaints have sometimes been made', he noted in his 1891 report, 'that the people at the Palace look well-to-do and are not ragged enough', a view that he felt 'betrays some ignorance of the circumstances of life at the East End':

> The casual poor class are frequently not so numerous as is sometimes represented, and those of them who care for any form of amusement that partakes of an improving or instructive character is of course not very large. A man or woman who has sufficient sense and restraint of mind to appreciate a concert of the most popular character rarely long remains among the class of the casual poor, who are to be found chiefly at the lower music halls, which are to a great extent the cause, as well as the result, of their abasement. These people it is very difficult to attract, except at the cost of lowering the entertainments till they cease to become in any sense improving.[91]

Social workers regarded the respectable artisans, small-scale tradesmen, factory workers with regular wages, their wives and families as the settlements' natural constituency among working people. 'The proper work of [Toynbee] Hall', commented a perceptive visitor in 1890, 'is not among the miserably poor, but it is rather to cultivate intelligence and self-respect among those who are fairly independent. A wider intellectual outlook brings with it many suggestions of hope and self-help, and so vastly illuminates a way of life which, surrounded by modern conditions of luxury and splendour, would otherwise be increasingly dreary.'[92] William How, the liberal-minded Bishop of Bedford, agreed that Toynbee Hall, with its 'singularly energetic, incessant, and many-sided activities', largely devoted itself to the 'class capable of receiving higher education and culture, consisting largely of the young teachers of Board schools, clerks, intelligent mechanics, and the like...'[93] This 'fairly independent' class had supplied the students at Whitechapel's university extension courses since the mid-1870s. The LSEUT secretary R. D. Roberts felt the Whitechapel classes were exemplary in their 'mixed character' of artisans, young clerks and local elementary school teachers,[94] with a relatively high proportion of the first category compared to other extension centres. Henrietta Barnett remembered them with some exasperation:

> They were very trying, some of those early students: young ladies whose affectations when 'seeking cultivation' made one long to shake them; prigs who quoted Browning on all occasions; excellent persons whose little learning made them mad – with conceit; pretentious youths who patronised all who had not read the few books they had perused, and who killed by bad manners the belief that education made equality.[95]

Her memory was coloured by an unblushing conviction that, after 1884, 'the Toynbee men unconsciously taught them nobler standards', but informed observers like W. E. Forster also cited the Whitechapel lectures as the best example in London of working men taking up extension courses.[96] When these were extended to other centres in Tower Hamlets in the 1890s the occupational profile was also encouraging: of the 260 students that bought tickets for the 1894 autumn term or attended through weekly fees, 40% were working men and artisans, 14% were teachers, 17% were clerks or agents, and the remaining 29% were 'either women or men belonging to miscellaneous occupations, or who have not recorded their occupation at all. We may assume that, on the whole, most of the 260 belong to the poorer classes; for we find that 93 per cent. are residents in the Tower Hamlets', an extension conference was told in 1894.[97] Ernest Aves, interviewed at the settlement by his fellow-investigators on Charles Booth's inquiry in 1898, indicated that while Toynbee Hall drew students from a wide area of London's eastern half, '[n]one of course are of the poorest class but it will be safe to say that nearly all of them have been educated in a public elementary school and that a large proportion would be described as of the working rather than of the lower middle class'.[98]

Generally speaking it seems clear that settlement workers, their sponsors and supporters did not entertain any illusions that their work would 'reach' the 'lowest' on the social scale in practical terms. James Adderley, the warden of Oxford House, acknowledged the criticism that Toynbee Hall only catered to 'well-to-do' East Londoners; if this was so, he felt, it was only a natural consequence of its educational emphasis. Even though many Toynbee Hall residents came 'into immediate contact with some of the lowest on the social scale' through charity organisation work, sanitary aid and so on, the settlement was 'not a bit ashamed to say that it does aim at working from the top rather than from the bottom. It recognises what too many philanthropists overlook – that if you raise the upper class [among working people] the lower will move up too.'[99]

In a similar way, as soon as the People's Palace opened its doors debate commenced over its apparent failure to attract the most impoverished and 'demoralised' residents of the district. '[T]he class of girls that has come there [to use the Palace facilities]', commented Cunynghame in 1890, 'is almost too well off, and I do not believe there are any below the rank of workroom girls'.[100] Threepence music concerts in the Queen's Hall attracted large audiences drawn almost entirely, it seemed, from the respectable working class of the district. 'The hearers came, no doubt', commented one observer of a Palace concert, 'from the higher ranks of "the people". They looked, for the most part, like the families of small tradesmen and prosperous artisans.'[101] For this reason supporters like Cunynghame urged 'the founders of such institutions [on the Palace and polytechnic model] should not be disappointed because their audiences do not come dirty or in rags, because, as a rule, even the poor will clean themselves up a little to go to public performances'.[102] But they remained sensitive to suggestions that their work was missing its mark and only catered to middle-class patrons. After the Palace Library had been open for three months, a review of its register suggested that of the 1,239 readers that had nominated their occupations, 'more than half may be described as mechanics or artisans (skilled or unskilled), while only 130 belong to the shop-keeping and professional classes. Of the remainder, 180 are schoolboys, and 202 are clerks, shop employés, etc.'[103] Like the impressions that prevailed among most observers, the rudimentary statistics we have suggest an audience of employed, respectable and self-improving East Enders, none of them affluent but none in desperate poverty either.

The Palace sponsors rejected suggestions that on this evidence they were failing to reach their intended audience. 'I am often asked whether the benefits of the People's Palace really reach the genuine poorer classes', reported Currie in 1890,

> and I am glad to be able to always reply that they most certainly do. I believe that this question often rises in the minds of good friends of the Palace, who visit the institution with the expectation of finding the halls and corridors swarming with ragged men and women with no boots. An impression exists among many people that poverty and rags are synonymous; an impression which a short residence in the East End and some personal intercourse with its inhabitants would very completely eradicate.[104]

The Palace librarian held a similar view: '"All Sorts and Conditions" implies no class grade, or distinction', she insisted. 'We do not get *"gutter snipe"* or *"gaol birds"*, if that is what is meant by *the people*, but we do not consider we have altogether failed to reach the People because of this.'[105] In considering the youngsters at the Palace Institute, some 3,600 in number, Walter Besant was sure

> they belong, with the exception of a few clerks, absolutely to the working classes. They are not of the lowest class; that has been thrown in our

teeth; if they were they would not stay in so orderly and civilized a place; but they are 'respectable'. They are of those who work with their hands; both girls and lads...they have a trade; they belong to the 'better class' of labour.[106]

Contemporary accounts of the audiences at the Bermondsey Settlement also dwelt on these nuanced social distinctions. A promotional meeting held by the settlement's sponsors two months before the building opened was mainly attended by shop assistants, who responded with applause to the suggestion that shorter working hours and an 8 pm closing would enable many of them to attend evening classes at the settlement.[107] As it transpired attendance numbers proved healthy, and seemed to represent a genuine cross-section of local people. 'The students have been almost entirely residents in Bermondsey and Rotherhithe', Lidgett reported of the first session of classes that drew some 1,566 students in the spring and summer terms of 1892, 'and between the ages of 16 and 25. They have fairly represented the various sections of the local population – except that we have not yet reached the Dockers. Artizans, warehousemen, clerks and shop assistants, have all been present in considerable strength.'[108] One observer, William Hunt, writing in 1900, felt sure that as well as providing a model of decent conduct and cleanliness to the 'careless, slovenly poor of the slums', Lidgett's settlement had a more direct audience among the 'respectable poor'. These were the men and women, Hunt explained,

> who upon a small wage try to extract a certain amount of dignity out of life – the people who, while facing daily the burden of want, yet aspire to the maintenance of a large measure of self-respect; in Bermondsey and Rotherhithe there are thousands of these who find in the Settlement that friendliness and good comradeship which is indispensable to the development of their ideals.[109]

In practice, then, the distinctive rhetoric of the charitable appeals – with their vague conceptions of 'the poor', 'the toiling masses', 'all sorts and conditions of men' and so on, that were used to promote these philanthropic agencies at their conception – typically gave way in practice to much more constrained and focussed social categories. The larger social rationale behind the cultural mission pivoted sharply as these reformist proposals became practical realities, and the optimistic language of a universal appetite for culture's benefits gave way to more nuanced social distinctions. But this did not represent a failure of the liberal programme of practical reform through popular education and moral amelioration. The audiences at cultural philanthropic events were drawn from the shades of grey at the upper margins of working-class independence and the lower divisions of modest middle-class status, from among wage-earning artisans, apprentices and shop assistants, factory workers, tradesmen and clerks across this indistinct spectrum. Whatever their precise social and economic situation, such men and women were absolutely the target for late-Victorian liberal social reform: none were affluent, and despite their independence all had a need for greater social security. Accordingly, they were unified by an earnest interest in their own self-improvement. E. M. Forster's fictional Leonard Bast comes easily to mind as the archetypical aspiring clerk, but equally representative were autodidact Whitechapel working men like bookbinder Frederick Rogers and the basket weaver Thomas Okey, both great enthusiasts for Toynbee Hall's extension classes and faithful to the ideals of liberal education for the many rather than the few.

Far from any chagrin at their failure to attract the 'outcast poor' to these centres of cultural philanthropy, as we see on pp. 229–31 and pp. 242–5 reformers implemented deliberate measures to exclude the casual poor, the homeless, unemployed and 'demoralised' altogether. Demonised as parasitic 'loafers', threatening and shiftless, the truly 'outcast' among the poor were closely watched at the People's Palace, and it seems they rarely ever crossed the threshold into the charmed atmosphere of the Whitechapel and Bermondsey settlements.

Notes

1 D. Weiner, *Architecture and Social Reform in Late-Victorian London* (Manchester: Manchester University Press, 1994), p. 165.
2 LMA: F/BAR/6, letter to F. G. Barnett of 29 March 1884.
3 DRO: Gell Papers, D3287/B2, letter to P. L. Gell of 4 August 1884. Aspects of the construction contract and on-site problems and decisions are obliquely referred to in this correspondence during 1884.
4 Weiner, *Architecture and Social Reform*, p. 168; see also her 'The Architecture of Victorian Philanthropy: The Settlement House as Manorial Residence' *Art History* 13:2 (June 1990), p. 212; and A. Briggs and A. Macartney, *Toynbee Hall: The First Hundred Years* (London: Routledge and Kegan Paul, 1984), p. 22.
5 L. Matthews-Jones, 'Centres of Brightness: The Spiritual Imagination of Toynbee Hall and Oxford House' (Ph.D. thesis, University of Manchester, 2009), chapter 5.
6 As argued by S. Koven, 'Culture and Poverty: The London Settlement House Movement' (Ph.D. thesis, Harvard University, 1987), pp. 112–116.
7 F. Arnold, 'Oxford House and Toynbee Hall' *Leisure Hour* (1888), p. 276.
8 *Charity Organisation Reporter*, 13 (October 1884), p. 333.
9 R. A. Woods, *English Social Movements* (London: Swan, Sonnenschein and Co., 1892), pp. 86–7.
10 R. A. Woods, 'The Social Awakening in London' *Scribner's Magazine* 11 (April 1892), p. 412.
11 W. F. Aitken, *Thirty Years in the East End: A Marvellous Story of Mission Work* (London: S. W. Partridge and Co., 1906), p. 148.
12 Cited in M. E. Sadler 'University Extension in England' *Quarterly Review* 172 (April 1891), p. 419.
13 *Toynbee Journal* 1:9 (June 1886), p. 71.
14 'The People's University in Whitechapel' *London* (October 3, 1895), p. 835.
15 H. Barnett, *Canon Barnett: His Life, Work, and Friends* (London: John Murray, 1918), vol. 2, p. 42.
16 Arnold, 'Oxford House and Toynbee Hall', p. 276.
17 F. F. Vane, *Agin the Governments: Memories and Adventures* (London: Sampson Low, Marston and Co., 1929), p. 60.

18   C. R. Ashbee, *The Building of Thelema* (London: J. M. Dent and Sons, 1910), p. 170.

19   C. R. Ashbee, *School and Guild of Handicraft: Statement of its Nature and Purpose* (pamphlet) (London, 1888), n. p.

20   'An Evening in the Library' *Toynbee Record* 5:5 (February 1892), pp. 54–5.

21   BL: Cockerell Papers, Add. Mss. 52626, Diary (1889), f. 62; entry of 12 November.

22   Durham Cathedral Archives, Herbert Hensley Henson diaries, Journal 4 entry for 23 January 1888, cited in L. Matthew-Jones, 'St Francis of Assisi and the Making of Settlement Masculinity, 1883–1914' in J. H. Arnold and S. Brady (eds), *What is Masculinity? Historical Dynamics from Antiquity to the Contemporary World* (London: Palgrave Macmillan, 2011), p. 295.

23   D. Vincent (ed.), *The Crawford Papers* (Manchester: Manchester University Press, 1984), p. 14, entry of 21 July 1892.

24   Vincent, *The Crawford Papers*, p. 14, entry of 21 July 1892.

25   S. A. Barnett, 'University Settlements' *Nineteenth Century* 38 (December 1895), p. 1020.

26   Woods, *English Social Movements*, p. 86.

27   Barnett, *Canon Barnett*, vol. 2, pp. 78–9.

28   Arnold, 'Oxford House and Toynbee Hall', p. 276.

29   'Special Edition: The People's Palace: Opening by the Queen' *Evening Standard* 14 May 1887.

30   Weiner, *Architecture and Social Reform*, p. 193.

31   Weiner, *Architecture and Social Reform*, p. 201.

32   Weiner, *Architecture and Social Reform*, p. 187.

33   QMUL: QMC/PP/7/1, letter from Robson of 5 June 1885.

34   QMUL: QMC/PP/7/1, letter dated June 1885, f. 4.

35   QMUL: QMC/PP/7/1, letter from Robson of 10 June 1885.

36   QMUL: QMC/PP/7/1, letter from Robson of 7 July 1885.

37   QMUL: QMC/PP/2/12, appeal leaflet returned as anonymous correspondence.

38   'I have just received instructions to prepare plans for the Beaumont Trust scheme at once', Robson wrote to Henry Tate, a potential donor: QMUL: QMC/PP/2/13, letter of 17 December 1885.

39   *PMG* 28 June 1886.

40   *Daily News* 12 January 1886.

41   'The People's Palace: Laying the Foundation Stone by the Prince and Princess of Wales' *ELO* 3 July 1886.

42   QMUL: QMC/PP/7/1, letter to the Beaumont Trust of 20 March 1886.

43   QMUL: QMC/PP/7/1, letter from Robson of 20 March 1886.

44   See DCA: MB 56–58, Minute Books, Court of Assistants (1883–1893) where matters relating to the Beaumont Trust's financial affairs are documented, and G. Ginn, 'Gifts of Culture, Centres of Light: Cultural Philanthropy in the late-Victorian East End' (Ph.D. thesis, University of Queensland, 2001), Appendix Four: 'Completing the People's Palace Façade', pp. 410–15.

45   DCA: Court of Assistants Minute Book MB 58 (1890–93) f. 65, report dated 12 June 1890.

46   Particularly Beaumont Trust, *Opening of the People's Palace for East London* (pamphlet) (London, 1887).

47   *Lend a Hand: A Record of Progress* 8 (March 1892), pp. 154–5.

48   QMUL: QMC/PP/4/8, 'Programme of the Ceremonies', n. p.

49   *Illustrated London News* 21 May 1887.

50   *The Times* 16 May 1887, p. 10.

51   *The Musical Times* 1 February 1888, p. 91.

52 DCA: People's Palace Box 2: 'Extract from [Beaumont Trust] Minute Book'. The booklet was prepared by a special sub-committee, appointed on 21 April 1887 and consisting of three members including Samuel Barnett.

53 Beaumont Trust, *Handbook to the People's Palace* (pamphlet) (London, 1887), p. 10.

54 S. S. Blanchard, 'The People's Palace in London' *Lend A Hand* 9:5 (November 1892), p. 342. For Queen Victoria's practical and symbolic contribution to philanthropic work, see F. Prochaska, *Royal Bounty: The Making of a Welfare Monarchy* (New Haven: Yale University Press, 1995), chapters 3 and 4.

55 *Daily Telegraph* 14 May 1887.

56 The following are from Beaumont Trust, *Handbook to the People's Palace*, pp. 29–46.

57 T. Richards, 'The Image of Victoria in the Year of Jubilee' *Victorian Studies* 31:1 (1987), p. 10.

58 Beaumont Trust, *Handbook to the People's Palace*, p. 10.

59 Beaumont Trust, *Handbook to the People's Palace*, p. 10.

60 DCA: MB/SS1, People's Palace: General Purpose Committee Minutes, 1893–1895, ff. 49, 67.

61 C. Bermant, *Point of Arrival: A Study of London's East End* (London: Eyre Methuen, 1975), p. 182. Local rumour suggested the College principal was 'responsible for the complete success of the fire' to facilitate the College's ownership of the whole site: *East London Papers* 3:1 (April 1960), pp. 9–10.

62 A. P. Laurie, *Pictures and Politics: A Book of Reminiscences* (London: International Publishing Company, 1934), p. 74.

63 'Notes of the Week', *Palace Journal* 2:30 (6 June 1888), p. 462.

64 M. S. R. James, *A Sketch of the People's Palace and its Library* (pamphlet) (London, 1893), p. 12.

65 'Correspondence', *The Library* 1 (1889), p. 39.

66 M. S. R. James, 'The People's Palace Library' *The Library* (n. d.), THLHL: Clippings Box 830.1. The initial collection of 7,332 volumes, including only 350 to 400 volumes inherited from the defunct Beaumont Institution and loaned to Toynbee Hall while the Palace Library was erected, grew slowly by donation and a limited purchase of stock to its peak of 12,423 in 1891. When the library closed on 31 January 1902, the collection of only some 11,000 volumes was transferred to the new rate-supported Mile End Library in Bancroft Road. P. M. Brading, 'A Brief History of the People's Palace Library, East London, 1888–1902' (M.A. thesis, University of Sheffield, 1976), p. 26.3, and 'Appendix A: Comparative Statistics – Admissions, Issues, Books', p. A1.3.

67 J. S. Lidgett, *The Aims and Work of the Bermondsey Settlement* (London, 1891), p. 8.

68 D. Weiner, *Architecture and Social Reform*, p. 168. Her discussion of the Bermondsey Settlement follows, pp. 169–75.

69 'The Lord Mayor in Bermondsey' *South London Press* 18 July 1891.

70 M. Girouard, *Sweetness and Light: The 'Queen Anne' Movement 1860–1900* (Oxford: Clarendon Press, 1977), p. 64.

71 Girouard, *Sweetness and Light*, p. 63.

72 'The Lord Mayor in Bermondsey' *South London Press* 18 July 1891.

73 Bermondsey Settlement, *Third Annual Report* (London, 1894), p. 20.

74 B. Frost, 'God Cares Also for Minds: John Scott Lidgett, the Bermondsey Settlement and Methodist Educationalists' in his *Pioneers of Social Passion: London's Cosmopolitan Methodism* (Peterborough: Epworth Press, 2006), p. 48.

75 'The Bermondsey Settlement', *London* (9 January 1896).

76 M. Simmons, *Report of the Bermondsey Settlement: Some Account of the Women's Work* (London, 1897), p. 35.

77 *Monthly Record* 1:2 (February 1895), pp. 14–15.
78 Cited in Girouard, *Sweetness and Light*, p. 64.
79 W. Besant, *East London* (London: Chatto and Windus, 1901), p. 348.
80 *The Times* leader, October 1886, reprinted in Beaumont Trust, *The People's Palace for East London* (pamphlet) (London, 1886). LMA: A/BPP/2/1.
81 W. Besant, *All Sorts and Conditions of Men* (London: Chatto and Windus, 1894 [1882]), p. 309.
82 Blanchard, 'The People's Palace in London', p. 342.
83 The electrical installation, noted as the only one within several miles, was described in the journal *Engineering* 21 October 1892.
84 W. Schivelbusch, *Disenchanted Night: The Industrialization of Light in the Nineteenth Century* (Angela Davies trans.) (Oxford: Berg Publishers, 1988), p. 54.
85 James, *A Sketch of the People's Palace and its Library*, p. 6.
86 Cited in Barnett, *Canon Barnett*, vol. 2, p. 78.
87 Schivelbusch, *Disenchanted Night*, p. 169.
88 'Band Concerts', *St Jude's* 1:8 (August 1889), p. 74.
89 'The People's University in Whitechapel' *London* (3 October 1895), p. 835.
90 Koven, 'Culture and Poverty', p. 117, fn. 41.
91 QMUL: QMC/PP/6/5, H. Cunynghame, 'Assistant Commissioner's Memorandum on the Present Condition of the People's Palace' (15 August 1891), p. 14.
92 'A Visitor', 'Three London Charities' *Unitarian Review* 34 (October 1890), p. 343.
93 W. W. How, 'The East End' *Contemporary Review* 54 (1888), p. 801.
94 Parlt. P: *Royal Commission on a University for London: Minutes of Evidence* XXXIX [c.5709-I] 1889, p. 189.
95 Barnett, *Canon Barnett*, vol. 1, p. 326.
96 W. E. Forster, 'Extension of University Teaching' *The Times* 26 April 1883, p. 8.
97 W. G. de Burgh, in 'Annual Meeting of the London Society: Conference on Working-men Centres' *UEJ* 5 (December 1894), p. 38.
98 BLPES: Booth Collection, B/227, f. 205.
99 J. G. Adderley, 'University Settlements' *East London Magazine* 1:6 (January 1891), p. 69.
100 H. Cunynghame, 'Memorandum on the Social, Physical, and Intellectual Improvement of the Poorer Classes of London'; Parlt. P.: *Accounts and Papers* 1890 (142), p. 129.
101 A. R. Buckland, 'The People and the People's Palace' *Sunday Magazine* 20 (1891), p. 681.
102 Cunynghame, 'Assistant Commissioner's Memorandum', p. 14.
103 'The Library', *Palace Journal* 1 (25 January 1888), p. 158.
104 E. H. Currie, 'The Working of "The People's Palace"' *Nineteenth Century* 27 (1890), p. 350.
105 James, *A Sketch of the People's Palace and its Library*, p. 12.
106 'The People's Palace', *North American Review* 147 (1888), p. 59.
107 'The Bermondsey Settlement' *Southwark and Bermondsey Recorder* 18 November 1891.
108 Bermondsey Settlement, *First Annual Report* (London, 1892), p. 14.
109 W. Hunt, 'Some Aspects of Settlement Life' *The Wesleyan-Methodist Magazine* 123 (1900), p. 763.

8   Uniting sentiment, common feeling

This chapter and the next develop a sense of cultural philanthropy in action, as we see social workers engineering highly artificial social occasions at these centres of their cultural mission. They brought a panoply of moralising influences to bear through art exhibitions, evening classes, clubs and reading groups, recitals and concerts, and opportunities for refined, improving social intercourse such as garden parties, excursions, dances, *soirées* and *conversaziones*. Again we focus on matters 'as reformers perceived them to exist', because in blunt terms we have little direct evidence to re-construct the view from the other side. We have no eyewitness accounts from working-class East Londoners of an art exhibition at the People's Palace, for example, nor diary entries written by local 'neighbours' after a concert recital in Bermondsey or Whitechapel. There are some near misses: the *Palace Journal* spoke of five essays written by the elocution class about their experiences of the People's Palace, but sadly did not print them. Some working-class autodidacts wrote memoirs, and there is some correspondence in the surviving administrative records, as we see on pp. 231–2, for example; there are also traces in the magazines and published reports that give voice to plebeian perspectives. But these are overwhelmed in the documentary record by the abundant descriptions and accounts written by reformers about their practical activism. As we would expect, they tend to the positive, and we need to weigh up carefully their competing impulses of candour and self-interest. Certainly there is a lot of wishful thinking on show in these sources, but also much sincere reportage and open-minded reflection. Privately, in letters and journals, as well as the more candid reflections of later years, the doubts and frustrations that simmered beneath the surface were vented. Through these sources we gain some access to these obscure historical moments when the description, diagnosis and propositional rhetoric explored in earlier chapters gave way to action.

As we will see, much care was taken to discriminate, mediate and supervise. The rhetoric of broad conciliation between 'rich' and 'poor' favoured when promoting these schemes gave way to more hard-nosed distinctions: an old-fashioned distinction between 'deserving' and 'undeserving' was insisted upon, as 'the loafer', 'the idler', the 'roughs' and their sort were monitored and at times carefully excluded from culture's benevolent embrace. 'Real compassion for the poor when distributing charity demanded selectivity', Thomas Brydon observes. 'Targets had to be chosen carefully in the hope that the respectable among the poor might be "raised", "elevated", or "picked up"'.[1] In the same way, the reformist cultural mission to the slums was not offered unconditionally as an abstract entitlement, but rather with care and precision as a 'gift'. It remained highly personal and mediated, as our philanthropists adopted positions of authority to ensure order and suitable propriety at these events. As teachers and supervisors, they interpreted the culture on display and regulated proceedings to ensure that the gifts they offered were properly delivered and received. One objective, then, in these last two chapters is an understanding of the techniques of intervention and regulation involved, and a recognition of the problems that ensued for reformers in situations where a mediating personal influence was not possible. We see this particularly at the People's Palace, as the improving social idealism that lay behind the Beaumont Trust's efforts in improving recreation and popular education was ratcheted up to support mass events on an impersonal scale.

Their efforts can only be sampled here, and activities like the Whitechapel Fine Art Exhibitions that have previously attracted historical attention are discussed only in truncated terms. We concentrate rather on the more elusive and ephemeral moments such as the evening classes, debates and discussion groups, entertainments, 'At Homes' and conversaziones, music concerts and club activities held at Toynbee Hall and the Bermondsey Settlement. Events at the People's Palace were typically mounted on a grander scale, resulting in large-scale entertainments, concerts, exhibitions and dances that generated genuine dilemmas of supervision and management for reformers.

Despite the airy ideals of their sponsors, then, and the often bizarre juxtapositions and contrasts that arose when these ideals came to practical fruition, these occasions and encounters warrant a careful consideration. 'The sheer wishfulness of the enterprise evokes contempt as much as admiration', Koven comments of the Barnetts' Whitechapel Fine Art Exhibition, but he counsels against dismissing the effort 'as a kind of mad hatters' tea party emblematic of misguided Victorian do-gooders'.[2] Indeed, as we look closer we find a coherence to these occasions and encounters as the social idealism behind cultural philanthropy swung into action. We see high-minded yet practical efforts that, building on the patterns of late-Victorian voluntarist social work at a moment when conceptions of the role of the state in welfare and education were enlarging, animated the civic and social energies of progressive social workers. When we look closely we see that, in its essence, cultural philanthropy was a progressive project of individual emancipation through adult education and the imagined potential of an integrated, participatory civic life.

Settlement lectures and evening classes

The most rudimentary and widespread arena of improving self-culture in our period was the evening lecture. Whether offered on isolated occasions as a single event, or accompanied (as in university extension) by recommended reading, discussion classes and submitted work, educational lectures were ubiquitous, much like the correspondence courses of later decades. Many lecturers reported a great appetite for knowledge and higher learning being at least partly satisfied by a well-organised and expertly delivered lecture. There was 'no better audience than one of working men and women', wrote one settlement worker, Will Reason. 'None follow a lecture more closely, none are so hearty in their genuine applause, and, if it be a debatable matter none so ready and frank in questions and criticism.'[3]

As we saw above, university extension emerged in the 1870s as a liberal reforming movement to take higher education to the nation at large. But when extension lectures were advertised in neighbourhoods like Whitechapel, Mile End and Bermondsey they joined a much older tradition of 'penny readings' and evening addresses that had long been a feature of Mechanics' Institutes, the Temperance and Co-operative movements and trade unionism, in music hall programmes and popular exhibitions, because, as Jonathan Rose notes, late-Victorian working class culture 'was saturated by the spirit of mutual education'.[4] Occasional lectures had limited educational value, of course: topics were not necessarily consistent or systematically treated, and the educational effectiveness of individual speakers could not be guaranteed. Lecturers performed rather than taught, and audiences were not students. But from these unpromising foundations some attempts at systematic evening lectures arose. At Red Cross Hall in 1888, for instance, a committee of working men was formed to organise occasional lectures and entertainments which, Octavia Hill reported, were successful and well attended.[5] The men of the committee 'leaned to questions bearing on modern life, and this would point to Professor Dicey or Mr Marriott [as suitable speakers]', she wrote to Sydney Cockerell. 'I am a little afraid about getting an audience for lectures of the more interesting kind without magic lanterns or explosions, but if anyone would give us a trial I should be very glad.'[6] But Cockerell recorded decidedly mixed results for their first winter programme of evening lectures. Things began well with Arthur Laurie, the Toynbee Hall resident, who spoke on 'Ice and Snow' using magic lantern illustrations and personal stories of alpine climbing in Switzerland to an appreciative audience. But a much less successful effort followed the week after, when another invited lecturer, a J. P. Osmaston, lectured on the themes of leisure and idleness in what we can only imagine was a hectoring tone. 'Poor lecture and scanty audience', recorded Cockerell that evening in his diary, 'Altogether very dispiriting.'[7]

The key principle for the Barnetts, their parish volunteers and the Toynbee Hall circle that gathered around them in the mid-1880s, was that lectures and evening classes needed to be comprehensive, sustained and systematic, but also encourage a personal connection between teacher and student through tutorials rather than didactic lectures alone. This was standard practice for the LSEUT, but had special resonance for their Whitechapel work. Affordable fees were another consideration, set in the mid-1880s at a standard one shilling fee for a term of ten lectures and accompanying tutorials, but as the *Toynbee Record* reported, 'many who can afford more take 5s. and guinea tickets'.[8] Better-off students were expected to contribute more to ensure their continuation. Student representatives were also obliged to run the local organising committee. These had to be 'large and representative', the Toynbee resident and extension lecturer W. G. de Burgh reported after a decade of Toynbee Hall's extension work, embracing vestries, trade unions, friendly societies, clergy, teachers, representatives of all political opinion and especially students. But ultimately, he concluded, '[t]he only truly satisfactory Committee is one formed in the main of past and present Students at the Lectures'.[9]

In a sense, then, Toynbee Hall began as transplanted college for the Barnett's ambitious programme of local adult education in Whitechapel, but one that had important qualities of self-governance and civic participation. Previously held in the cramped, drab St Jude's schoolrooms, the classes shifted to the new settlement for the 1885 session and expanded rapidly. The low fees attracted more than 300 students to the classes, male and female, rising in the following year to 455. A pattern emerged whereby four courses were offered in parallel in both the autumn and spring terms, two of them literary and two scientific, run by accredited LSEUT lecturers. 'The students are drawn from all classes, and from all parts of London'; it was reported in 1888, and although it could not be denied that 'the majority are schoolmasters, schoolmistresses, and clerks...[t]here is a considerable and increasing proportion of artisans, especially in the science courses'.[10] The pattern of four concurrent courses each term at Toynbee Hall continued until the summer session of 1892, when a fund was established to take the work further afield. An existing centre at Limehouse was absorbed and another commenced at Poplar. In this the organising committee pursued 'an ideal of continuity in these Courses – continuity of Lecturer, as far as should be possible, and continuity of subject', so that consecutive courses on history and science were offered in Limehouse, and economics and economic history in Poplar.[11] Numbers continued to rise until peaking at 916 enrolments during the winter and spring of 1897, followed by more than 500 attending weekly classes during the summer that followed.[12] The two student residences, Balliol and Wadham Houses, were going well, and together with another satellite centre at Millwall, Toynbee Hall was now approaching Samuel Barnett's ardent hopes as a 'University for East London', something to which he had aspired as a Beaumont Trustee in 1882. But the settlement's report that year noted that extension lectures were no longer drawing increasing enrolments, 'which may be partly accounted for by the increase in the range and number of our Classes, Clubs and Reading Parties'.[13] Enrolment figures suggested the two were in inverse proportion: as the drawing power of formal lectures ebbed, the appeal of smaller discussion groups and tutorials – something always dear to Barnett's heart, and central to the Toynbee model – correspondingly gained strength.

These informal classes met at Toynbee Hall with individual residents to study particular topics and texts. Nine separate 'Reading Parties' commenced during 1885; four years later these had grown to more than fifty classes and reading groups overseen by the settlement's Education Committee.[14] All were encouraged to use Toynbee Hall's library, opened in 1886 with the appointment of a professional librarian to act as a reader's advisor. 'It has been the view of the promoters of the Toynbee Library', stated the annual report that followed, 'that a mere collection of books, however copious it may become by the generosity of benefactors, loses half its value to inexperienced readers unless it is supplemented by a Librarian, who can offer literary counsel and direction to those who come'.[15]

The special courses of study were classed in five groups: A and B covered 'Language, Literature and Morals', with C (Science), D (Music and Art), and E (Technical Education). In some cases only a handful of members met weekly in each class according to the traditional university term calendar, working on the small and intimate scale Barnett had had in mind when he first conceived the settlement. In these gatherings personal friendship was 'as much kept in sight as the positive communication of knowledge'. 'Whilst instruction is given and received', his third report on the settlement's work continued, 'the main object in view is the establishment of friendship and sympathy between the teachers and the taught'.[16] Science teaching covered topics in geography, geology, chemistry, botany, astronomy, natural history more broadly, microscope work, entomology and practical histology. Music and art teaching was more modest: a singing class mounted with the Popular Ballad Concert Committee attracted around fifty members and violin lessons about twenty-five students, but freehand drawing could only muster eight students across two terms. Some technical classes in carpentry, wood-carving, clay modelling and musical drill were offered, attracting around seventy men and boys as an average weekly attendance.

By the winter of 1886–7, some 182 students were attending informal weekly classes for courses in groups A and B alone. Along with courses in modern languages, moral philosophy, history and Latin, Ernest Aves taught two separate classes in economics, Charles Ashbee took a Ruskin class through *Time and Tide* and *Fors Clavigera,* there were multiple classes in literature taught by residents like Thory Gage Gardiner and Francis Fletcher Vane, and Bolton King explained the life and achievements of Mazzini. The first two terms of 1887 saw Ashbee add a class on decorative illustration (the beginnings of his Guild of Handicraft) and the appearance of a small Greek language class, while Vane surrendered his pedagogical ambitions to concentrate on the settlement's cadet corps. The philosophy class, meanwhile, was re-constituted as a club.[17] E. B. Sargent met with trainee teachers in a literary class, attempting to stoke broader intellectual concerns than what was required in their narrow and utilitarian syllabus; reading through

> first, Charles Kingsley's *Water Babies*, which they began with thinking a
> silly nursery book, and ended with finding too deep for them; then some

Tennyson, and lastly More's *Utopia*, which seemed to please them very much by its anticipation of modern problems of education and politics, though they originally chose it as bearing on the period of history for their scholarship examination in that thought of 'what will pay', which is bound up with all their studies.[18]

Bolton King used Kingsley's *Alton Locke* 'to hang literary or moral criticisms and dissertations on,...trying to give them a wider view of educational and social problems, and a new insight into the important part they are themselves called upon to play in training the children under them'.[19] Years later, some recalled their efforts (and their apparent success) with amazement. Nevinson remembered how 'for a long time I myself held readings in *Paradise Lost*, the queerest thing about which, and by far the most instructive, was that large numbers of men came all the way from those dull but deserving districts [around the settlement] to attend'.[20]

A good number of readers and students pounced on the literary opportunities with zeal. We have already noted the example of Frederick Rogers, but he was not alone. Thomas Okey, a Spitalfields basket-weaver and night-time student of Italian, also attended extension lectures by the historian S. R. Gardiner 'whose broad and impartial treatment of history', he later recalled, 'genial manner, range of view, and ease and clarity of diction, were a rich intellectual endowment to us Toynbee students'.[21] At the Bermondsey Settlement, where similar activities were legion, one literature student relished the intellectual company as much as the stimulation. 'The reading of Shakespeare in a class is a revelation to one who has always studied alone', they explained to the settlement's magazine. '[I]nsignificant words contain meanings undreamed of until they come under discussion, and the fine wit which is found in the most tragic of Shakespeare's plays seems to gain an added zest when interpreted by a reader who thoroughly enters into the spirit of the play.'[22] Seventeen students in the Bermondsey Settlement's elocution class formed themselves into a weekly study group dedicated to Browning, known as the 'Brown Owls', 'a name chosen at the suggestion of one of the members, on account of the owl being the bird of wisdom, symbolical of learning, the companion of the golden Minerva, and accustomed to take its higher flights in the night time'.[23] Another 'Bermondsey boy', Charles Welch, was aged about 16 in the mid-1890s and working twelve hours a day in a small South London workshop sewing leather bags when he developed an unlikely passion for Greek. Calling at the Bermondsey Settlement, he was originally encouraged to enrol in a more practical modern language but insisted on joining the Greek class – the numbers of which soon dwindled down to himself alone. 'Now', he later wrote, 'let the reader consider the selfless devotion that enabled an elderly lady to come late at night, in all weathers, prepared to give what amounted to private tuition to a Bermondsey boy.' It was an experience that imprinted Welch for life. He remembered other formative experiences through the classes and clubs of the settlement:

I joined the Art class, and the latent desire to express myself in line and colour was stimulated. There were the elocution classes, too. Here language became alive, Shakespeare both a feast and a stimulus. Here I shed what little stage fright a Bermondsey boy could have, and felt the thrill of playing such roles as 'Shylock' and 'King Lear'.[24]

Toynbee Hall's model of 'Oxbridge' tutorials, reading groups and small classes was echoed on a more modest scale at the Bermondsey Settlement (see Figure 8.1). While the first term of teaching there in 1892 included some bible classes and general popular lectures, the programme had genuinely challenging academic elements. Mathematics and science courses ranged from algebra and arithmetic to botany, electricity and magnetism, and mechanics. Of these, a university extension course in the 'Chemistry of Everyday Life' taught by Professor Vivian Lewes proved the most popular, attracting some 220 students. Commercial courses on book-keeping, shorthand, typewriting and so on had around 260 in attendance, alongside the art and technical classes in clay modelling, first aid, cookery and dressmaking that also tended to be practical and skills-focussed. Importantly, although some courses appealed directly to either men or women, the general classes enrolled both male and female students. Lidgett acknowledged that this was partly on grounds of economy, but there was also a higher aim. 'The union of the sexes in higher education and recreation is itself a refining influence', he insisted, 'and it is time that the one-sided devotion to the needs of men and youths should cease, and women, often harder worked and with drearier lives, should be able to count on equal care'.[25]

By the 1896 session, with the Bermondsey extension classes in full swing, an autumn course offered by Hugh de Havilland of Peterhouse, Cambridge on 'Vegetable and Animal Life' was considered to have enjoyed the greatest success of any to that time. 'Easy to follow, beautifully illustrated, and given by a lecturer with great personal charm', the settlement magazine wrote, 'they have united instruction with true recreation, to a remarkable degree'.

> Nothing can be better for those of us who are hard-worked and live far away from nature, than to spend an hour or two each week studying natural history. Full of wonder and practical interest as the subject is, it is also a restful pursuit after busy days, and has little or nothing of the grind of some scientific studies.[26]

Eighty-six tickets were sold, and about ten weekly papers were submitted in this class. 'The students seemed to take a considerable interest in the subject', de Havilland noted at its conclusion. 'The audience was small, but very attentive, and I hope the Physiology [course] next term will draw a larger audience.'[27] More mixed results came in the settlement's courses on literature, history, languages and music. In 1892, the first year of offerings, 123 attended the classes associated with the choral society, for example, and eighty-two the violin classes run by the Popular Musical Union. Introductory Latin,

Shakespeare and English parliamentary history each attracted around twenty students; German had twenty-six enrolments and French gained sixty-three.[28] These numbers were promising, and in 1893–4 the university extension offerings continued with a two-part course, of ten weeks each, by the Fabian Graham Wallas on 'The English Citizen, past and present'. The lectures were timely and informative, Lidgett enthused in the Settlement's annual report, dealing as they did with issues of local government and welfare being addressed in Westminster with the Parish Councils Bill, 'and though Mr Wallas is understood to have well-marked political opinions of his own, these were never allowed to become in the least degree apparent to the class'.[29] The first course attracted considerable interest at first, with 109 tickets sold in advance, but attendance proved disappointing. Only fourteen students regularly attended the tutorial classes, and of these only five or six – four of them female – submitted regular papers. The exam results were likewise of a very poor standard according to the external examiner, F. W. Maitland, the celebrated legal historian. 'University Extension is, I believe, very new in Bermondsey', Wallas reflected at the end of the first class. 'Therefore although the writers of papers showed great industry and care the results [were] sometimes a little disappointing'.[30] He also taught these courses at Morley College, attached to Emma Cons' Royal Victoria Hall in Lambeth,[31] having more success with eighty-five enrolments of whom more than fifty attended weekly classes regularly. 'This course interested me extremely', he noted. 'Nearly all my class were young men between 19 and 25 who did a great deal of reading and took a genuine interest in the subject. I expect very good work from them in the spring term.'[32] Back at Bermondsey only science courses were offered during 1894, but the next year saw a return to the Warden's favoured topics when H. Boyd Carpenter, the son of the Bishop of Ripon, taught two consecutive courses on the history of British colonialism, illustrated by lantern slides. Perhaps wary of repeating Wallas' relative failure, Lidgett was keen to drum up interest, and reminded readers of the settlement magazine 'how growingly important the Colonies and India have become in questions of our foreign politics and trade'. The principle of active citizenship was again at the forefront:

> It is quite impossible to enter intelligently into many of the most important subjects of present every-day interest, without having some knowledge of the history of British conquest and colonisation. The subject is full of stirring incident, and is so close to the present time as to impose no very severe strain upon the ordinary hearer or reader. With such a lecturer as Mr Boyd Carpenter it can be neither dull nor difficult…we confidently hope that a large number will show their interest in the subject by attending these lectures, and will thereby fit themselves more intelligently to discharge the duties of British citizenship.[33]

But numbers again proved very disappointing. Nearly 100 students enrolled for the first survey of British colonialism to 1857, but the lectures were largely homiletic, dealing with England as a land of sailors, how trade followed the flag and many colonies began as havens for religious freedom, according to a summary prepared by one of the students.[34] The response was muted as only six students on average submitted weekly written work. Numbers more than halved after Christmas, when the lectures concentrated on British India. Only forty-four enrolled this time, a handful submitting weekly papers and only two, Mary and Elizabeth Chambers, sitting the final examination. As classes concluded Carpenter wrote somewhat ruefully: 'The lecturer cannot help but think, that considering the neighbourhood, scientific work is more likely to succeed than historical and literary courses.'[35]

Extension advocates thus had occasion to reflect on their own effectiveness as teachers, the extent of basic demand for their classes, the nature of their audiences and how best to work with them to secure genuine adult education in poor and working-class neighbourhoods. Most remained convinced that the personal dimension was paramount: Canon Browne's closing comments at an 1894 conference to explore the challenges involved, for example,

> dwelt upon the extreme importance of securing Lecturers for University Extension work who should not only be able to instruct their audiences... but also get themselves into the hearts and souls of those whom they were teaching; when such a Lecturer had learnt to know a district, he should by all means be retained there, sympathy and mutual understanding being most essential to success in work of this kind.[36]

But this did not necessarily equate to paternalism by a new generation of 'gentleman settlers', as many critics of the settlement ethos have assumed. While historians have debated the point at considerable length, as Geddes Poole summarises, many insist the university extension ethos 'largely reflected the essentially moderate, socially conservative and upwardly mobile aspirations of much of the British working class of this period'.[37] As Goldman argues, '[t]here is no evidence that any of [the extensionists] were party to deliberate strategies of political incorporation...[and if] intellectuals shared certain fundamental ideological positions with their students, it is hard to argue that they grafted onto the adult education movement their own distinctive (and anti-radical) positions'.[38]

Indeed, as we have seen, a clear recognition of self-management – of students serving on committees to ensure that the programme met their needs – was very evident in the extension work of this period, another embodiment of the social idealism that animated extension efforts at large. It was a key theme in the LSEUT conference on working-class centres in 1894, for example, as when a LSEUT worker in the Deptford extension classes spoke practically 'of the necessity of appointing a strong working-men Committee to supervise the local arrangements'.[39] Canon Browne, like Barnett a key Anglican voice for the conciliatory potential of liberal adult education, repeated the point in closing the conference. His own lengthy experience, he stated unequivocally, had demonstrated 'the necessity of having in artisan districts an "Attendance Committee" composed wholly of working-men, who should make the lecture known among their fellows, and bring the audience together'.[40]

As the Victorian century drew to a close the appeal of the extension model, with its Oxbridge overtones and lecture hall hierarchy of teacher over learner, began to wane. Barnett's sub-warden, E. J. Urwick, observed in 1899 that 'the centre of attraction had shifted; it is no longer to be found in the lecture-hall so much as in the meetings of reading-parties, societies, and [tutorial] classes. A few years ago a good University Extension Society course was sure to attract an audience; now the attendance will not be more than two-thirds of what it was...'[41] Educational provision for working people was shifting as the polytechnics and evening schools proliferated, while tutorial classes and close-knit reading and discussion groups came to the fore in the Workers' Educational Association after 1903. This celebrated effort towards democratic adult education began with a meeting at Toynbee Hall in July that year, a reminder that the ideal of educational association and popular higher education through tutorials and reading groups was something Barnett had advocated in Whitechapel since the mid-1870s.

Classes and lectures at the People's Palace

During the early 1880s, when the People's Palace was taking shape as a 'Besantian' vision of educational opportunity and improving recreation, some hoped that the principles of university extension would underpin the whole endeavour. In 1881, as the terms of the Beaumont Trust were being revised to establish Currie's as-yet-unnamed institution, the LSEUT (through Barnett and his Tower Hamlets committee) applied for use of the funds to support their work in the neighbourhood. Numbers at their classes in the Medical School of the London Hospital had climbed from twenty in 1877 to more than two hundred, and they hoped that when new Trustees were appointed they should be 'acquainted with the work of the Society in the East of London, and...[so] will make provision for holding its lectures and classes in the Beaumont Hall, the small rooms of which are described as being well suited for class rooms, and the large Hall for lectures attended by large numbers'.[42] But by this time Beaumont Institution was virtually derelict and would play little part in the charity scheme's future. Currie, revealingly, was sceptical about university extension work in East London, airing doubts at a meeting with the Charity Commission in May 1881 'that the locality which was the object of this Charity is fitted for higher teaching, and it would be almost a sin to devote this fund for any such purpose, at least to such a purpose alone'. He felt the LSEUT was 'very theoristic and doctrinaire', and failed to comprehend the pragmatic needs of the district and its population.[43]

With university extension decisively marginalised, trade skills and 'useful knowledge' came to the fore at the Palace taught by instructors from bodies such as the Society of Arts, the City and Guilds of London Institute and the

Science and Art Department for fees of between a shilling and 7/6 per session. Courses in what became the Palace Technical School commenced in workshops in the old Bancroft School buildings, remodelled under the direction of Robert Mitchell of the Regent Street Polytechnic. By November around 1,500 students were attending classes there, beginning with trades such as joinery, tailoring, plumbing, metal turning, general carpentry and boot-making. More theoretical classes in engineering, telegraphy, mathematics, geometry and chemistry were offered, as were courses in clerical composition, elocution, modern languages, arithmetic and shorthand. Most were to assist students into paid employment, but at the end of 1887 the *Palace Journal* reiterated that a second aim, that of inculcating a love of knowledge for its own sake, was an 'undercurrent...which we ought to do our utmost to extend and encourage'.[44] Evening classes in music prospered alongside these pragmatic offerings: nearly 120 had joined singing classes within a month, the piano lessons were fully subscribed with fifty students, and a Monday night violin class had attracted seventeen more.[45]

Literary study through directed reading had featured in Besant's fictional 'Palace of Delight', an emphasis that the Beaumont Trust tried to maintain in the realised scheme. Three qualified librarians were appointed to the library: chief librarian Frances Low, Constance Black (sister of the celebrated trade union leader Clementina Black) and Miss M. S. R. James who arrived with the opening of the new library building in August 1888. Apart from G. F. Hilcken at the Bethnal Green Free Library, these women were probably the only qualified librarians working in the East End at this time, and to begin with they looked to voluntary assistance to inculcate a love of reading. 'To those who have not far advanced along the road to knowledge', the first handbook to the Palace explained, volunteer advisers would suggest 'travels, tales, and picture books, while the thoughtful will be told of essays and biographies, and the student directed on to literature of which otherwise he would not have heard...'[46] They imagined tutorial-style reading parties led by these advisors meeting in alcoves off the main library, where 'in sympathy with the mental attitude of the class...[the advisers would] divine ways of introducing them to the more subtle meanings of the author, or of guiding them through those passages which are sometimes rendered obscure by want of knowledge or experience'.[47] It is unclear whether any volunteer-led groups materialised, but Sunday openings were managed with voluntary help. Miss Low looked ahead to a course of evening lectures by other volunteers on literary topics to draw readers from the fiction of Marryat and Rider Haggard towards Thackeray, Scott, Shakespeare and Goethe as exemplars of a more demanding literature, authors that 'remain unknown [to most readers], and their books unread because it is wrongly believed their works would prove dry and uninteresting'.[48]

Meanwhile the 'Popular Lectures for the People' in the Queen's Hall were well-attended, as the appreciative audience for a two-hour lecture 'Across America' illustrated by slides in January 1890 attests.[49] But educational lectures in the Queen's Hall were hampered by the enormous capacity of the auditorium itself. One old friend of the polytechnic idea, Assistant Charity Commissioner Henry Cunynghame, felt that this was a fatal flaw. By 1891, and with the Palace's finances in a disastrous state, he lamented how the Hall's vast dimensions had 'rendered it almost impossible to get lecturers who can be heard in it', and that consequently the Palace had been denied the lucrative speaking engagements that might have buttressed its income.[50] One speaker, Harold Spender, found the setting so inhospitable and vast that he suggested partitioning the main hall to bring audiences closer to the lectern. 'I lectured there last Wednesday', he told the Drapers' Company secretary in March 1894, 'and though my voice is pretty tough, I have had a sore throat ever since'.[51]

A 'common life' in clubs and associations

Self-improving study, whether in class-rooms, lectures or the technical work-shops, was never imagined by these promoters as an isolated, self-absorbed activity. Self-culture was intended to be sociable, as when Lidgett saw a cor-porate spirit coalescing in the Bermondsey students so that 'attachment to the Settlement is steadily growing, and we are gradually overcoming that spirit of isolation, which is so evil a feature of London life'.[52] In this spirit all three centres encouraged active participation by students in clubs and associations. As soon as classes and conditions of membership were being formulated for the opening of the People's Palace in mid-1887, for example, self-managed clubs were encouraged 'for the purpose of consolidating sociability amongst Members', specifically football and harriers clubs, orchestral and choral societies, a military band and fife and drum band, chess club, sickness benefit club and savings bank.[53] With the building incomplete, several temporary iron buildings previously used to house an industrial exhibition were pressed into service as a gymnasium, and games rooms for billiards and social clubs were set up in the old school buildings that remained on the Palace site. The settlement ethos of civic participation and active citizenship, meanwhile, meant that clubs and societies loomed just as large for Barnett, Lidgett and their co-workers in Whitechapel and Bermondsey. 'The Whitechapel Centre aims at being more than a mere lecturing agency', explained the *Toynbee Record*. 'It endeavours to unite the students into something of a common life.'[54]

These efforts echoed a major theme in late-Victorian social work. Histor-ians are attracted to formal movements like the Boys' Brigade and the later Boy Scouts and Girl Guides, but in fact the ordinary social clubs for young people, permeating into working-class communities from a host of churches, chapels and philanthropic ventures, were probably more influential in an everyday sense. Attached to workplaces, churches or educational institutes, philanthropic clubs were modest in their size and facilities, but as a reformist phenomenon they were remarkably ubiquitous. 'I think I am not exaggerating when I say that nearly every parish in London has its girls' club as well as an institution of like nature for young men', wrote one philanthropist, Mary

Jeune, in 1893. 'A few of the clubs are fairly flourishing, some even almost smart; but the majority are very poor.' She described the typical arrangements:

> They all have a quiet and clean room, with a bright fire, and pretty prints and pictures on the walls, and are in charge of a decent woman, who supplies what refreshment the members may require; and there a tired work-girl, who is a member, can go from seven to ten of an evening and spend her time reading, gossiping, or, if she is studious and not too tired, taking up some branch of instruction. There are gymnastic classes, sewing and cooking classes if she is so minded; and gymnastics are very popular, as is also singing and part-singing.[55]

The fraternity of club life was intended to counter narrow experience and limited education, and the sense of fellowship and common purpose gained there might, it was hoped, nourish social connections and build communities of interest. 'In the clubs', wrote James Adderley of Oxford House's work in this area,

> the working man and the University man can meet each other in the best of all ways, as friends and as the members of one society....Half our social troubles nowadays are due to misunderstandings between one class of society and another. These clubs should be a meeting ground where each class would get to know the opinions and feelings of the other.[56]

Such aspirations put the supervised philanthropic social clubs at the very heart of the settlement enterprise. Their self-managed social clubs, with elected office bearers and committee but supervised by social workers, were important local entities that often attracted wholehearted support from working men and women. Frank Foster, a riverside worker and member of the Dockers' Union, was elected secretary of the St George's Social Club run by the Bermondsey Settlement in early 1896 and had no doubt that a 'well-conducted Club has power to do good, *i.e.*, to elevate and educate certain classes of workmen, greater than that of any other association in existence'. He listed four key aspects of their own club: games of skill like billiards and bagatelle 'in which...the heart of the average British working-man delights', the relaxed tone of their musical evenings that encouraged all to contribute a song and join in the chorus, the availability of newspapers and the chance to discuss current affairs. Perhaps most essential to Foster was their members' 'sense of proprietorship, a consciousness that a part of the concern is his, that he has a share in the management, and has the right to suggest improvements, and he swells out with pride if his suggestions are adopted by his fellow members'.[57] These hopes and expectations united club promoters and many of their members. One unnamed volunteer involved in youth work for girls in Bermondsey, convinced the clubs were 'an embodiment of Settlement aims', captured neatly the balancing ambitions of physical, moral and social amelioration:

> in their gymnastic classes, [clubs supplied] that strength of body and increased vitality the lack of which is one of the initial difficulties in all work that involves 'self-help' among South Londoners; quickening an honest healthy love of nature and real beauty by long rambles in the country and visits to Picture Galleries; strengthening the sense of mutual dependence and obligation, which is the guiding principle of a club; and, above all, bringing about, in the most simple and complete manner, that companionship and confidence between classes which it is the first object of the Settlement to promote.[58]

In Whitechapel a rich profusion of clubs sprang up at Toynbee Hall after 1884. Less ambitious philanthropic centres might have been content with a social club for evenings indoors, and perhaps sporting clubs and a few musical societies. Toynbee Hall supported all these and more as its social and recreational clubs flourished in a quite remarkable abundance. Each one had some involvement from residents or other settlement volunteers; but at the same time they were largely self-managed, electing their own committees to be responsible for their own procedures, membership matters, finances and meetings. A Guild of Compassion, Sanitary Aid Society and Vigilance Society directed local energies to charitable ends, but most of the Toynbee Hall clubs addressed specialised interests, encouraging intellectual growth and advanced (if informal) study. The Adam Smith Club debated economics, while the Library Readers Union and Literary Association, the Ethical Society and Philosophical Society, the Natural History Society and Shakespeare Society all conducted spirited meetings. J. M. Dent, the self-made publisher of popular classics, joined the last-named club in the mid-1880s and remembered discussing Shakespeare's plays 'with great avidity, reading a scene and then discussing each item...we did not only argue about philological items and little differences in the readings and so on, but we discussed the living spirit of the play and every character was criticised as a live man'.[59] More practical and vocational clubs catered for art students, photography enthusiasts, nursing, life-saving and ambulance, and groups like the Orchestral Society and Pupil Teachers' Debating Society emerged from classes taught in the settlement. Games and physical activity were catered for through the Athletic Association, football and swimming clubs, and clubs for chess and cycling. Groups like the Natural History Society read and discussed scientific papers and had monthly country excursions to examine geology, plants and wildlife, but several others were entirely devoted to organised excursions: the Antiquarian Society, Leonardo Sketching Club, and perhaps most notably the Toynbee Travellers' Club (TTC).

Only this last-named, the best-known of the settlement's clubs, has received any substantial historical attention. The TTC existed for educational purposes rather than simple tourism, 'providing co-operative travel for those who were studying together' in Henrietta Barnett's description, and undertaking numerous overseas and domestic trips before dissolving in 1913.[60] It grew out of Bolton King's Mazzini class when a member suggested a pilgrimage to the great democratic patriot's tomb at Genoa.[61] Thus their first trip to Italy in 1888 can be understood, Sutcliffe argues, as an affirmation of Mazzini's democratic liberalism, a secular pilgrimage 'as the Toynbee Hall pilgrims – travelling representatives of the adult education movement – followed itineraries which targeted the symbols affirming the republican, democratic identity of liberal Italy'.[62] But Henrietta Barnett remembered the origins of this first trip rather differently, growing 'out of the resolve we registered in St Peter's at Rome [during a holiday], to show the St Jude's workers some of the marvels we were enjoying'.[63] Indeed, as Maltz suggests, if a moralising exposure to high culture sat comfortably alongside these progressive leanings, there may well have been tensions as the first major tour unfolded. The scrapbook maintained during their first trip to Italy, a bold experiment in taking eighty-one University Extension male and female students (mostly clerks, Board School teachers and junior civil servants, and quite a few of them unmarried) to Florence, Pisa and Genoa, indicates a divided party, 'one faction unashamedly "artistic" and "intense", the other perplexed and cynical over their companions' aesthetic effusions'.[64] Certainly when Barnett evaluated the benefits of this first excursion abroad he made little reference to the republican virtues of Italy's modern democracy. 'Brought face to face in Florence with a life which expressed itself in building, in painting, in sculpture', he wrote characteristically, 'they felt of course a quickening of brain as they strove to understand this new language, and a widening of sympathy as they realised that success cannot always be measured by one standard; but chiefly, perhaps, they felt an increase of humility'.[65]

Nothing nearly as ambitious crowned the club life of the new settlement in Bermondsey, but a rash of social and recreative clubs sprang up there too. The major club, the St George's Social Club, was founded in April 1894 and within a year had 162 members, twenty of them female. The settlement magazine marvelled at its progress: 'It has met, talked, discussed, read, listened to lectures, organised concerts, completed a billiard handicap, and started an athletic club, all before it was nine months old'.[66] In May 1895 one of its rooms was decorated and turned over for members' exclusive use for conversation and reading. 'There is oilcloth on the floor', the settlement magazine reported, 'a table and chairs, pictures and a bookshelf, already partially filled with books....Plans are already being discussed for making bright and happy evenings, and for enabling those who come to derive as much pleasure as possible, with, perhaps, a dash of profit'.[67] No drinking or gambling were permitted, but its rules allowed meetings and social activities on Sundays provided these were 'such as are calculated to promote the religious, moral, intellectual or social good of the members'.[68] The female presence was distinctive, and represented another of Lidgett's cherished ambitions. He had advanced views on gender equity, and in extolling the virtues of the club he ventured that

> when the principle of introducing women to the membership is recognised, and the club becomes in addition the meeting place of men and women in different ranks of life, the great drawbacks to ordinary clubs are removed, and it is possible to work enthusiastically for its success, without fearing either injury to the home life of the members, or the narrowing influence of cliques.[69]

When a female auditor was appointed by vote at the first annual meeting in April 1895, it was regarded as an unprecedented achievement among London's philanthropic social clubs.[70] Bolstered by a donation of books from the Kyrle Society, the club set up its own library for members, where titles by Thomas Carlyle, Samuel Smiles, Jules Verne's *Great Explorers*, Dickens and Kingsley ensured an earnest and self-improving tone.[71] 'We feel and know that our respectability is assured', wrote a committee member in mid-1896. 'There is plenty of mirth in this Club, but no ribaldry, plenty of fun and jokes; but nothing coarse, or remotely suggestive.'[72]

A dedicated club for factory girls associated with the settlement had been commenced earlier, in October 1893, by Mary Simmons and Miss E. A. Barrs. This met three nights a week at the Southwark Park schoolrooms near the women's residences of the settlement, and concentrated on gymnastics and drill, dress-making, debating, singing and painting under the encouraging hand of the settlement ladies. The dress-making class was held to be popular, its members sewing the red and blue uniforms worn in the drill sessions. Miss Barrs ran a painting class for club members on Saturdays, and a local newspaper was struck with 'the quickness with which many of these girls – nearly all factory hands – have learned to copy water-colour drawings of flowers and simple landscapes'. Again we see a balance struck between supervision and self-reliance, and the encouragement to sociability and civic participation:

> Games, music and tea – the latter, prepared by two of their number, is sold at halfpenny a cup, and halfpenny a slice of bread and butter – are appreciated; but the most popular class is that for gymnastics, taught by a trained instructor, who was once a factory girl herself, and who thoroughly understands and sympathises with her pupils. This, more than anything else, has improved the girls' physique. The material for their costumes is supplied at half-price, and they are taught to make it up, as well as their own clothes, while discussions on subjects of civic and local interest are held.[73]

Within eighteen months the club had over sixty regular members, becoming known as the 'Beatrice Club' to recognise Beatrice Dunkin, a young woman bed-ridden by spinal injury who Lidgett had known since his time in

Cambridge. While staying at a convalescent home Dunkin had met a young woman from South London who worked at the Peek, Frean and Co. factory. When the latter returned to Bermondsey, she took Dunkin's advice and called on Mary Simmons at the settlement, who 'told her about the Club and of her anxiety to secure enough girls to ensure a good start'. It seems she actively set about recruiting among her co-workers, assuring its success, and Lidgett was delighted to tell Miss Dunkin 'that just when she was complaining that her life was useless, she was founding a Girl's Club as surely as if she had been busily tramping the streets of Rotherhithe'.[74] Lidgett saw an exemplary narrative of philanthropic generosity in Beatrice Dunkin's efforts, stimulating as they did a corresponding self-help among the Bermondsey factory workers that transcended barriers of distance, class and personal affliction.

St Christopher's Club, a weekly play and activity group for boys too young for the Boys' Brigade, was organised by another of the settlement's female residents, Ethel Emuss, at her lodgings on Sundays. The girls' division of the St George's Social Club, meanwhile, continued to meet weekly in West Lane, with gymnastic drill and ballad-singing, stories and reading, 'sometimes Hans Andersen's "Fairy Tales", sometimes Kingsley's "Heroes", and generally end up a pleasant evening with a lively game'.[75] It was joined several years later by the St Olave's Guild run by the female social workers to help local girls find employment and encourage them into the settlement's gymnasium for games and gymnastics. The Guild's social aspirations could stand for the Settlement's club activities in general: 'To bring them into touch with others' was cited as a primary objective, 'to let them feel that they belong to something and somebody; that life is not all work, all drudgery, with no change; but that there is a life with interests outside their work'.[76] The settlement's Parliamentary Debating Society also flourished, attracting around eighty students to join and debate political measures and mock bills with Lidgett agreeing to serve as Speaker. 'Of course, they are open to some objection on the ground either of pretentiousness or of playing at Parliament', he acknowledged.

> But on the other hand they train public speakers, they teach members to understand and respect the rules of debate, they promote in political opponents kindliness and intelligent appreciation of different points of view, and encourage study and ingenuity in drafting bills and resolutions for discussion. Above all they tend to foster a civic spirit, and this we feel to be most important.[77]

By the mid-1890s a chess club, tennis, cycling and cricket clubs, a group excursion to Switzerland in the summer of 1895, a Choral and Orchestral Union, *conversazione* and 'At Homes', performances of Shakespeare by the elocution class, concerts, debates and recitals had blossomed in Bermondsey's unpromising soil. A Rambling Club organised weekend expeditions into the countryside, and others were mounted through the efforts of residents and

BERMONDSEY . . .
. . SETTLEMENT,

Farncombe Street, Jamaica Road, S.E.

(Near SPA ROAD STATION, S.E.R.)

Warden = **REV. J. SCOTT LIDGETT, M.A.**

Secretary = **MISS KNOWLES.**

Membership Subscription	1/- each Term.
General Class Fees	I/- ,,
Additional Subjects	6d. each.

The Evening Educational Classes:

ART.—Art Needlework, Clay Modelling, Drawing and Colour, Freehand Drawing, Geometrical Drawing, Metal Work, Wood Carving.

COMMERCIAL.—Book-keeping, Commercial Geography, Type-writing, Shorthand, Writing and Dictation.

LANGUAGES, LITERATURE, &c.—English Grammar and Literature, Literary Society, French, German, Latin, Greek, Elocution.

MATHEMATICS and PHYSICAL SCIENCE.—Arithmetic, Algebra, Euclid, Chemistry, Electricity and Magnetism, Sound, Light and Heat, Advanced Mathematics, Botany.

MUSICAL.—Choral Society, Orchestra, Glee Part-Song Choir, Solo Singing, Sight Singing, Violin and other Instruments.

TECHNICAL.—Ambulance, Cooking, Dressmaking, Millinery, Nursing, Use of Tools, Drawing for the Workshop, Building Construction.

THEOLOGICAL.—Biblical Study, Church History, Greek Testament, Sunday School preparation.

UNIVERSITY EXTENSION LECTURES.

ADVANTAGES TO MEMBERS.

Reading Room and Library, Smoking Room, Gymnasium and Athletic Clubs Popular Lectures and Concerts, Social and Excursion Clubs, Choral and Orchestral Union, Parliamentary Debating Society.

Figure 8.1 Bermondsey Settlement leaflet, *c.* 1897

volunteers at local schools, taking students on Saturdays to London land-marks like Westminster Abbey, the Houses of Parliament and the national museums. 'These afternoons not only supply much enjoyment to those who take part in them but are of genuine educational value', Lidgett reported. 'To widen the interest taken by the young in the great city to which they belong, quite apart from the increase in knowledge afforded by visits to places of historic or scientific importance, is of very great advantage.'[78] The Factory Girls' Club started their own fortnightly excursions during the summer months in 1897. 'We have already visited the exhibition of Mr Watts' pictures in Whitechapel', its supervisor Miss I'Anson reported, 'and the very excellent collection of pictures in the Art Gallery of the Guildhall, amongst which we made many friends, and [also] visited Hampstead, in response to an invitation by Mrs Vaughan Nash, who very kindly entertained us for tea and afterwards accompanied us on to the Heath. There we strolled about enjoying the bright, clear air, the fresh, tender green of the trees, and the extensive views in various directions, coming home tired but well contented, and with happy memories of a very delightful time to cheer us in our work during the week.'[79]

Among Bermondsey's philanthropic clubs were two remarkable pioneering attempts to encourage games and pastimes among children. Efforts began modestly enough with two residents organising weekly sessions of games, singing and recitation during the winter of 1892–3 at two local Board Schools, assisted by members of the settlement's classes. One volunteer, a Miss Crawford, set up another weekly playgroup on summer afternoons with rounders and team sports. Given that working families in Bermondsey and Rotherhithe occupied cramped houses, with most in two rooms only, without parks or playgrounds suited to games, Lidgett voiced the common anxiety that children had 'no games at home. They are driven out into the streets, an inhospitable nursery on a winter evening at the best, but, too often, a school for the undoing of all the intellectual and moral education of the day time, where manners are coarsened and corrupted.'[80] For several years this work sputtered along fitfully, with no shortage of willing volunteers but always lacking, as Mary Simmons put it, '[a] worker who had...health, energy, the spirit of play and the gift of organisation combined, to take the lead' until taken up vigorously by Grace Hannam when she arrived at the Settlement at the end of 1895 to establish her 'Guild of Play'.[81] Traditional English dances, songs, games and pastimes were taught to Bermondsey children in an environment that focused on teamwork and individual responsibility. 'We sing, and march, and play together', 'Sister Grace' wrote in explanation, 'and from start to finish we show the children that it lies very largely in their own hands to make or mar the evening's fun. We treat the children rationally and respectfully, acknowledging their individuality, encouraging them to do right for right's sake as much as possible; we have no rewards for good behaviour save those of working for others...'[82] The Guild hosted their first May Day gathering in 1896, when flowers and flags decorated the rooms of the settlement and children gathered around the maypole set up in the lecture room for their dances, 'the result of many an hour which the children have spent', the settlement magazine explained, 'substituting for the rough language and games of the street, the quaint and refining movements, with which our great-great grandmothers beguiled their hours of leisure'.[83] On subsequent occasions the children performed their dance routines for invited audiences, together with pantomimes and *tableaux* drawn from fairy stories. In Hannam's estimation the work of organised play for children was a vehicle for 'redeeming for the children of our courts and alleys "their right to their childhood",... not simply to amuse or spoil them, but to let our children's work be illustrative of the Settlement rule, which is to train them to train themselves'.[84]

In all this Sister Grace was a progressive advocate of play as a moralising element in children's education, citing the German theorist Friedrich Fröbel as she expounded a respect for their innate creativity and sociability that was rare in the educational practices of the day.[85] Deeper anxieties are also evident, however. 'Nothing could be happier than the sight of our children playing together contentedly and joyously the quaint old English song games', she wrote,

> which we teach them in place of the echoes of the West End Music Hall songs, with their vile meanings, so readily understood by our elder children, and explained to the younger ones, which we hear yelled in the streets at night. Our scheme for their playtime is a right one, and will play its own definite part in the great scheme for social reform.[86]

If the Guild of Play can fairly be accused of organising 'shows' of orderliness and elegance rather than true play, the open and participatory structure of its games and dances contrasted positively with the strict conformism and routine expected in London's infant schoolrooms at this time. Even so, moralising intentions were ever-present. 'We do believe that our love for the children should stimulate us to draw them upward to those heights of goodness only reached by the paths of self-sacrifice', Hannam declared, 'and that we should appeal to what is noblest in their natures; not by coercion, but by the mighty influence of a living spirit and a consistent example'.[87]

Similar motives infused her pioneering effort to establish a social club at the settlement for disabled children, adults and the elderly that grew into a national network of inter-connected societies as 'The Guild of the Brave Poor Things'. The name came from Juliana Ewing's sentimental 1885 novella *The Story of a Short Life*, a bestseller for young readers about a pampered and wilful boy from an aristocratic family crippled in a carriage accident while watching military manoeuvres. Despairing of ever taking arms like his ancestors, young Leonard 'gradually learns lessons of patience and self-control...helped by the thought that it may be as keen a fight to be a brave cripple as to be a brave soldier'.[88] He starts a scrapbook, a collection of 'Poor Things who've been hurt, like me'; he explains to his mother, '[or] had their legs or their arms chopped off in battle, and are very good and brave about it, and manage very, very nearly as well as people who have got nothing the matter with them'.[89] Borrowing her name from Leonard's scrapbook, Hannam established a weekly playgroup at the Bermondsey Settlement that valorised the endurance and fighting spirit of disabled people in the struggle of life. Although the term 'things' in the Guild's title provoked some disquiet (the local newspaper thinking it 'a peculiar word...to use in a titular phrase relating to human creatures'), it quickly became a noted feature of the Settlement's weekly programme.[90] Mary Simmons described how 'Friday after Friday the Settlement Hall is filled with members, the maimed, the halt and the blind, almost all very poor as well as crippled, but all vowed to courage and cheerfulness in spite of, and even through, the hardness of their lot.'[91] Several hundred gathered each week, some around

> tables plentifully furnished with newspapers and magazines, the blind cluster around the piano, there are toys for the children, facilities for painting mottoes and pictures, while a group of blind women will sit in a corner to knit and chat. Short lectures are given at times on scientific and other subjects. The object is to make the settlement a true 'Palace of Delight' for the day.[92]

'We have the merriest afternoons possible', Hannam explained, 'we play all sorts of games; musical chairs, dumb charades, proverbs, draughts, dominoes, and the children have dolls, and tops and Noah's Arks, and the time just flies....' The Guild began as a modest enterprise and essentially remained so throughout its life: small-scale, local and voluntarist, highly personal. But again we see a moralising hope for social interaction at its core. Through these simple games and pursuits, Simmons wrote, 'worn faces brighten, and even suffering is easier to bear, as they feel themselves drawn once more into "the swim of things", and brought into fellowship with the rest of the world'.[93]

In both of Hannam's pioneering endeavours there was an unflinching commitment to personal influence, and certainly a moral preference for order and decorum that might seem intrinsically paternalistic. We might also see an element of historicist fantasy, as pre-industrial, antiquated pastimes and games – suitably bowdlerised as orderly fun – were revived to restore lost social connections. But an essentially cogent sense of educational possibility through play and creativity is also present. 'We need organised play to go hand in hand with school work', Hannam explained in justifying her approach.

> We need it as a philanthropic agent, leading the child, ever so gently, into right ways of thinking, speaking, and acting, from the beginning. We need it, to help forward the social training, to give the opportunity of co-operation; it seems to me a plain duty to make the children feel part of the big plan which we mean to fight for to the teeth; for the spirit of these games, the losing sight of personal feeling for the good of the majority, the dependence of one upon the other for success, the vigorous

individuality brought into service for those less vigorous, all this, begun and grown in these play hours, will crystallize into action in the hereafter.[94]

These aspirations were shared by her co-workers at the Settlement, and not only her husband, the child psychologist and LCC inspector of education Charles Kimmins. When the time for fund-raising began to support her work for disabled children through a retreat in the countryside, the Chailey Heritage Craft School, Lidgett spoke in support, hoping that visitors to the Guilds' annual gala display at the Bermondsey Town Hall in May 1901 'had seen something of the possibilities of organised play and the part it could perform in the development of education'.[95]

Club life at the People's Palace

The People's Palace Institute made similar provision for adolescents and young adults through clubs and special interest societies. For a weekly rate of 1½ *d.* for boys and men and a penny for female members, the Institute conferred free admission to all concerts, entertainments, and exhibitions; evening use of the library, free access to the gymnasium, reduced fees at classes, membership of the Palace social club and subsidised issues of the *Palace Journal.*[96] These social and leisure opportunities were intended to draw the Institute members together in a sustaining corporate life, modelled once again on Quintin Hogg's success at the Regent Street Polytechnic. But its fees were set a little lower, because 'in its very different environment it seemed necessary for the Palace to make its amusing side more conspicuous than its sober educational side, and as a natural consequence the young people at first joined its Institute more for the entertainments and social diversions than for the classes'.[97] Within two weeks of the opening in early October 1887 a flood of sixteen hundred members had enrolled, nearly a quarter of them female, growing to 4,200 at the end of the first year as up to thirty new applications were received each day.[98] When Currie welcomed the 500 latest members in January 1888 at a reception tea, gymnastics display and a music concert in Queen's Hall, he 'strongly urged them to fraternise, and make sociability their aim – recommending for this purpose the various clubs that had sprung up in their midst'.[99]

By this time the Institute hosted more than twenty distinct clubs and societies, including the Chess and Draughts Club, Debating Society, Choral Society, Military Band, Orchestra, Sketching Club, Harriers' and Ramblers' Clubs, Photographic Society, a Ladies' Social Club, Dramatic Club, Literary Club and associations for swimming, football, cricket, lawn tennis, cycling, boxing and billiards.[100] As a range of activity it was truly 'Besantian' in flavour, promising to realise the manifold social benefits of self-culture, intellectual stimulation and mutual fellowship working in harmony. Besant hoped the Sketching Club would display their work every year as a 'Royal Academy of the East'. 'Before many years', he enthused in the Palace magazine, our concerts will be given by our own Members; the songs will be composed, written, and sung by our own musicians, poets, and vocalists; we shall play on our own stage plays written and acted by ourselves; this Journal...will be written by the Members. As for our own athletes, we have them already. But, in the realm of Art, Music, and Literature we are only making a beginning.[101]

For a time these hopes did not seem far-fetched: when a change of executive occurred in the Palace's mock parliament run by the Debating Society in May 1888, for example, the occasion was marked by a reception, co-ordinated by the Ladies' Social Committee, featuring a short Shakespearian piece performed by the Palace Dramatic Society.[102]

Perhaps most encouraging was the fact that each of these clubs appeared spontaneously, as potential members come together of their own accord, recruited fellow members and formed their own management committees, often involving young men and women working together. 'Some twenty years ago...no such thing was known as a joint committee of men and women', the *Palace Journal* commented, 'but the world is not as it was then, and women are now taking their share in active life, and in most of the modern philanthropic works we find men and women united in the committee work'. Offering some advice on meeting procedure, agendas and minutes for the many in the Institute who were new to this kind of role, the *Journal* was sure of the civic spirit that would thus be encouraged. By their very nature committee members

> are not thinking of themselves, but of the work itself, striving to bring to it their best experience and capabilities; and with such materials as the Palace possesses of enlightened and superior young business men and women, we doubt not that committees will be found equal to the task ... [so that] by harmonious and diligent work, the grand conception of a People's Palace may be developed to the utmost, through the energetic and united work of those toilers for whom it was erected.[103]

The social and moral advantages to be gained seemed self-evident. Currie reflected at the Institute's first anniversary dinner that 'the clubs which had been started in connection with the Palace, and which were in a flourishing condition, were a great help in binding the young people together, feeling, as they did, they had interests in common'.[104] To Sir Philip Magnus, the eminent educationalist, the Palace Institute seemed 'essentially a corporation of working men and women, bound together by the sympathy of kindred occupations, and bent on mutual improvement...to promote their intellectual, physical, moral and material well-being'; in this the self-governance through clubs and committees seemed an influence for 'making them more self-dependent, and by stimulating the taste for higher pleasures and amusements'.[105]

All this was highly pleasing to the promoters. But it quickly became evident that some members took the People's Palace 'merely as a house of call and lounging place', a casual and disaffected element that as Currie explained was entirely unwelcome:

> they played at billiards, smoked, put on ridiculous airs in their dignity as members towards the officials and attendants, never appeared in the gymnasium or worked at the classes, and, in short, generally lowered the tone of the Institute and filled places which might have been more profitably occupied by others; besides which many of them did not belong to the class for whom the Palace was primarily intended.[106]

These 'loafers', the unemployed and the apathetic, were seen as a problem. Casual in their manner, insufficiently diligent or appreciative of the opportunities on offer, these visitors were soon actively discouraged. At the Palace Library, to begin with 'the continual rambling in and out of that class of persons so well-known as "loafers", was a constant and grave annoyance'.[107] Weekly reader's tickets on the model of the British Museum reading room were soon introduced, 'to discourage sightseers and loafers and to encourage a sense of belonging to a distinct community of interest'.[108]

The Trustees were keen to exclude casual users from the Palace more broadly. They felt the problem had arisen because membership of the Institute could initially be taken up by anyone, who would then have a reduced fee for class attendance, rather than the other way around.[109] Membership of the Institute was summarily restricted to students attending the various classes of the Palace Technical Schools, the age limit was raised to sixteen years and a 'Junior Section' established 'for lads of from thirteen to sixteen years of age, who were in respectable employment'.[110] No new enrolments were admitted, and recently expired memberships were not reminded to renew their subscriptions. In September 1889 the Palace Institute was suspended altogether in order to resolve the problem of 'loafers' as the old Bancroft buildings that housed the clubs and class-rooms were demolished.[111] Students enrolled at the various classes and members of the Palace gymnasium, military band, chess club, choral and orchestral societies and other clubs were subsequently offered membership of the reformed Institute for an additional fee of sixpence a quarter. All this came to be seen as an instructive failure within the larger People's Palace experiment: after all, Currie admitted in 1890, 'a loyal *esprit de corps* could not be expected among a large number of young persons of different religions, tastes and habits, brought together suddenly, with only a common object of getting all the convenience and amusement which the Palace had to offer for as little payment as possible'. He considered the change, and the exclusion of the 'loafer element', to be highly satisfactory:

> These arrangements were, of course, greeted with murmurings among the class of members whose membership had been beneficial neither to themselves nor to the institution, but there can be no doubt whatever of the good effects of the change...it was not, indeed, from the *bona fide*

members of clubs that murmurs arose, but from those young men whom it was found desirable to exclude from the Institute until such time as it should please them to co-operate in the efforts of the trustees to improve their minds and bodies, and who resented the loss of their exclusive lounging place.[112]

With this adjustment the Palace clubs continued to supply the sociability and fellowship so dear to the Beaumont Trust's scheme. When the Institute students mounted their New Years' *conversazione* in early January 1891, the Palace was seasonably decorated, and entertainments included a vocal performance and short operetta on the main stage of the Queen's Hall, while a short dramatic sketch was staged by students in the adjoining lecture hall. Elsewhere, the ante-rooms to the Library were to be 'used for the purposes of refreshments, and promenading', with a nearby room designated as a 'Smoking Room' for the men. On these occasions, studious pursuits were put aside as Palace members were encouraged to adopt the polite manners and sociability of the middle-class parlour. Even so, as the arrangements for the *conversazione* were being finalised, it was thought that a 'descriptive exhibition of the Phonograph could be held in one of the Class Rooms for the studiously disposed'.[113]

Not all the Palace's philanthropic clubs enjoyed uninterrupted success, especially in the incomplete buildings of 1887–8. The Palace Debating Society struggled in a cramped space that was basically inadequate for meetings, let alone actual debates. 'The room to which we are relegated', the secretary wrote to Currie in early March 1888, 'is almost enough to stifle the Society at one blow. It is the room used as a cloak room, and with an attendance of about 25 the room is crowded...we may expect at least a dozen more and where we are to pack them passes my comprehension'.[114] Later meetings attracted up to eighty or more, but were held in spare rooms and even the basement of the old Bancroft School buildings at the rear of the Palace site.[115] Under these circumstances the enthusiasm of the Palace's debaters seems to have wilted. But when Harold Spender came across from Toynbee Hall and joined the Palace clerk in supervising an experimental debate in October 1890 to revive the society, the effort was well rewarded. He declared it 'a success in every way – orderly, large, keenly interested and temperate in word'. The new society would follow Toynbee Hall's policy of free admittance to all interested debaters, and Spender was confident that with a continuous series of debates and discussion topics 'there will grow up at the People's Palace a debating society of first-class quality – a school of dialectic for East London'. He was sure that moral and intellectual benefits would accrue over time. 'I think that such a meeting-place of ideas is peculiarly desirable for our working-classes', he wrote in seeking support from the Beaumont Trustees, 'who are apt to gather in their clubs and consider that there is no opinion in the wide world but their own that is worthy of consideration, and to grow narrow from very narrowness of sphere'.[116]

Such moralising intentions seem heavy-handed and patronising. Yet we do have clues that the Palace clubs' autonomous and democratic character was valued, and indeed jealously guarded, by their members. When a proposal was mooted in October 1887 to establish separate refreshments for the 'better sort' among the Palace members, it opened up a basic social fault line within the membership. According to one Palace user, those that favoured separate refreshment rooms 'seemed to form themselves into a little click [*sic*] to carry out their wishes. But other members, from a class that was 'looked [down] upon as though they were thought to be to[o] poor or beneath the aspiring Brothers' opposed the idea. This person, writing under the assumed name 'E. Patterson', was one of the latter and helped organise a petition to the Trustees to voice their opposition to the idea. A 'Higher Class refreshment room', it was asserted, 'would benefit a few, interested parties only, and more over [be] the means of setting up a class distinction and forming a gulf, which never should exist in a People's Palace and one which would prove utterly foreign to the now existing arrangements *via* [*sic*] one Library, 1 gymnasium, 1 games room, 1 set of Education Classes, and one admission fee to anything'. 'Patterson' lamented the decline of the original 'spirit of the undertaking, [*viz*] Education, recreation and co-operation of all classes rich and poor together', and hinted at other tensions within the Palace membership. The argument for a separate refreshment room, it seems, came from members

> who belong to the lower middle class of society, but mainly supported by Jews who feel the inconvenience of dress on their sabbath and other obvious reasons, Still I have not a word to say against Nationality (injustices except[ed]) only class distinctions in the People's Palace. If they can exercise, read, work and study together, why can they not sup together...[?][117]

The actions of the Trustees in response are unclear, but this episode casts a slim shaft of light on the elusive inner life of Palace members, their factions and preferences. Class, status, ethnicity, and membership privileges were all live issues. Perhaps most importantly, for these ardent subscribers to the Palace and its ethos the official 'Besantian' rhetoric of the enterprise represented something more than bland reformist platitudes. 'Patterson's' protest hints that the conceptions of corporate inclusion and social conciliation favoured by middle-class reformers had firm adherents from within the Palace membership itself.

'At home' at the settlements

The fellowship and mutual interest that reformers hoped to inculcate by club activities also animated the sociable events that quickly became the hallmark of the settlement movement. Barnett's initial proposal at Oxford in 1883 had promised that the new university settlement would provide frequent

receptions and parties, when 'whatever be the form of entertainment provided, be it books or pictures, lectures or reading, dancing or music, the guests
will find that their pleasure lies in intercourse',[118] an emphasis on sociability
that once again had been anticipated in his parish activities. 'My husband
counted it a religious duty to give parties', Henrietta Barnett remembered; his
logic being that 'through [social] intercourse comes friendship, through friendship comes love of men, and through love of men comes love of God'.[119] Their
parish entertainments, parties and musical recitals, he explained in a St Jude's
sermon in October 1876, were meant to introduce a social element that he
believed was missing when 'the poor go off to make pleasure'. Social interaction across the boundaries of class and status offered important moralising
benefits for all concerned. 'Parties should be signs of friendship and meetings',
he insisted, 'not to convert, but simply to show what good pleasure is'.[120]
Evenings of sandwiches, talk and parlour entertainment in the schoolrooms or
the vicarage were quintessential to the Barnetts' Whitechapel ministry for three
decades. 'Whatever was the result, the pleasure of welcoming the parish
people in our own home never palled'; Mrs Barnett insisted,

> the small annoyances of greasy heads leaning against Morris papers and
> dirty damp garments ruining furniture covers, were soon surmounted by
> placing chairs and backless sofas well away from the wall, and substitut-
> ing washable Liberty cottons for silk damasks. At every party care was
> taken to invite guests of different classes, and so horizons were widened,
> sympathies deepened, and sources of common interest discovered.[121]

The Barnetts organised summer visits to grand country houses in a similar
spirit: not merely excursions to 'see the sights', these were highly engineered
social encounters undertaken in the name of 'friendship'. 'The Vicar and Mrs
Barnett tell their friends among the rich how much their Whitechapel friends
would enjoy a day in their beautiful country homes', the parish magazine
explained, 'and the postman brings to the Vicarage, letters of invitation for
10, 20, 40, 50, 60 or 100 Whitechapel people [to] spend the day in the homes
of those whose lives are cast in pleasant places'. Railway fares and expenses
were either covered by the host or paid out of the parish Entertainment Fund,
'to which other friends contribute, for the desire is that the St Jude's party-day
should be a day free of expense and void of care'. But there was also a prim
insistence that 'higher' purposes should be kept in view:

> But though pleasure is very good, yet there is something more than
> pleasure, and it would be well perhaps, if we could remember this on our
> Party-days. We might all learn more from our visits to the country; and
> those hosts who teach us by music or books, or microscopes, or intro-
> ductions and talks with people who know more than most of us, do for us
> all a greater service than those who, with all their kindness, only amuse
> us with games, or swings, or laughter-making acts.[122]

The pattern continued at Toynbee Hall, when the settlement buildings were opened up to the labouring poor as a venue for concerts, debates, club meetings, magic-lantern shows, 'smoking concerts', tea parties and formal dinners. These events came to epitomise the Barnetts' hopes for social intercourse through improving entertainments, as working-class neighbours were welcomed into the carefully crafted environment of Whitechapel's transplanted university college. 'In the four months past between three and four thousand neighbours have been entertained', reckoned the settlement's first annual report, but only in separate gatherings that were small enough to ensure intimacy. 'As entertainers we have welcomed parties of our neighbours, parties of students, parties of pupil-teachers, and parties from workmen's clubs'.[123] These occasions collectively came to be known as the 'At Homes', when the settlement was opened for East London 'neighbours' as a 'hospitable home.... All that [Toynbee Hall] includes of earnestness, learning, skill, and whatever may rise out of a spirit of friendliness, is meant to be put at the service of the people of the East End.'[124] Local co-operative societies, trade unionists, sporting organisations such as the Tower Hamlets Cricket Club, and the students of various classes and educational efforts were entertained on this basis.[125] 'Teachers, Co-Operators, East End Club Members', explained the Entertainment Committee in 1889,

> University Extension Students, Working Men, Politicians, Men and Women of Science, Street Orderly Boys, Needlewomen, Policemen, Railway Porters, Clergy and Philanthropists have met in [the settlement's] rooms; friendships have been made, pleasure has been given, the bonds of sympathy between many representing widely separated spheres of life have been strengthened, and many have learnt what gain may come from the meeting and friendly intercourse of those whose lives seemed far apart.[126]

The key personality in Toynbee Hall's entertainment programme was Henrietta Barnett, who argued that in East London 'more artificial methods for gaining and keeping life must be adopted' than were needed in 'gentler places, where folk get the aid of some of Nature's beauties...'[127] She emphasised the value of the settlement's social life and entertainments in the surrounding urban context – depicted in explicitly 'Besantian' terms, we notice – of dull mediocrity and materialism:

> A modern novelist has made the reading-public familiar with the difficulties of social intercourse in East London. Large factories and yards are rare, and isolation is the prevailing feature of a life, which in other respects also is a life of dulness and monotony. 'They keep themselves to themselves, and do not mix with their neighbours.' There are therefore two or three entertainments every week during the winter at the Hall, and to supply that 'drawing-room element' which has been felt to be so necessary; these parties take the form of suppers, conversaziones,

gatherings of the Student Union, etc., besides the private hospitality of individual residents.[128]

Thus the settlement's entertainments were conceived as intimate affairs. A large gathering of the members of various associated clubs at Toynbee Hall in late 1887 for distribution of prizes and awards was, Barnett explained to his brother, 'not a successful party as it did not lead to anything. There is not much object in entertaining those who are not friends and cannot be friends'.[129] The most effective social occasions hosted at the settlement, he felt, were those that managed to retain a personal, companionable character. Accordingly, during the winter months, 'some sort of recreative instruction, either in the form of a concert, a magic lantern, or a variety entertainment' was given each Monday evening for groups called together from the various settlement classes.[130] Light meals of lemonade and sandwiches were followed by parlour games, dances, performances of different kinds and brief speeches. Summer evenings saw music concerts by lantern-light in the Toynbee quadrangle, and in the early autumn each year, on the grandest of all the social occasions at the settlement, extension students numbering in their hundreds were invited to a reception to mark the resumption of the Toynbee evening classes.

These parties and 'At Homes' had explicitly moralising intentions, as East End 'neighbours' were drawn into the settlement's charmed atmosphere, with its collegial elegance and didactic furnishings open to guests who had been invited, as Henrietta explained unblushingly, 'in order to give them pleasures and to increase their interests'. The settlement's didactic interior came into its own on these occasions:

> The artists, of which those who care can learn, as they turn over the portfolios, look at the photograph books, or study the gift pictures on the walls. The great, also, in the musical world are pressed into the service, as the musically generous among the friends of Toynbee Hall pass on the plaintive ideas of Schumann, or the soul-stirring aspirations of Beethoven and Mozart.[131]

The aim always was not 'to entertain for entertainment's sake, but, in as far as possible, to create and deepen friendships and to widen sympathies'.[132] The residents served quite literally as a social conduit, as they personally introduced their peers to the Whitechapel labouring poor, giving rise to the mutual understanding and sense of common purpose that was the essential currency of social idealism. 'How now can it be told what was done and said at the thousand and one parties given in Toynbee Hall?' Henrietta Barnett asked in 1888.

> The tale is hidden in the closer friendship and better understanding of the many rich and poor who have found a meeting place in its drawing room and an introducer in their common friend, the Resident, who is their

host. People of all sorts have there found their kinship, have joined their aspirations, blended their hopes, and seen in each other the common heart which beats beneath all kinds of coats and gowns, be their texture ever so various.[133]

Reflecting in hindsight on Toynbee Hall's social occasions, however, some residents were bemused by what they had attempted in their youthful enthusiasm. Francis Fletcher Vane remembered an innate resistance and reserve that had to be overcome: 'Get a crowd of Britons of various classes together and it is wonderfully difficult to move them, or to get them to move as a team'.[134] He and Ingham Brooke colluded on one occasion to liven things up: 'He took the piano, and I chose the prettiest girl for a partner... [in] a rollicking polka' to the delight of the Whitechapel guests. The two residents, however, were 'called to account for this innovation'. The usual pattern was far more sedate and dispiriting, as word-games were suggested and 'apathetically accepted....As the game proceeded dullness was increased. Few of the poorer guests spoke (what they thought I cannot imagine). As an entertainment it was hopeless.'[135] We are probably right to share this scepticism. But the settlement's commitment to social *rapprochement* through hospitality never faltered during Barnett's tenure as warden, perhaps reaching its apogee in the receptions for Whitechapel working-men organised in the houses of Toynbee Hall's wealthy West End patrons and supporters. Social distance would be overcome, the settlement's sponsors were convinced, as the universal pleasures of fellowship were enjoyed together across the barriers of social class. At one reception at Devonshire House for East London's university extension students in February 1895, for instance, according to the *Toynbee Record* the Toynbee students loitered awkwardly in the vast rooms until their 'shyness and stiffness soon yielded to the cordial and unaffected courtesy of the host and hostess and the friends who had been invited to help in the entertainment'. Revealingly, it was the guests who were depicted as stilted and awkward, trapped within their upbringing and background, while the social graces of their magnanimous hosts helped them to span the class divide with ease. Ironically, after visiting Chatsworth House (the Devonshires' vast country seat) a decade earlier, Samuel Barnett had been appalled by the Duke's ostentatious luxury. 'Wealth had ransacked the world to make great rooms', he reported scornfully to his brother, 'buy Italian art, frame the biggest conservatories and plan rocks into wild forms. The effect was after all very small...It is not a house to represent a home, and its things had better be in a museum nearer town.'[136]

Eleven years later, with Barnett pleading his absence through illness, the plutocratic Duke's townhouse was thrown open for a grand reception for Toynbee Hall's students. The 700 students were met formally by the Duke and Duchess at the top of marble stairs to the long ball-room. A group of aristocratic ladies were on hand to provide musical diversion as the evening progressed, and one volunteered to take the guests around the Duke's collection of old masters.

The *Toynbee Record* was sure this entirely artificial social encounter had mutual benefit for the participants: 'The ladies sang and played in the Draw-ing-room, and the music, which was admirable, was received with an applause and an evident appreciation which we hope gave some pleasure in return.' While dancing began 'to perfect music, and on the best of floors' and the guests 'unthawed' in the ball-room,

> The rest of us fell into groups and talked, or wandered through the rooms feasting our eyes on the pictures and the decorations. The House was built at the beginning of the last century...and the beautiful ceilings belong, as the Duke told an enquirer, to that period, and have never been touched, except for re-gilding, since.[137]

In all the occasion was considered a tremendous success, and it was regretted that 'Toynbee Hall appeared without its natural head'.[138] Henry Nevinson was there too, however, and held a more critical view of proceedings that supplies an instructive contrast to the *Record*'s blithe narrative. Nevinson recorded biting descriptions of the hosts in his diary, the Duke 'in ribbon and star, benevolently bored' and his wife with 'a fixed and artificial smile...I could see no trace of charm or love or any of the noble passions which par-dons what is called sin'.[139] Devonshire House, for Nevinson, was a vast aris-tocratic obscenity encrusted with the worst excesses of privilege. Going from room to room he 'came now and then upon a diamonded duchess seated in style as at Madame Tussaud's. Mostly very graceful and very aristocratic, but there was [one] man a terrible example of noble breeding, chinless, boneless, brainless and swivel-eyed'.[140] He was unconvinced that any moralising benefits would be imparted through this highly engineered encounter. Self-consciously intellectual and a struggling writer, Nevinson's viewpoint was as distant from his aristocratic hosts as it was from the 'swarming mob of Toynbee students'. His account of the latter, in fact, is sharp and contemptuous:

> Barbarian urges of Toynbee students broke out in supper rooms. Every-thing was swept clean off as by locusts and the carpet left strewn with orange peel and chicken bones. At the last they fell to devouring the ornamental strands of white of egg etc. used to garnish the meats. I myself had taken them for iced potatoes. The port flowed perhaps too freely. Everything served in silver which I hope is still the owner's. Hun-garians fiddled, countesses sang, the plebs danced.[141]

The sight which for Nevinson encapsulated the increasingly bizarre occasion was provided by a disoriented, half-drunk East Ender reeling on the steps of Devonshire House as the evening came to a close, 'appealing to the footmen and stars' for directions to the Blackwall bus.

Although never elaborated to this extent, an enthusiasm for entertainments and sociability was also central to the improving work of the Bermondsey

Settlement. But here too it needed to be enacted with care. 'Amusements and entertainments are necessary [to settlement work]', Lidgett wrote in his 1894 report, 'but if they are not to demoralise they must grow out of intellectual interests and the friendships which [those interests] create'.[142] The interests he had in mind were demonstrated when members of the Bermondsey Settlement's elocution class, having earlier prepared for examinations, performed selections from their repertoire at the St George's Social Club and a local infirmary during 1894, followed by a similar performance at the settlement's Christmas *soirée* and a comedietta for the Students' Concert two months later, in February.[143]

As a consequence 'At Homes' much like those at Toynbee Hall punctuated life at the Bermondsey Settlement each term during the programme of evening classes. Its magazine reported on two evenings in November 1894, where '[m]usic formed a harmonious background for conversation and games: clumps, dumb charades, and a strange contest called parlour tennis caused much fun'. These were followed shortly afterwards by the Christmas *soirée*, another attempt to entertain and encourage fellowship through gymnastic displays, humorous recitations by the elocution class, refreshments, and 'an apparently endless programme of music, songs, and recitations in the drawing-room'.[144] The pattern was repeated the following year, when some eight hundred visitors from the settlement's classes and clubs 'were entertained by several displays', explained the *Monthly Record*, 'wherein the sister arts "Gymnastike" and "Mousike", vied in friendly rivalry for the first place in popular favour'. The occasion captured the settlement's social programme in full: while the gymnastic class 'disported itself in the Gymnasium, giving various performances, including horse-vaulting, dumb-bell exercises, and varieties on the horizontal and parallel bars', the rest of the building was brimming with activity.

> Simultaneously, in the Lecture Hall the music of a loud Orchestra delighted many more. Particularly deserving of note were the singing of Miss Morgan, and the solos on violin and cornet. Anon the Elocution Class shewed how they had progressed rhetorically under the untiring efforts of Mr Jones. The sections from Sheridan's 'Rivals' given in the costumes of a by-gone age, were interpreted with real art. The Drawing-room, too, was enlivened by recitations from Dr Kimmins and Mr Masham, the former reciting 'Eugene Aram' with much tragic power, the latter some comic parodies from 'Bab-ballads'. Lastly we must not forget the charming musical sketch on the pianoforte (given by Mr and Mrs Champness), which was again and again encored. It was not till quite late that people began to disperse from a most enjoyable social evening, and we cannot but think that common interest in these mutually-improving gatherings may help not a little towards forging that link of Christian friendliness that should bind society yet more closely together.[145]

The intimate and personal character of all this work remained a touchstone for the reformist programme. 'Our parties are not public entertainments';

Lidgett reminded readers of his third report in 1894, 'they are "At Homes" in our Drawing Room, and the student who is specially interested in his subject gradually finds his teacher, if a Resident, in that teacher's private room. And thus to intellectual interests and helpfulness we are able to add homely warmth.'[146]

'Attractions innumerable' at the People's Palace

The intimate, domestic flavour of the social occasions at the settlement houses, and the personal influences they were supposed to mobilise, contrasted with the flamboyant opening ceremonies of the People's Palace in May 1887, when a round of lavish entertainment was mounted to announce the Palace's improving cultural mission in bold terms. Ten thousand local girls were entertained there on the Thursday night after its opening; a similar number of boys attended the following night, and over three thousand workmen and their wives came on the Saturday evening.[147] According to Bishop How, who attended on all three occasions, the entertainment was carried off 'with great munificence and was admirably organised', although he was unconvinced about its quality and lasting effect. 'Plenty of food and all manner of amusements were going on', he reported to his daughter, creating quite a carnival atmosphere in the Palace grounds: 'conjurers, performing dogs, vanishing lady, sailors singing and dancing, performing goats, Punch and Judy, Corney Grain, etc. etc. I stood by the side of the vanishing lady and saw her plop down through a trap door...'[148] In the same manner between three and four thousand local working men were invited as guests of the Drapers' Company to an evening *conversazione* to accompany the stone-laying ceremony for the Palace Library in the Jubilee Week, June 1887. Drawn from the permanent workforces of the dock companies, the East London railways, the gasworks and other large East End firms, those invited were carefully screened in order to ensure an assemblage of the respectable labouring poor. 'In each case', the press reported, 'a list of the men employed earning from 20s. to 30s. a week, and, if possible, having a record of at least four years' service in their present situations, was furnished, and from these lists the invitations were made out'.[149] The chosen thousands were received at the Queen's Hall by Sir John Jennings, Master of the Drapers' Company, and were entertained by bandsmen of the Grenadier Guards, a minstrel troupe and the eminent vocalist Mme Antoinette Sterling, who was later to perform regularly at the Palace.

Grand occasions of mass audiences remained the Palace's characteristic mode of activity during its glittering first few years. 'Sir Edmund began his operations with a "show"', it was commented in 1890, 'and he has been giving shows ever since. That he has succeeded in supplying a want is sufficiently attested by the fact that *a million and a half* of people attended his entertainments in the first year, 1887–88.'[150] There was some exaggeration in this, but the Palace became famous for its exhibitions and displays, drawing thousands to see local manufacturing exhibits, exotic flowers and time-honoured East End pets and hobbies such as costermongers' donkeys, dogs, pigeons and poultry. In its first year, 36,500 people attended a Poultry and Pigeon Show over two weeks in October 1887, a Dog Show attracted 15,000 in three days in March 1888, and a further 24,225 people attended the Cats and Rabbits Show on Easter Monday and Tuesday.[151] The royal and aristocratic patronage continued: HRH the Princess Christian opened the Palace's Show of Chrysanthemums in November 1887; the Prince of Wales opened the Apprentices Exhibition on 10 December, and the Duke of Westminster opened the Workman's Exhibition the following May. The latter two exhibitions attracted 86,000 and 96,436 visitors respectively, and set the pattern for the Palace's grandest event, the 1888 Autumn Fête and Art Exhibition held over six weeks in August and September. This promised 'attractions innumerable all day long, picture-gallery, organ recitals, entertainments, displays, shows, bands, etc....Venetian masts, Chinese lanterns, and all the gay appurtenances which go to make up a *fête* will be found: but the switchback railway will be conspicuous by its absence'.[152] Nevertheless it attracted an extraordinary 310,000 visitors, paying either sixpence or a penny to attend in the evening.

The practical problem faced by Currie and his co-managers was that their careful screening of attendees to the stone-laying ceremony could not be kept up. If the Palace was to remain true to its 'Besantian' ideals, the expansive and all-encompassing rhetoric that had infused the public appeals of 1884–7, it could not routinely rely upon selective invitations to ensure decorous audiences from among respectable working families. Currie and his managers faced two particularly knotty problems: their obligation (as they saw it) to police the separation of younger men and women at the Palace, and the difficulty of supervising and regulating behaviour at these large popular events.

Policing gender at the People's Palace

'This experiment is very interesting', observed Henry Cunynghame of the Palace scheme in 1887, 'because it is the first instance on a large scale in which the interests of girls have been considered as well as those of boys. Experience will dictate how far it is expedient to separate the sexes.'[153] It was, in other words, an experiment that required supervision and regulation. Like others involved in the Palace scheme, Walter Besant understood sexual difference in conventional 'separate spheres' terms,[154] and in a pamphlet addressed directly to local working men he codified their basic expectations. Each man could 'sit and take your tobacco with conversation, books or newspapers', he promised. 'Here, if you prefer, you may devote your evenings to the pursuit of knowledge, to amusements, or to learning one of those arts in which some men find the greatest pleasure of their lives.' Their sons would meanwhile gain a profitable education in the Technical Schools and absorb improving codes of manly conduct. 'Friendships are made which will be life long'; Besant hoped, 'the lads are finding out each other as young men do at Oxford or Cambridge. Already they like better to be boxing and cudgel playing in the gymnasium, or running with the harriers, than walking up and down the street with a girl: already they are beginning to understand that social life which they have never before had the chance of enjoying.'[155] Even if the Palace facilities cost a younger man a shilling a week, Besant felt he would otherwise 'spend five times that sum in beer, music halls and theatres for himself and his girl. It is not one of the least advantages of membership, that it separates a lad from the society of his sweetheart while he is at the Palace'.[156] Meanwhile, he assured the working-class fathers of East London, 'your wives, your daughters, and your sisters will also find a pleasant or profitable way of passing their evenings, exposed to no dangers or temptations, and be enabled, like yourselves, to learn what they please, and to enjoy the entertainment of the Palace'.[157]

In practice the Palace worked on these lines as a series of gendered realms, where conventional distinctions of sexual difference were carefully regulated. From its classes and club rooms to the public spaces of the Queen's Hall and Winter Garden, men, women, boys and girls were organised into distinct groups, and scrutinised carefully in areas such as the Queen's Hall, the library and gardens where segregation was not feasible. This applied particularly in the old buildings of the Bancroft School that served as club-house for the members of the Palace Institute. 'The lower floor was appropriated for the use of the young women', explained Currie, 'and the upper to that of the young men, communication between the two being blocked, and separate entrances being provided'. The distinctions resulted in a men's club upstairs and a ladies' realm below:

> The billiard-tables were transferred...and parts of the upper floor were fitted up as reading and smoking rooms, committee rooms, billiard and bagatelle rooms, and one room as a small library; while on the ground floor the young women were given a sitting-room, needlework-rooms, a reading-room, cloak-rooms, and a music-room.[158]

Other areas and activities of the Palace were similarly gendered by official sanction. The male students of the Palace Institute used the gymnasium proper every evening, while their female counterparts received gymnastic instruction in the Queen's Hall on the evenings that it was not required for concerts.[159] Clubs such as the chess and debating societies, which were not necessarily exclusive to either sex, were in fact restricted to men and boys only. Conventional assumptions prevailed: both the abstract calculations of chess and the pressing public questions that occupied the debating society were deemed the exclusive preserve of the 'masculine' intellect. This thinking was so commonplace as to rarely require justification, yet traces of a dissenting view are occasionally to be found. One petitioner to the Beaumont Trust chairman wondered aloud, for example, whether the male members of Palace clubs might be consulted to determine the validity of the ban on female membership. 'Why do I suggest such [?]', he asked rhetorically, before answering the question with some vigour:

because Lady and Gentleman Philanthropists think it wise to bring the sexes up together in a rational way[;] also many social thinkers and Phrenologists and Mr Walter Besant. Chess is a quite [*sic*] game and would cultivate females mode of thinking. [D]ebating: many ladies can talk but although they may not do in Parliament they could in such a gathering give Earnest thoughtfull [*sic*] expression to their views and [p]leas[e] them to take an interest in the government of the country and many other reasons and why [the] Ramblers [Club –] because ladies like and should have [an] interest in museums, countries, objects, etc, etc.[160]

We have no sense of how widespread these views were, but they had little visible effect on the Palace and its operation. Thus for the period in 1887–8 that the Queen's Hall was used as a temporary library, it was proposed that a portion be set aside for females only, with appropriate magazines to hand and a lady supervisor 'so as to exercise an influence over the girls'.[161] Besant envisaged that the ante-rooms to the library at the rear of Queen's Hall would be 'given over entirely for the use of the girls who form the 'Lady Members'. They will then have it all to themselves, under the government of their own committee, their own music room, tea room, reading and writing room, and conversation room'.[162] There was a separate boys' room at the Palace Library for its Sunday opening, later used as the Wilkie Collins Memorial Library.

Given the intensive supervision applied to events at the Queen's Hall and in the Library, these arrangements left the Winter Garden as the only section of the Palace where free socialising between the sexes could occur. Henry Nevinson visited the People's Palace in April 1893, and noted that as a 'dull-ish concert' proceeded in the Queen's Hall there were 'pupils flocking about in the Winter Garden', with much intermingling of the sexes in evidence. 'I had no such place to meet my lover', commented his female companion drily. In an oblique criticism of the Palace's stated intention to reach the poor and working families of the district and its codes of sexual propriety, the two agreed that the Palace's 'main result would be a large increase of population among the lower middle classes'.[163]

Crowd behaviour at the People's Palace

The larger gatherings at the Palace were crowded, noisy and potentially volatile, presenting managers with a second problem. The scale of the Palace's activities were difficult enough: one neighbour felt that much disruption had been tolerated with little complaint during construction, but the first Palace Fête in the summer of 1888 had been 'a veritable pandemonium'.

At intervals during the day we hear a steam whistle [and] also a steam organ rolling out the latest *classical* music (not mentioning several others), but my children after having gone to bed are roused and greatly frightened by a violent explosion, somewhat resembling that of a cannon...[and] sufficiently violent to shake my house.[164]

More troubling was the risk of disorder and vandalism. On Whit Monday in June 1889, when a crowd of 15,000 thronged the Palace and its surrounds for the Workmen's and Apprentices' Industrial Exhibition, a finger was apparently deliberately broken off one of the marble statues in the Queen's Hall; 'not, it is reassuring to know', John Knight (Besant's sub-editor on the *Palace Journal*) editorialised sternly, 'by any responsible, full-aged East-ender, but by a few unclean ruffians of about sixteen years of age or so'. Nevertheless this, it was feared, was a pivotal moment:

> Packed as it has been at times with thousands of excited and heavy-limbed Mile-Enders and Whitechapellers to witness boxing competitions and gymnastic displays, the Queen's Hall has always remained undamaged, and in every way the visitors to the Palace have shown their anxiety to preserve untarnished their splendid gift. But the spell has it seems at last been broken....What continued interest in the East End can be expected from those with the means to give it practical effect when they find their finest gifts treated in this manner?[165]

At the Donkey Show a month later, the crowds made it difficult to spot an organised gang of pickpockets loitering at a side door into the Queen's Hall, at least according to W. J. Orsman of Hoxton's Christian Mission who reported them to an attendant. No-one alerted a nearby constable, however, who seems to have been indifferent to the purported threat. The attendant, Orsman reported indignantly to Currie, 'actually allowed these men a few minutes afterwards to snatch a gold presentation watch from one of the party arriving with the Earl of Aberdeen. This constable ought to be reprimanded. I heard afterwards of two other robberies.'[166]

Currie and his co-managers were thus caught in a dilemma when it came to the large-scale attractions at the Palace. They needed to be grand and all-encompassing if they were to match the 'Besantian' rhetoric of their appeal campaign, but there was a high risk of the kind of disorderliness that would fatally undermine the whole philanthropic exchange promised by the Palace scheme. In fact it was only these attractions at very cheap rates of entry that succeeded in drawing a genuine cross-section of the East End population. Currie commented that, among the crowds that attended their first fête, 'it was particularly noticeable that the very poor, to whom even a charge of twopence or threepence is at times almost prohibitive, flocked in very large numbers through the turnstiles at the lower price of a penny – very poorly-dressed men, women, and children indeed forming the bulk of the visitors'.[167] But adding to the dilemma was the fact that it was the scale and expense of the shows that fatally eroded the Palace's shaky finances. Cunynghame's investigation into the Palace's financial position in 1891 indicated that £9,455 had been spent on exhibitions and shows in the Palace's first year (1887–8), offset by only £4,248 in gate receipts. The situation worsened, with costs staying at the same high level the following year but takings falling to £2,864. Despite the enormous attendance for the 1888 Fête and Exhibition, the low entry fee and extensive outlays resulted in a crippling overall loss of £650–8–10 for this event alone. Coupled with earlier losses of £73 for the Cat, Rabbit and Guinea Pig Shows, £203 for the workman's exhibition, and £419 for the Christmas Fête, the shows and exhibitions represented a drain on resources that the Palace simply could not afford.[168]

Indeed they were part of a brief Indian summer of reckless spending before an inevitable winter of austerity. Under Currie's leadership, the Palace staff numbered nearly 40 people in 1887, a total annual wages bill of £2,315, and salaries at the Technical School and for the evening classes added over £4,600, even before the expensive entertainments and exhibitions were taken into account. With expenses running far beyond the funding arrangements supplied by the Drapers' Company and through the City Parochial funds, this expenditure rapidly sank the Trust's palatial philanthropy. After some of the trustees signalled concern at the financial state of the whole enterprise, the Charity Commission intervened into the Palace's management in 1890. Their report identified unserviced debt, poor budgeting and profligate spending; the measures imposed included better auditing, debt reductions and a shift to cash expenditure only. The year that followed saw cuts to salaried staff and the end of un-guaranteed entertainments and exhibitions, and the shows and entertainments that had successfully attracted 'all sorts' from East London were discontinued. Total expenditure on entertainments was thus reduced from over £9,000 in 1888–9 to a strictly limited budget of £1,800 in 1890–91.[169] Any entertainments would have to be self-sustaining, a new direction formalised in a revised administrative scheme of 1892 that enabled 'entertainments and exhibitions at higher scales of prices' in Queen's Hall and the Winter Garden with a view to benefit the financial position of the Trust.[170]

The experience highlighted that mass recreation at the Palace had surpassed the Trust's capacities for moralising supervision. Teachers could run their classes, and volunteers might assist with clubs and societies, but who was to supply a moralising personal example at these large, undiscriminating gatherings? If the regular concerts, entertainments, the annual Autumn Fête and Art Exhibition, and facilities such as the library and baths were liberally open to all with cheap admission prices, many observers felt that problems would inevitably follow. The *Birkbeck Institution Magazine*, for one, regretted the Palace's undiscriminating welcome, because it undermined what could be achieved with the more promising full-time members and students. This was 'not merely the criticism of an individual who would prefer the doors of the People's Palace to swing less freely in admitting every comer, but it points to the all-important question of influence.' The efficacy of the Palace and its activities as a force for genuine education and thus personal 'elevation' was questioned:

If an Institute partakes ever so faintly of a 'garden walled round', its power of reforming the individual character is proportionately greater. The People's Palace is unquestionably one of the best expressions of the democratic spirit of our time, but it would be well to guard against the possibility of its being merely a reflex of the sidewalk where all may mix, irrespective of interest or common feeling.[171]

* * *

In practice, then, we see that the philanthropic gift of culture was not an isolated and eccentric endeavour. Rather, it was deeply embedded in a range of social, educational, and recreational activities mounted at these various centres of moralising reformist effort. Classes and lectures presented opportunities for higher education, sometimes on the university extension model, but in other places more irregularly. Sociability and associational life was a vital element, encouraged in dozens of clubs and special interest societies. The entertainments and social occasions hosted by the settlements in Whitechapel and Bermondsey aimed to encourage personal connections and friendship in small and intimate ways, humanising (as reformers thought) a dreary setting of urban routine. Grace Hannam, explaining the value of the concerts and entertainments delivered as part of her Guild of the Brave Poor Things in mid-1896, put it very simply: 'Only those living in Bermondsey and Rother-hithe know to the full how much a bit of colour is appreciated in such a dull place'.[172] The People's Palace, meanwhile, struggled to manage (and perhaps more pertinently, to afford) its more elaborate programme of lavish entertainment as it took these ambitions to the level of grand public spectacle, with attendant problems of supervision and regulation. It suffered from a larger problem, distinct from its financial fortunes or the shift to technical education narrowly understood. Put simply the scale of its operations could never be properly regulated to achieve the moralising intentions of its founders and advocates. 'The trouble is that it is so much, and yet fails of being somewhat more', wrote Robert Woods in 1892.

> There has been from the beginning a lack of that element of soul which one finds in [Quintin Hogg's] Polytechnic. There is no uniting sentiment, no common feeling. The number of students is altogether over 5,000. The students' association, though it enrols 2,000 members, does not accomplish much. The fees for instruction are higher than they should be; but even at the concerts or entertainments, which either are free or have a very small charge for admission, the poorer grades of working people do not come in any such numbers as it was hoped they would.

Woods endorsed the characteristically moralising stance favoured at the settlements and extension classes, a more interventionist approach, ironically enough, than that of the Palace Trustees and administrators. 'The great secret of this', he observed, 'is that in connection with any such work there must be strong, organised influences which shall teach these less hopeful classes to appreciate the healthful pleasures of life – which shall, in fact, go out into the highways, and hedges, and compel them to come in.'[173]

Notes

1   T. R. C. Brydon, 'Charles Booth, Charity Control, and the London Churches, 1897–1903' *The Historian* 68:3 (2006), p. 494.
2   S. Koven, 'The Whitechapel Picture Exhibitions and the Politics of Seeing' in D. J. Sherman and I. Rogoff (eds), *Museum Culture: Histories, Discourses, Spectacles* (Minneapolis: University of Minnesota Press, 1994), p. 44.
3   W. Reason, 'Settlements and Education', in W. Reason (ed.), *University and Social Settlements* (London: Methuen, 1898), p. 56.
4   J. Rose, *The Intellectual Life of the British Working Classes* (New Haven: Yale University Press, 2010 [2001]), p. 83.
5   O. Hill, *Letter to My Fellow-Workers* (London, 1888), p. 6.
6   WAC: Octavia Hill Papers, letters to Sydney Cockerell, D. Misc. 84/2, ff. 63–4.
7   BL: Cockerell Papers, Add. Mss. 52625, ff. 62 and 65, diary entries for 7 November and 28 November 1888.
8   'University Extension in Whitechapel', *Toynbee Record* 1 (October 1888), p. 10.
9   W. G. de Burgh, in 'Annual Meeting of the London Society: Conference on Working-men Centres' *UEJ* 5 (December 1894), p. 38.
10   'University Extension in Whitechapel', p. 10.
11   'Annual Meeting of the London Society: Conference on Working-men Centres', p. 37.
12   H. Barnett, *Canon Barnett: His Life, Work, and Friends* (London: John Murray, 1918), vol. 1, p. 337.
13   Toynbee Hall, *Thirteenth Annual Report* (London, 1897), p. 18.
14   Toynbee Hall, *Fifth Annual Report* (London, 1889), p. 22. A later report listed the subjects in classes and reading groups as History, Politics, Economics, Literature, French, German, Italian, Latin, Greek, Biology, Physiology, Botany, Geology, Astronomy, Chemistry, Mathematics, Musical Analysis, Singing, Violin and Drawing. Toynbee Hall, *Eighth Annual Report* (London, 1892), p. 19.
15   Toynbee Hall, *Third Annual Report* (Oxford, 1887), p. 10.
16   Toynbee Hall, *Third Annual Report*, p. 15.
17   Toynbee Hall, *Third Annual Report*, pp. 15–16.
18   Toynbee Hall, *Second Annual Report* (Oxford, 1886), Supplement, p. 37.
19   Toynbee Hall, *Second Annual Report*, p. 38. The authors of these articles are identified by Vicars Boyle's manuscript annotations in LMA: A/TOY/5.
20   H. W. Nevinson, *Changes and Chances* (London: Nesbit & Co., 1923), p. 80.
21   T. Okey, *A Basketful of Memories* (London: J. M. Dent, 1930), p. 50.
22   'A Student', 'The Literature Class' *Monthly Record* 2:9 (November 1896), p. 98.
23   'The Brown Owls' *Monthly Record* 3:3 (March 1897), p. 42.
24   C. Welch, 'The Tribute of a Bermondsey Boy' in P. Scott (ed.), *The Lasting Victories* (London: Lutterworth Press, 1948), pp. 190–2.
25   Bermondsey Settlement, *First Annual Report* (London, 1892), p. 15.
26   'The University Extension Lectures', *Monthly Record* 3:1 (January 1897), p. 9.
27   ULL: EM 2/23/23, LSEUT Lecturers' and Examiners' Reports, 1896, Bermondsey (Michaelmas Term), n. p.
28   Bermondsey Settlement, *First Annual Report*, pp. 13–14.
29   Bermondsey Settlement, *Third Annual Report* (London, 1894), p. 21.

30 ULL: EM 2/23/17, LSEUT Lecturers' and Examiners' Reports, 1893, Bermondsey (Michaelmas Term), n. p.
31 ULL: EM 2/23/18, LSEUT, *Report of the Council for the Session 1893–94* (London, 1894), pp. 3, 7. For Morley College, see A. Geddes Poole, *Philanthropy and the Construction of Victorian Women's Citizenship: Lady Frederick Cavendish and Miss Emma Cons* (Toronto: University of Toronto Press, 2014), chapter 5.
32 ULL: EM 2/23/17, LSEUT Lecturers' and Examiners' Reports, 1893, Morley College (Michaelmas Term), n. p.
33 J. S. Lidgett, 'The Settlement University Extension Lectures' *Monthly Record* 1:7 (October 1895), pp. 78–9.
34 'One of the Class', 'The Settlement University Extension Lectures' *Monthly Record* 1:8 (November 1895), pp. 95–6.
35 ULL: EM 2/23/22, 'Lecturers' and Examiners' Reports Lent & Summer Terms 1896', 'Lecturer's Report', undated, and 'Report of the Council for the Session 1895–96', pp. 6–7.
36 Canon Browne, in 'Annual Meeting of the London Society: Conference on Working-men Centres', p. 40.
37 Geddes Poole, *Philanthropy and the Construction of Victorian Women's Citizenship*, p. 161.
38 L. Goldman, 'Intellectuals and the English Working Class 1870–1945: The Case of Adult Education' *History of Education* 29:4 (2000), p. 299.
39 'Annual Meeting of the London Society: Conference on Working-men Centres', p. 39.
40 Canon Browne, in 'Annual Meeting of the London Society: Conference on Working-men Centres', p. 40.
41 Cited in Barnett, *Canon Barnett*, vol. 1, p. 338.
42 TNA: Charity Commission CHAR7/5, copy of letter of 31 January 1881.
43 TNA: Charity Commission CHAR 7/5, 'Interview Memorandum' of 5 May 1881.
44 'Our Educational Work', *Palace Journal* 1:6 (21 December 1887), p. 69.
45 'The Palace at Work' and 'Musical Arrangements', *Palace Journal* 1:1 (November 1887), pp. 3, 5.
46 Beaumont Trust, *Handbook to the People's Palace* (London, 1887), pp. 13–14.
47 Beaumont Trust, *Handbook to the People's Palace*, p. 14.
48 'The Library and Reading Room' *Palace Journal* 2:45 (19 September 1888), p. 642.
49 *Evening News*, 30 January 1890, cited in A. Chapman, 'The People's Palace for East London' (M.Phil. thesis, University of Hull, 1978), p. 204.
50 QMUL: QMC/PP/6/5, H. Cunynghame, 'Assistant Commissioner's Memorandum on the Present Condition of the People's Palace', (15 August 1891), pp. 7, 11.
51 DCA: People's Palace Box 3, correspondence dated 15 March 1894.
52 Bermondsey Settlement, *Third Annual Report*, p. 22.
53 LMA: A/BPP/2, *People's Palace for East London (Beaumont Trust)* [scheme of management, 'arrangements suggested by Mr Robert Mitchell'], (London, 1887), n. p.
54 'University Extension in Whitechapel', *Toynbee Record* 1 (October 1888), p. 10.
55 M. Jeune, 'Amusements of the Poor' *National Review* 21 (May 1893), pp. 311–12.
56 J. G. Adderley, 'University Settlements' *East London Magazine* 1:4 (November 1890), p. 37.
57 F. Foster, 'Clubs and Club Life' *Monthly Record* 2:1 (January 1896), p. 8.
58 Cited in M. Simmons, *Report of the Bermondsey Settlement: An Account of the Women's Work* (London, 1897), pp. 12–13.
59 J. M. Dent, *The House of Dent 1888–1938* (London: J. M. Dent & Sons, 1938), p. 51.
60 Barnett, *Canon Barnett*, vol. 1, p. 364.

61   Okey, *A Basketful of Memories*, p. 66.
62   M. P. Sutcliffe, *Victorian Radicals and Italian Democrats* (Woodbridge: Boydell Press, 2014), pp. 179–80. See also M. P. Sutcliffe, 'The Toynbee Travellers' Club and the Transnational Education of Citizens, 1888–90' *History Workshop Journal* 76:1 (2013), pp. 137–59.
63   Barnett, *Canon Barnett*, vol. 1, p. 359.
64   D. Maltz, *British Aestheticism and the Urban Working Classes, 1870–1900: Beauty for the People* (Basingstoke: Palgrave Macmillan, 2006), p. 80.
65   'From Whitechapel to Florence' (letter) *The Spectator* 23 June 1888, p. 850. See also J. Browne, 'The Toynbee Travellers' Club' *History of Education* 15 (1986), pp. 11–17, and Okey, *A Basketful of Memories*, pp. 66–91.
66   *Monthly Record* 1:1 (January 1895), p. 10.
67   *Monthly Record*, 1:5 (May 1895), p. 57.
68   *Monthly Record* 1:2 (February 1895), p. 23.
69   'The Bermondsey Settlement' *London* (9 January 1896).
70   *Monthly Record* 1:6 (June 1895), p. 69.
71   *Monthly Record* 1:2 (February 1895), pp. 22–3.
72   'St George's Club', *Monthly Record* 2:4 (April 1896), p. 47.
73   *The Echo*, 11 June 1895, cited in 'Working Girls' Club', *Monthly Record* 1:6 (June 1895), p. 71.
74   J. S. Lidgett, 'The Beatrice Club' in E. M. Haslam, *Beatrice Club for Women and Girls* (pamphlet) (London, n. d. [*c.*1932]), n. p.
75   L. I'Anson, 'The Working Girls' Clubs' *Monthly Record* 3:6 (June 1897), p. 94.
76   Simmons, *Report of the Bermondsey Settlement*, p. 29.
77   Bermondsey Settlement, *Second Annual Report* (London, 1893), p. 16. The information above on classes and attendances is sourced from this report, pp. 14–15.
78   Bermondsey Settlement, *Second Annual Report*, pp. 24–5.
79   I'Anson, 'The Working Girls' Clubs', p. 94.
80   Bermondsey Settlement, *Second Annual Report*, pp. 25–6.
81   Simmons, *Report of the Bermondsey Settlement*, p. 17.
82   'The Women's Settlements of London: The Wesleyan Settlement at Bermondsey' *The Sunday at Home* 41 (March 1898), p. 321.
83   'Editorial Notes' *Monthly Record* 2:5 (May 1896), p. 49.
84   Simmons, *Report of the Bermondsey Settlement*, p. 18.
85   G. Hannam, 'Childhood: An Appeal' *Monthly Record* 2:5 (May 1896), p. 53. See J. Read, 'Free Play with Froebel: Use and Abuse of Progressive Pedagogy in London's Infant Schools, 1870–1904' *Pedagogica Historica* 42:3 (2006), pp. 299–323 and K. Brehony, 'A "Socially Civilising Influence"? Play and the Urban "Degenerate"' *Pedagogica Historica* 39:1/2 (2003), pp. 87–106.
86   'Sister Grace', '"Appy Evenin'!' *Monthly Record* 2:9 (December 1896), p. 101.
87   Hannam, 'Childhood: An Appeal', p. 52.
88   A summary of the novel's plot is in 'The Women's Settlements of London: The Wesleyan Settlement at Bermondsey' *The Sunday at Home* 41 (March 1898), p. 321.
89   J. Ewing, *The Story of a Short Life* (London: SPCK, 1885), p. 54.
90   'Lady Mayoress in Bermondsey' *Southwark and Bermondsey Recorder*, 18 May 1901.
91   Simmons, *Report of the Bermondsey Settlement*, p. 27.
92   'The Women's Settlements of London', p. 322.
93   M. Simmons, *Report of the Bermondsey Settlement: Some Account of the Women's Work* (London, 1897), p. 27.
94   Hannam, 'Childhood: An Appeal', pp. 53–4.
95   'Lady Mayoress in Bermondsey', *Southwark and Bermondsey Recorder* 18 May 1901.
96   W. Besant, 'The People's Palace' *North American Review* 147 (1888), p. 58; E. H. Currie, 'The Working of "The People's Palace"' *Nineteenth Century* 27

(February 1890), p. 345; DCA: People's Palace Box 2, E. H. Currie, 'To the Beaumont Trustees' [first report on the People's Palace], 1 October 1888, p. 6.

97   A. Shaw, 'London Polytechnics and People's Palaces' *Century Magazine* 40 (June 1890), p. 176.

98   Chapman, 'The People's Palace for East London', p. 205.

99   'Admission of New Members' *Palace Journal* 1:9 (January 1888), p. 126.

100   Currie, 'To the Beaumont Trustees', p. 7.

101   'Notes of the Week', *Palace Journal* 2:50 (24 October 1888), p. 702.

102   QMUL: QMC/PP/16/5, letter to E. H. Currie, received 5 May 1888.

103   'Committees' *Palace Journal* 1:5 (December 1887), p. 58.

104   'Our Anniversary Dinner' *Palace Journal* 2:49 (October 1888), p. 691.

105   P. Magnus, 'The New Polytechnic Institutes' *Good Words* 30 (December 1889), p. 622. Chapman comments on the spontaneous and self-managed character of the Palace clubs, 'The People's Palace for East London', pp. 205–06.

106   Currie, 'The Working of "The People's Palace"', p. 346.

107   M. S. R. James, 'The People's Palace Library' *The Library* n. d., p. 343. THLHL: clippings box 330.1.

108   P. M. Brading, 'A Brief History of the People's Palace Library, East London, 1882–1902' (M.A. thesis, University of Sheffield, 1976), p.12.1.

109   Chapman, 'The People's Palace for East London', pp. 205–10.

110   Currie, 'The Working of "The People's Palace"', p. 346.

111   Announced in the *Palace Journal* 4 (July 1889), p. 134.

112   'The Working of "The People's Palace"', pp. 348–9.

113   DCA: People's Palace Box 2, C. E. Osborne, 'Proposed New Year's Conversazione' [typescript].

114   QMUL: QMC/PP/11/1, letter from H. J. Hawkins of 5 March 1888.

115   QMUL: QMC/PP/11/1, letters from J. W. Norton dated 30 March 1888 and W. Marshall dated 17 April 1888.

116   DCA: People's Palace Box 3, ms. correspondence from H. Spender, n. d.

117   QMUL: QMC/PP/16/6, 'A Petition to Sir Edmund Hay Currie' dated 22 October 1887.

118   S. A. Barnett, *Settlements of University Men in Great Towns* (pamphlet) (Oxford, 1884), repr. as Appendix A in J. A. R. Pimlott, *Toynbee Hall: Fifty Years of Social Progress 1884–1934* (London: J. M. Dent and Sons, 1935), p. 270.

119   Barnett, *Canon Barnett*, vol. 1, p. 156.

120   LMA: Barnett Papers, F/BAR/497 f. 149, sermon delivered at St Jude's Evensong, 1 October 1876.

121   Barnett, *Canon Barnett*, vol. 1, p. 153.

122   'Summer Parties', *St Jude's* 1:8 (1889), p. 70.

123   *First Annual Report of the Universities Settlement in East London* (pamphlet) (Oxford, 1885), pp. 12, 16.

124   R. A. Woods, 'The Social Awakening in London' *Scribner's Magazine*, 11 (April 1892), p. 412.

125   Toynbee Hall, *Second Annual Report* (Oxford, 1886) p. 28.

126   Toynbee Hall, *Fifth Annual Report* (London, 1889), p. 25.

127   Toynbee Hall, *Second Annual Report*, p. 26. Henrietta Barnett is identified as the author by Vicars Boyle's manuscript annotation in his bound copy of the annual reports, LMA: A/TOY/5.

128   *Toynbee Hall: General Information* (pamphlet) (London, 1887), n. p.

129   LMA: F/BAR/62, letter to F. G. Barnett of 3 December 1887.

130   *Toynbee Journal and Students Union Chronicle* 1:8 (May 1886), p. 63.

131   Toynbee Hall, *Second Annual Report*, pp. 26–7.

132   Toynbee Hall, *Third Annual Report* (Oxford, 1887), p. 22.

133   'Entertainment Echoes', *Toynbee Record* 1 (October 1888), p. 6.

134   F. F. Vane, *Agin the Governments: Memories and Adventures* (London: Sampson, Low, Marston and Co., 1929), p. 60.
135   Vane, *Agin the Governments*, pp. 60–1.
136   LMA: F/BAR/16, letter to F. G. Barnett of 26 July 1884.
137   'An Evening at Devonshire House', *Toynbee Record* 7:6 (March 1895), p. 78.
138   'An Evening at Devonshire House', p. 78.
139   Bod. L.: Nevinson Papers, MSS Eng. Misc. e 610/2, f. 28; entry of 20 February 1895.
140   Bod. L.: Nevinson Papers, MSS Eng. Misc. e 610/2, f. 29.
141   Bod. L.: Nevison Papers, MSS Eng. Misc. e 610/2, ff. 29–30.
142   Bermondsey Settlement, *Third Annual Report* (London: 1894), p. 20.
143   *Monthly Record* 1:2 (February 1895), p. 21.
144   *Monthly Record* 1:1 (January 1895), p. 3.
145   'J. E. M.', 'The Christmas Conversazione' *Monthly Record* 2:1 (January 1896), p. 10.
146   Bermondsey Settlement, *Third Annual Report*, p. 20.
147   These were memorable enough to feature in A. S. Richardson (ed.), *Forty Years' Ministry in East London: Memoirs of the Rev. Thomas Richardson* (London: Hodder and Stoughton, 1903), p. 170.
148   F. D. How, *William Walsham How: A Memoir* (London: Isbister, 1893), p. 220, reprinted letter of 28 June 1887.
149   *The Times* 27 June 1887, p. 7.
150   A. Shaw, 'London Polytechnics and People's Palaces' *Century Magazine* 40 (June 1890), p. 176.
151   Currie, 'To the Beaumont Trustees', 1888, pp. 1–2.
152   'Palace Gossip', *Palace Journal* 2:37 (25 July 1888), p. 550.
153   H. Cunynghame, 'Memorandum upon the Social, Physical, and Intellectual Improvement of the Poorer Classes of London, especially in relation to Institutions that unite Recreation with Education' dated 3 December 1887, in Parlt. P.: *Return of certain Memoranda and Reports by Charity Commissioners or their Assistant Commissioners on Technical Instruction, on Institutions combining Recreation with Education and on Free Libraries* 1890 (142) LV, p. 167.
154   'Woman is woman and man is man', Besant editorialised in the *Palace Journal* on the subject of suffrage reform, 'One works and creates; fights every day and all day long…the other sits down, receives and distributes. She cannot really work – that is, do productive work, – and she cannot fight.' 'Notes of the Week' *Palace Journal* 4 (May 1889), p. 26.
155   W. Besant, 'The People's Palace', *North American Review* 147 (1888), pp. 62–3.
156   Besant, 'The People's Palace', p. 58.
157   Beaumont Trust, *To the Working Men of East London: The People's Palace* (pamphlet) (London, 1887), p. 2.
158   'The Working of "The People's Palace"', p. 347.
159   That is, Tuesdays, Wednesdays and Fridays. Currie, 'To the Beaumont Trustees', 1888, p. 8.
160   QMUL: QMC/PP/16/6, letter from 'E. Patterson' of 24 October 1887.
161   LMA: A/BPP/2/1, report of Robert Mitchell to meeting of Beaumont Trustees, 12 July 1887.
162   Besant, 'The People's Palace', p. 57.
163   Bod. L.: Nevinson Papers, MSS Eng. Misc. e 610/1, f. 58, journal entry for 22 April 1893.
164   QMUL: QMC/PP/16/6, letter of 15 August 1888.
165   'Palace and Institute Notes' *Palace Journal* 4 (June 1889), p. 51. Besant remained honorary editor of the *Journal* at this time, assisted by John Knight and Arthur Morrison.

166 QMUL: QMC/PP/16/5, letter of 29 July 1889. The parallels between this incident and Arthur Morrison's fictional account (when Dicky Perrot steals the Bishop's watch at the opening of the 'East End Elevation Mission') are striking. A. Morrison, *A Child of the Jago* (London: MacGibbon and Kee, 1969 [1896]), p. 57.

167 Currie, 'To the Beaumont Trustees', 1888, p. 3.

168 H. Cunynghame, 'Assistant Commissioner's Memorandum', p. 16. Of the large shows at the People's Palace in 1888–9, only the smaller Easter Fête and the Cage Bird Show returned profits for the Beaumont Trust, of £25–5–7 and £43–9–0 respectively.

169 See QMC/PP/16/4, financial report of 29 July 1890, followed by Cunynghame, 'Assistant Commissioner's Memorandum', p. 10.

170 THLHL: L.P.4303, 'People's Palace and East London College' (report to Court of Assistants, Drapers' Company, 1926, from H. T. Mason, chairman), p. 2.

171 'C. J. P.', 'Social and Educational Centres of the Metropolis: III – The People's Palace' *Birkbeck Institution Magazine* 1:7 (March 1893), p. 57.

172 'The Guild of the Poor Things' *Monthly Record* 2:4 (April 1896), p. 46.

173 R. A. Woods, *English Social Movements* (London: Swan Sonnenschein and Co., 1892), pp. 254–5.

9 The gift of culture, properly understood

Reformist attempts to supply fine art and classical music to the late Victorian urban poor – as we finally encounter them in this last chapter – were in a sense an apotheosis of all the efforts outlined above. Cultural philanthropy was not something isolated and distinct, a quixotic Ruskinian tilting at windmills some scholars have called 'missionary aestheticism': with a few exceptions, the men and women we have been discussing were not 'aesthetes' in any critically meaningful sense of that term, and their aspirations were not confined to the cultivation of artistic appreciation for moral benefit. Furthermore their work was not the ideas of the great social critics – Carlyle, Ruskin, Arnold, Morris – put into action to produce concrete results: our reformers were not automatons dancing to someone else's tune. It was not as simple as the social philosophy of T. H. Green, germinated at Balliol College and then flowering as practical social policy: it shared many affinities with Green's ideas, as it did with those that crystallised politically as the 'New Liberalism', but it was not identical to either programme either in conception or execution. Nor was it driven by a narrow sense of class self-interest, an attempt to enforce moral conformity through respectable recreation: the range and nuance of this intervention into the daily sphere of urban poverty are much diminished if seen only in these reductive terms.

The gift of culture arose, rather, as a vivid late-century climax of the deep and quintessentially liberal project of Victorian social idealism. Far from being an eccentric effort on the margins, a 'fantasy of remedying slum chaos and slum brutality through communal aesthetic revelation', it sat in close and comfortably among the primary reformist concerns of the later nineteenth century.[1] In conception and deed, it was a precise expression of 'the positive impulse to build character and promote social betterment by collective means of some kind [that] permeates the diverse liberal thought' of our period.[2] The closer we look at this educational effort through moralising culture the more we realise that aestheticism had relatively little to do with it, just as we are struck by the absence of evidence that class-bound impulses of *embourgoisement* or conformist respectability were at its heart. Rather, it was 'an education to citizenship', that imagined and then aimed to inculcate mutually sustaining relationships in a fully realised civic life. It was an effort towards commonality, conciliation and social integration by an active process of individual moral amelioration and improving sociability. Needless to say reformers prosecuted these ideas from a position of class influence and with an awareness of their own status as educated onlookers to the social problem – they had no opportunity historically to do otherwise. But when they spoke of respect and obedience it was not in terms of social status, of due regard for dutiful subordination to one's social 'betters', but to the abstract authority of liberal culture in the name of citizenship and harmonious development of the individual within a social and moral community. Cultural philanthropists, if we can take them as a whole, did not look back to a pre-industrial order, but forward to a reconciled, moralised modern community of the future, infused with a broad appreciation of liberal culture. They had begun the journey, even if they had not gone far down the road, to the very modern position whereby the state takes a solemn responsibility (in principle at least) to nurture the critical intelligence of its citizens. Recent work has demonstrated how Emma Cons' Morley College – arising out of her own philanthropic 'Temperance Coffee House' and opera venue, the Royal Victoria Hall in Lambeth – also expressed this liberal ethos of worker emancipation through education, corporate life and the liberal arts.[3] If Geddes Poole argues that Emma Cons' egalitarian style made for a contrast with the Barnetts' more high-minded efforts in Whitechapel or the Oxbridge model of university extension, it is nevertheless hard to deny a basic affinity among these efforts in comparison to other modes of improving social work. When viewed through a wider lens, it is evident that they correlated in many more ways than they diverged.

In the moralising gift of culture, then, we see the underlying social idealism of the late-Victorian period – a set of impulses behind what Harris calls the 'popular vocabulary of social reform', and which increasingly came to shape public policy in welfare and education – distilling into immediately practical activities. The loan of valuable artworks to the East End and industrial South London emerged as the supreme emblem of late-Victorian cultural philanthropy, most notably at Samuel and Henrietta Barnett's Whitechapel Fine Art Exhibitions. Essentially the same reformist impulses propelled reformers to mount musical concerts, in *soirées* and chamber recitals at the settlements and at isolated venues like Red Cross Hall or the Royal Victoria Hall, or on a mass footing at the People's Palace, to complement the social intercourse of 'At Homes', dances, dinners and club events discussed in Chapter 8. Both efforts, as we see them briefly in this final chapter, arose directly alongside the educational work seen in earlier chapters and shared their underlying purposes. They were sustained by this generation of philanthropic reformers because they seemed to be a spiritualising, moralising solvent against an urban environment of dull respectability and weary routine. At the same time, they promised to encourage sociability and corporate interaction against class insularity, and to establish the bonds of mutual feeling and interests that might sustain a meaningful civic life. With this delicate balance of promise and possibility the philanthropic gift of culture found favour, for a time at least, as a part of the moralising, civic-minded and progressive repertoire of liberal social reformers.

One gospel of music for rich and poor

Concerts of high-class music were integral to Samuel Barnett's attempts at social and spiritual renewal in Whitechapel. The 'Oratorio Services' he and his wife introduced there within a year of arriving in 1873 were sponsored by West End sympathisers and aimed to dramatise and beautify parish services through sacred song and musical accompaniment. 'Grand music, heard in a Church with which many associations of a higher life are connected, seems to have the power of expressing the aspirations and holding the attention of those whose lives are for the most part low and uncontrolled', he reported a year later. 'The music would, I think, help many whom sermons failed to touch, to possess their souls.'[4] Free Sunday evening concerts in the St Jude's schoolrooms followed, organised by Clement Templeton of the Harrow Music School: two recitals in December 1877 were followed by six the following year as their work took solid form as the People's Concert Society (PCS). Aiming 'to increase the popularity of good music by means of cheap concerts', by 1895 the PCS had delivered some 800 concerts of classical chamber music to audiences across London. After their first efforts in Whitechapel Barnett called the music 'perfect of its kind, very unlike any commonly heard in these parts. It seemed, though, entirely to capture the minds of the audience, and during some of the difficult pieces there was not a movement in the room'.[5] He repeated this verdict to anyone that cared to listen, assuring the Church Congress at Carlile in late 1884, for example, that philanthropic concerts of fine music met a genuine need. He denied the common notion that working people and the poor 'had no capacity for appreciation beyond a catchy music hall chorus'. Among East End audiences, he insisted, many had an ear for fine music:

> They have listened to and apparently taken in difficult movements of Beethoven, Schumann, and Chopin. The loud applause which has followed some movement and the strained, rapt attention have proclaimed the universal feeling and shown that among the people of East London many may be found who care for high-class music.[6]

The irony is that Barnett himself was tone deaf just as he was colour blind. Henrietta wrote that her husband 'could not sing, and had no ear for either time or tune. Indeed, neither he nor I were ever quite sure of "God save the Queen" until other people stood up.'[7] But any doubts he had about the moral benefits of fine music were only ever privately expressed. Prompted by a musical evening with his brother's family in Bristol, for example, Barnett wondered in a letter to his wife whether the Whitechapel poor, lacking the education to fully appreciate fine music, 'rejoice simply in the sensation, or feel that music opens the view of a life in which they themselves live or might live'.[8] That was the essential question they tried to resolve through many years of effort organising oratorios, concerts and recitals, not least in their university settlement after 1884. The People's Entertainment Society and the Popular Ballad Concert Society regularly hosted musical evenings at Toynbee Hall; their volunteers supervising music classes and encouraging local musicians to perform.[9] Demand threatened on occasion to exceed the capacity of the settlement's music room. Recent concerts had been well attended, it was reported in 1885, featuring Beethoven's sonatas for violin and piano, presented with other 'songs rather above the concert-room level', that together provided 'evidence...of the sufficiency of one gospel of music for rich and poor'.[10] Concerts by this time were no longer entirely a matter of philanthropic provision, as singing and violin classes run by the Popular Musical Union (PMU) as part of the St Jude's evening classes nurtured local musicians. As Alice Hart explained in 1886, proficient students were recruited into the settlement's orchestra or choir; the latter, 'composed entirely as it is of working people, have during the past year sung...in Whitechapel and Mile End, at benefit concerts and in the *Messiah* at St Jude's Church, on Easter Thursday'.[11] By 1889 the parish magazine lauded the success 'of our own choir, soloists, organist, pianist and conductor' in mounting a polished performance of Alfred Gaul's modern oratorio *The Holy City*.[12] On this basis, and although the numbers involved were inevitably small, Geddes Poole's supposition that the Whitechapel concerts were failures, allegedly 'frequently rebuffed and occasionally reviled' because of their philanthropic character, is perhaps rather hasty.[13]

As the university and social settlements appeared, one by one, on Toynbee Hall's model in the years that followed, many followed its example in hosting philanthropic concerts but few as avidly or effectively as the Bermondsey Settlement in the 1890s. Within a few years the settlement's musical societies and choral groups could point to a string of successful performances mounted by their own musicians: after the premiere of *Judas Maccabeus* in April 1893, performances of celebrated oratorios by Haydn, Mendelssohn, Rossini, Handel and Sullivan followed at half-yearly intervals.[14] Lidgett measured the local benefit as much by the spirit of enterprise and self-sufficiency displayed, as local people mounted complex and challenging choral and orchestral works in the Bermondsey Town Hall, as by the moralising influence of the music itself. When some 200 local musicians and vocalists, all members of the settlement's music clubs and choirs, gathered on the stage to perform Haydn's *The Creation* and Mendelssohn's *St Paul*, it was a production 'on a scale unknown in Bermondsey before', Lidgett wrote enthusiastically. 'The public rendering of the great musical works is of much benefit [in a neighbourhood] where "variety entertainments" are the usual order of the day', he continued, 'but still more [beneficial is] the efficient local production of such concerts and the tastes which their preparation promotes.'[15] When the settlement staged a performance of Handel's *Messiah* at the Bermondsey Town Hall in December 1895 it was with a pronounced degree of local pride; this was followed shortly after in April 1896 by an ambitious staging of Sir Arthur Sullivan's cantata *The Golden Legend*, a complex orchestration of Longfellow's poem of the same name and a mainstay of amateur choral societies in Britain since its premiere in 1886. Listeners were promised a performance in which 'all the most dramatic, humorous, delicate and *piquant* effects' familiar from Sullivan's comic operettas would be 'shown in more serious and lofty music'.[16] Meanwhile the settlement's programme of concerts continued apace. The People's Concert Society organised a series of chamber concerts in the Bermondsey Settlement's lecture hall, in the weeks leading up to Christmas 1895, at a subsidised rate of 3*d.* for each, 'partly to give an opportunity to lovers of good music, and partly to assist the work of musical education at the Settlement'.[17] The first saw the lecture hall filled for a programme of two trios by Schumann and Beethoven for piano and strings, solo pieces for violin and cello, and vocal renderings of Beethoven's 'Creation's Hymn' and Schubert's 'Erlkönig', the latter an adaptation of Goethe's dramatic ballad delivered with piano accompaniment.[18]

But were these recitals really as 'fine' as reformers hoped? We have many concert bills, newspaper reports and promotional descriptions but virtually no candid accounts from eyewitnesses on which to judge. Sydney Cockerell was a *habitué* at the concerts and exhibitions at the major centres of cultural philanthropy in Southwark and Whitechapel, especially at Red Cross Hall where he volunteered as Octavia Hill's secretary and administrator. His diary entries for 1888–90 give us a sense of the variable quality that was probably typical of these philanthropic and amateur concerts. The first major event organised there, a dramatisation by George MacDonald of Bunyan's *The Pilgrim's Progress* in September 1888, was pronounced a success on every level, right down to the workings of their untested stage. 'Very much pleased with it', Cockerell recorded that night in his diary. 'First performance of any kind in our Hall and a very good beginning. All arrangements satisfactory – audience gratified – curtain an entire success.'[19] In early December a choral concert failed to attract good numbers on a cold night of dense fog, but Cockerell felt the bill and performance had been excellent fare, 'magnificent music – splendid violin, good part-songs and glees, zither, flute, recitations etc.'[20] By 1890 he was a seasoned observer, and less easily impressed. He attended a series of Sunday afternoon and Thursday night concerts and theatricals at Red Cross Hall that proved a mixed bag. The first, in early February, attracted only a 'small audience, but suitable songs – Robin Adair and Scotch ballads'; later that week he was back for performances of 'two little plays prettily acted by Goulding's friends, before a crowded and appreciative audience'. A week later the Hall hosted a vibrant performance from the 'ABC White Minstrels' from Richmond: 'here ladies and two gentlemen...dressed in white with powdered hair', he wrote in his diary. 'An excellent programme and everything done with wonderful confidence and spirit. We never had a better entertainment.' A week after that a concert and cantata 'given by a party of schoolgirls from heaven knows where' was rather wayward: 'well meaning people', he thought, 'but nowise brilliant except in the colours of their dresses, which might better be described as gaudy'. Things deteriorated again on Thursday evening, 27 February, when Cockerell struggled through a 'very insipid and mediocre concert given by the St Celicia Choir', and 'rather a poor concert' followed on 2 March. With some relief he recorded that the last mid-week concert of the season, on Thursday 13 March had passed off very well. He had felt similar relief the previous Sunday: 'In afternoon [went] to last of this year's concerts at the Red Cross Hall, a very good one indeed – Sunday afternoons free in future as well as Sunday mornings – hurrah again!'[21]

There were few such misfires, however, in the grand concerts staged in the Queen's Hall at the People's Palace. In its early years the Palace enjoyed considerable lustre as a high-class musical venue, the Trust's philanthropic largesse supporting concerts at a very professional standard. No fewer than fifty-six musical events were staged in the gleaming new venue during the summer of 1887, Chapman notes, 'mainly ballad and orchestral concerts, and capacity audiences were reached. For this first season the *artistes* offered to play to the poor at the Palace without accepting any fees…[including] the Handel Society, the Welsh Vocal Union, Viscountess Folkestone's Ladies String Band, and the Popular Musical Union'.[22] Many celebrity vocalists offered to appear in the East End as a philanthropic gesture, or enjoyed the implied status an invitation conferred. A booking for a reduced fee at the People's Palace was its own reward: after being told that he was too famous for the Queen's Hall, one *artiste* declared theatrically 'Am I though? I have just been playing to the Queen, and now I want to play to the People.'[23] Performers' names could be recited with some pride: 'Madame Valleria, Madame Antoinette Stirling, Miss Alice Gomes, Mr Alfred Capper, and a host of other well-known performers, have given their services'[24] as the Palace offered concerts and recitals on Wednesday and Saturday nights, 'open to the public at very low fees'.[25]

The star vocalists had popular drawing power, certainly, but so too did the grand orchestral and choral pieces. 'The music given is not of the "music-hall" character', Besant explained in 1888, 'but is uniformly good; the *Messiah*, for instance, which was lately given – the chorus consisting of the Palace choir – attracted an audience which packed the hall completely'. Sunday organ recitals of sacred music also attracted good audiences of working men who (Besant thought) needed something to do away from home as their Sunday dinner was prepared.[26] The Rev. Thomas Richardson, a vehement critic of the Palace's 'irreligious' influence from his church immediately next door,[27] meanwhile, was convinced Sunday concert audiences were mostly middle-class anti-sabbatarian conspirators, and waited in the street to personally inspect the crowds attending Sunday music concerts at the Palace. 'He is of the opinion', it was reported, 'that more than two-thirds of the of the audience wore gloves; that they were not only not of the working class, but did not even belong to the East End population, or at least not of the neigh-bourhood of the Palace, but came from a distance all round London in order, as he supposed, to give an appearance of success to this Sunday entertainment.'[28]

Sensitive to this kind of attention, the Palace administrators scheduled their Sunday concerts with care. The 12.30 p.m. organ recitals, accompanied by the Palace Choral Society, were repeated later in the afternoon and early eve-ning,[29] and as such were deliberately timed, both to attract a working-class audience prior to the opening of the public-houses at 1 p.m. and to rebut criticism of the Palace's Sunday opening from church bodies. 'It will be observed', Currie indicated in response to some religious censure, 'that the times at which all this music takes place are carefully regulated so as to leave no chance of their interfering with any person's attendance at either church or Sunday-school....In the vocal music nothing of a sectarian character is allowed, and no music is ever performed which is not regularly performed in churches.'[30] The recitals showcased the splendid pipe organ donated by T. Dyer Edwardes in 1887, a majestic aural and visual presence at one end of the Queen's Hall. Many years later, the Palace's long-serving organist was 'quite sure that we fully have realized the wish of Mr Dyer Edwardes who in his inscription on the organ says that he hopes "that its sweet strains and solemn tones might bring peace and rest to many a weary mind". Whether few or many come, I trust that his wish has always been carried out.'[31] By 1890, the success of the Palace's musical events appeared to speak for itself. 'It is interesting to know that our two years' experience at the People's Palace teaches us that the inhabitants of East London have every appreciation and enjoyment of high-class music', Currie could confidently proclaim.

> It is, indeed, most surprising to observe the enthusiasm with which a good performance of refined music is received among people whose taste (if, indeed, they could be reasonably expected to have any) might be supposed to have been not improved by what little popular music they have hitherto been accustomed to.[32]

'There is no doubt', agreed the Palace librarian in 1893, 'that...the musical taste of East London has made, and is making rapid strides....Beethoven's 'Adelaide' is a very great favourite, and Brahms' music is listened to with rapt attention.'[33] Performances accompanied by solo and part-singing were the most popular, she noted, and oratorios such as the *Messiah* and *Elijah* attracted larger audiences than the average ballad concert. Other Palace entertainments had a more directly popular flavour such as selections from comic operas and costume recitals, and even minstrel troupes and novelty acts. The Palace managers sought to engage 'Professor Golding' at one time, whose programme advertised 'Extraordinary and Astonishing Ven-triloquism – the cackling of fowls, bleating of sheep, barking of dogs in the distance, sawing and planing without tools, the snappy dog under the table, voices heard in all directions – in the cellar, on the roof, etc.'[34] Similarly, the comic entertainer A. G. Pritchard performed at various times at the Palace in 1888–9, and staged a *tableau vivant* and magical lantern display to replace the usual Wednesday night concert of classical music on one occasion in mid-January 1889. The results should have given the Queen's Hall managers food for thought. Pritchard's Wednesday performance attracted an audience of 1,908, which swelled to 3,280 when the performance was repeated the following Saturday at a 3d. entrance fee. The latter figure was, by quite a margin, the largest attendance for the Palace entertainments that year.[35]

But after that time, as the Palace's finances collapsed and management responsibility was increasingly assumed by the Drapers' Company, commercial imperatives came to the fore. Novelty acts and cheerful amusements grew more prominent as the Palace shifted to a more commercial footing, a trend that filled reformers with dismay. 'What is needed in London', commented Henry Cunynghame on the Palace entertainment programme,

> is the encouragement of sensible and sober habits of life rather than the excitement of plays and performances. Thus, for instance, violin and choral classes are far better for the young men and women than performances of Christy Minstrels or ventriloquists. The former train them for home life and its pleasures; the latter encourage them to be ever gadding after novelties which please for the moment but leave no after result.[36]

This moralising element was fading in the 1890s, but as late as 1892 a summer choir recital in Queen's Hall, performed by five hundred local children 'under an able and efficient leader', provided a self-evidently instructive contrast for one observer. Here was a true 'People's Palace', fostering a nobility of spirit and purpose in a new democracy, surrounded on all sides by the infamous 'Gin Palaces' of ill repute:

> To the looker-on of that vast crowd of people, of fathers and mothers, whose hearts must have been thrilling as the sweet voices of their children rung and echoed through the hall, what a contrast was here presented to those whose leisure is spent in those terrible pests of all London, whose scarlet bedezined walls and brilliant lights flash out from the corners of almost every street.[37]

The true artist paints for all

If late-Victorian cultural philanthropy could be imagined as a symphony, we would hear it reach its crescendo in the provision of fine art to the slums in loan exhibitions over the last two decades of the century. The initiative that defined the type and remains its best-known example is the Whitechapel Fine Art Exhibition, mounted annually by the Barnetts and their co-workers in the parish and settlement from 1881 to 1898. As a highly visible and sustained 'gift of culture' to the East End poor, their efforts have garnered considerable historical attention.[38]

Each exhibition, often featuring very valuable paintings loaned by wealthy patrons, was held for two weeks (after 1886, for three) during the Easter vacation period[39] in the St Jude's schoolrooms adjacent to the vicarage. All this cost around £200 to stage, if we take 1889 as an example, funded by sale of explanatory catalogues (£24), donations made on the floor (£64) and £110 from wealthy sponsors.[40] Each year, the Barnetts and their supporters assembled a range of paintings from private donors and established collections, arranged insurance for damage or theft, decorated the prosaic rooms with textiles and ornaments, organised volunteers as 'watchers' for each of the daily sessions, compiled and printed an innovative penny catalogue of descriptions for the viewer, and shepherded thousands of visitors through the cramped schoolrooms (see Figure 9.1). The task of crowd control was itself enormous: attendances rose from around 9,000 at the modest opening exhibition of 1881, to 26,492 the following year, 55,300 in 1886, and peaked at over 73,000 in 1892.[41] On any given day at the Exhibition, the *Toynbee Record* commented in 1889, 'an outsider is almost as interested in observing the visitors as in looking at the pictures. The mixture of the classes is very noteworthy. There are Jews and gentiles; representatives of West End culture and East End respectability; working men in their working clothes; and poorly-clad mothers with babies in their arms.'[42]

ART IN WHITECHAPEL—LOAN EXHIBITION OF PICTURES IN ST. JUDE'S SCHOOL HOUSE, COMMERCIAL STREET, E.

Figure 9.1 Art in Whitechapel, 1884

The pictures shown at the Whitechapel exhibitions were as far removed from the prosaic world of poor relief and charity as visitors could imagine. 'On entering the upper rooms of the Schoolhouse where the Exhibition is held', one observer wrote in 1887, 'one is struck by the contrast between the ideal and the real, the past and the present. Behind us are the dying Christian and the furious tigers of Briton Rivière's "Roman Holiday", and in front, through the windows is seen a block of the Model Lodging Houses with which the neighbourhood has been covered.'[43] Between 1881 and the turn of the century, visitors to the Whitechapel exhibition faced the most celebrated artworks of the age. Virtually every major British artist of the period featured; over two decades, hundreds of illustrious paintings by artists such as Holman Hunt, Millais, Burne-Jones, Watts, Leighton, Waterhouse, Rossetti and Herkomer were displayed in Whitechapel.[44] Contemporary masterpieces such as Holman Hunt's *The Light of the World*, and Rossetti's *The Annunciation of the Virgin*, were exhibited in 1883 and 1885 respectively. The 1893 show had many particularly fine pictures, after Henrietta Barnett's typically forthright requests had secured many from a single donor. 'Was there ever such a loan?' she asked. 'The Committee had to insure it for £50,000; and crowds lingered before the Billets, the Mauves, the Israels, the Millets, the Corots, the Daubignys, the Jacques, dumb before their elusive, permeating, mind-awakening, spirit-satisfying beauty.'[45] These impulses remained strong enough to culminate in the permanent foundation of the Whitechapel Art Gallery at the turn of the century. Once more the Barnetts were the driving force, their presence ensuring the new gallery's first object was to maintain free loan exhibitions of 'high class modern pictures' previously shown at exhibitions in the wealthy districts of London.[46]

The whole event was self-evidently a supremely tangible expression of late-Victorian cultural philanthropy. If indeed they supplied, as Matthews-Jones argues, an 'alternative religious space' for Barnett to exercise his 'spiritual authority',[47] the exhibitions were also a vehicle through which liberal reformers aimed to apply a great principle in social work: namely, as the Marquis of Ripon explained in opening the 1886 Exhibition, that 'real, solid, and permanent educational work among the masses of the people' could be achieved by 'giving them the very best which the country was able to supply'. Like Barnett, Ripon was an ardent supporter of the University Extension movement, and saw many of its principles reflected at the Whitechapel exhibition. He perceived that in an age of evident and growing political discontent,

> those who enjoyed the many advantages of life – wealth, instruction, position, works of art and fine libraries – could only hope to retain them by doing their best to disseminate the fruits of that learning which had made their own lives bright and happy. It was, in truth, no paradox to say that if they wished to alleviate the condition of those who were most depressed in their outward circumstances, they could only effectively do so by offering them the best which they themselves possessed.[48]

The valuable works of art loaned to Whitechapel each year, in other words, had much more than a merely 'aesthetic' value. As a token of their owners' broad social sympathies, the paintings became a kind of moralised collateral exchanged between the worlds of wealth and poverty, something with the potential to inspire and educate, but also to rehearse the deeper interconnections so precious to the holistic social ideal. The artists and paintings were famous throughout the world, visitors to the Exhibition were reminded, and by loaning them for the common benefit their owners were in effect seeking a bond of trust. The enlightened appreciation of the Whitechapel audience was expected in return, as the only response that could make the exchange meaningful. As one local advocate, professing to speak on the exhibition audience's behalf in Barnett's parish magazine in 1889, put it:

> we East Londoners can hardly feel too grateful to our West London friends for despoiling their homes and trusting their treasures into our keeping for many days, in order that we may share their pleasure in them, and that we may feel that the pictures are, in a sense, ours also, since the true artist paints for all, and gives his work to the world.[49]

When new picture rooms were opened in 1886, at a cost of £2,000 raised by donations, Barnett felt it was an indication that 'East London was beginning to care for culture, and that West London was beginning to recognise that men might have other needs than those which relief funds and missions could meet.'[50]

The success of Barnett's efforts at the Whitechapel Loan Exhibition supplied a model for similar efforts at other settlements and polytechnics. The first 'Exhibition of Modern Pictures' at the People's Palace, curated by staff of the New Gallery, Regent Street, was formally opened by HRH the Duchess of Albany on 4 August 1888, and featured 150 paintings by Millais, Landseer, Watts, Richmond, Crane and other artists. This was the Palace's premier cultural event, and the benevolent luxury embodied in its buildings and grounds was heightened to emphasise the occasion. The spaces around the Queen's Hall and Palace Library were temporarily converted to gardens and palm-houses, with platforms for music performances, stalls, refreshments and amusements. Any vacant ground 'was occupied by a steam roundabout, swings, and numerous shows…[with] a band-stand being erected in the space in front of Queen's Hall, and a large number of flags and Chinese lanterns being hung about this space'.[51] The gymnasium building nearby was also hung with Chinese lanterns and featured another band platform for nightly performances. A Flower Show was installed to fill the vast auditorium space of Queen's Hall, with the paintings mounted on the walls at either side. For the second exhibition and fête in 1889, the walls of the Hall and the Palace Library were again filled to capacity with paintings. 'When [the paintings] had been hung up…and a crowd of Easterners flocked in', one of the Beaumont Trustees remembered, 'not a picture was scratched or injured. They were all hung "on the line", within easy reach of those who enjoyed them'.[52]

The *Palace Journal* announced shortly before the opening of the second exhibition that the 'rich friends of the People's Palace (and they are many and generous) have stripped their walls of all that is good in pictures, and the great living artists have emptied their studios for the benefit of East London'.[53] More than 400 pictures were hung for this exhibition, 'by far the largest and finest ever seen in the East End', Currie boasted with one eye in the direction of Whitechapel. 'Applications for loans of pictures were made to the principal picture owners and artists in the country with most gratifying results.'[54] Old Masters by Rubens, Reynolds, Canaletto and Rembrandt were represented, alongside contemporary favourites such as Briton Rivière, Watts, Frith, Millais, Leighton and Landseer. The Palace's attractions were further boosted by a show of live monkeys, while the gymnasium, 'fitted with fountains and rockeries, and set with palms and shrubs', hosted nightly concerts and other entertainments. Over six weeks an extraordinary attendance of 211,111 was registered at the gates, 'a falling-off of attendance as compared with the fete of the previous year', the chairman acknowledged, 'but this was entirely due to the great dock strikes, which, beginning half way through the progress of the fête, seriously diminished the audience'.[55] Not all were there for the artworks, of course, but the audience interest and response to the fine art on display was still considered very satisfactory.

The Bermondsey Settlement did its best to match these glamorous rivals across the river. Spearheaded by the energies of the newest resident, H. Boyd Carpenter, planning for their own loan exhibition got underway in early 1896 with promises of contributions from supporters and a similarly eminent list of major artists. The event was opened by HRH Princess Louise, herself an amateur painter, who donated two landscapes that were numbered first and second in the catalogue and hung in the drawing room, evidence of 'her sympathy with all efforts to bring works of art within reach of the people'.[56] The main rooms of the settlement were filled with 139 paintings large and small, that perhaps did not rival the other exhibitions but included a fair smattering of RAs, a study by Botticelli, G. F. Watts' *Love and Death*, work by Burne-Jones and several paintings by William Holman Hunt, by this time an ageing Pre-Raphaelite who attended the opening in person and moved the vote of thanks to the princess. Admission was free to all comers, with donation boxes in each room, and Sunday afternoons were turned over to a private viewing for members of the settlement's classes and clubs. For his part, Lidgett encapsulated the guiding motives and ambitions of this first exhibition in terms that again capture for us the urban imagery, the social reconciliation and the moralising influences of art and nature that all infused their cultural philanthropy. There is a basic Romanticism here, certainly, but rather than any tangible 'missionary aestheticism' we find instead a conventional social idealism given concrete effect:

> Whatever other virtues our part of South-east London may have, it is not beautiful, and most of us are engaged in hard toil through the day,

returning to monotonous surroundings and influences at night. If it is good for our wealthy friends to visit at their leisure the great collections of art treasures at the West End, and to adorn their own walls with beautiful pictures, although they live within reach of and can easily enjoy, from time to time, all the glories of land and sea, how much more do we need to have beautiful sights brought to us occasionally, with all their gracious suggestions, their memories, perhaps, of days long gone by, their appeal to the imagination, and the restful influences which they exert. Ugliness is always present with us, it depresses us, deadens the imagination, puts a hurtful mark upon our manners.[57]

As always for Lidgett, the idea of social conciliation and mutual welfare through civic integration was foremost. A political progressive with one eye on Spring Gardens, the headquarters of the LCC, he saw it as much as a municipal objective of the near future as it was a voluntarist endeavour in the present. 'Some day our administrators will try to make London the fair City it might be', he prophesied, 'but the motive power which will demand of them such an improvement, can only come by patiently educating the tastes of growing numbers of our citizens, so as to perceive and enjoy what is beautiful, that they will combine against squalid and sordid surroundings, because they will recognise that mind and imagination need feeding as well as bodies and souls'.[58]

* * *

This at least is how liberal reformers understood their gift of culture, and in the process they looked ahead to a far more universal provision of art, music and literature for British cities through municipal initiative. But this high-minded, moralising philanthropy offered little, critics contended, to resolve the abyss between rich and poor. 'It is difficult, perhaps, for the ladies and gentlemen who work in Whitechapel to recollect that their *protégés* regard their surroundings with a different eye from that which the visitor casts, revolted and disgusted, round the narrow street or narrower court', a *Spectator* columnist offered in 1890.

> Virtue blooms in a cracked pot at an attic window as well sometimes as in majolica on a balcony of the most artistic work, – and a seamstress looking out over it sees heaven as well, perhaps, as the pretty lady whose kind heart is sick for her, and eager to share with her the luxuries, or at least the cleanliness, of Mayfair.[59]

For many, the self-importance and condescension that seemed to hang about these improving schemes of cultural uplift like noxious vapour was an irresistible target, and *Punch* was not alone in making fun at their expense. Working-class critics like the teetotal Anglican, radical Liberal turned socialist and later Labour MP for Bow and Bromley George Lansbury tended to regard Toynbee Hall and other settlements as aloof and condescending.[60] A similar scepticism features in the period's fiction. One novelist of the late-century 'Cockney' school, Arthur Morrison, had spent years as secretary to the People's Palace, and he began the second chapter of his *A Child of the Jago* (1896) with a scathing account of the deluded self-importance that attended the 'East End Elevation Mission and Pansophical Institute', modelled on Toynbee Hall and the People's Palace. At the Elevation Mission, he wrote, the 'aspiring East Ender' might find

> the Higher Life, the Greater Thought, and the Wider Humanity: with other radiant abstractions, mostly in the comparative degree, specifics all for the manufacture of the Superior Person. There were many Lectures given on still more subjects. Pictures were borrowed and shown, with revelations to the Uninformed of the morals ingeniously concealed by the painters. The Uninformed were also encouraged to debate and to produce papers on literary and political matters, while still unencumbered with the smallest knowledge thereof.[61]

Such denunciations capture the essence of the basic critique against cultural philanthropy, and echo those against social idealism more generally: if 'superior persons' were occasionally manufactured among the 'Uninformed' by the airy metaphysics and complacent ideals of their benevolent betters, the whole process achieved little or no genuine educational result while the social distance between the two remained unbridgeable. But as Hunter demonstrates, even if this was a sincere personal view, Morrison's fiction was a self-conscious intervention against sentimental charity and needs to be understood in the context of the philanthropic debates of the early and mid-1890s. In many ways this antipathy signalled his own emancipation from low-level bureaucratic anonymity in Mile End and his advent, via invitations to write for W. E. Henley's *National Observer* and *New Review*, into a sphere of critical and literary life in which he hoped to prosper.

Notwithstanding this antagonism – and without denying its vigour – we have seen the extent to which the philanthropic 'gift of culture' was a significant and enduring feature of social work in the late-Victorian period. We have seen something of its range, diversity and logical coherence. What it ultimately achieved is not really at issue here, in the same way that we are not trying to judge whether in fact the fine arts are indeed 'civilising influences'. We are more properly concerned with what it represented in its immediate context, rather than with what it achieved in the short, medium or long term. What conclusions, then, can be drawn?

The most important misconception about the cultural mission to metropolitan slums is the art historians' notion that it was in essence a Ruskinian 'missionary aestheticism'. There is no doubt that avid followers of Ruskin across the country sought to make his views prevail through practical initiatives large and small. Eagles has documented vividly their associational work in 'the places and networks where Ruskin was feted, admired, and celebrated, and through which his influence was spread' in the societies, museums, guilds and workshops that proliferated across the country.[62] This influence can be traced in the provincial art museums of Manchester, Birmingham and Liverpool, all of which, as Woodson-Boulton demonstrates, emerged as a direct result of these networks, as 'reformers in all three cities... engaged with Ruskin personally on some level' and were 'deeply committed to translating his writings into action'.[63] But this explanation simply does not fit the instances of cultural provision in the London slums explored in this book. Ruskin's ideas were an 'influence' on the work we have discussed above, certainly, but only in a very diffused and imprecise sense. Octavia Hill was a former disciple and Cockerell a young enthusiast, but Besant, Currie and the Beaumont Trustees were not remotely 'Ruskinian'; they were not 'aesthetic ideologues' and in no sense did their work proceed from first principles laid down by the Sage of Coniston. In Bermondsey, the robust educational culture around Lidgett and his co-workers likewise bears little trace of Ruskin's social paternalism: a moralising Nonconformist social liberalism constitutes its distinctive tone. So too with the Barnetts (Henrietta Barnett does not make a single direct reference to Ruskin in her copious memoir), and the vast majority of the Toynbee Hall residents. Perhaps the only true Ruskinian in that group, Charles Ashbee, found the prosaic realities of Whitechapel work repellent, and soon moved his Guild and School of Handicraft out of Barnett's orbit altogether.

The larger point is that the influence of Ruskin's ideas and example was in some sense present, but not everyone who felt that cultural provision had a place in social work was working under his influence in any historically meaningful sense. His influence alone is not a sufficient explanation for their activism. 'Artists are preachers', explained Samuel Barnett's parish magazine just before the Whitechapel exhibition of 1889, 'they see a thought greater than can be put into words, they throw it on to the canvas, and then those who have eyes to see look and find something which speaks of them, rouses them or comforts them'.[64] The language reminds us of Ruskin, but the sentiment is entirely conventional: most Broad Church Anglicans imbued with the Romantic values of the age would have said something similar. Like Borzello, we might be tempted to see this as evidence how 'Ruskin's linking of art, society and Christianity in a complete and convincing artistic philosophy was a gift to the Anglican reformers of the 1880s and 1890s who found themselves in church or settlement houses surrounded by the poor in desperate need of improvement'.[65] But this moralising habit was endemic to conventional nineteenth-century conceptions of pictorial art; exemplified by Ruskin in some respects but by no means unique to him. Artworks, indeed, were not valued in the first instance on aesthetic grounds, in terms of the aesthetic sensibility they evoked or induced among audiences. What mattered was their ability to convey deeper meanings and 'higher truths' that had moralising potential, but this was a habit by no means due to Ruskin's influence alone. The philanthropic schemes we have discussed here, moreover, went well beyond art appreciation; it makes no sense, accordingly, to label their work 'Ruskinian' when it included such diverse 'non-Ruskinian' elements as political debating clubs, reading groups, ballad concerts, magic lantern shows and violin classes. Typecasting their work as 'missionary aestheticism' might supply a delicious sense of historical distance, but in the process we sidestep a large part of their reformist effort and distort our understanding of its essential character. On proper inspection, indeed, it appears far closer to an enduring ideal of humanistic liberalism in a participatory modern democracy than it was a throwback to paternalistic condescension.

* * *

If this reforming effort is poorly comprehended by the label 'missionary aestheticism', how then should it characterised? In the broadest sense the cultural mission was a florid expression of the fundamental High Victorian faith in education. The slum journalist George Sims spoke for many in his conviction that the 'next generation will be more cultured, more intellectual, and more refined; mental faculties will be exercised which have been dormant in the poor of to-day....Education will make even the lowest of our citizens something better than they are at present – mere animal reproducers of their species.'[66] This commonplace view energised a host of reforming efforts on a range of fronts: from the Mechanics' Institutes and evening lectures to the extension of elementary education through legislation and local rates from 1870, to the Free Libraries movement of the 1890s and the Sunday Society's attempts to liberalise access to public museums and galleries. The amelioration of the urban poor through moralising culture was thus only one manifestation of this characteristic nineteenth-century belief in the immense emancipatory power of education. As Harrison observes, education remained the favoured middle-class social reform in the late-Victorian period because 'it seemed to offer a way to effect real social change that was non-revolutionary, immediately practical, and in harmony with the ideals of rationality, improvement and progress'.[67]

In more specific terms we have seen how the cultural philanthropic mode shared a close relationship with contemporary developments in university extension and enhanced proposals for technical education on the polytechnic model. Like these pioneers in adult and working-class higher education, the cultural philanthropists rejected an instrumentalist approach to popular learning through utilitarian 'instruction'. Rather, they took the learning experience to be morally transformative. They agreed with Lord Playfair, who in speaking in 1894 of the progress of university extension put the matter plainly:

> The main purpose is not to educate the masses, but to permeate them with a desire for intellectual improvement, and to show them methods by

which they can attain this desire. Every man, who acquires a taste for learning and is imbued with the desire to acquire more of it, becomes more valuable as a citizen, because he is more intelligent and perceptive. As Shakespeare says:

Learning is but an adjunct to ourself...
It adds a precious seeing to the eye.[68]

This permeation of moral ideals to support active citizenship in a modern democracy was as intrinsic to the provision of cultural access as it was to university extension. When he first arrived as a university settler in White-chapel, W. G. de Burgh recalled, 'I remember being told that working men needed imagination. I did not at the time quite realise what that saying meant. A little experience showed its truth.' He elaborated on his idealist sense of the importance of a moral vision imparted through a liberal education, something that he called a 'disciplined imagination':

> What working men need is the power of conceiving an ideal in definite relation to present conditions, and of preserving that definite relation amid the experiences of active life. It is a rare gift for any man to be able to weld in an ideal purpose among hard realities without becoming either a materialist or a dreamer. To grasp Utopia and modern London at one glance without losing touch of the one or the other requires something more than enthusiasm for progress. It requires a disciplined imagination, and this discipline is what the University Extension Movement is uniquely qualified to impart.

Like others at the settlement he looked ahead to a time when comprehensive and consistent extension classes would supply 'a system of higher intellectual teaching which may so train the imagination of London working-men that they may learn to value knowledge for its own sake, and that not only as an enjoyment for the leisure of the moment, but as an effectual discipline for the discharge of the highest duties of citizenship'.[69]

Our discussion has indicated the importance of the urban setting in con-figuring these larger, abstract social concerns into an active programme of social reform through cultural provision. In the reformist imagination, Lon-don's poor neighbourhoods were a backdrop – and not a passive one – for the human misery of the residuum and the labouring poor, seen (as the conven-tional argument goes, following Stedman Jones) as being primarily the result of moral failure, of weaknesses of 'character', that by the 1880s was shifting through a range of environmental and socio-biological anxieties to a diag-nosis of urban degeneration. But the urban dimension in this shift – with the 'black spot' slums of the Booth survey apparently seen as breeding grounds for a dangerous residuum of the casual poor – has arguably been exaggerated by historians' over-attention to the sensational rhetoric of slum journalism.

When we turn to the diagnoses of impoverished neighbourhoods offered by active reformers, we find a much less alarmist picture. The poverty of White-chapel, Mile End, Bermondsey and Southwark was largely seen by active reformers as a problem of dreary, repetitive materialism – in the monotonous topography, the 'dull streets', the absence of natural beauty and local historic character, altogether lacking a nourishing spiritual presence. It was also a problem of social disconnection, as in the 'wilderness of disconnected lives' of Beatrice Potter or the absence of public institutions lamented by Walter Besant, that spoke to the absence, he felt, of a nourishing civic spirit. Afflicted in these ways, in the reformist view these neighbourhoods lacked the supportive social connections and the integrated unity of outlook – the 'disciplined imagination', to use de Burgh's term – that made for a mean-ingful human existence. This is why they were convinced that the circum-stances of London's 'nameless toilers' (men and women who, for all their improving living standards and evident respectability, continued to subsist in a cycle of daily labour, isolated and alienated) was a problem that called for urgent effort to resolve. They never saw poverty as entirely a matter of individual moral failure and intemperate habits, as our Victorian stereotype suggests, and (needless to say) nor was it ever approached as entirely a question of impersonal economic factors and free of moral considerations altogether. Rather, they looked on poverty in holistic terms: economic opportunity, material realities and local social relationships were taken to be inter-fused in a way that set the character of impoverished neighbourhoods, in the same way that moral, spiritual and educational qualities were all seen as inter-fused to define an individual. Seen in this way, urban poverty was a problem well attuned to the assumptions and preoccupations of social ide-alism, because after all the problem and its solution were the two sides of the same coin. Building wider communities, wider opportunities and wider horizons in the pinched, utilitarian settings of modern London supplied, they felt, an important part of the solution. These themes have a strikingly contemporary ring, but they were as much a part of this work as the cen-sorious and moralising language of improvement we expect and deplore in these late-Victorian social reformers.

* * *

But by the turn of the century the commitment to moralising, redeeming and reconciling modes of social work and adult education had begun to ebb. 'The wave of enthusiasm which created the modern settlement has ceased to advance'; the journalist, social worker and later Liberal MP Charles Mas-terman wrote in 1901, 'the buildings remain and a few energetic toilers, and the memory of a great hope'.[70] The first phase of settlement work, with its high idealism and moralising ambitions grounded in a personal ethos of community and connection, was drawing to a close, symbolised at Toynbee Hall by William Beveridge's time as Sub-Warden from 1903 and Barnett's resignation in 1906. Nigel Scotland explains the transition in terms of a dwindling supply of undergraduates from the universities, the uptake of more egalitarian socialist ideas among working people, and the increasing municipal provision of local welfare services.[71] These factors were in fact symptomatic of something larger as moral preoccupations drained out of social policy, in Himmelfarb's characterisation,[72] and as social idealism, with all its contradictions, failed to prosper as an immediate programme of practical activism. This was in turn part of a larger uncertainty. 'It is not possible to identify a single turning point', writes Michael Roberts, 'but, sometime in the life of the generation which had reached independent adulthood in the 1880s, "moral reform" lost its resonance in public debate...it was partly a matter of being elbowed to the side of the stage, partly of losing the attention of the audience, partly also, among some, of losing faith in the message being delivered'.[73]

The shift is most visible in the steadily weakening efforts of local social work agencies. In Cox's terms, the decades after the turn of the century witnessed a 'disintegration of the civilising mission', as the 'diffusive Christianity' and its attendant social services attempted by churches and charities in the epicentres of metropolitan poverty like Lambeth, the focus of his study, visibly eroded. The provision of adult education, housing improvements, benefit societies, penny dinners and home visits (among other things) either withered away or were supplanted by social services administered by state and municipal agencies, signs of 'a highly significant transformation of attitudes about the relationship between churches and society which reached a crisis point between 1906 and 1914'.[74] If the character of church and charitable social work was changing, we might also see this shift in generational and conceptual terms: the passing of a particular generation of reformers, the waning of their particular analysis of the urban crisis and its possible solution, and the eclipse of a moralising imperative of personal service and social conciliation between rich and poor, was also underway. As Cox puts it with regard to the churches, 'during the Edwardian decade the very definition of the social problem changed, and the churches simultaneously began to think of their own social role in a different way'.[75]

His point applies equally to the quasi-secular, quasi-spiritual social work of cultural provision. The basic animating ideas of this reforming intervention into the lives and neighbourhoods of the London poor – of educational uplift and social conciliation through exposure to moralising culture – that we have seen running strongly in reforming circles from the mid-1870s was losing momentum as the century drew to a close. If on the one hand social idealism had prompted an increased openness to state regulation and provision, there was concurrently the rise of more environmental, determinist conceptions of the social problem, its severity and possible solution, that drained the moralising agenda of much of its credibility. Whatever credibility it retained by the turn of the century, we suspect, was absorbed into the reforming energies of municipal progressivism.

But a foundation had been laid, and not every reforming effort at cultural improvement withered into dust. The direct links between Barnett's Whitechapel reformers, for example, and the cultural policies of the London County Council under the Progressive majority after 1889 have not yet been fully considered. The influence the cultural philanthropists had in the loose coalition of liberal and socialist opinion, the Progressive fusion of 'Gladstonian, New Liberal, Fabian, and trade-union interests' and its resultant cultural politics demand closer attention.[76] Certainly Barnett was an active voice in the ear of his personal associates on the LCC, as when he urged regulation of the latest salacious amusements of the street. In 1899 he wrote to his close friend John Burns, the radical unionist, borough councillor for Battersea and a leading campaigner against unregulated music halls:

Your eye has doubtless noticed the prevalence of these 'mutascopes'. There is one near here [i.e. Whitechapel] which shows suggestive, if not dirty, pictures. Boys and girls go in and get corrupted. The police, whom I have consulted, cannot touch the evil. The only thing that occurs to me is to extend the control of the County Council, so as to cover all places of entertainment – mutascopes and gaffs included. The County Council could then do for these places what it has done for Music Halls...[77]

It is likely that, given his wide network of associations, Barnett's engagement with municipal cultural policy was more than the occasional 'voice in the ear'. The policies and themes he and Henrietta laid out in *Practicable Socialism* could well prove on closer inspection to have had more contemporary resonance than has hitherto been recognised. As Chris Waters has recognised, in matters such as the development of parks and open spaces, Council policy drew heavily from the success of voluntary organisations such as the Kyrle Society and the Metropolitan Public Gardens Association, and it would be surprising if the diffuse experiments in cultural philanthropy we have seen prospering in the 1880s had little or no resonance in the municipal reformism of the Progressive era that followed.[78]

Certainly many of the schemes of cultural provision discussed in this book – local lectures, *soirées* and dances, fine music concerts, art exhibitions and galleries, readings rooms and libraries – proved ephemeral and short-lived, but others had substantial legacies into the twentieth century. The settlements endured as neighbourhood community centres, working with disadvantaged groups in attempting to supply their social and educational needs. We cannot trace their institutional evolution in detail here, but the Whitechapel Art Gallery, the modern polytechnics that arose from the City Parochial Charities reforms of the 1880s and 1890s, the Royal Victoria Hall or 'Old Vic' that later gave rise to the National Theatre, the neighbouring institute that became Morley College, the philanthropic promenade concerts at the Queen's Hall, Langham Place now revered as 'The Proms', and the adult education classes later adopted by the WEA and the Department of Extra-Mural Studies in the University of London all have their roots in the late-Victorian cultural mission. In Mile End in 1934, the vestiges of Currie and Besant's People's Palace became a true university for East London as Queen Mary College.

* * *

Finally, what of the tricky issue of class relations, which after all was the essential and ultimately unresolved problem of Victorian social reform? Historical assessments of leisure, entertainment and intellectual provision as part of the voluntarist social work of the nineteenth century in Britain have typically followed Peter Bailey's 'rational recreation' approach, treating reforming efforts as an attempt to suppress older leisure patterns to meet the labour needs of industrial capitalism, accompanied by corresponding attempts to inculcate appropriate habits of deference, time-discipline and orderliness through respectable leisure. Many would see cultural philanthropy as little more than a late-century elaboration of this larger project, oriented around the fault-lines of social class and power, into the sphere of art and culture. 'These days', Borzello tells us, 'words like "refine", "elevate" and "civilise" in the context of art are seen as patronising examples of the powerful telling the ordinary what to think.'[79] Her point is perhaps attractively blunt, but our discussion illustrates the benefits to be gained by an approach that is not confined to these themes alone.

The 'rational recreation' paradigm consistently ignores, undervalues or confuses the complex motivations that underpinned social activism. It fails to account properly for idealist or 'spiritualising' impulses amid the secular business of social work and practical education, an aspect that distinguished late-Victorian reformism. It overlooks emerging notions of civic responsibility for intangible human 'needs' rather than material 'wants' that had long-term implications in the evolution of conceptions of the public good. One endorsement of the value of the concerts staged by the People's Entertainment Society nicely captures the kind of moralised social connection that seemed possible to liberal reformers. The 1879 plea of Lady Lindsay, the aristocratic wife of the Earl of Crawford and later the mother of an Oxford House man, evokes the moral landscape of social anxiety, perceived obligation, improving ambition, and hopes for class conciliation in which cultural philanthropy prospered:

> Surely, in these days of class opposition, of smouldering animosity between rich and poor, it is something to establish a sense of friendship and sympathy; surely, in these days, when the sufferings of the denizens of distant lands, who are not English, who are not our own, meet with the responsive English generosity that is a source of surprise and admiration to the whole world, we shall not refuse to spare a little of this generosity to those who dwell at our very doors, who speak our own mother-tongue, whose interests, many of them, are the same as ours, and upon whose

dark and sunless lives we can shed with so little trouble such true and kindly beams of sunlight and sympathy?[80]

We tend to think this patronising, especially considering Lady Lindsay's wealth and privilege and the casual, grating imperialism of her language. But we should remember that John Scott Lidgett, an ardent reforming politician, a powerful force for social improvement and the enlargement of educational access in South London, brought essentially the same motives into action when he founded a new settlement in Bermondsey, where efforts in cultural uplift, educational inspiration and social connection were united by the common emphasis in all three on the idea of civic participation. For Lidgett, knowledge was power. The Bermondsey Settlement's university extension lectures 'strengthen our powers of thought and reasoning...enlarge our stores of information, and increase our understanding of the world in which we have to live'. Their Parliamentary Debating Society helped its members to acquire 'the gifts of self-possession, public speaking and debate, the art of expression and the rules of public discussion, without which it would have been impossible for them to take the part which they may now legitimately hope to do in the future in civic life', and musical concerts gave 'elevating pleasure...the refreshment and the refinement which the fine arts produce, and both of these improve our general power of helping others'. 'If dingy and monotonous London has a need', he concluded, bringing the characteristic urban imagery of cultural philanthropy to bear with his customary *élan*,

> it is to multiply citizens of high intelligence, broad sympathies and ele-
> vated tastes, who will wed all these to the public service and form a
> political force, compelling legislative and administrative bodies to make
> the city a place where not only physical life can be safe, but where the
> higher life of intellect, heart and character can thrive by being awakened,
> satisfied, and then inspired to extend its influence to ever widening circles
> of less favoured men.[81]

Many observers, then and now, would not share this faith. But we should not on this account disregard the socially progressive force of liberal humanism and social idealism that took these concerns from idea to fruition, in the process anticipating and helping precipitate conceptions of the 'common good' that needed broad currency before the public provision of the fine arts and liberal education could be possible in the twentieth century. Britain would be poorer place, then and now, had people like Lidgett, Lady Lindsay, Samuel Barnett and Walter Besant remained inactive.

Perhaps the ultimate gain for us in putting the 'rational recreation' para-digm to one side comes in the richness of our historical insight. By taking these aspirations seriously – romantic, flowery, frequently sentimental and unrealistic though they might be at first sight – and listening to them with care, we grasp what reflective, articulate and socially progressive men and women among the late-Victorians actually thought and did when confronted with the vast, daunting spectre at their feast, by the unsettling presence of urban poverty and entrenched disadvantage. There was a class politics tied up in cultural philanthropy, certainly, but it was nothing so simplistic as a middle-class attempt to impose *bourgeois* values and inculcate docility in an urban working class whose 'true' interests lay elsewhere.

Frederick Rogers, the Whitechapel bookbinder and secretary to the local extension classes, is one audible voice among the many that we have lost. He dismissed Walter Besant's worries that working men lacked decent leisure, and in doing so spoke up as a passionate advocate of self-improvement through cultural opportunity. Men like himself had ample pleasures, he suggested, and none of them brutalising: clubs, brass bands, elocution and recital classes, rowing and swimming clubs, amateur drama groups and theatricals (although, he noted, 'if workmen like theatricals at all, they like them good, and are merciless critics'). Working people knew the difference, he insisted, between mediocre 'temperance entertainments', songs and music accompanied by exhortations and speeches, and the 'higher work' done by the Kyrle Society, the People's Concerts and People's Entertainment Societies, the Popular Ballad Concert Committee and the Royal Victoria Hall, 'work which has for its aim the bringing of the best within the reach of the poorest. Now and again it misses its mark, and the blessing falls to the giver rather than the receiver; but very often it is useful and helpful to both'. He even found value and merit in the most ridiculous figure of all, that of the priggish philanthropic aristocrat, Nevinson's 'good young man in a shiny top hat', the pious advocate of culture's enlightening mission to working men.

> A very different picture is presented by the handsome young aristocrat who stands on the platform of the workman's club, and interprets to his hearers the music of Beethoven and Mozart, to that which is seen when the tired workman stands there after his day is done, and gives such talents as he may possess to the amusement of his fellows. Very different outwardly are these two, but they are united in the same unselfish task and are each learning to lose self in something greater than self, through the simple method of helping their fellows to amusement.[82]

Notes

1 D. Maltz, *British Aestheticism and the Urban Working Classes, 1870–1900: Beauty for the People* (Basingstoke: Palgrave Macmillan, 2006), p. 1.
2 L. Goodlad, *Victorian Literature and the Victorian State: Character and Governance in a Liberal Society* (Baltimore: Johns Hopkins University Press, 2003), p. viii.
3 A. Geddes Poole, *Philanthropy and the Construction of Victorian Women's Citizenship: Lady Frederick Cavendish and Miss Emma Cons* (Toronto: University of Toronto Press, 2014), esp. chapter 5 'The Citizens of Morley College'.
4 S. A. Barnett, *Second Parish Report, 1875* cited in H. O. Barnett, *Canon Barnett: His Life, Work, and Friends* (London: John Murray, 1918), vol. 1, p. 93.

5 S. A. Barnett, *Fifth Parish Report, 1878* cited in Barnett, *Canon Barnett*, vol. 1, p. 96. See also 'People's Concert Society', *Monthly Record* 2:1 (January 1896), p. 10.
6 'Classical Music for the People', *Magazine of Music* 1:8 (November 1884), p. 4.
7 Barnett, *Canon Barnett*, vol. 1, p. 95. Koven also notes that Barnett's colour-blindness did not impair his conviction about the moral benefits of pictorial art: 'The Whitechapel Picture Exhibitions and the Politics of Seeing' in D. J. Sherman and I. Rogoff (eds), *Museum Culture: Histories, Discourses, Spectacles* (Minneapolis: University of Minnesota Press, 1994), p. 32.
8 Quoted in Barnett, *Canon Barnett*, vol. 1, p. 95.
9 *First Annual Report of the Universities' Settlement in East London* (Oxford 1885), p. 16.
10 'Staccato' [regular feature], *Magazine of Music* 2:15 (June 1885), p. 64.
11 'The Missionaries of Music' *Toynbee Journal* 1:12 (September 1886), p. 98. For the PMU classes, see S. A. Barnett, *Fifteenth Pastoral Address and Report of Parish Work* (London, 1888), p. 16.
12 *St Jude's* 1:3 (March 1889), p. 29.
13 Geddes Poole, *Philanthropy and the Construction of Victorian Women's Citizenship*, p. 136.
14 'Editorial Notes' *Monthly Record* 2:5 (May 1896), p. 50.
15 Bermondsey Settlement, *Third Annual Report* (London: 1894), pp. 21–2.
16 J. E. Borland, 'The Golden Legend' *Monthly Record* 2:4 (April 1896), p. 41.
17 *Monthly Record* 1:8 (November 1895), p. 92.
18 *Monthly Record* 1:9 (December 1895), p. 97.
19 BL: Cockerell Papers, Add. Mss. 52625, f. 56, diary entry of 22 September 1888.
20 BL: Cockerell Papers, Add. Mss. 52625, f. 67, diary entry of 11 December.
21 BL: Cockerell Papers, Add. Mss. 52627, ff. 20–26, diary entries of various dates.
22 A. Chapman, 'The People's Palace for East London' (M.Phil. thesis, University of Hull, 1978), p. 200.
23 M. S. R. James, *A Sketch of the People's Palace and its Library* (London, 1893), p. 10.
24 J. G. Adderley, 'What is the People's Palace Doing?' *Eastward Ho!* 7 (August 1887), p. 226.
25 E. H. Currie, 'The Working of "The People's Palace"' *Nineteenth Century* 27 (February 1890), p. 345.
26 W. Besant, 'The People's Palace' *North American Review* 147 (1888), p. 61; Currie, 'The Working of "The People's Palace"', p. 351.
27 Richardson was the foremost campaigner for temperance restrictions and against Sunday opening at the Palace. See A. S. Richardson (ed.), *Forty Years Ministry in East London* (London: Hodder and Stoughton, 1903), pp. 170–4.
28 J. Williams, 'Sunday at the People's Palace' *Lend a Hand* 3 (1888), p. 322.
29 Currie, 'The Working of "The People's Palace"', pp. 345–6.
30 'The Working of "The People's Palace"', pp. 351–2.
31 DCA: People's Palace Box 3, ms. correspondence dated 15 July 1907.
32 Currie, 'The Working of "The People's Palace"', p. 351.
33 James, *A Sketch of the People's Palace and its Library*, pp. 9–10.
34 QMUL: QMC/PP/10/32, ms. correspondence and enclosed playbill, n. d.
35 QMUL: QMC/PP/6/5, H. Cunynghame, 'Assistant Commissioner's Memorandum on the Present Condition of the People's Palace', (15 August 1891), pp. 25–7.
36 Cunynghame, 'Assistant Commissioner's Memorandum', p. 13.
37 S. S. Blanchard, 'The People's Palace in London', *Lend a Hand* 9:5 (1892), p. 342.
38 See F. Borzello, 'The Relationship of Fine Art and the Poor in Late Nineteenth Century England' (Ph.D. thesis, University of London, 1980), her subsequent *Civilising Caliban: The Misuse of Art 1875–1980* (London: Faber and Faber, 2014

[1987]) and S. Koven, 'The Whitechapel Picture Exhibitions and the Politics of Seeing'. Gavin Budge sees the Barnetts' exhibitions as a Ruskinian call to mental work in 'Poverty and the Picture Gallery: The Whitechapel Exhibitions and the Social Project of Ruskinian Aesthetics' *Visual Culture in Britain* 1:2 (2000), pp. 43–56, and Maltz, *British Aestheticism and the Urban Working Classes*, pp. 73–9, explores Henrietta Barnett's evocations of visitor responses to the exhibitions as an exercise in bourgeois self-affirmation. Lucinda Matthews-Jones ('Lessons in Seeing: Art, Religion and Class in East London, 1881–1898' *Journal of Victorian Culture* 16: 3 (2011), pp. 383–403) considers the exhibitions as an arena for Christian spirituality.

39 Koven suggests that the link between Easter and the exhibition 'implied a kind of equivalence between the expression of God's universal and impartial truth and love of the people through communion and through viewing great art'. 'The Whitechapel Picture Exhibitions and the Politics of Seeing', p. 34.
40 'Our Enquiry Column', *St Jude's* 1:6 (June 1889), p. 59.
41 Matthews-Jones, 'Lessons in Seeing', p. 389. Other attendance figures can be found in local press reports, the returns of attendances in the Barnett's periodical articles, and Samuel Barnett's annual pastoral address and accounts. See also Borzello, 'The Relationship of Fine Art and the Poor', pp. 50–1.
42 'Occasional Notes', *Toynbee Record* 1:8 (May 1889), p. 95.
43 'Hope for the East End', *Magazine of Music* 4:38 (May 1887), p. 33.
44 Borzello, 'The Relationship of Fine Art and the Poor', p. 56, and see for example the list in Barnett, *Canon Barnett*, vol. 2, pp. 167–8.
45 Barnett, *Canon Barnett*, vol. 2, p. 158.
46 Charity Commission, *Scheme for the Whitechapel Art Gallery* (pamphlet) (London, 1899), p. 3.
47 Matthews-Jones, 'Lessons in Seeing', p. 396.
48 'The Fine Art Exhibition', *Toynbee Journal* 1:8 (May 1886), p. 65.
49 *St Jude's* 1:5 (May 1889), p. 50.
50 'The Fine Art Exhibition', *Toynbee Journal and Students Union Chronicle* 1:8 (May 1886), p. 64.
51 DCA: People's Palace Box 2, E. H. Currie, 'To the Beaumont Trustees' [first report of the People's Palace] 1 October 1888, p. 3.
52 H. Jones, *Fifty Years, or Dead Leaves and Living Seeds* (London: Smith, Elder and Co., 1895), p. 95.
53 *Palace Journal* 4 (July 1889), p. 134.
54 DCA: People's Palace Box 2, E. H. Currie, 'To the Beaumont Trustees' [second report of the People's Palace] 1 October 1889, p. 2.
55 Currie, 'To the Beaumont Trustees', 1889, p. 2.
56 'The Opening of the Picture Exhibition', *Monthly Record* 2:6 (June 1896), p. 62.
57 J. S. Lidgett, 'The Approaching Loan Exhibition of Paintings at the Settlement' *Monthly Record* 2:4 (April 1896), p. 38.
58 Lidgett, 'The Approaching Loan Exhibition', p. 38.
59 'A Commentary in an Easy-Chair' *The Spectator* 16 August 1890, p. 211.
60 See N. Scotland, *Squires in the Slums: Settlements and Missions in late-Victorian London* (London: I. B. Taurus, 2007), pp. 197–8.
61 Cited in A. Hunter, 'Arthur Morrison and the Tyranny of Sentimental Charity' *English Literature in Transition, 1880–1920* 56:3 (2013), p. 307.
62 S. Eagles, *After Ruskin: The Social and Political Legacies of a Victorian Prophet, 1870–1920* (Oxford: Oxford University Press, 2011), p. 3.
63 A. Woodson-Boulton, *Transformative Beauty: Art Museums in Industrial Britain* (Stanford: Stanford University Press, 2012), p. 3.
64 *St Jude's* 1:4 (April 1889), p. 38.
65 Borzello, *Civilising Caliban*, p. 28.

66 G. Sims, *How the Poor Live, and Horrible London* (London: Chatto and Windus, 1889), p. 124.

67 J. F. C. Harrison, *Late-Victorian Britain 1870–1901* (London: Fontana, 1990), p. 199.

68 Lord Playfair, 'The Evolution of University Extension as a Part of Popular Education' in *Aspects of Modern Study* (London: Macmillan and Co., 1894), p. 8.

69 W. G. de Burgh, in 'Annual Meeting of the London Society: Conference on Working-men Centres' *UEJ* 5 (December 1894), p. 39.

70 C. F. G. Masterman, *The Heart of the Empire* (1901), cited in K. Inglis, *Churches and the Working Classes in Victorian England* (London: Routledge and Kegan Paul, 1963), p. 173.

71 Scotland, *Squires in the Slums*, pp. 209–10.

72 G. Himmelfarb, *Poverty and Compassion: The Moral Imagination of the Late-Victorians* (New York: Alfred A. Knopf, 1991), pp. 381–9.

73 M. J. D. Roberts, *Making English Morals: Voluntary Associations and Moral Reform in England, 1787–1886* (Cambridge: Cambridge University Press, 2004), p. 287.

74 J. Cox, *The English Churches in a Secular Society: Lambeth, 1870–1930* (New York: Oxford University Press, 1982), p. 201; see esp. chapter 4 'Diffusive Christianity' and chapter 6 'The Disintegration of the Civilizing Mission'.

75 Cox, *The English Churches in a Secular Society*, p. 201.

76 S. Pennybacker, '"It was not what she said but the way in which she said it": The London County Council and the Music Halls' in P. Bailey (ed.), *Music Hall: The Business of Pleasure* (Milton Keynes: Open University, 1986), p. 119.

77 BL: Burns Papers, Add. MSS. 46297, vol. 17, f. 148, letter from Samuel Barnett of 20 May 1899.

78 C. Waters, 'Progressives, Puritans and the Cultural Politics of the Council, 1889–1914' in A. Saint (ed.), *Politics and the People of London: The London County Council, 1889–1965* (London: Hambledon Press, 1989), p. 53.

79 Borzello, 'Preface to the 2014 Edition', *Civilising Caliban*, p. xvi.

80 Lady Lindsay, 'The People's Entertainment Society' *Time* 1 (1879), p. 474.

81 J. S. Lidgett, 'Ideals of the Settlement and how to Realise Them: II – Self-Improvement' *Monthly Record* 1:9 (December 1895), p. 98.

82 F. Rogers, 'Working Men and their Amusements' *Eastward Ho!* 1:3 (July 1884), pp. 234, 237.

Additional bibliography

Archives and collections

Ashbee Papers, Kings College Archive Centre, University of Cambridge:
CRA/A/1/1–3: Charles Ashbee Journals, 1884–1887

Ashbee Collection, National Art Library, Victoria and Albert Museum:
MSL/1959/2168: Ashbee Memoirs (typescript), vol. 1, 'The Guild Idea 1884–1902'

Barnett Papers, London Metropolitan Archives:
F/BAR/1–114: letters to F. A. Barnett, 1883–1892
F/BAR/460–465: Miscellaneous clippings, notes, correspondence
F/BAR/466: S. A. Barnett: Parish Circular, 1873
F/BAR/484: S. A. Barnett: 'The Ideal City' (pamphlet) Bristol, n. d.
F/BAR/493–511: Sermon notebooks, 1875–1888
F/BAR/514–516: Sermon notes, 1876–1877, 1884–1885
F/BAR/517: Notes for lectures at Bristol Cathedral, 1894
F/BAR/524–526: Typescript lectures on 'Christ and Workmen's Problems'
F/BAR/540: Sermon notes 'Class Relations in East London', 1889
F/BAR/553: Notes on 'Toynbee Hall and local government', n. d.
F/BAR/554: Notes on speech of thanks, n. d.
F/BAR/560–595: Miscellaneous pictures and photographs
ACC/3816/02/0101–01–3: Barnett correspondence, 1874–1936
ACC/3816/02/01/003: misc. photographs and notes re. Barnett memorial

Barnett Papers, Lambeth Palace Library:
MSS. 1463–6: Miscellaneous notes, clippings and correspondence

Beaumont Trust People's Palace Collection, London Metropolitan Archives:
A/BPP/1/1–4: Reports, letters, accounts and programmes relating to the Beaumont Institute and J. T. Barber Beaumont, 1842–1873
A/BPP/2/1–3: Reports, letters, accounts and programmes relating to the Beaumont Trust and People's Palace, 1881–1891

Walter Besant Correspondence, Dr Williams' Library, London:

24.110: letters to Henry Allon, 1871–1884

Beveridge Papers, British Library of Political and Economic Science, London School of Economics:

BEVERIDGE1/C/1: Appointments diary, 1903
BEVERIDGE/9A/36/A: transcriptions of correspondence, *c*. 1900–1909
BEVERIDGE/10/1: pamphlets and offprints, 1904–1914

Charles Booth Collection, British Library of Political and Economic Science, London School of Economics:

Group A: Loose Papers: vols. 28, 32–34, 38–39, 45–47, 56, 58
Group B: Notebooks: 155–157, 173–174, 178–179, 182, 221–229, 279–283, 365–367, 381–392

Booth Papers, University of London Library:

MS.797: I/47, 4911–12: Miscellaneous correspondence, 1903
MS.797: II/30: draft paper: 'Condition and Occupations of the People of East London and Hackney', 1888
MS.797: II/90/6ii: Obituary and report of service for Ernest Aves, 1917

Oscar Browning Papers, Kings College Archive Centre, University of Cambridge:

EAD/GBR/0272/PP/OB/1/101/A: letters from S. A. Barnett, 1888–1906
EAD/GBR/0272/PP/OB/1/99/A: letters from H. O. Barnett, various dates

Bryce Papers, Bodleian Library, Oxford:

Vols 183, 302: Miscellaneous speeches, notes re. the City of London Parochial Charities Bill, 1881–1882

Burnett Archive of Working-Class Autobiographies, Brunel University Library:

1:229 Leonard Ellisdon, 'Starting from Victoria', *c*. 1960
1:24 James Ashley, [untitled memoir], *c*. 1908
2:114 J. L. Bull, 'Reflections in Retirement', *c*. 1979
1:274 Jack Goring, [untitled memoir], *c*. 1938
1:371 Alfred Ireson, [untitled memoir], *c*. 1929
1:571 Thomas Rayment, 'Memories of an Octogenarian, 1864–1949', *c*. 1949
1:586 Elizabeth Rignall, 'All So Long Ago', n. d.
1:593 E. Robinson, 'I Remember', *c*. 1982
1:600 George Rowles, 'Chaps among the Caps', n. d.
1:891 L. Taylor, [untitled memoir], n. d.

Burns Papers, British Library:

Add. Mss. 46297: ff.148–149, 259–260, letters from S. A. Barnett, 1899–1900

Charity Commission, National Archives:

CHAR 7/5: 'Philosophical Institution at Beaumont Square, Mile End'

Children's Country Holidays Fund Records, London Metropolitan Archives:

LMA/4040/01/001–013: Executive Minutes, 1884–1914
LMA/4040/02/001/004: Executive Council Minutes, 1887–1914
LMA/4040/03/001–009: Annual Reports, 1884–1914

Cockerell Papers, British Library:

Add. Mss. 52623–7: Diaries, 1886–1890
Add. Mss. 52722: miscellaneous letters, notes, and clippings

Courtney Collection, British Library of Political and Economic Science, London School of Economics:

COURTNEY/21–4: Diary of Kate Courtney, 1875–1891

Drapers' Company Archive, Drapers' Hall:

MB 56–58: Court of Assistants Minute Books, 1883–1893
Boxes 1–4 of uncatalogued material relating to the People's Palace, Mile End
MB/SS1: People's Palace: General Purpose Committee Minutes, 1893–1895

Family Welfare Association (formerly COS) Records, London Metropolitan Archives:

A/FWA/C/A3/17–39: COS Enquiry Committee Minute Book, 1884–1903
A/FWA/C/A3/48–49: Notes on Children's Country Holidays Fund Work
A/FWA/C/A49/1–21: COS Enquiry Committee Districts Sub-committee Minute Books, 1877–1899

Class D: COS Enquiry Department:

A/FWA/C/D31/1–2: Finsbury Polytechnic, 1888–1889
A/FWA/C/D140/1–3: Children's Country Holidays Fund, 1884–1960
A/FWA/C/D155/1: School of Handicrafts for Destitute Boys, Chertsey, 1886–1938
A/FWA/C/D161/1: Working Lads' Institute and Home, Whitechapel, 1887–1931
A/FWA/C/D164/1: Oxford House, Bethnal Green, 1887–1961
A/FWA/C/D185/1–2: Bethnal Green Free Public Library, 1889–1926
A/FWA/C/D187/1: Royal Victoria Hall
A/FWA/C/D207: Robin Society, 1897–1931
A/FWA/279/1: Guild of Brave Poor Things

Fulham Papers, Lambeth Palace Library:

Misc. correspondence of Frederick Temple, Bishop of London: vols 6, 7, 10, 18, 23, 35–37, 47–48, 50–52, 55
Letters from W. W. How, Bishop Suffragen for East London, on parishes: vols 35–39, 47–48
Correspondence re. Young Men's Friendly Society: vol. 47

Gell Papers, Derbyshire Record Office:

Part VII: P. L. Gell: Correspondence and Papers: A: Gen. Corresp. 1869–1923: 1–6: Arnold Toynbee and Toynbee Hall

Octavia Hill Papers, British Library of Political and Economic Science, London School of Economics:

Coll. Misc. 512: various correspondence

Octavia Hill Papers, Westminster Archives Centre:

D. Misc. 84/2, 1–190: letters to Sydney Carlyle Cockerell
Letter to My Fellow Workers (printed pamphlets), 1877–1886

London County Council and Greater London Council Records, London Metropolitan Archives:

GLC/AR/BR/19/1021: Architects Department: Royal Victoria Hall
GLC/AR/BR/19/0253: Architects Department: People's Palace
GLC/AR/BR/19/1444: Architects Department: Whitechapel Picture Gallery
LCC/MIN/7330/E9: Minutes and Papers of the Housing of the Working Classes Committee, 1889–1892
LCC/MIN/7784: Minutes of the Lodging Houses Sub-Committee, 1893–1895
LCC/MIN/7814: Minutes of the Improvements Committee
LCC/MIN/10,876: Theatres and Music Halls Committee: People's Palace, Mile End, 1889–1910
LCC/MIN/10,882: Theatres and Music Halls Committee: Queen's Hall, 1891–1907
LCC/MIN/10,895: Theatres and Music Halls Committee: Royal Victoria Hall, 1886–1909
LCC/MIN/10,929: Theatres and Music Halls Committee: Sunday Entertainments (general papers), 1893–1909
LCC/MIN/12,787: Special Committee on Technical Education, 1890–1893

London Society for the Extension of University Teaching, University of London Library:

EM 1/1: LSEUT, minutes of the University Board
EM 1/3/1: LSEUT, Annual Reports, 1877–1886
EM 1/3/2: LSEUT, Annual Reports of Council, 1887–1888, and additional publications
EM 1/7/1: Reports to London Parochial Charities, vol. 1, 1892–1893 to 1920–1921
EM 1/8: LSEUT pamphlets, 1890–1899
EM 1/15/1: LSEUT List of Centres, 1877–1878 to 1945–1946
EM 2/23/1–15: Lecturers' and Examiners' Reports, 1883–1892
LSEUT/1–29: Appeals for funds, 1882–1892
LSEUT/39–40: Leaflets, 1888–1891

Marvin Papers, Bodleian Library, Oxford:

MS. Eng. lett. e.104–106, correspondence, 1885–1891
MS. Eng. lett. d.248–250: correspondence, 1889–1891

Milner Papers, Bodleian Library, Oxford:

MS. MILNER dep. 4: correspondence with P. L. Gell, 1873–1899
MS. MILNER dep. 25: miscellaneous correspondence, 1872–1885
MS. MILNER dep. 57: diaries and notes, 1882, 1885–1886
MS. MILNER dep. 59: diaries and notes, 1883, 1885, 1890–1892

Nevinson Papers, Bodleian Library, Oxford:

MSS. Eng. Misc. e.610/1: Journal, 2 January to 22 May 1893
MSS. Eng. Misc. e.610/2: Journal, 1 January to 15 May 1895
MSS. Eng. Misc. e.610/3: Journal, April 1896 to March 1897

Passfield Papers, British Library of Political and Economic Science, London School of Economics:

PASSFIELD/2/1/2/8, ff. 556–619: Beatrice Potter, misc. correspondence
PASSFIELD/7/14A: 'A Lady's view of the unemployed at the East [End]'
PASSFIELD/7/1/6, ff. 1–37: 'Personal observation and statistical inquiry' (1887)

People's Palace Archive, Queen Mary, University of London Library:

QMC/PP/2/3 Letter from Sir. E. H. Currie and minutes of Mansion House meeting, 23 June 1885
QMC/PP/2/1-5 Beaumont Trust: miscellaneous pamphlets and appeals
QMC/PP/2/15-16 Beaumont Trust: general correspondence relating to fundraising
QMC/PP/16/1-6 Beaumont Trust: miscellaneous correspondence
QMC/PP/10/31 correspondence re. East London Industrial Exhibition, 1887
QMC/PP/4/8 'Programme for Opening of the People's Palace by the Queen' 14 May 1887
QMC/PP/4/2 Laying of foundation stone at Queen's Hall: general papers and correspondence
QMC/PP/2/8 Correspondence and general papers re. royal patronage, 1886
QMC/PP/4/1 Enquiries regarding Sunday opening and sale of intoxicating drinks
QMC/PP/18/5 Letters from Beaumont family members, 1883–1886
QMC/PP/11/1 General correspondence re. clubs and societies
QMC/PP/6/1-6 Papers re. Charity Commission and People's Palace

Society of Authors Archives, British Library:

Add. Mss. 57040: misc. notes re. H. W. Nevinson, 1941

Southwark Local History Library:

File 360–76: Bermondsey Settlement

Toynbee Hall Papers, London Metropolitan Archives:

A/TOY/5: Annual Reports, 1884–1894
A/TOY/8/1: Toynbee Hall Financial Reports, 4–29 (1888–1915)

A/TOY/9/1: Universities Settlement in East London: Memorandum and Articles of Association, 1884
A/TOY/17/2: Toynbee Hall Visitors Book, 1885–1927
A/TOY/21/3–4: Memorial to S. A. Barnett
A/TOY/22/3/6: C. M. Lloyd: 'What Toynbee Hall does for East London'
A/TOY/25/1: Plan: site for club room, Toynbee Hall
A/TOY/26: Miscellaneous

Toynbee Hall (Additional Records), London Metropolitan Archives:

ACC: 2486/009: Bye-laws and regulations of the Council, 1887
ACC: 2486/010: Annual Report of the Council, 1886
ACC: 2486/201–202: Toynbee Hall centenary

Tower Hamlets Local History Library, general collection (830–1) and archives:

TH/8326: Bethnal Green Free Library letter-book
'People's Palace: Queen Alexandra's visit to St. George's-in-the-East and the People's Palace, July 14th 1904' [scrapbook]
'Toynbee Hall: University Extension' scrapbook compiled by S. A. Barnett, 1888–1894

Wallas Papers, British Library of Political and Economic Science, London School of Economics:

WALLAS/1/9–21: misc. correspondence, 1890–1898
WALLAS/6/4: university extension lectures and syllabus
WALLAS/6/2: Lecture on 'Education in England', 1892

Mary Ward Papers, University of London Library (National Archives):

MS Add. 303/39–42: Dorothy Mary Ward diaries, 8 vols, various dates [*c.* 1889–1910]

Contemporary published sources

Adcock, A. St. J., *East End Idylls* (London: James Bowden, 1897).
Aitken, G. H., *Fellow-workers with God and other Sermons* (London: Methuen and Co., 1921).
Ashbee, C. R., *From Whitechapel to Camelot* (London: Guild of Handicraft, 1892).
Ashbee, C. R., *The Survey of London: Vol. I: The Parish of Bromley-by-Bow* (London: P. S. King and Son, 1900).
Barnett, H. O., *The Making of the Home: A Reading-book of Domestic Economy for School and Home Use* (London: Cassell and Co., 1885).
Barnett, S. A., *The Service of God: Sermons, Essays, and Addresses* (London: Longmans Green and Co., 1897).
Barnett, S. A., *Worship and Work: Thoughts from the Unpublished Writings of the Late Canon S. A. Barnett* (H. O. Barnett ed.) (Letchworth: Garden City Press, 1913).
Barnett, S. A., *Perils of Wealth and Poverty: By the Late Canon Barnett* (V. Boyle ed.) (London: George Allen and Unwin, 1920).
Besant, W., *Children of Gibeon* (London: Chatto and Windus, 1887).

Besant, W., *London North of the Thames* (London: Adam and Charles Black, 1911).

Booth, C., *East London* (*Life and Labour of the People in London* Vol. 1) (London: Macmillan, 1889).

Booth, C., *Condition and Occupations of the People of the Tower Hamlets 1886–1887; Being a Paper Read before the Royal Statistical Society in May, 1887* (London: Edward Stanford, 1887).

Booth, C., *Life and Labour of the People in London: First Series: Poverty* (London: Macmillan, 1902), 4 vols.

Booth, C., *Life and Labour of the People in London: Third Series: Religious Influences* (London: Macmillan, 1902), 4 vols.

Booth, W., *In Darkest England, and The Way Out* (London: The Salvation Army, 1890).

Cunynghame, H., *Assistant Commissioner's Financial Report* [*on the People's Palace*] (29 July 1890) (London: Charity Commission, 1890).

East London Exhibition, [People's Palace], *Official Daily Programme* (London, 1896).

Gilman, D. C. (ed.), *The Organization of Charity; being a Report of the Sixth Section of the International Congress of Charities, Corrections and Philanthropy* (Baltimore: The Johns Hopkins Press, 1894).

Green, T. H., *The Witness of God and Faith: Two Lay Sermons* (London: Longmans, Green, and Co., 1885).

Hadden, R. H., *An East-End Chronicle: St George's-in-the-East Parish and Parish Church* (London: Hatchards, 1880).

Harwood, P., *The Object of the Sunday Lectures at the Philosophical Institution, Beaumont Square, Mile End* (London: Charles Fox, 1842).

Hill, O., *Homes of the London Poor* (London: Macmillan and Co., 1875).

Hill, O., *Colour, Space and Music for the People* (London, 1884).

Hodson, A. L., *Letters From a Settlement* (London: Edward Arnold, 1909).

Ingham, J. A., *City Slums: A Political Thesis* (London: Swan Sonnenschein and Co., 1889).

Jay, A. O., *Life in Darkest London: A Hint to General Booth* (London: Webster and Cable, 1891).

Jay, A. O., *The Social Problem: Its Possible Solution* (London: Simpkin, Marshall, Hamilton, Kent and Co., 1893).

Jay, A. O., *A Story of Shoreditch* (London: Simpkin, Marshall, Hamilton, Kent and Co., 1896).

Jones, H., *Attitude and Aim of the English Church in Social and Humanitarian Movements* (London: SPCK, 1891).

Keating, P. (ed.), *Into Unknown England 1866–1913: Selections from the Social Explorers* (Manchester: Manchester University Press, 1976).

Kimmins, G., *Polly of Parker's Rents* (London: James Bowden, 1899).

Knapp, J. M., *The Universities and the Social Problem* (London: Rivington, Percival and Co., 1895).

Leighton, B., *Letters and Other Writings of the Late Edward Denison, MP for Newark* (London: Richard Bentley and Son, 1872).

London, J., *People of the Abyss* (London: Journeyman Press, 1992 [1903]).

Manners, Lady J., *Some of the Advantages of Easily Accessible Reading and Recreation Rooms and Free Libraries* (London: William Blackwood and Sons, 1885).

Masterman, C. F. G., *The Condition of England* (J. T. Boulton ed.) (London: Methuen, 1960 [1909]).

Mackinder, H. J. and Sadler, M. E., *University Extension: Has it a Future?* (London: H. Froude, 1890).

Mackinder, H. J. and Sadler, M. E., *University Extension: Past, Present, and Future* (London: Cassell and Co., 1891).

[Mearns, A.], *The Bitter Cry of Outcast London* (London: James Clark, 1883).

Montague, F. C., *Arnold Toynbee* (Baltimore: John Hopkins University Studies in Historical and Political Sciences, 1889).

Moulton, R. G., *The University Extension Movement* (London: Bemrose and Sons, n. d. [1885]).

Nettleship, R. L. (ed.), *Works of Thomas Hill Green* (London: Longmans, Green and Co., 1906), 3 vols.

'Pearl Fisher', *The Harvest of the City, and the Workers of Today* (London: John F. Shaw and Co., 1884).

People's Palace, *Opening of the Queen's Hall and Stone-laying* (London, n. d. [1887]).

People's Palace, *Handbook and Guide: An Account of its Origin and Recreative Work* (London, 1911).

Peppin, T. S., *Club-land of the Toiler* (London: J. M. Dent and Co., 1895).

Pike, G. H., *An East-End Free Library* (London, 1888).

Polytechnic Reception Bureau, *The Social Centres of London: Being a Comprehensive Guide to the Social, Educational, Recreative and Religious Institutes and Clubs of the Metropolis* (London: Polytechnic Reception Bureau, 1892).

Ragged School Union, *The Dens of London: Forty Years' Mission Work among the Outcast Poor of London* (London, n. d. [1884]).

Reason, W., *Our Industrial Outcasts* (London: Andrew Melrose, n. d. [1905]).

Roberts, R. D., *Eighteen Years of University Extension* (Cambridge: Cambridge University Press, 1891).

Roberts, R. D., *Education in the Nineteenth Century* (Cambridge: Cambridge University Press, 1901).

Rogers, F., *The New Movement at the Universities, and What May Come of It* (London, n. d. [c. 1886]).

Ross, E. (ed.), *Slum Travelers: Ladies and London Poverty, 1860–1920* (Berkeley: University of California Press, 2007).

St Jude's, Whitechapel, *Annual Pastoral Address and Report on Parish Work* (London, 1873–1892).

School of Handicraft, *Annual Report* 1–7 (1888/89 to 1894–1895).

Shand, Lord, *Technical Education: What such Education is, and by what Means it can best be Given* (Edinburgh: W. Green, 1882).

Toynbee, A., *'Progress and Poverty': A Criticism of Mr Henry George* (London: Kegan Paul, 1883).

Toynbee, A., *Lectures on the Industrial Revolution of the Eighteenth Century in England* (London: Rivington's, 1884).

Toynbee Hall, *Annual Report* 2–46 (1885/86 to 1931/32).

Toynbee Hall, *Toynbee Hall: General Information* (London, 1887).

Tuckwell, W., Leland, C. G., and Besant, W., *Art and Hand Work for the People: being three Papers Read before the Social Science Congress, September 1884* (Manchester: J. E. Cornish, 1885).

Universities' Settlement Association, *The Universities' Settlement in East London* (printed circular) May 1884.

Universities' Settlement Association, *First Report of the Universities Settlement in East London* (Oxford, 1885).

White, A., *The Problems of a Great City* (London: Remington, 1886).

Williams, M., *Round London: Down East and Up West* (London: Macmillan and Co., 1892).
Woods, R. A. (ed.), *The Poor in Great Cities: Their Problems and What is Being Done to Solve Them* (London: Kegan Paul, Trench, Trubner and Co., 1896).
Working Men's Club and Institute Union, *The Conditions on which Local Societies will be Received into Membership* (London, 1863).

Memoirs and reminiscences

Addams, J., *Twenty Years at Hull-House, with Autobiographical Notes* (New York: Macmillan, 1938).
Adderley, J., *In Slums and Society: Reminiscences of Old Friends* (London: T. Fisher Unwin, 1916).
Benson, E. F., *As We Were: A Victorian Peepshow* (London: Longman's, Green and Co., 1930).
Beveridge, J., *Beveridge and His Plan* (London: Hodder and Stoughton, 1954).
Beveridge, W., *Power and Influence* (London: Hodder and Stoughton, 1953).
Barberton, R., *The Diaries of Mary, Countess of Meath* (London: Hutchinson, 1928), 2 vols.
Bruce, M. L. (comp.), *Anna Swanwick: A Memoir and Recollections 1813–1899* (London: T. Fisher Unwin, 1903).
Burnett, J., *Destiny Obscure: Autobiographies of Childhood, Education and Family* (London: Allen Lane, 1982).
Burnett, J. (ed.), *Useful Toil: Autobiographies of Working People from 1820s to 1920s* (London: Allen Lane, 1984).
Chase, E., *Tenant Friends in Old Deptford* (London: Williams and Norgate, 1929).
Catchpool, E. St J., *Candles in the Darkness* (London: Bannisdale Press, 1966).
Dudley Ward, C. H. and Spencer, C. B., *The Unconventional Civil Servant: Sir Henry H. Cunynghame* (London: Michael Joseph, 1938).
Grinling, C. H., 'Fifty Years of Pioneer Work in Woolwich' [pamphlet] (London, 1922).
Hall, B. T., *Our Fifty Years: The Story of the Working Men's Club and Institute Union* (London: Working Men's Club and Institute Union, 1912).
Holiday, H., *Reminiscences of My Life* (London: William Heinemann, 1914).
Lang, C. G., [1913 reminiscence of Samuel Barnett] extracted in Barnett, S.A., *Worship and Work: Thoughts from the Unpublished Writings of the Late Canon S. A. Barnett* (H. O. Barnett ed.) (Letchworth: Garden City Press, 1913), pp. ix–xiv.
Lansbury, G., *Looking Backwards – and Forwards* (London: Blackie and Son, 1935).
MacKenzie, N. (ed.), *The Letters of Sidney and Beatrice Webb* (Cambridge: Cambridge University Press, 1978), 3 vols.
Mansbridge, A., *An Adventure in Working-class Education, being the story of the Workers' Educational, Association, 1903–1915* (London: Longman's Green and Co., 1920).
Martin, H. (ed.), *Christian Social Reformers of the Nineteenth Century* (London: Student Christian Movement, 1927).
Milner, A., 'Reminiscence' [of Arnold Toynbee] in Toynbee, A., *Lectures on the Industrial Revolution of the Eighteenth Century in England* (London: Longman's Green and Co., 1925 [1884]), pp. ix–xxx.
Roberts, R., *The Classic Slum: Salford Life in the First Quarter of the Century* (London: Penguin, 1990 [1971]).

Salter, J., *Memoirs of a Public Servant* (London: Faber and Faber, 1961).
Sims, G. R., *My Life: Sixty Years' Recollections of Bohemian London* (London: Eveleigh Nash Company, 1917).
Spender, J. A., *Life, Journalism and Politics: An Autobiography* (London: Cassell and Co., 1927).
Stuart, J., *Reminiscences* (London: Chiswick Press, 1911).
Thorp, J. E., *With Lads in Whitechapel through Fifty Years* (London: Epworth Press, 1938).
Ward, M., *A Writer's Recollections* (London: Collins, 1918).
Webb, B., *The Diary of Beatrice Webb* (N. and J. Mackenzie eds) (London: Virago Press, 1982).

Selected periodical articles and essays

Adderley, J. G., 'Is Slumming Played Out?' *English Illustrated Magazine* 119 (August 1893), pp. 834–841.
Barnett, H. O., 'Passionless Reformers' *Fortnightly Review* n. s. 21 (August 1882), pp. 226–233.
Barnett, H. O., 'Women as Philanthropists' in T. Stanton (ed.), *The Woman Question in Europe* (New York: G. P. Putnam's Sons, 1884), pp. 108–138.
Barnett, H. O., 'Pictures for the People' in S. A. Barnett and H. O. Barnett, *Practicable Socialism* (second ed.) (London: Longmans Green and Co., 1895), pp. 175–187.
Barnett, H. O., 'The Beginning of Toynbee Hall' in S. A. Barnett and H. O. Barnett, *Towards Social Reform* (London: T. Fisher Unwin, 1909), pp. 239–254.
Barnett, S. A., 'A Democratic Church' *Contemporary Review* 46 (November 1884), pp. 673–681.
Barnett, S. A., 'The Duties of the Rich to the Poor' in H. Jones (ed.), *Some Urgent Questions in Christian Lights* (London: Rivington's, 1889), pp. 66–81.
Barnett, S. A., 'Hospitalities' in J. M. Knapp (ed.), *The Universities and the Social Problem* (London: Rivington, Percival and Co., 1895), pp. 53–66.
Barnett, S. A., 'Sensationalism in Social Reform' in S. A. Barnett and H. O. Barnett, *Practicable Socialism: Essays on Social Reform* (London: Longman's Green and Co., 1895), pp. 228–234.
Barnett, S. A., 'University Settlements' *Nineteenth Century* 38 (1895), pp. 1014–1024.
Barnett, S. A., 'The Failure of Philanthropy' *Macmillan's Magazine* 73 (March 1896), pp. 390–396.
Barnett, S. A., 'The Ways of Settlements and Missions' *Nineteenth Century* 42 (December 1897), pp. 975–984.
Barnett, S. A., 'Twenty-five Years of East London' *Contemporary Review* 74 (August 1898), pp. 280–289.
Barnett, S. A., 'A Retrospect of Toynbee Hall' in S. A. Barnett and H. O. Barnett, *Towards Social Reform* (London: T. Fisher Unwin, 1909), pp. 255–270.
Bennett, O., *A Bright Spot in Outcast London* (London: Hatchards, 1884).
Besant, W., 'The Amusements of the People' *Contemporary Review* 45 (March 1884), pp. 342–355.
Besant, W., 'The People's Palace' *Contemporary Review* 51 (February 1887), pp. 226–233.
Besant, W., *To the Working Men of East London: The People's Palace* (London: Beaumont Trust, 1887)
Besant, W., 'The Farm and the City' *Contemporary Review* 72 (December 1897), pp. 792–807.

Besant, W., 'One of Two Millions in East London' *Century Illustrated Monthly Magazine* 59 (1899), pp. 225–243.

Besant, W., 'Is This the Voice of the Hooligan?' *Contemporary Review* 77 (January 1900), pp. 27–39.

Besant, W., 'Art and the People' in his *As We Are and As We May Be* (London: Chatto and Windus, 1903), pp. 246–269.

Besant, W., 'The Associated Life' in his *As We Are and As We May Be* (London: Chatto and Windus, 1903), pp. 296–314.

Bindon, E., 'An East-End Club' *Eastward Ho!* 5 (July 1886), pp. 285–288.

Bisland, E., 'The People's Palace in London' *The Cosmopolitan* 10:3 (January 1891), pp. 259–268.

Black, C., 'Labour and Life in London' *Contemporary Review* 60 (August 1891), pp. 207–229.

Blanchard, S. S., 'The People's Palace in London' *Lend A Hand* 9:5 (November 1892), pp. 340–344.

Brockett, F. W., 'The People and Their Friends' *Fortnightly Review* 45 (March 1886), pp. 306–317.

Buckland, A. R., 'Bank Holiday at Bethnal Green' *Cassell's Family Magazine* 9 (1883), pp. 299–301.

Buss, S., 'Aspects of East London' *Eastward Ho!* 1:2 (June 1884), pp. 81–86.

Collings, T. C., 'The Settlements of London: What they are, and what they are doing' *Leisure Hour* (1895) pp. 600–606, 739–744, 796–802.

Dixon, E., 'A Whitechapel Street' *English Illustrated Magazine* 77 (February 1890), pp. 355–360.

'The Dwellings of the London Poor: An Interview with the Rev. Samuel Barnett' *Cassell's Family Magazine* 13 (1886), pp. 396–399.

'E. M. E.', 'Women's Settlements' *Hearth and Home: An Illustrated Weekly Journal for Gentlewomen* 435 (14 September 1899), pp. 717–718.

Fawcett, H., 'Bethnal Green Museum' *Eastward Ho!* 1:2 (June 1884), pp. 149–151.

Fish, A., 'Metropolitan Art Schools: the People's Palace' *Magazine of Art* (May–October 1897), pp. 252–256.

Gilman, J. B., 'Toynbee Hall, Whitechapel, the Universities' Settlement in East London' *Lend a Hand* 2:5 (May 1887), pp. 255–256.

Gregory, R., 'The Inhabitants of East London' *Quarterly Review* 169 (October 1889), pp. 431–459.

Greville, V., 'The Use of Music' *Eastward Ho!* 2:1 (November 1884), pp. 607–610.

Hayward, G., 'Sunday Art' *Eastward Ho!* 5 (May 1886), pp. 26–29.

Hill, T., 'The Local Separation of Classes' *Eastward Ho!* 6 (February 1887), pp. 341–347.

Holmes, F. M., 'Toynbee Hall and the Rev. S. A. Barnett' *Great Thoughts* 19 (1893), pp. 348–350.

How, W. W., 'Eastward Ho!' *Eastward Ho!* 1:1 (May 1884), pp. 1–2.

'J. R.', 'Music and Culture' *Magazine of Music* 2:5 (June 1885), pp. 69–70.

James, M. S. R., 'The People's Palace and its Library' *Library Journal* (October 1893), pp. 427–430.

Jebb, E. L., 'Recreative Learning and Voluntary Teaching' *Contemporary Review* 48 (October 1888), pp. 526–536.

Jeune, M., 'Amusements of the Poor' *National Review* 21 (May 1893), pp. 303–314.

Jones, H., 'The Amusements of the People' *Good Words* 32 (1891), pp. 163–166.

Kemp, E. A. L., 'A Great Gulf Fixed' *Eastward Ho!* 1:1 (May 1884), pp. 59–62.

Lambert, B., 'The Outcast Poor – I. Esau's Cry' *Contemporary Review* 44 (December 1883), pp. 916–923.

Lambert, B., 'Jacob's Answer to Esau's Cry' *Contemporary Review* 46 (September 1884), pp. 373–382.

Lister, H., 'Manliness and Manly Sports' *Eastward Ho!* 1:4 (August 1884), pp. 283–290.

'London Music-Halls' *Magazine of Music* 3:29 (August 1886), pp. 89–91.

Marshall, F., 'Music and the People' *Nineteenth Century* 8 (December 1880), pp. 921–932.

Medhurst, B., 'A Musical Mission for Christmas' *Eastward Ho!* 6 (December 1886), pp. 120–6.

Morrison, A., 'Whitechapel' *Palace Journal* 3 (April 1889), pp. 1022–1023.

Reaney, G. S., 'Outcast London' *Fortnightly Review* n. s. 40 (December 1886), pp. 687–695.

Sims, G. R., 'Sunday's Dinner' *Eastward Ho!* 1:1 (May 1884), pp. 10–14.

Smith, S., 'The Industrial Training of Destitute Children' *Contemporary Review* 47 (January 1885), pp. 107–119.

Stuart-Wortley, J., 'The East End as Represented by Mr Besant' *Nineteenth Century* 127 (1887), pp. 361–377.

'The Palace of Delight: A Possible Story' *Eastward Ho!* 1:1 (May 1884), pp. 65–66.

'The People's University in Whitechapel' *London* (3 October 1895), pp. 835–836.

Tunis, J., 'The People's Palace: A Palace of Joy' *Lend a Hand* 8 (1892), pp. 151–158.

White, A., 'The Nomad Poor of London' *Contemporary Review* 47 (May 1885), pp. 714–726.

Williams, J., 'Sunday at the People's Palace' *Lend a Hand* 3 (1888), pp. 321–323.

Wills, F., 'Recreative Evening Schools' *Nineteenth Century* 20 (July 1886), pp. 130–138.

Wills, F., 'What I Found in the East End' *Eastward Ho!* 7 (January 1888), pp. 504–507.

'Working Men's Concerts' *Magazine of Music* 3:31 (October 1886), p. 131.

Monographs

Alderman, G., *London Jewry and London Politics, 1889–1986* (London: Routledge, 1989).

Altick, R. D., *The English Common Reader: A Social History of the Mass Reading Public 1800–1900* (Chicago: University of Chicago Press, 1957).

Altick, R. D., *The Shows of London* (Cambridge, MA: Harvard University Press, 1978).

Altick, R. D., *Writers, Readers, and Occasions: Selected Essays on Victorian Literature and Life* (Columbus: Ohio State University Press, 1989).

Anderson, P., *The Printed Image and the Transformation of Popular Culture* (Oxford: Clarendon Press, 1991).

Anderson, R. D., *Universities and Elites in Britain Since 1800* (London: Macmillan, 1992).

August, A., *The British Working Class, 1832–1940* (Harlow: Pearson Longman, 2007).

Ausubel, H., *In Hard Times: Reformers among the Late-Victorians* (New York: Columbia University Press, 1960).

Ball, A., *The Public Libraries of Greater London: A Pictorial History, 1856–1914* (London: Library Associations, 1977).

290   *Additional bibliography*

Baldick, C., *The Social Mission of English Criticism 1848–1932* (Oxford: Clarendon Press, 1983).

Bivona, D. and Henkle, R. B., *The Imagination of Class: Masculinity and the Victorian Urban Poor* (Columbus: Ohio State University Press, 2006).

Blyth, J. A., *English University Adult Education 1908–1958: The Unique Tradition* (Manchester: Manchester University Press, 1983).

Bradley, K., *Poverty, Philanthropy and the State: Charities and the Working Classes in London, 1918–79* (Manchester: Manchester University Press, 2009)

Briggs, A., *Victorian Cities* (Harmondsworth: Penguin Books, 1968).

Britain, I., *Fabianism and Culture: A Study in British Socialism and the Arts, c.1884–1918* (Cambridge: Cambridge University Press, 1982).

Brinton, C., *English Political Thought in the Nineteenth Century* (New York: Harper and Row, 1962).

Cacoullos, A. R., *Thomas Hill Green: Philosopher of Rights* (New York: Twayne, 1974).

Carey, J., *The Intellectuals and the Masses: Pride and Prejudice among the Literary Intelligentsia, 1880–1939* (London: Faber and Faber, 1992).

Carpenter, S. C., *Winnington-Ingram* (London: Hodder and Stoughton, 1949).

Carroll, J., *The Cultural Theory of Matthew Arnold* (Berkeley: University of California Press, 1982).

Checkland, O., *Philanthropy in Victorian Scotland: Social Welfare and the Voluntary Principle* (Edinburgh: John Donald, 1980).

Collini, S., *Liberalism and Sociology: L. T. Hobhouse and Political Argument in England 1880–1914* (Cambridge: Cambridge University Press, 1979).

Conway, H., *People's Parks: The Design and Development of Victorian Parks in Britain* (Cambridge: Cambridge University Press, 1991).

Crocker, R. H., *Social Work and Social Order: The Settlement Movement in Two Industrial Cities 1889–1930* (Urbana: University of Illinois Press, 1992).

Davies, A., *The East End Nobody Knows: A History, a Guide, an Exploration* (London: Macmillan, 1990).

Davis, A. F., *Spearheads for Reform: The Social Settlements and the Progressive Movement, 1890–1914* (New York: Oxford University Press, 1967).

Davis, H. W. C., *A History of Balliol College* (Oxford: Blackwell, 1963).

Davis, J., *Reforming London: the London Government Problem, 1855–1900* (Oxford: Clarendon Press, 1988).

Devereux, W., *Adult Education in Inner London 1870–1980* (London: Shepeard-Walwyn and London Education Authority, 1982).

Digby, A., *Pauper Palaces* (London: Routledge and Kegan Paul, 1978).

Donakowski, C., *A Muse for the Masses: Ritual and Music in the Age of Democratic Revolution 1770–1870* (Chicago: Chicago University Press, 1977).

Draper, W. H., *University Extension: A Survey of Fifty Years 1873–1923* (Cambridge: Cambridge University Press, 1923).

Ellis, A., *Educating the Masters: Influences on the Growth of Literacy in Victorian Working Class Children* (Aldershot: Gower, 1985).

Englander, D., *Landlord and Tenant in Urban Britain, 1838–1918* (Oxford: Clarendon Press, 1983).

Feldman, D., *Englishmen and Jews: Social Relations and Political Culture, 1840–1914* (New Haven: Yale University Press, 1994).

Francis, M. and Morrow, J., *A History of English Political Thought in the Nineteenth Century* (New York: St Martin's Press, 1994).

Fraser, D., *Urban Politics in Victorian England: The Structure of Politics in Victorian Cities* (Leicester: Leicester University Press, 1976).

Godwin, G., *Queen Mary College: An Adventure in Education* (London: Queen Mary College, 1939).

Golby, J. M. and Purdue, A. W., *The Civilisation of the Crowd: Popular Culture in England 1750–1950* (London: Batsford Academic, 1984).

Gosden, P. H. J. H., *Self-Help: Voluntary Associations in Nineteenth Century Britain* (London: Batsford, 1973).

Harrison, B., *Peaceable Kingdom: Stability and Change in Modern Britain* (Oxford: Clarendon Press, 1982).

Harrison, J. F. C., *Learning and Living 1790–1960: A Study in the History of the English Adult Education Movement* (London: Routledge and Kegan Paul, 1961).

Harrop, S. (ed.), *Oxford and Working-Class Education* (Nottingham: University of Nottingham Department of Adult Education, 1987).

Hartley, H., *Balliol Men* (Oxford: Blackwell, 1963).

Hay, J .R., *The Development of the British Welfare State, 1880–1975* (London: Edward Arnold, 1978).

Hayley, B., *The Healthy Body and Victorian Culture* (Cambridge, MA: Harvard University Press, 1978).

Heyck, T. W., *The Transformation of Intellectual Life in Victorian England* (London: Croom Helm, 1982).

Hilton, B., *The Age of Atonement: The Influence of Evangelicalism on Social and Economic Thought, 1795–1865* (Oxford: Clarendon Press, 1988).

Himmelfarb, G., *The Idea of Poverty: England in the Early Industrial Age* (New York: Alfred A. Knopf, 1984).

Hobsbawm, E. J., *Industry and Empire* (Harmondsworth: Penguin Books, 1969).

Holloway, J., *The Victorian Sage: Studies in Argument* (London: Macmillan, 1953).

Horowitz, H., *Culture and the City: Cultural Philanthropy in Chicago from the 1880s to 1917* (Lexington: The University Press of Kentucky, 1976).

Hurt, J. S., *Education and the Working Classes From the Eighteenth to the Twentieth Centuries* (London: History of Education Society, 1985).

Jepson, N. A., *The Beginnings of English University Adult Education – Policy and Problems* (London: Michael Joseph, 1973).

Johnson, A. H., *The History of the Worshipful Company of Drapers Vol. 3: 1603–1920* (Oxford: Clarendon Press, 1922).

Jones, P. d' A., *The Christian Socialist Revival in England, 1877–1914* (Princeton: Princeton University Press, 1968).

Joyce, P., *Work, Society, and Politics: The Culture of the Factory in Later Victorian Britain* (Brighton: Harvester Press, 1980).

Joyce, P., *Visions of the People: Industrial England and the Question of Class, c.1848–1914* (Cambridge: Cambridge University Press, 1990).

Joyce, P., *The Rule of Freedom: Liberalism and the Modern City* (London: Verso, 2003).

Keating, P., *The Haunted Study: A Social History of the English Novel 1875–1914* (London: Secker and Warburg, 1989).

Keating, P., *The Working Classes in Victorian Fiction* (London: Routledge and Kegan Paul, 1971).

Keating, P. (ed.), *Working-class Stories of the 1890s* (London: Routledge and Kegan Paul, 1971).

Kelly, T., *Outside the Walls: Sixty Years of University Extension at Manchester 1886–1946* (Manchester: Manchester University Press, 1950).

Kelly, T., *A History of Adult Education in Great Britain* (Liverpool: Liverpool University Press, 1970).

Kelly, T., *A History of Public Libraries in Great Britain 1845–1965* (London: The Library Association, 1973).

Kitson Clark, G., *Churchmen and the Condition of England 1832–1885* (London: Methuen, 1973).

Koven, S., *The Match Girl and the Heiress* (Princeton: Princeton University Press, 2014).

Lee, A., *The Origins of the Popular Press in England 1855–1914* (London: Croom Helm, 1978).

Lees, A., *Cities Perceived: Urban Society in European and American Thought, 1820–1940* (Manchester: Manchester University Press, 1985).

Leslie, W. B., *Gentlemen and Scholars: College and Community in the 'Age of the University' 1865–1917* (University Park, PA: Pennsylvania State University Press, 1992).

Lester, J. A., *Journey Through Despair, 1880–1914: Transformations in British Literary Culture* (Princeton: Princeton University Press, 1968).

Levy, C. (ed.), *Socialism and the Intelligentsia 1880–1914* (London: Routledge and Kegan Paul, 1987).

Livesey, R., *Socialism, Sex and the Culture of Aestheticism in Britain, 1880–1914* (Oxford: Oxford University Press, 2007).

Lockhart, J. G., *Cosmo Gordon Lang* (London: Hodder and Stoughton, 1949).

Lynd, H. M., *England in the 1880s: Towards a Social Basis for Freedom* (London: Frank Cass and Co., 1968 [1945]).

Magnusson, N., *Salvation in the Slums: Evangelical Social Work, 1865–1920* (Metuchen, NJ: Scarecrow Press, 1977).

Marriott, S., *A Backstairs to a Degree: Demands for an Open University in late Victorian England* (Leeds: University of Leeds Department of Adult Education and Extramural Studies, 1981).

Martin, D. E. and Rubenstein, D. (eds), *Ideology and the Labour Movement: Essays presented to John Saville* (London: Croom Helm, 1979).

McGaskell, S. M. (ed.), *Slums* (Leicester: Leicester University Press, 1990).

McIlhiney, D. B., *A Gentleman in Every Slum: Church of England Missions in East London 1837–1914* (Eugene, OR: Wipf and Stock, 1988).

McKibbon, R., *The Ideologies of Class: Social Relations in Britain 1880–1950* (Oxford: Clarendon Press, 1990).

McLeod, H., *Religion and the Working-Class in Nineteenth Century Britain* (London: Macmillan, 1984).

Maclure, S., *One Hundred Years of London Education 1870–1990* (London: Allen Lane, 1990).

Meacham, S., *A Life Apart: The English Working Class, 1890–1914* (Cambridge, MA: Harvard University Press, 1977).

Mowat, C. L., *The Charity Organisation Society, 1869–1913: Its Ideas and Works* (London: Methuen and Co., 1961).

Moyes, C., *A History of the Mothers' Union: Women, Anglicanism and Globalisation, 1876–2008* (Woodbridge: Boydell and Brewer, 2009).

Mumford, L., *The City in History* (Harmondsworth: Penguin Books, 1991 [1961]).

Nead, L., *Victorian Babylon: People, Streets and Images in Nineteenth-Century London* (New Haven, CT: Yale University Press, 2000).

Newman, A. (ed.), *The Jewish East End 1840–1939* (London: Jewish Historical Society of England, 1981).

Norman-Butler, B., *Victorian Aspirations: The Life and Labour of Charles and Mary Booth* (London: Allen and Unwin, 1972).

Noyce, J., *Libraries and the Working Class in the Nineteenth Century* (Brighton: Smoothiee Publications, 1974).

O'Day, R. and Englander, D., *Mr Charles Booth's Enquiry: Life and Labour of the People in London Reconsidered* (London: Hambledon, 1993).

Olsen, D. J., *The Growth of Victorian London* (Harmondsworth: Penguin Books, 1979).

Olsen, D. J., *The City as a Work of Art: London, Paris, Vienna* (New Haven, CT: Yale University Press, 1986).

Owen, D., *English Philanthropy 1660–1960* (Cambridge, MA: Harvard University Press, 1965).

Palmer, A., *The East End: Four Centuries of London Life* (London: John Murray, 1989).

Palmer, I., *Matthew Arnold: Culture, Society and Education* (London: Macmillan, 1979).

Pelling, H., *Popular Politics and Society in Late-Victorian Britain* (London: Macmillan, 1968).

Pemberton, J. E., *Politics and Public Libraries in England and Wales, 1850–1970* (London: Library Association, 1977).

Pennybacker, S. D., *A Vision for London 1889–1914: Labour, Everyday Life and the LCC Experiment* (New York: Routledge, 1996).

Perkin, H., *The Rise of Professional Society: England since 1880* (London: Routledge, 1990).

Phillips, K. C., *Language and Class in Victorian England* (Oxford: Blackwell, 1984).

Pope, R., Pratt, A. and Hoyle, B. (eds), *Social Welfare in Britain 1885–1985* (London: Croom Helm, 1986).

Prest, J. (ed.), *Balliol Studies* (London: Leopard's Head, 1982).

Pritchard, R. J., *Thomas Greenwood: Public Library Enthusiast* (Biggleswade: Clover Publications, 1981).

Reid, A. J., *Social Classes and Social Relations in Britain, 1850–1914* (London: Macmillan, 1991).

Richards, T., *The Commodity Culture of Victorian England: Advertising and Spectacle, 1851–1914* (Stanford: Stanford University Press, 1990).

Roach, J., *Social Reform in England 1780–1880* (London: B. T. Batsford, 1978).

Roderick, G. W. and Stephens, M. D., *Post School Education: Educational Values in America and England in the Nineteenth Century* (Beckenham: Croom Helm, 1984).

Rose, J., *For The Sake of the Children: Inside Dr Barnardo's: 120 Years of Caring for Children* (London: Hodder and Stoughton, 1988).

Rose, M., *The East End of London* (London: Cresset Press, 1951).

Rose, M. E., *The Relief of Poverty, 1834–1914* (London: Macmillan, 1972).

Rose, M. E. (ed.), *The Poor and the City: The English Poor Law in Its Urban Context* (New York: St Martin's Press, 1985).

Rothblatt, S., *The Revolution of the Dons* (London: Faber, 1968).

Sadlier, M. E., *Michael Ernest Sadler* (London: Constable, 1949).

Sanderson, M. (ed.), *The Universities in the Nineteenth Century* (London: Routledge and Kegan Paul, 1975).

Schwarzbach, F. S., *Dickens and the City* (London: Athlone Press, 1979).

Sennett, R., *The Fall of Public Man* (London: Faber and Faber, 1986).

Sharpe, W. and Wallock, L. (eds), *Visions of the Modern City: Essays in History, Art and Literature* (Baltimore: The Johns Hopkins University Press, 1987).

Simey, M., *Charity Rediscovered: A Study of Philanthropic Effort in Nineteenth-Century Liverpool* (Liverpool: Liverpool University Press, 1992).

Simon, B., *Education and the Labour Movement, 1870–1920* (London: Lawrence and Wishart, 1965).

Sinclair, R., *East London* (London: Hale, 1950).

Smith, S. M., *The Other Nation: The Poor in English Novels of the 1840s and 1850s* (Oxford: Clarendon Press, 1980).

Smith, W. S., *The London Heretics 1870–1914* (London: Constable, 1967).

Snape, R., *Leisure and the Rise of the Public Library* (London: Library Association, 1995).

Springhall, J., *Youth, Empire and Society: British Youth Movements, 1883–1940* (Hamden, CT: Archon, 1977).

Springhall, J., *Coming of Age: Adolescence in Britain, 1860–1960* (Dublin: Gill and Macmillan, 1986).

Stedman Jones, G., *Languages of Class: Studies in English Working Class History 1832–1982* (Cambridge: Cambridge University Press, 1983).

Stocks, M. D., *Fifty Years in Every Street. The Story of the Manchester University Settlement* (Manchester: Manchester University Press, 1945).

Stocks, M. D., *The Workers' Educational Association: The First Fifty Years 1903–1953* (London: Allen and Unwin, 1953).

Summerfield, P., and Evans, E. J., *Technical Education and the State since 1850: Historical and Contemporary Perspectives* (Manchester: Manchester University Press, 1990).

Sutcliffe, A. (ed.), *Metropolis, 1890–1914* (London: Mansell, 1984).

Sutherland, G. (ed.), *Matthew Arnold on Education* (Harmondsworth: Penguin, 1973).

Swafford, K., *Class in Late-Victorian Britain: The Narrative Concern with Social Hierarchy and Its Representation* (Youngstown: Cambria Press, 2007).

Tawney, R. H., *The WEA and Adult Education* (London: Athlone Press, 1953).

Terrill, R., *R. H. Tawney and His Times: Socialism as Fellowship* (London: Andre Deutsch, 1974).

Thompson, F. M. L. (ed.), *The University of London and the World of Learning 1836–1986* (London: Hambledon Press, 1986).

Thompson, F. M. L., *The Rise of Respectable Society: A Social History of Victorian Britain, 1830–1900* (London: Fontana, 1988).

Thompson, F. M. L. (ed.), *The Cambridge Social History of Britain* (Cambridge: Cambridge University Press, 1990), 3 vols.

Thompson, P., *Socialists, Liberals and Labour: The Struggle for London 1885–1914* (London: Routledge, 1967).

Treble, J. H., *Urban Poverty in Britain, 1830–1914* (London: B. T. Batsford, 1979).

Vance, N., *The Sinews of the Spirit: The Ideal of Christian Manliness in Victorian Literature and Religious Thought* (Cambridge: Cambridge University Press, 1985).

Vicinus, M., *The Industrial Muse: A Study of Nineteenth Century British Working Class Literature* (New York: Barnes and Noble, 1974).

Vincent, A. and Plant, R., *Philosophy, Politics and Citizenship: The Life and Thought of the British Idealists* (Oxford: Blackwell, 1984).

Vincent, D., *Bread, Knowledge and Freedom: A Study of Nineteenth Century Working Class Autobiographies* (London: Europa Publishing, 1981).

Vernon, J., *Distant Strangers: How Britain Became Modern* (Berkeley: University of California Press, 2014).

Wagner, G., *Barnardo* (London: Weidenfeld and Nicolson, 1979).

Walton, J. K. and Walvin, J. (eds), *Leisure in Britain, 1780–1939* (Manchester: Manchester University Press, 1983).

Ward, W. R., *Victorian Oxford* (London: Frank Cass, 1965).

Wardle, D., *English Popular Education 1780–1970* (Cambridge: Cambridge University Press, 1970).

Watson, I., *Song and Democratic Culture in Britain: An Approach to Popular Culture in Social Movements* (London: Croom Helm, 1983).

Welsh, A., *The City of Dickens* (Oxford: Clarendon Press, 1971).

White, J., *Rothschild Buildings: Life in an East End Tenement Block, 1887–1920* (London: Routledge and Kegan Paul, 1980).

Williams, R., *The Country and the City* (London: Hogarth Press, 1985).

Wohl, A. S., *The Eternal Slum: Housing and Social Policy in Victorian London* (London: Edward Arnold, 1977).

Wright, A., *R. H. Tawney* (Manchester: Manchester University Press, 1987).

Yelling, J. A., *Slums and Slum Clearance in Victorian London* (London: Allen and Unwin, 1986).

Young, G. M., *Victorian England: Portrait of an Age* (New York: Doubleday Anchor, 1954).

Articles, essays and book chapters

Aalen, F. H. A., 'Lord Meath, City Improvement and Social Imperialism' *Planning Perspectives* 4 (1989), pp. 127–152.

Abel, E., 'Middle-Class Culture for the Urban Poor: The Educational Thought of Samuel Barnett' *Social Service Review* 52:4 (1978), pp. 596–620.

Abel, E., 'Toynbee Hall, 1884–1914' *Social Service Review* 53:4 (1979), pp. 606–632.

Alvey, N., 'The Great Voting Charities of the Metropolis' *Local Historian* 21 (1991), pp. 147–155.

Auerbach, S., '"A Right Sort of Man": Gender, Class Identity, and Social Reform in Late-Victorian Britain' *Journal of Policy History* 22 (2010), pp. 64–94.

Bailey, P., '"A Mingled Mass of Perfectly Legitimate Pleasures": The Victorian Middle Class and the Problem of Leisure' *Victorian Studies* 21 (1977), pp. 7–28.

Bales, K., 'Reclaiming "Antique" Data: Charles Booth's Poverty Survey' *Urban History Yearbook* 13 (1986), pp. 75–80.

Bales, K., 'Charles Booth's Survey of *Life and Labour of the People in London*, 1889–1903' in M. Bulmer *et al.* (eds), *The Social Survey in Historical Perspective, 1880–1940* (Cambridge: Cambridge University Press, 1991), pp. 66–110.

Benvenuto, R., 'The Criminal and the Community: Defining Tragic Structure in *A Child of the Jago*' *English Literature in Transition, 1880–1920* 31 (1988), pp. 153–161.

Bernstein, S. D., 'Reading Room Geographies of Late-Victorian London: the British Museum, Bloomsbury and the People's Palace, Mile End' *19: Interdisciplinary Studies in the Long Nineteenth Century* 13 (2011).

Billinge, M., 'A Time and Place for Everything: An Essay on Recreation, Re-Creation and the Victorians' *Journal of Historical Geography* 22:4 (1996), pp. 443–459.

Boege, F. W., 'Sir Walter Besant: Novelist' *Nineteenth Century Fiction* 10 (March 1956), pp. 249–280; 11 (June 1956), pp. 32–60.

Bradley, K., '"Growing up with a City": Exploring Settlement Youth Work in London and Chicago, c. 1880–1940' *London Journal* 34:3 (2009), pp. 285–298.

Briggs, A., 'The Language of "Class" in Nineteenth Century England' in A. Briggs and J. Saville (eds), *Essays in Labour History: In Memory of G.D.H. Cole* (London: Macmillan, 1960), pp. 43–73.

Bulmer, M. and Kish Sklar, K., 'The Social Survey in Historical Perspective' in M. Bulmer, K. Bales, Kathryn Kish Sklar (eds), *The Social Survey in Historical Perspective 1880–1940* (Cambridge: Cambridge University Press, 1990), pp. 1–48.

Cahill, M. and Jowitt, T., 'The New Philanthropy: the Emergence of the Bradford City Guild of Help' *Journal of Social Policy* 9:3 (1980), pp. 359–382.

Calder, R., 'Arthur Morrison: A Commentary with an Annotated Bibliography of Writings about him' *English Literature in Transition, 1880–1920* 28 (1985), pp. 276–297.

Cannadine, D., 'The Context, Performance and Meaning of Ritual: The British Monarchy and the "Invention of Tradition", *c.*1820–1977' in E. Hobsbawm and T. Ranger (eds), *The Invention of Tradition* (Cambridge: Cambridge University Press, 1983), pp.101–164.

Clarke, P. F., 'The Progressive Movement in England', *Transactions of the Royal Historical Society* (Fifth Series) 24 (1974), pp. 159–181.

Collini, S., 'Idealism and "Cambridge Idealism"' *Historical Journal* 18:1 (1975), pp. 171–177.

Collini, S., 'Sociology and Idealism in Britain, 1880–1920' *European Journal of Sociology* 19 (1978), pp. 3–50.

Collini, S., 'The Idea of "Character" in Victorian Political Thought' *Transactions of the Royal Historical Society* 35 (1985), pp. 29–50.

Collins, P., 'Dickens and the City' in W. Sharpe and L. Wallock (eds), *Visions of the Modern City: Essays in History, Art and Literature* (Baltimore: The Johns Hopkins University Press, 1987), pp. 101–121.

Creedon, A., 'A Benevolent Tyrant? The Principles and Practices of Henrietta Barnett (1851–1936), Social Reformer and Founder of Hampstead Garden Suburb' *Women's History Review* 11:2 (2002), pp. 231–252.

Crossick, G., 'From Gentleman to the Residuum: Languages of Social Description in Victorian Britain' in P. J. Corfield (ed.), *Language, History and Class* (Oxford: Blackwell, 1991), pp. 150–178.

Davis, W. A., 'Mary Jeune, Late-Victorian Essayist: Fallen Women, New Women, and Poor Children' *English Literature in Transition, 1880–1920* 58:2 (2015), pp. 181–208.

Dennis, R., 'The Geography of Victorian Values: Philanthropic Housing in London, 1840–1900' *Journal of Historical Geography* 15:1 (1989), pp. 40–54.

Dewey, C. J., '"Cambridge Idealism": Utilitarian Revisionists in Late-Nineteenth-Century Cambridge' *Historical Journal* 17:1 (1974), pp. 63–78.

Domville, E., 'Gloomy City or the Deeps of Hell: The Presentation of the East End in Fiction between 1880–1914' *East London Papers* 8:2 (1965), pp. 98–109.

Donajgrodzki, A. P., 'Introduction' in A. P. Donajgrodzki (ed.), *Social Control in Nineteenth Century Britain* (London: Croom Helm, 1977), pp. 9–26.

Dunne, P. A., 'Penny Dreadfuls: Late Nineteenth-Century Boys' Literature and Crime' *Victorian Studies* 22 (1979), pp. 133–150.

Dyos, H. J., 'The Slums of Victorian London' *Victorian Studies* 11 (1967), pp. 5–40.

Feltes, N. N., 'Misery or the Production of Misery: Defining Sweated Labour in 1890' *Social History* 17 (1992), pp. 441–452.

Foster, J., 'How Imperial London Preserved Its Slums' *International Journal of Urban and Regional Research* 3 (1979), pp. 93–114.

Garside, P. L., 'West End, East End: London, 1890–1940' in A. Sutcliffe (ed.), *Metropolis 1890–1940* (London: Mansell, 1984), pp. 221–258.

Gatens, W. J., 'John Ruskin and Music' *Victorian Studies* 30 (1986), pp. 77–97.

Graff, H. J., 'Pauperism, Misery and Vice: Illiteracy and Criminality in the Nineteenth Century' *Social History* 11 (1977), pp. 245–268.

Hapgood, L., 'Urban Utopias: Socialism, Religion and the City, 1880 to 1900' in S. Ledger and S. McCracken, *Cultural Politics at the Fin de Siècle* (Cambridge: Cambridge University Press, 1995), pp. 184–201.

Harris, W., 'H. W. Nevinson, Margaret Nevinson, Evelyn Sharp: Little-Known Writers and Crusaders' *English Literature in Transition, 1880–1920* 45:3 (2002), pp. 280–305.

Harrison, B., 'Religion and Recreation in Nineteenth-Century England' *Past and Present* 38 (1967), pp. 98–125.

Hennock, E. P., 'Poverty and Social Theory in England: The Experience of the Eighteen-eighties' *Social History* 1 (1976), pp. 67–91.

Himmelfarb, G., 'Lionel Trilling: The Moral Imagination' in her *The Moral Imagination* (Chicago: Ivan R. Dee, 2006), pp. 219–229.

Johnson, P., 'Conspicuous Consumption and Working-class Culture in late-Victorian and Edwardian Britain' *Transactions of the Royal Historical Society* 38 (1988), pp. 27–42.

Kadish, A., 'University Extension and the Working Classes: The Case of the Northumberland Miners' *Historical Research* 60 (1987), pp. 188–207.

Kearney, A., 'John Churton Collins and the University Extension Movement' *Notes and Queries* 26 (1979), pp. 328–331.

Keeson, C. A. G. C., 'Barber Beaumont' *East London Papers* 1:3 (1960), pp. 13–21.

Kidd, A. J., 'Outcast Manchester: Voluntary Charity, Poor Relief and the Casual Poor 1860–1905' in A. J. Kidd and K. W. Roberts (eds), *City, Class and Culture: Studies of Social Policy and Cultural Production in Victorian Manchester* (Manchester: Manchester University Press, 1985), pp. 48–73.

Kidd, A. J., 'Philanthropy and the "Social History Paradigm"' *Social History* 21 (1996), pp. 180–192.

Kiernan, V., 'Labour and the Literate in Nineteenth-Century Britain' in D. E. Martin and D. Rubenstein (eds), *Ideology and the Labour Movement: Essays Presented to John Saville* (London: Croom Helm, 1979) pp. 32–61.

Kijinski, J., 'Ethnography in the East End: Native Customs and Colonial Solutions in *A Child of the Jago*' *English Literature in Transition, 1880–1920* 37 (1994), pp. 490–501.

Laybourn, K., 'The Guild of Help and the Changing Face of Edwardian Philanthropy' *Urban History* 20 (1993), pp. 43–60.

Lees, L. H., 'Poverty and Pauperism in the Nineteenth Century (The H. J. Dyos Memorial Lecture)' University of Leicester, Victorian Studies Centre, 1988.

Lewis, J., 'The Place of Social Investigation, Social Theory and Social Work in the Approach to Late Victorian and Edwardian Social Problems: The Case of Beatrice Webb and Helen Bosanquet' in M. Bulmer, K. Bales and K. Kish Sklar (eds), *The Social Survey in Historical Perspective 1880–1940* (Cambridge: Cambridge University Press, 1990), pp. 148–169.

Lummis, T., 'Charles Booth: Moralist or Social Scientist?' *Economic History Review* 24 (1971), pp. 100–105.

MacMaster, N., 'The Battle for Mousehold Heath 1857–1884: "Popular Politics" and the Victorian Public Park' *Past and Present* 127 (1990), pp. 117–154.

McKean, M., 'Rethinking Late-Victorian Slum Fiction: The Crowd and Imperialism at Home' *English Literature in Transition, 1880–1920* 54:1 (2011), pp. 28–55.

McKibbon, R., 'Social Class and Social Observation in Edwardian England' *Transactions of the Royal Historical Society* 28 (1978), pp. 175–199.

McKibbon, R., 'Working-class Gambling in Britain: 1880–1939' *Past and Present* 82 (1979), pp. 147–178.

Mann, P. H., 'Octavia Hill: An Appraisal' *The Town Planning Review* 23:3 (1952), pp. 223–237.

Marriott, S., 'Extensionalia – the Fugitive Literature of Early University Adult Education' *Studies in Adult Education* 10 (1978), pp. 50–72.

Marriott, S., 'Oxford and Working-class Adult Education: A Foundation Myth Re-examined' *History of Education* 12 (1983), pp. 285–299.

Marriott, S., 'The Whisky Money and the University Extension Movement: "Golden Opportunities" or "Artificial Stimulus"?' *Journal of Education Administration History* 15 (1983), pp. 7–15.

Marriott, S., 'The Journalism of the University Extension Movement in its Political Context, 1889–1926' *History of Education* 20 (1991), pp. 341–357.

Martin, M., 'The Romance of the Slum: Gender and Cross-class Communication of Religious Belief, 1880–1920' *Studies in Church History* 42 (2006), pp. 394–405.

Mowat, C. L., 'Charity and Casework in Late Victorian London: The Work of the Charity Organisation Society' *Social Service Review* 31:3 (1957), pp. 258–270.

Nord, D. E., 'The Social Explorer as Anthropologist: Victorian Travellers among the Urban Poor' in W. Sharpe and L. Wallock (eds), *Visions of the Modern City: Essays in History, Art and Literature* (Baltimore: The Johns Hopkins University Press, 1987), pp. 122–134.

Nord, D. E., 'The City as Theatre: From Georgian to Early Victorian London' *Victorian Studies* 31 (1988), pp. 159–188.

O'Day, R., 'Interviews and Investigations: Charles Booth and the Making of the Religious Influences Survey' *History* 74 (1989), pp. 361–376.

O'Day, R., 'Before the Webbs: Beatrice Potter's Early Investigations for Charles Booth's Inquiry' *History* 78 (1993), pp. 218–342.

Potts, A., 'Picturing the Modern Metropolis: Images of London in the Nineteenth Century' *History Workshop Journal* 26 (1988), pp. 28–56.

Rainbow, B., 'The Rise of Popular Music Education in Nineteenth-Century England' *Victorian Studies* 30 (1986), pp. 25–49.

Reed, J. S., '"Ritualism Rampant in East London": Anglo-Catholicism and the Urban Poor' *Victorian Studies* 31:3 (1988), pp. 375–403.

Reinders, R. C., 'Toynbee Hall and the American Settlement Movement' *Social Service Review* 56:1 (1982), pp. 39–54.

Richter, M., 'T. H. Green and his Audience: Liberalism as a Surrogate Faith' *Review of Politics* 18:4 (1956), pp. 444–472.

Rodger, R., 'Political Economy, Ideology, and the Persistence of Working-Class Housing Problems in Britain, 1870–1914' *International Review of Social History* 32 (1987), pp. 109–143.

Royle, E., 'Mechanics' Institutes and the Working Classes, 1840–1860' *Historical Journal* 14:2 (1971), pp. 305–321.

Saint, A., 'Technical Education and the Early LCC' in A. Saint (ed.), *Politics and the People of London: the London County Council 1889–1965* (London: Hambledon Press, 1989), pp. 71–91.

Sanderson, M.., 'Literacy and Social Mobility in the Industrial Revolution in England' *Past and Present* 56 (1972), pp. 75–104.

Sanderson, M., 'The English Civic Universities and the "Industrial Spirit", 1870–1914' *Historical Research* 61 (1988), pp. 90–104.

Savage, M., 'Urban History and Social Class: Two Paradigms' *Urban History* 20 (1993), pp. 61–77.

Senelick, L., 'Politics as Entertainment: Victorian Music-Hall Songs' *Victorian Studies* 19 (1975), pp. 149–180.

Shiman, L. L., 'The Band of Hope Movement: Respectable Recreation for Working-class Children' *Victorian Studies* 17 (1973), pp. 49–74.

Simhony, A., 'T. H. Green: The Common Good Society' *History of Political Thought* 14 (1993), pp. 225–247.

Smith, T. B., 'In Defence of Privilege: the City of London and the Challenge of Municipal Reform, 1875–1890' *Journal of Social History* 27 (1993), pp. 59–83.

Soffer, R. N., 'The Revolution in English Social Thought, 1880–1914' *American Historical Review* 75:7 (1970), pp. 1938–1964.

Springhall, J., 'Building Character in the British Boy: The Attempt to Extend Christian Manliness to Working Class Adolescents, 1880 to 1914' in J. A. Mangan and J. Walvin (eds), *Manliness and Morality: Middle-class Masculinity in Britain and America, 1880–1940* (Manchester: Manchester University Press, 1987), pp. 52–74.

Stapleton, J., 'Political Thought, Elites and the State in Modern Britain' (review essay) *Historical Journal* 42:1 (1999), pp. 251–268.

Stedman Jones, G., 'Working-class Culture and Working-class Politics in London, 1870–1900: Notes on the Remaking of a Working Class' in his *Languages of Class: Studies in English Working Class History, 1832–1982* (Cambridge: Cambridge University Press, 1983), pp. 179–238.

Summers, A., 'A Home from Home – Women's Philanthropic Work in the Nineteenth Century' in S. Burman (ed.), *Fit Work for Women* (London: Croom Helm, 1979), pp. 33–63.

Smith, T. H., 'The Jago' *East London Papers* 2:1 (1959), pp. 39–47.

Stone, L., 'Literacy and Education in England 1640–1900' *Past and Present* 42 (1969), pp. 61–139.

Thompson, P., 'Liberals, Radicals and Labour in London, 1880–1900' *Past and Present* 27 (1964), pp. 73–101.

Ward, D., 'The Victorian Slum: An Enduring Myth?' *Annals of the Association of American Geographers* 66 (1976), pp. 323–336.

Welch, E., 'Oxford and University Extension' *Studies in Adult Education* 10 (1978), pp. 39–49.

White, P., 'Ministers of Culture: Arnold, Huxley and Liberal Anglican Reform of Learning' *History of Science* 43:2 (2005), pp. 115–138.

Wohl, A. S., 'The Bitter Cry of Outcast London' *International Review of Social History* 13 (1968), pp. 189–245.

Wright, F., 'F. C. Mills and the Broad Street Boys Club' *East London Record* 13 (1990), pp. 18–22.

Yelling, J. A., 'The Selection of Sites for Slum Clearance in London, 1875–1888' *Journal of Historical Geography* 7 (1981), pp. 155–165.

Yeo, E. and S. Yeo, 'Ways of Seeing: Control and Leisure versus Class and Struggle' in E. Yeo and S. Yeo (eds), *Popular Culture and Class Conflict 1590–1914: Explorations in the History of Labour and Leisure* (Brighton: Harvester Press, 1981), pp. 128–154.

Index

For Product Safety Concerns and Information please contact our EU
representative GPSR@taylorandfrancis.com
Taylor & Francis Verlag GmbH, Kaufingerstraße 24, 80331 München, Germany